THE RISE OF THE ENTREPRENEURIAL STATE

LA FOLLETTE PUBLIC POLICY SERIES

The Robert M. La Follette
Institute of Public Affairs

Robert H. Haveman, Director

State Policy Choices: The Wisconsin Experience
Sheldon Danziger and John F. Witte, editors

The Midwest Response to the New Federalism
Peter K. Eisinger and William Gormley, editors

*The Rise of the Entrepreneurial State: State and Local
Economic Development Policy in the United States*
Peter K. Eisinger

The Rise

of the

Entrepreneurial

State

State and Local Economic Development Policy
in the United States

PETER K. EISINGER

The University of Wisconsin Press

The University of Wisconsin Press
114 North Murray Street
Madison, Wisconsin 53715

The University of Wisconsin Press, Ltd.
1 Gower Street
London WC1E 6HA, England

Library of Congress Cataloging-in-Publication Data
Eisinger, Peter K.
    The rise of the entrepreneurial state.
    (La Follette public policy series)
    Bibliography: p. 345–369.
    Includes index.
    1. Industrial promotion—United States—States.
2. United States—Economic policy—1981–
3. Regional planning—United States.   4. Federal government—United
States.   5. Intergovernmental fiscal relations—United
States.   I. Title.   II. Title: Entrepreneurial state.   III. Series.
HC110.I53E56   1988   338.973   88-40184
ISBN 0-299-11870-3
ISBN 0-299-11874-6 (pbk.)

To my mother and father,

Marjorie and Chester Eisinger

Contents

Illustrations

Tables

Preface

THIS book was conceived and written in many different places over the past several years, so much so that I read in it with nostalgic pleasure the record of a satisfying academic itinerary across the national landscape. The genesis of this study lies in research I conducted in Atlanta and Detroit in the mid-1970s on the transition to black mayoralties in those cities. I was struck at the time that a major way both mayors, Maynard Jackson and Coleman Young, attempted to reach out to white elites was to promote private investment opportunities, mostly in the downtowns of their cities. That the mayors in these cities concentrated so avidly on commercial construction in their respective central business districts had a certain irony in these racially divided cities. Yet both men justified their attentiveness to what were overwhelmingly white interests by arguing that the jobs and tax revenues generated by these projects would benefit their black constituents both directly and indirectly.

Whatever skepticism or curiosity this argument aroused remained on hold until a visiting appointment at Columbia University in 1982–83 gave me an opportunity to begin to read the literature in the fields of urban and regional economic development, industrial location determinants, and job creation. From that year's reading I developed a course in the politics of economic development policy that I taught in two subsequent years at Wisconsin, once at the undergraduate level and once to graduate students in the La Follette Institute of Public Affairs.

It was in the classroom that my education in this policy domain began in earnest: some of my graduate students were actually employed at the time in the Wisconsin Department of Development (the state's economic development arm); others had worked as local public officials and had first hand experience with tax increment financing districts, UDAGs, and other arcana of the trade. In front of these students, and with their help, I framed what I believed to be the key questions that challenged social science scholars as well as practitioners in this field. Periodic reality tests were provided by visitors from state and local government and the private development community whom we asked to come to tell us how economic development really worked.

In 1984–85 I was asked to serve on the Advisory Committee of the Wisconsin Strategic Development Commission. The SDC, appointed by Governor Tony Earl, was charged with developing an analysis of the Wisconsin economy and a plan for its revitalization. The committee on which I served functioned principally as a sounding board for the commission staff, though the SDC executive director, Robert Milbourne, and assistant director, Carol Toussaint, surely taught me far more about economic development than I taught them. Both provided able and patient instruction on the limits and possibilities of state intervention in the local economy in the context of Wisconsin politics. In addition to my duties on the Advisory Committee that year, I was also commissioned to write several research papers on various topics, including tax abatements, industrial location determinants, and high technology job growth, for several of the specialized policy groups into which the Strategic Development Commission was organized.

In the summer of 1985 the La Follette Institute of Public Affairs at Wisconsin and its director and my colleague, Dennis Dresang, provided generous support for me to begin to outline this book. Then in the fall I moved westward to the Center for Advanced Study in the Behavioral Sciences in Palo Alto where I spent a golden year writing the first two-thirds of the manuscript. It is scarcely a novel observation among social scientists to say that there is probably no place on earth more pleasant or supportive to work than the Center. There is certainly no more stimulating group of colleagues, no better lunches, no more cutthroat volleyball. Partial support that year came from the National Science Foundation (grant number BNS-8011494), while the remainder came from the Wisconsin Alumni Research Foundation. I am grateful to both sources. I also wish particularly to thank Gardner Lindzey and Bob Scott of the Center for their encouragement and the CASBS librarians, Margaret Amara, Rosanne Torre, and Bruce Harley, for their efficient and good-natured help.

The thought of being coast-less after a year in California led me to the other edge of the country to accept a generous offer to join Brown University's Taubman Center for Public Policy as a visitor in 1986–87. Aided by the fine resources of the Taubman Center and two thoroughly competent undergraduate research assistants, Sandy Roth and Diana Edensword, I finished the book. Then I went home to Wisconsin.

During the years of writing this work I have presented segments in various lectures and conferences in the United States and Canada, and various people have read and commented on my work. Among the latter

I wish especially to thank Tom Anton, Bob Bates, Dick Bingham, Otis Graham, Bob Milbourne, Nelson Polsby, John Portz, and Graham Wilson. I wish also to thank Gordon Lester-Massman, my editor at the University of Wisconsin Press, for his loyal stewardship, and Robin Whitaker for her meticulous and helpful editing.

Finally, I wish to thank my family: between 1982 and 1987 my two children, Jesse and Sarah, went to a new school every year as we trekked back and forth across the country. They survived the modest traumas of annual dislocation with a wonderful equanimity and a perpetual sense of adventure. They even seem to have learned something in the process. I am genuinely grateful for their capacity for adjustment. And of course I am grateful to Erica, whose appetite for this journey was easily as great as my own.

Part I

GROUNDWORK

CHAPTER 1

An Introduction to State and Local Economic Development Policy

SOMETIME after the mid-1970s there emerged on the state and local scene an intense preoccupation with economic development that has been marked by a level of consensus and expectation unusual in American politics. Other domestic policy issues have swept in similar fashion to the top of the political agenda in recent decades, commanding nearly universal engagement or interest: civil rights, the environment, energy, and even the "social agenda" of the New Right are examples. But the divisions that characterize politics in these passionate arenas stand in contrast to economic development, in which common purpose, the public interest, and partnership are key terms of discourse.

This is not to claim that there are neither disagreements about means nor competition for resources among places and interests in the politics of economic development. Rather it is to suggest that this policy domain is marked by an extremely broad agreement as to the desirability of substantial government involvement in the creation of private-sector employment. Acceptance of this proposition is not, of course, universal, but nevertheless it comfortably crosses partisan lines, urban-rural divisions, the racial cleavage, and regional boundaries. Many Americans seem convinced that they can truly help to shape the economic destinies of their states and communities through public intiatives. In the technical language of tax abatements, venture-capital pools, industrial revenue bonds, tax incremental financing, and high-tech incubators, people see hope for salvation from a world of harsh competition and impersonal economic transformations. If those other policy arenas that so dominated American politics in their time entailed deep conflicts, sacrifice, and for some the prospect of defeat, economic development appears to hold out the possibility of prosperity for all.

Economic development policy refers to those efforts by government to encourage new business investment in particular locales in the hopes of directly creating or retaining jobs, setting into motion the secondary employment multiplier, and enhancing and diversifying the tax base. In the United States, economic development involves efforts to foster subnational economies, even when economic development policies originate with the federal government. Questions of national economic efficiency or well-being are often lost in the competitive struggle to achieve local prosperity and security. The result of such a focus in practical terms is that the national economy is to some degree the sum of its subnational parts, some developed and prosperous, some not, and all in mutual competition for private investment and resources.

To the extent that Americans in the modern period have sought deliberately to foster *national* economic development (the word "national" almost never modifies "economic development" in American politics), it has been largely through the blunter tools of macroeconomic tax and spending policy and monetary controls. Development models that involve selective national intervention at the firm or industry level—commonly a component of national industrial policies—have failed to take hold in national politics in the United States. The reasons for this outcome are manifold, but the failure is at least partly a function of the uneven geographical distribution of particular industries. A national industrial policy would thus have the effect of forcing the federal government to make politically unacceptable choices among *regions* as it went about favoring certain industrial "winners." This is one constraint that does not inhibit states and cities, however; firm- and industry-specific instruments of intervention, applied in varying degrees according to strategic considerations, have proliferated at the subnational level.

These policy instruments have emerged so quickly and in such variety that the field has outpaced broad-gauged efforts to reflect upon it from a global perspective. The purpose of this book is to do just that, namely, to characterize and analyze the policy domain of subnational economic development as a whole by exploring its modern origins, its justifications and practical elements, and the basis of its dynamics.

There are at least three important reasons for this enterprise. One is that economic development is an increasingly important government activity—a point I shall amplify in the next chapter—but we know surprisingly little about it of a systematic nature. Much literature is pitched to the needs of practitioners, and scholarly work on the subject is often narrowly focused and fragmentary. There are no established frameworks. The field lacks an analytical synthesis and a critical interpretation.

A second reason for this effort is to document an unusual development in the way in which government in America relates to the economy. Government involvement with the market in the United States has typically been described in terms of a "weak state" model: one of its crucial distinguishing features is that investment and production decisions are left almost entirely to the private sector (Zysman, 1983, p. 19; Krasner, 1978, p. 61). Government pursues no conscious development strategy. Its primary economic role is to provide a supportive macroeconomic and regulatory climate for business.

The weak state is contrasted with European and Japanese models of public intervention, in which government action is informed by long-term market developments (Johnson, 1982). Among other initiatives, governments set up pools of public money to invest in particular economic sectors, offer loans at favorable rates to selected firms or industries, and subsidize civilian research, all in response to the elements of centrally planned strategic guidelines. Unlike the macroeconomic manipulations that more or less define the limits of American intervention in the economy (the Chrysler loan notwithstanding), intervention in the strong state is as likely to occur at the level of the economic sector or the firm. As Krasner writes of the Japanese strong state, such a level of intervention blends "a high regard for private enterprise . . . with a belief that the government should act as a well-intentioned guide" (1978, p. 60).

What is taking place in American subnational politics in the economic development domain falls somewhere between the strong- and weak-state models, a distinctive mix of elements much influenced by its American environment and limitations. But on balance it is apparent, even as this nascent development that I have called the entrepreneurial state takes shape, that its dominant features owe more to the tradition of intervention that marks the strong state. Entrepreneurial-state policies represent a clear departure from the system of public support for company-led economic decision-making that has typically characterized joint public–private-sector relationships in the American political economy.

A third reason for this study is to suggest the importance of attending to subnational policy developments in the United States, for to overlook these generally in favor of a focus on Washington, particularly in the field of economic policy-making, is to come away with only a partial grasp of the nature of American political impulses and possibilities. What is so striking about the domain of economic development policy, aside from the sheer fireworks of policy invention, is the disjunction between subnational and national economic strategies. Although some of this disjunction is the product of rhetorical flourishes, it nevertheless reflects genuinely different levels of engagement. At the national level during years in which the entrepreneurial state took shape, the critical ideas were deregulation, privatization, the free market, voluntarism, and the supply-side macroeconomic doctrine. Yet the entrepreneurial state is based on a strategy of intervention, guidance, and initiative in the economy. The 50 states and many of their communities are in the process of fashioning, with varying degrees of vigor and coherence, separate little industrial policies, self-conscious attempts to foster selected industries judged to provide comparative local advantage or to be critical to the local economic future.

The case of economic development policy thus demonstrates several points about American politics. It illustrates the versatility of a federal arrangement that permits governments at the two different levels to pursue quite different (though not necessarily conflicting) courses of policy. It provides yet more evidence of the pragmatism of American politics, where policy choices may be less governed by ideology than necessity and the desire for results. And it suggests finally that much of the effort to shape the American economic future has devolved to the state capitals.

The Idea of a Policy Domain

The focus of the present analysis is the substance and context of a distinctive policy domain. The term has a simple, though particular, meaning. A policy domain is an arena in which actors seek to craft and implement solutions and responses to one or a set of given public problems. The ultimate problem in the economic development domain in the simplest terms is to oversee the creation of sufficient, stable, well-paid employment to ensure and enhance the collective well-being.

The relevant actors who populate this domain constitute a fairly small elite. At the center are political chief executives, governors and mayors, for whom economic development has become a major responsibility. Their function is to articulate development goals and create the coalitions to generate and implement policy initiatives. In addition, they have long functioned as major promoters of the state or local business climate. They also serve as zealous sales representatives abroad for local products and even particular firms. Development professionals in both the private and public sectors—economic planners, state labor economists, industrial-site development specialists, corporate officers charged with government liaison, chamber of commerce officials and the like— are also constant and critical actors. Their functions include the invention, promotion, and implementation of economic development policy initiatives. Other actors are specialists or episodic participants: labor leaders, real estate developers, bankers, state legislative and city council representatives, university administrators, and university and corporate scientists. Aside perhaps from the state officials and the scientists, the cast of characters is little different from that which made up the postwar "progrowth coalitions," described by Mollenkopf (1983), that were instrumental in the renewal of urban downtowns.

It is useful to think of the policy domain in which these figures operate in architectural terms, a metaphor I propose to use only for the moment for its value in organizing the analysis. To speak of architecture is immediately to suggest a concern with design. In *The Sciences of the Artificial* Herbert Simon speaks of "design" as "action aimed at changing existing situations into preferred ones" and "devising artifacts to attain goals" (1981, pp. 129, 131). Design is, in other words, policy. The elements of design in a policy domain are programs and strategies.

A policy domain, like a piece of architecture, is not simply a presentation of surface aesthetics: its basic contours are defined by its structural features. These support, determine, and constrain design possibilities, though they can sustain considerable design variation. In a policy domain these structural features include principles of operation that establish the framework within which policy is crafted; they also include justifications for actions and theories of action, that is, propositions about cause and effect in regard to particular sorts of public initiatives. Structural technology is sensitive to the particular historical, cultural, and economic environment of which it is a product. As aspects of the environment change in profound ways, so too may certain elements of structure undergo transformation, as the Roman arch gave way to the Gothic, as cast iron gave way to steel beams, opening new design possibilities to the imagination. It is the contention of this book that the economic policy domain is in the midst of such an environmental transformation, the effect of which has been to change some of these structural elements, especially attitudes toward strategic planning and theories of action. The result has been the emergence of a new set of design elements that define the entrepreneurial state.

The Entrepreneurial State

The notion of the entrepreneurial state[1] owes much to Schumpeter's classic discussion of the entrepreneurial function. "The fundamental im-

---

1. Stuart Holland (1972) used the term "state entrepreneurship" to describe the Italian

pulse that sets and keeps the capitalist engine in motion," Schumpeter wrote in *Capitalism, Socialism and Democracy* (1962, p. 83), "comes from the new consumers' goods, the new methods of production or transportation, the new markets, the new forms of industrial organization that capitalist enterprise creates." It is the function of the entrepreneur, a risk-taker, an actor with vision, to animate the economic engine "by exploiting an invention or, more generally, an untried technological possibility for producing a new commodity or producing an old one in a new way, or by opening up . . . a new outlet for products . . ." (p. 132).

The entrepreneur encounters resistance, however, for such activity has a disequilibrating impact, threatening established, even if stagnating, patterns of productivity. Such resistance may range from skepticism to refusals to finance a new undertaking. Yet, Schumpeter writes, "To act with confidence beyond the range of familiar beacons and to overcome that resistance . . . define the entrepreneurial type as well as the entrepreneurial function" (ibid.). The entrepreneur not only identifies new opportunities—new products to invent and sell, new markets to penetrate—but also mobilizes, organizes, and may even supply the resources necessary to exploit those possibilities.

Schumpeter's entrepreneur is a private actor. But there are certain social and economic conditions under which private entrepreneurial activity may not suffice to provide the basis for the sustained and high economic growth that a society may have come to expect. The failure of private-sector entrepreneurialism may be a function of myopic vision, sheer timidity, a lack of resources, or a preoccupation with "paper capitalism"—mergers, buy-outs, takeovers (Reich, 1983)—to the detriment of production and industrial innovation. Under these circumstances there

---

Institute for Industrial Reconstruction, a multisectoral public enterprise group. Managers run the public companies in this group with great flexibility, that is, responsively to market considerations. I use the term "entrepreneurial" in a slightly different way: in the American context entrepreneurial interventions fall short of public ownership, although the state may coinvest in firms. A similar diagnosis led to state entrepreneurial solutions in both Italy and the United States, however: insufficient investment capital, regional growth disparities, and insufficient consumption or demand levels to ensure a desirable rate of growth. A concept related to the notion of the entrepreneurial state is Chalmers Johnson's categorization of Japan as a "developmental state." Here the "dominant feature" is a concern with what "industries ought to exist and what industries are no longer needed," with the overriding goals the enhancement of the nation's international competitiveness and high-speed growth (1982, pp. 19, 22). The degree of central control, the overwhelming focus on the international market, and the careful enunciation of grand strategic goals distinguish the developmental state from its looser relative, the entrepreneurial state.

is a role, in a flexible society, for the state to serve an entrepreneurial function.[2]

The entrepreneurial state in America performs roles much like those of Schumpeter's figure, but it does so in partnership with private economic actors. The difference between Schumpeter's entrepreneur and the entrepreneurial state is that the latter seeks to identify market opportunities not for its own exclusive gain but on behalf of private actors whose pursuit of those opportunities may serve public ends. In its role of partner the state has become a risk-taker, a path-finder to new markets, the midwife to joint public-private efforts to develop and test untried technology. The state increasingly functions as a "company former" (Shapero, 1981, p. 28), supplying the necessary wherewithal to stimulate new private-business formation. By its interest in underwriting and encouraging new product development, basic and applied high-tech research, and the adoption of new methods in "mature" industries, the entrepreneurial state seeks, in the words that Premus and his colleagues use to define the individual entrepreneur, "to exploit opportunities that are generally not apparent to other decision-makers" (1985, p. ix).

What guides the entrepreneurial state is attention to the demand side of the economic growth equation. Underlying the actions of the entrepreneurial state is the assumption that growth comes from exploiting new or expanding markets. The state role is to identify, evaluate, anticipate, and even help to develop and create these markets for private producers to exploit, aided if necessary by government as subsidizer or coinvestor. The policies of the entrepreneurial state are geared to these functions. They include the generation of venture capital for selected new and growing businesses, the encouragement of high-technology research and product development to respond to emerging markets, and the promotion of export goods produced by local businesses to capitalize upon new sources of demand.

Among the states, degrees of self-conscious entrepreneurialism vary, as does the willingness to experiment in this newer policy realm. No state, however, represents a pure type, exclusively committed to either entrepreneurial or traditional policy approaches. Most states proffer a mix of traditional location inducements with one or more programs designed in response to market demands. However, some states—for

---

2. One reason the United States has never needed a strong state based on the European model, according to Krasner, is that "the American economy has performed extraordinarily well without much direct government intervention" (1978, p. 66).

example Massachusetts, Connecticut, Michigan, Pennsylvania—have either staked a claim as pioneers in entrepreneurial experimentation or shifted decisively across a broad front to the newer strategy.

The Argument in Brief

The thesis of this book is that subnational economic development policy has undergone a recent shift from an almost exclusive reliance on supply-side location incentives to stimulate investment to an approach that increasingly emphasizes demand factors in the market as a guide to the design or invention of policy. The mastery of demand factors requires a sensitivity by the state to the structure and possibilities of the market, an entrepreneurial sensibility.

There are several important implications of this shift in approach. Demand-based policies hold out the prospect of genuine capital formation and lessened interstate competition. In addition the rise of the entrepreneurial state heralds the involvement by state governments as participants in the market economy to a degree to which Americans in modern peacetime are unaccustomed.

The source of this shift from supply-side or traditional approaches to demand-side entrepreneurialism is, in good measure, a product of the influence of shifts in three great environmental forces. Shifts in the distribution of people and jobs across the landscape, changes in the federal political arrangement, and deep transformations in the nature of the American economy are primarily responsible for changes in the theory and practice of economic development.

The shift of population and jobs southward and westward has posed a competitive challenge to the North. To all appearances the success of the South in particular has seemed to be a function of the cheaper costs of doing business in that region, an advantage created to some degree by the lower taxes imposed by southern states and the land and capital subsidies they offer. Since the condition of a state's economy is regarded as a state responsibility (the decentralized federal system in America has eschewed serious regional development policies), northern states have been compelled to respond in order to capture their share of mobile capital.

The conditions of competition suggested at first a simple model for the design of policy initiatives. The model assumed a supply-side process of economic development: investment, which in turn generates jobs, would be attracted to those locales where the costs of factors of production—entered on the supply side of the economic-growth equation—are lower. Thus, northern states have set out to match their competition by offering the same or even more generous location inducements to mobile firms. But the putative value of these inducements, whose efficacy economists have doubted from the beginning, have diminished as more and more states have offered them, creating incentives to experiment with new policies that promoted development in noncompetitive ways. The result has been the profusion of policies identified with the entrepreneurial state, which emphasize local resources as the basis for growth rather than the competitive engagement with other states for mobile capital.

A second transformation has occurred in the federal system, where the decline in real purchasing power of federal aid to states and localities since the late 1970s has heightened incentives to nurture indigenous local tax bases to provide a growing source of revenue. Since there is not enough mobile capital to satisfy the employment needs of every state, states have turned to their local economies as a source of growth, particularly to the small business sector and to the pool of latent entrepreneurs, a substantially different set of economic actors from those which had been the object of supply-side location incentives.

A third set of transformations has occurred in the structure of the American economy. Two very different changes are at issue. One involves the increasing involvement of the American economy in the international marketplace. The other concerns the shift in the ways in which Americans earn their livelihoods.

The rise of the international market, both as a source of competition and as a growing market outlet for American goods, has stimulated the states to think about the competitiveness of their industries and about the possibilities of export. Policies addressed to both concerns are central to the activities of the entrepreneurial state.

The steady decline of manufacturing employment in certain traditional heavy industries and the concomitant growth of service-sector jobs mark an economic sea change that raises a variety of questions about the American economic future. What elements of the growing service sector can be expected to provide the basis for a stable and prosperous economy? What will be the structure of demand for industrial goods in the future? What, indeed, *are* the industries of the future?

The response to these questions by the entrepreneurial state has first been a tentative embrace of principles of strategic planning in order to focus resources on the economic activities that appear to build for the future. As we shall see, strategic planning at the state level is neither well developed nor universally practiced, but some of its assumptions have

Chart 1-1.   Contrasts between Traditional Supply-Side Policy and Demand-Side
Entrepreneurial Policy

Supply Side	Demand Side
Growth is promoted by lowering production-factor costs through government subsidies of capital and land and through low taxes.	Growth is promoted by discovering, expanding, developing, or creating new markets for local goods and services.
Main focus is on established, potentially mobile capital.	Main focus is on new capital
Strategies focus on stimulating capital relocation or capital retention.	Strategies focus on new business formation and small business expansion.
Development involves competition with other jurisdictions for the same investment.	Development proceeds by nurturing indigenous resources.
Government supports low-risk undertakings.	Government becomes involved in high-risk enterprises and activities.
Any employer is a suitable target for development assistance.	Development assistance is offered selectively according to strategic criteria.
Government's role is to follow and support private-sector decisions about where to invest, what businesses will be profitable, and what products will sell.	Government's role is to help identify investment opportunities that the private sector may either have overlooked or be reluctant to pursue, including opportunities in new markets, new products, and new industries.

been widely adopted. In addition, demand-side economic development policy in the entrepreneurial state has focused on fostering new industries through subsidized research and product development in a wide number of advanced technology fields assumed to be the industries of the future.

The growth of demand-side entrepreneurial activities has not displaced supply-side strategies: lowering taxes, for example, remains a compelling means to development ends for state politicians, and states and communities still aggressively pursue booster campaigns to publicize the virtues of their respective business climates. Nevertheless, the rise of state entrepreneurialism represents a genuine reordering of long-established relations between the public and private sectors. Some of the differences between the supply-side traditional approach to development and the demand-oriented entrepreneurial approach are summarized in Chart 1-1.

The Plan of the Book

Chapter 2 summarizes the rise of economic development as a policy issue and discusses the framework principles of operation that provide certain of the contours of this policy domain. Many of these framework elements—the idea of a public-private partnership, for example, and the principle of decentralization—are relatively stable and support both supply- and demand-side policies. Other elements—attitudes toward economic planning, for example—appear to be changing, and the consequence is to shift the balance in the mix of supply policy and demand policy.

Chapter 3 explores another feature of structure, the justifications for action. Theories of action—that is, propositions about what sorts of policies are necessary to produce the desired ends—are treated mainly in Chapters 4 and 9. These appear to be less stable structural elements than the others. The context of the economic development policy domain— its environment—is discussed in Chapter 4.

Supply-side policies—their origins, variety, and effects—are examined in Chapters 6 through 8. The major policy initiatives of the entrepreneurial state are the subjects of most of the remainder of the book: Chapter 10 explores the various venture-capital programs, Chapter 11 the efforts to encourage high-technology research, and Chapter 12 the states' attempts to penetrate foreign markets. Chapter 13 deals with the emergence of state efforts to hold business accountable for the effects of its decisions to move or shut down.

A brief note on methods is appropriate here. The analysis that follows is based mainly on a review of primary and secondary sources— federal, state, and local government documents, hearings and reports, consultants' analyses, and scholarly literature—as well as interviews and less formal discussions with public officials, business people, and development practitioners from California to Rhode Island. Material was collected from virtually every state on their respective economic development efforts. My own service both as a member of the Advisory Commission to the Wisconsin Strategic Development Commission and as a consultant to that body gave me a modest taste of economic development policy-making firsthand.

The analytical strategy has been first to provide an account of the historical development of particular programs or approaches and to relate these to the larger argument about the emergence and transformation of the economic development policy domain. I have then attempted to offer a running critical commentary on various policy options, paying particular attention to the justifications for intervention, the claims of program advocates and doubters, and the evaluation literature, where it exists.

I have used aggregate data on the incidence and characteristics of programs to give a sense of their growth, relative importance, and nature. Sometimes these data are reported by others; sometimes I have gathered them. There is, of course, much to learn by examining individual programs in detail. To gain a more intimate understanding of policy I have chosen to discuss the pioneer programs, the prototypes, and the widely acknowledged successes and failures. I have tried to alert the reader to which of these is typical and which is not.

The time span of the study runs generally from the depression era to 1985, but the principal focus is on the last decade of this period. Data on some programs are not available for the latter year; what appears in the book is the latest available material as of mid-1987.

CHAPTER 2

The Framework of Economic Development Policy

STATE and local economic development is not a new governmental function in the United States. Distant ancestors of modern policy initiatives may be traced back at least to the New Jersey legislature's decision in 1791 to incorporate Alexander Hamilton's private company, the Society for Establishing Useful Manufactures, as a vehicle for industrial development. Strengthened by a state tax exemption, a grant of power to condemn property for its own use, and control over much of the water supply of northern New Jersey, the society proceeded to create by the falls of the Passaic River the nation's first industrial park (Norwood, 1974, p. 37). Others have documented similar efforts of other young states in this period (e.g., Handlin and Handlin, 1969; Heath, 1954). The direct progenitors of contemporary economic development policies date from the Great Depression of this century, during which southern states in particular sought to lure industry to their region with offers of tax relief, cheap capital, and subsidized plants and land.

If economic development is not an entirely novel government concern, the character of this policy domain is qualitatively different from efforts in the years before the 1970s. The shift from an emphasis on supply-side location incentives to demand-oriented market-sensitive entrepreneurial policies as the means to growth has been accompanied by other shifts as well. No longer a limited regional activity of industrially underdeveloped southern and New England states, economic development is now a universal public function. Furthermore, the domain is marked by an increasing degree of institutionalization and policy elaboration, as the narrowly focused arrangements of the postdepression decades have given way to bureaucratic management of a complex array of technical programs. Finally, economic development has grown from a relatively marginal item on the political agendas of state and local officials to a central—even pivotal—issue among prevailing concerns.

The elevation of economic development to the standard array of governmental functions is a recent phenomenon. Writing particularly of its penetration of the planning profession, Edward Bergman has observed, "It is now widely accepted that economic development has taken its place among the principal planning activities carried out at state and local levels. Acceptance came so rapidly and so completely that long-time planners now overlook the fact that very few of them would have posed it as an important planning activity a decade ago" (1983, p. 260). Scholars estimate that by the mid-1980s more than 15,000 state and local officials in the United States were engaged in domestic economic development activities as their primary responsibility, and countless others dealt with development problems in tangential or episodic fashion (Beaumont and Hovey, 1985).

Twentieth-century forerunners of modern state economic development bureaus can be found in the early efforts of Alabama, North Carolina, Florida, and Maine, each of which established agencies between 1923 and 1927 to encourage industrial development and attract investment (Gilmore, 1959, p. 29). Economic development planning was part of the function of the state comprehensive planning agencies established by every state but Delaware during the depression as a condition of receiving federal public works funds. Development planning was limited in the 1930s mainly to taking inventories and coordinating the location of public works facilities with industrial development needs. A number of states, mainly in the South, continued to maintain parallel agencies devoted to encouraging industrial relocation (Cobb, 1982). When the National Resources Planning Board was disbanded in 1943, the state planning agencies disappeared in its wake.

State bureaus designed to implement efforts to stimulate industrial and other economic development spread after the war but did not become a universal element of state government machinery until recently. Today each of the 50 states has a department of economic development or its equivalent. Yet of the 44 states responding to a Council of State Governments survey in 1982, 13 reported that they had established economic development agencies as recently as the 1970s, and 8 said that they had formed such units only in the 1980s (Reinshuttle, n.d., p. 1). A number of states maintain one or more additional specialized authorities, commissions, or quasi-public corporations to complement their primary economic development unit.

Most large cities and urban counties also established or greatly expanded economic development offices in recent years.[1] New Haven created its Office of Economic Development in 1979, Minneapolis its Community Development Agency in 1981, and Chicago its Department of Economic Development in 1982, to give several examples. Detroit has an older agency, but as late as 1970 it employed only two people, whose tasks were limited to commercial- and industrial-site planning. By the middle of the decade, however, the number of employees had expanded to more than 40 and their tasks had greatly diversified. The elaboration of functions is also found at the state level, as the following passage from a report by the Utah Department of Community and Economic Development (1985) suggests:

Fifteen years ago promotional efforts of the Department of Community and Economic Development were limited to tourism and to responding to out-of-state industrial clients. Today the on-going programs of the Department . . . include: the Urban Development Program which recruits business to the metropolitan areas of the state; the Rural Development Program which coordinates with rural areas of Utah for recruitment of industry; the Business Development Program which is charged with helping existing businesses and with developing state financing initiatives; the International Development Program which works to attract foreign investment in Utah, to encourage export of Utah products to foreign markets and to promote Utah as a destination for the Pacific Rim tourist; . . . and the Centers of Excellence Program which encourages greater ties between Utah's colleges and universities and the private sector. (pp. 5–6)

The virtually universal institutionalization of the economic development function has also been accompanied by a proliferation of policy tools and a rapid intensification of their use. Conducting a detailed census of state and local policy initiatives, particularly over time, is a daunting and perhaps impossible task. No comprehensive catalogue exists; even the partial compendia are out of date at the time of publication, so fast is the pace of innovation in this policy domain.[2] One source, how-

---

1. No census of municipal economic development agencies exists to my knowledge. The Washington-based Council for Urban Economic Development reports, however, that many cities in the 1980s moved economic development functions out of planning departments and created new agencies headed by "cabinet level" administrators (interview, CUED, Apr. 14, 1987).

2. Two sources that provide reasonably thorough coverage of supply-side location-incentive programs by state include Northeast-Midwest Institute, *The 1983 Guide to Government Resources for Economic Development* (Washington, DC: Northeast-Midwest Institute, 1982) and National Association of State Development Agencies, *Directory of Incentives for Business Investment and Development in the United States* (Washington, DC:

ever, the *Industrial Development and Site Selection Handbook,* a trade periodical, does track the annual shift in the number of states offering various financing subsidies, tax incentives and exemptions, and special development services. Beginning in 1966 the survey reported on the incidence of 44 different incentive programs; the number of programs tracked rose to 53 in 1976 and 55 in 1985.

If we sum all the separate programs in the 50 states in any given year and take that sum as a percentage of all *possible* programs (the number of states [50] multiplied by the number of different types of programs), we get a simple index over time of the increasing penetration of these largely supply-side location-incentive programs tracked in the survey. Between 1966 and 1985 this penetration score went from .382 to .594. The actual number of programs in existence increased by 94.4 percent in these years (see Table 2-1). Table 2-2 shows, for illustrative purposes, the growth in the number of states offering selected programs from this survey.

Many policy innovations in economic development (including most of those associated with the entrepreneurial state) are not tracked annually. Urban enterprise zones and municipal land banks do not appear in the *Site Selection Handbook* survey, nor do product-development corporations or state venture capital funds. High-tech centers of excellence, mayoral trade missions abroad, and state export-financing programs are other examples of important program initiatives not enumerated in any annual survey.[3]

The growth in the simple number of programs, of course, fails to convey the increasing intensity of their use. Even programs long available in principle show sharply increased rates of use in the 1970s and 1980s. One dramatic example concerns tax-exempt bonds for industrial development financing, pioneered in the South in the 1930s. In 1975 cities, states, and other public authorities issued a total of $1.3 billion worth of such bonds to finance private firms, a sum that had grown to this level in modest increments since the early 1950s. By 1984, however, the vol-

---

Urban Institute, 1986, 2d ed.). Neither is published annually. The federal government publishes specialized directories of more recent entrepreneurial programs, including the following by the U.S. Small Business Administration: *State Activities in Capital Formation: Venture Capital, Working Capital, and Public Pension Fund Investments* (1985); *State Export Promotion Activities* (1984); and *State Policies and Programs to Enhance the Small Business Climate* (1984).

3. The growth of each of these programs, as well as others, is covered in Chapters 7, 10, 11, and 12.

Table 2-1. The Penetration of Supply-Side Location
Incentives, 1966–85

	1966	1976	1985
Total programs	840	1213	1633
Total possible programs	2200	2650	2750
Penetration percentage	.382	.458	.594
Programs per state	16.8	24.3	32.3

Sources: *Industrial Development and Manufacturers Record* 135 (Dec. 1966, 26–27; *Site Selection Handbook* 21 (May 1976), 106–8; *Industrial Development and Site Selection Handbook* 154 (Jan.–Feb. 1985), 52–54. (The different titles simply reflect name changes and the merger of two publications by the same publisher.) In addition to the tax incentives, capital and land subsidies, and technical assistance programs tracked in this survey, several regulatory programs (6 in 1966 and 1976, 4 in 1985) were tracked, but they are not included in these calculations, because they are not regarded as incentives to business location.

ume had risen to $17.4 billion, an explosive increase of more than 1200 percent (U.S. Congress, Joint Committee on Taxation, 1985, p. 60). Other examples abound. New York City's J-51 tax abatement, designed to stimulate investment in rehabilitated housing, was established in 1955. By 1979 the city had foregone a cumulative total of approximately $40 million in property taxes in the first 24 years of the program. Only three years later the amount of foregone tax revenues under J-51 had doubled to approximately $80 million (Avens et al., n.d., p. 13). Increases of virtually exponential proportions can be observed in other programs, such as the use of tax increment financing arrangements, the number of publicly supported research parks for high-tech industries, the number of foreign trade missions undertaken by governors and mayors, and so on.

Economic development has not only become functionally and organizationally embedded in subnational government in recent years, but it has also achieved a high, often unique, place on state and local political

Table 2-2.   Number of States Offering Selected Economic Development Programs

Policy	1966	1976	1985
City or county revenue bond financing[a]	28	43	50
State loans for building construction	11	15	30
Accelerated depreciation of industrial equipment	9	21	36
State loan guarantees for building construction	11	14	20
City or county loan guarantees for building construction	1	0	7
State aid for existing-plant expansion	14	27	37
Local tax exemption or moratorium on land or capital improvements	11	21	32
State tax exemption on manufacturers' inventories	19	34	43
State tax exemption to encourage R&D	3	7	19
City or county provision of free industrial land sites	—	13	19

Sources: Same as Table 2-1.
[a]Local government programs are normally dependent on state enabling legislation.

agendas. Economic development and growth concerns were not even included as such among the major policy issues that students of state politics discussed as recently as 1965. The policy areas of "taxation, education, welfare, and highway programs . . . ," wrote the editors of the classic *Politics of the American States,* "taken together, . . . constitute much of the substance of politics at the state level" (Jacob and Vines, 1965, p. 289). And an analysis of issues most frequently mentioned in gubernatorial state-of-the-state, inaugural, and budget speeches between 1970 and 1983 found no references to economic development until 1976, when it ranked sixth along with such concerns as election-law reform and government reorganization (Herzik, 1983). But then the issue began to rise in importance: in 1979 it ranked in fifth place on the list of concerns, and by 1981 it had risen to second. Later surveys of governors and their staffs conducted by the National Governors' Association found the issue in first place in both 1983 and 1984. Most governors also ranked it as the major priority of the future (Beyle, 1983; *State Policy Reports,* Sept. 21, 1984; Balderston, 1986, p. 4). Surveys among urban officials have turned up similar findings. For example, a 1983 National League of Cities survey found that of the top six "most serious issues" mayors said they were facing, three were related to economic development: unemployment, inadequate job base, and inadequate local revenue sources (Roberts, 1984, p. 12).

In many states and cities economic development is viewed, not simply as a discrete issue competing for attention and resources with other issues on the political agenda, but rather as a pervasive "framework issue" that bears in some way on all other major policy concerns. The possibilities for effective transportation, human services, and education initiatives are dependent in this view on the success of economic development policy, while tax policy, environmental regulation, and labor policy cannot be considered apart from their potential impact on prospects for economic development. The critical role of economic development is reflected in gubernatorial rhetoric: an analysis of 40 recent state-of-the-state messages found them studded with new development proposals—an average of about a dozen per speech (*State Policy Reports,* Mar. 1985, pp. 3–4).

These various indicia of the rise of economic development policy suggest that the issue has undergone a recent transformation from an occasional item on the agendas of a few industrially underdeveloped states to a concern of central and universal importance. Policy tools and programs, once relatively simple and few in number, have become exceedingly complex and varied, while policy development and implementation in this realm have become increasingly bureaucratized. In a variety of ways, then, economic development concerns and programs have penetrated the political world of states and communities.

Framework Elements of Economic Development Policy

For more than half a century subnational economic development policy has been shaped by a constant structural framework. The elements of this framework include the idea of a public-private partnership as the preferred vehicle for the pursuit of development goals, decentralized responsibility, avoidance of government economic planning, a preference for capital- rather than labor-based solutions to employment problems, and pragmatism. These elements have constituted a congenial matrix for the development of both supply-side and demand-oriented policy approaches.

PUBLIC-PRIVATE PARTNERSHIP

The idea that certain social goals can be achieved best through private-sector activity supported in some way by government has been and still is a central structural feature of economic development policy. The union of government and business in common effort, called a partnership in the economic development domain, is said to unite the greater vision, expertise, and management skills of the private sector with the risk-bearing capacity and resources of the public sector. At one extreme this collaborative principle precludes reliance on fully socialized economic forms as a strategy for development, and at the other it rejects a laissez-faire approach that maintains a solid wall between public authority and the private economy.

"Partnership" is a loose term for a range of types of collaborations. It may be invoked to describe the efforts of government to create a congenial business climate through, for example, general tax and labor policies. This sort of diffuse, indirect "partnership" contrasts with more focused relationships cemented by grants of subsidies to specific firms, where government plays the role of subordinate or junior partner, and with a range of actual joint ventures, where government and one or more specific firms share risks and even equity interests on a relatively equal footing.

Partnerships between government and business are justified on the grounds that private investment is essential to the economic health of a community or state but without public inducements it will not or cannot take place in sufficient quantity or in those ventures most likely to produce collective economic benefits. As Charles Lindblom argues in *Politics and Markets,* "Governments . . . must . . . offer benefits to businessmen in order to stimulate the required performance" of tasks that range from maintaining full employment to regional development. Without inducements, business will not perform those "indispensable functions" (1977, pp. 133–37).

Supply-side economic development policy sought to create partnerships with mobile capital through location inducements of various sorts—low taxes, tax exemptions, cheap land, and capital subsidies. Historically, these inducements have been offered on a unconditional basis, suggesting that government in the supply-side tradition fills a subordinate and quite vulnerable role in any partnership. Business recipients are under no obligation in the typical arrangement to produce a set number of new jobs or to remain in a location for a specified period of time. Once public assistance is provided, government can only hope in the usual case that the public interest will be served by the firm's economic decisions.

The partnership principle is equally critical to the entrepreneurial approach, but it is a partnership where government has attempted to focus its resources on firms or industries that promise growth, to play a more decisive role in influencing the behavior of target firms by identifying and then surmounting critical barriers to private investment, and, increasingly, to hold the private partner responsible for meeting performance obligations. Partnership is thus still important, but the balance of power between the two partners, I shall argue, has become more equal.

DECENTRALIZATION

The invention and implementation of economic development policies are the responsibilities chiefly of numerous state and local governments. The task is shared by countless private organizations, such as chambers of commerce, and quasi-public bodies, such as industrial development corporations. Most of these actors operate independently of one another. There is no federal department of economic development to offer guidance, nor is there a national development plan or coordinating body. Federal programs do exist, but their exploitation and implementation are left mainly to state and local officials and citizens' groups.

The very idea of the modern business inducement—the offer of public resources to reduce the costs of business operations in return for industrial employment—was crafted at the community level during the depression. These incentives were gradually adopted, refined, and expanded by the states.

Federal initiatives have been important at various times for establishing policy models or for stimulating state and local experimentation. Urban renewal in the 1950s, for example, introduced on a broad scale the use of eminent domain for economic development. Programs and conferences sponsored by the U.S. Small Business Administration helped to spur state interest in the small business sector. In addition, federal resources passed down to state and local governments in the form of grants-in-aid for economic development have been substantial at times, though they have diminished in importance since 1980. But despite Washington's record of policy invention and fiscal assistance, the federal role in subnational economic development has been dwarfed by the sheer energy, density, and ingenuity of state and local efforts.

This is not, of course, to overlook the fact that in the American federal system the maintenance and enhancement of economic well-being is a shared responsibility. It is simply a function carried out by the two levels of government in different ways. The federal government establishes the parameters of subnational efforts through its fiscal, monetary, and trade policies. Although states and localities also attempt to influence investment behavior through tax policies, the bulk of their efforts to create employment, stimulate new investment, and encourage new industries is carried out through microeconomic interventions.

One problem with placing a major burden for addressing such critical problems of economic performance or nonperformance on the shoulders of subnational government is that Americans enter the field of economic development policy without the full benefit of the superior resources that Washington is able to marshal. Moreover, the pattern of decentralized economic development means that this policy domain is subject to a classic weakness of a federal system, namely that regional inequalities affect the ability to fashion policy, thus, potentially perpetuating uneven rates of growth. Uneven patterns of prosperity and policy development exist, of course, in nations with centralized growth and development strategies (Rodwin, 1970). But in those societies it is a *national* goal to bring depressed regions up to the national norm. In the United States the achievement of this goal is mainly a state and local responsibility pursued by jurisdictions with very different capacities.

There are at least two additional consequences of the decentralization of responsibility worth noting: policy variety and interjurisdictional competition. Although there are several basic models that influence economic development policy design, there is not only much variation within these but also a great deal of idiosyncratic effort.

One important explanation for the variety of policy initiatives in this field is the response to the fact that states typically learn what their neighbors and major competitors are doing and prudently seek to match those efforts. This creates a problem of market differentiation insofar as a state is interested in attracting mobile domestic and foreign capital, for if every state offers the same menu of programs, how can any state stand out? How is it possible under those conditions for policy to make a difference in stimulating or attracting development? Investors of capital will make their decisions about how much, when, and where to invest without having to consider the differential impact of policy. This situation, then, creates incentives for program invention in order to create interstate differences. Policy variety is a product of competitive dynamics.

In addition, program variation reflects to some extent the lack of a strong consensus about what works and what does not in this policy domain. Much program design is frankly experimental, as states try alternative ways of wielding leverage in the economy.

Decentralization of responsibility for development also accounts for interjurisdictional competition. As one urban economist observed more than 20 years ago, "It seems rather useful to view the city not so much as a trading or producing area but rather as a center competing with all other places within the national economy for job-creating investments" (Stanislaw Czamanski, quoted in Conroy, 1975, p. 49). The supply-side tradition particularly is a response to the contest for mobile industries and branch operations of existing firms. The rise of the entrepreneurial state, however, with its emphasis on homegrown firms and entrepreneurs, promises to dampen interstate competition for investment.

State and local officials still devote substantial energies and resources to the competition for footloose firms, despite indications, discussed later, that such businesses do not constitute the main sources of employment growth in a state's economy. Much of this effort is no doubt spurred by the sheer excitement of the hunt, though other key factors are the need to counteract the efforts of other states and the fact that attracting the rare major employer from another place seems to pay enormous political dividends.

ABSENCE OF PLANNING

When economic development first emerged as an activity of state and local government, officials sought to encourage economic growth by pursuing targets of opportunity. Rumors that a particular firm was interested in relocating, inquiries from firms to local chambers of commerce about potential sites, or notices of relocation plans in the business press would mobilize local and state officials and business leaders in an effort to attract the prospect. Any business, no matter how small, no matter what the product or the wage structure, was considered a prize (Cobb, 1982, p. 70). States and cities still advertise the virtues of their respective business climates in the business media,[4] and inquiries generated by these ads may provide the basis for elaborate follow-up procedures (see, for example, Alabama Development Office, 1986, p. 56).

As competition became more intense, governors, mayors, and business leaders were no longer content to wait for firms to announce a desire to relocate. Instead, they formed "raiding parties" that traveled to other states prospecting for footloose firms. The city of Atlanta pushed this

---

4. Nearly every state advertises, but few report on their efforts as carefully as Oklahoma. The Oklahoma Department of Economic Development reports that its advertisements in such periodicals as *Fortune, Forbes, Barron's, Harvard Business Review,* and various airline magazines generated 7181 inquiries from businesses in 1984. The first two periodicals accounted for the largest number of inquiries (Oklahoma Dept. of Economic Development, 1985, Appendix XX).

practice to the extreme by establishing a permanent office in New York City in the 1970s from which to recruit northeastern businesses to Georgia (*New York Times,* Feb. 11, 1977). Although few states have matched Atlanta's particular brand of aggressiveness (Kentucky and Massachusetts are exceptions; both have New York offices), many still conduct vigorous prospecting campaigns outside the state. Mississippi, for example, reports 17 trips made by prospecting teams between July 1985 and June 1986 to New York, Chicago, Memphis, New Orleans, Los Angeles, San Francisco, Cleveland, and Mobile to make contact with "key decision makers in plant location" (Mississippi Dept. of Economic Development, 1985–86, pp. 11ff.).

To the extent that states have relied on random inquiries from out-of-state firms and saturation prospecting trips, the pursuit of economic development has been an essentially unplanned activity. Development goals under such a strategy are no more complex than attracting more jobs. It is no doubt the case that such an approach to economic development has been encouraged by the appearance of quantitative "scorecards" recording plant openings and closings, by state. These make the measurement of "success" and "failure" an apparently simple matter for the public (see, for example, *Industrial Development and Site Selection Handbook,* Nov.–Dec. 1985, pp. 28–29). These short-term considerations converge, of course, with the historic American suspicion of central economic planning (Kantrow, 1983, pp. 80–84). American individualism is more comfortable with the combination of liberties and disorder that obtain in the relatively unimpeded market than with the strictures of central planning (Wildavsky, 1986).

These cultural predispositions notwithstanding, an interest in more consciously planned approaches to development has begun to emerge. In its mildest version the planned approach involves simply targeting a broad range of industries on which to focus promotional efforts. Oklahoma provides an illustration: the state hired an outside consultant to identify various industries in advanced technological fields that might flourish in the state's particular setting, and these now provide the target firms for the state's prospecting efforts (Oklahoma Dept. of Economic Development, 1985, p. 14 and Appendix II). A number of communities and states also produce lists of development activities and goals in more or less random fashion that they label "economic development plans." The Advisory Commission on Intergovernmental Relations, for example, reports that in 1984 70 percent of 570 local chambers of commerce said that their communities had such "plans" (Roberts et al., 1985, p. 24).

A number of states and a few cities have embraced a more vigorous focused approach in the form of strategic economic development planning. Strategic planning is an exercise borrowed from the private corporate sector. Its key elements at the state and local level are the establishment of long-term economic goals that may realistically be met, an audit and analysis of internal strengths and weaknesses, and an assessment of opportunities in the external world that may be exploited by the state's or city's particular mix of economic resources and capabilities. The plan is designed to focus resources over the long term on a state's comparative advantages vis-à-vis other states and to prevent diffusion of effort (Sorkin et al., n.d.; Olsen and Eadie, 1982). A crucial aspect of state strategic planning is the identification of certain industries likely both to provide high economic development benefits and to flourish in that particular state's environment. As the director of Michigan's Department of Commerce describes the strategic planning process, it is as though the state of Michigan were an industrial park with certain given resources and advantages. The object of the managers—the state government—is to exploit these for the maximum collective economic effect. To fill up the park with tenants and encourage their growth, the state must do a "market analysis" to assess the range of external opportunities for firms likely to do well in the state economy, and it must perform an audit of internal resources—labor market characteristics, capital availability, the nature of the local industrial agglomeration, and so on—on which firms may draw. This exercise in Michigan actually led to the targeting of automotive-parts manufacturers and certain specific high-technology industries with special application to the auto industry (Douglas Ross, speech made at Wayne State University, Apr. 16, 1987).

The emphasis in strategic planning is on specific feasible goals attained according to a timetable. Normative objectives—what ought to be—and grand speculations about the future play no role in strategic planning.[5] The strategic planning process varies from strictly in-house, professional, bureaucratic participation to an elaborate, consensus-building, "corporatist" effort among labor leaders, business people, and government bureaucrats and elected officials.

By 1986 at least 17 states had written some sort of strategic plan

---

5. Strategic planning efforts in the public sector are distinguished from the "futures" commissions that many states and cities sponsored in the 1970s (e.g., the Goals for Dallas Commission, Oregon 2000, and so on). Futures reports generally deal with more than economic development, they offer alternative scenarios, they seldom specify timetables or policy options, and they generally ignore resource constraints (see Chi, 1983).

Chart 2-1.   State Strategic Economic Development Plans, 1985

Arizona	1983	*Arizona Horizons: A Strategy for Future Economic Growth*
California	1984	*Job Creation for California in the Decade of the Eighties*
Hawaii	1985	*Hawaii's Economic Future*
Illinois	1985	*Illinois Jobs for the Future: Five Year Economic Development Strategy*
Indiana	1983	*In Step with the Future*
Iowa	1984	*We Are Iowans First*
Michigan	1984	*The Path to Prosperity*
Minnesota	1985	*Minnesota: A Strategy for Economic Development*
Montana	1983	*Montana Economic Development Project*
Nevada	1985	*Nevada State Plan for Economic Diversification and Development*
New York	1985	*Rebuilding New York: The Next Phase from Recovery to Resurgence*
North Dakota	1985	*An Economic Development Plan for North Dakota*
Ohio	1983	*Toward a Working Ohio: Jobs and Ohio's Economy*
Pennsylvania	1985	*Choices for Pennsylvanians*
Rhode Island	1984	*The Greenhouse Compact*[a]
Utah	1985	*Developing Utah's Economy: Guidelines, Policies and Plans*
Wisconsin	1985	*The Final Report of the Strategic Development Commission*

[a]Defeated by voters in a referendum, June 1984.

designed to focus state resources on certain targeted industries of special significance to the state. Chart 2-1 lists the states and the titles of their plans. At least eight additional states reported in a 1985–86 survey that they were preparing strategic plans or had just been mandated to do so by their legislatures.[6] A number of other states have marketing plans in lieu of strategic plans, but these are short-term agendas that do not derive from an analysis of external opportunities for local industries and the state's resources.[7] Several cities, including San Francisco, Pasadena, and San Antonio, have also prepared strategic economic development plans.

Although Pennsylvania conducted the first state strategic planning exercise, it was Rhode Island's elaborate 976-page *Greenhouse Compact* several years later that achieved national attention. Orchestrated by Ira Magaziner, a private economic development consultant, the plan proposed by a representative commission appointed by the governor called for an array of new venture-capital programs, research centers, job-training efforts, and small business incubators. This complex plan, which contemplated public expenditures of $250 million over a seven-year period, was put before the voters and, to the surprise of its myriad backers

6. These included Alaska, Arkansas, Florida, Kansas, Nebraska, New Hampshire, New Mexico, and West Virginia. The survey of all states was conducted by telephone in 1985–86.

7. For example, Oklahoma, Mississippi, and Alabama.

in the statehouse and corporate and union headquarters, went down to overwhelming defeat (Magaziner, 1986; Anton and West, 1987). No other strategic plan has been the subject of a statewide popular referendum. Piecemeal implementation by legislative action and executive decree has been the rule.

Strategic planning in the public sector for economic development is clearly new. Most of the history of economic development is notable for the absence of planning. The growing interest in planning, which represents a genuine change in one structural element of the policy domain, has arisen out of the need to use public resources in a more focused, efficient way in a highly competitive environment. As states compete with other states, as local producers compete abroad, and as indigenous entrepreneurs compete with one another for public and private capital, state economic development officials have sought, out of necessity, ways of concentrating their efforts on those economic sectors and business people most likely to produce job growth. Strategic planning provides the guidelines for such efforts.

THE PRIMACY OF CAPITAL

A fourth critical element in the structure of economic development is the notion that the key to job creation, a primary goal, is to encourage and subsidize the investment of private capital. As new firms are born or as existing firms relocate or expand under the impetus of business subsidies, it is expected that the local demand for labor will increase. Employment goals are therefore pursued through a trickle-down process common to both supply-side and demand-oriented approaches to development.

An alternative strategy would, of course, focus directly on labor and take the form of public employment, wage subsidies to private industry, labor training, and labor mobility programs, that is, an "active manpower policy" in the Swedish mode (Ginsburg, 1983, Ch. 6). Some state and local governments do offer wage subsidies (they are often found in state urban enterprise zones, for example), and nearly all states administer job-training programs geared to the needs of specific enterprises. But these are essentially secondary elements in a policy domain in which the support of capital is the paramount consideration.[8]

---

8. The Congressional Budget Office reports that in fiscal year 1983–84 the states spent a total of $428 million on business promotion in the form of loans, loan guarantees, venture capital funds, and a variety of direct expenditures including job-training and labor services. Expenditures on all labor programs accounted for 28.3 percent of total spending. California alone, however, spent $68 million of the $121 million devoted to labor programs.

To assume in a capitalist society that capital is the engine of economic development is hardly surprising, but the implication of this assumption has been an occasional tendency not merely to devise policies that promote capital but to supplement them with others that have a distinctly antilabor cast, particularly in the supply-side tradition. This tendency emerged in part from a diagnosis of regional economic decline that focused on the ability of low-wage states and foreign nations to induce industrial relocation from high-wage areas. Since such movement by firms is assumed by many to represent a strain toward efficiency—highly rational behavior—the blame for economic woes was attributed not to mobile industries but to labor which had priced itself out of the market.

It followed that, in order to compete as an attractive site for industry, states had an interest in reducing the local price of labor. In the 1940s southern states pioneered right-to-work laws in the hopes of weakening union power, thus undercutting labor's leverage in setting wages. A central theme in state and local economic development campaigns in those years was that southern labor was not only cheap but *willing* to work for a low wage (Cobb, 1982, Ch. 4). Although right-to-work laws spread out of the South only into the central and northern plains, other states sought to reduce labor costs on the supply side through their policies on unemployment insurance and worker-compensation levels. Such thinking is still encouraged by certain "business climate" surveys in which comparative wage rates and other labor costs among states figure prominently.

Policies of the entrepreneurial state reject the assumption that low wages constitute a competitive advantage. Economic development is increasingly understood as a process that involves not simply employment growth but also increasing income (see Chapter 3). Furthermore, the new entrepreneurial strategy has begun to experiment with programs designed to protect workers against economic dislocation, interposing state power between labor and private employers who decide to relocate or shut down (see Chapter 13). But in common with the supply-side tradition, demand-oriented entrepreneurial policies focus primarily on capital investment as the key to stimulating employment growth. Labor policy remains marginal to the economic development process.

Eliminating this outlier provides a more meaningful picture. Remaining labor expenditures amounted to only $53 million. After removing California's outlays from the state total, labor expenditures for all other states constituted only 14.7 percent of business-promotion costs (CBO, 1984, pp. 4, 79).

PRAGMATISM

When the state of Mississippi initiated its Balance Agriculture With Industry program of industrial subsidies in the 1930s, a few doubters were concerned that such arrangements were "socialistic" (Cobb, 1982, P. 33). But in their desperation for economic development many Mississippians put aside such worries. As one Mississippi banker commented, "I'm so much concerned about real forms of Socialism that I can't worry much about that municipally owned but privately operated factory down the street" (Moes, 1962, P. 74; see also Cobb, 1982, p. 33).

In the subsequent half century, as economic development programs spread among the states and cities, neither ideology nor theory has exercised a very rigorous constraint on the inventiveness of official efforts to encourage business investment. Competition rather than abstract principles has been the major driving force in the design and evolution of policy. As Beaumont and Hovey write: "State and local economic development strategies typically evolve incrementally, without an underlying economic theory, except that more jobs are good and less jobs are bad. Local and state officials tend to deal with development pragmatically" (1985, p. 328).

The continual search for whatever appears to work has both advantages and disadvantages. As for the advantages, a pragmatic approach permits great flexibility and encourages innovation. It tends, particularly in a decentralized federal system, to maximize the possibility of tailoring policy to fit the particular conditions of a specific locale. This relatively unconstrained approach to policy design also offers the possibility for integrating a learning process into the business of policy-making. If effectiveness is a major criterion in the crafting of policy, rather than conformity to abstract economic or ideological orthodoxies, then policy-makers must also be watchful for evidence of ineffectiveness as a signal for the need to change.

In practice such a rationalized, if atheoretical, process of policy evolution is often impossible. The intensity of interjurisdictional competition has accelerated the pace of policy innovation to such a degree that evaluation efforts to determine what does and does not work may not always be practical. The evaluation process is hindered not only by the constant need to innovate, however, but also by a reluctance or inability to bring relevant economic theory to bear on policy design. In part this is a product of lack of information—few economic development officials are formally trained in the field—and in part it is caused by a lack of resources that enable analysts in the public sector to generate hypotheses and test them with data over time.

Although the absence of theory makes change and flexibility possible, it may also lock jurisdictions into policies for which there is no theoretical justification. Instead of developing evaluation criteria by reference to theory-based tests, policy-makers often rely in their evaluations on received wisdom, appearances, and their own hunches.

Conclusions

Insofar as it is possible to identify a particular starting point in history, modern state economic development policy may be said to have emerged in the 1930s in the South. As James Cobb has written, "By introducing a system wherein the state sanctioned and supervised the use of municipal bonds to finance plant construction, the BAWI [Mississippi's Balance Agriculture With Industry] program lifted the curtain on an era of more competitive subsidization and broader state and local involvement in industrial development efforts" (1982, p. 5). The rise of economic development as a public policy issue may be charted from that moment by following its increasing penetration in various ways of state and local politics.

Since the depression the invention and elaboration of economic development have been shaped and constrained by certain relatively constant structural features of this policy domain. Their origins may be traced mainly to two major elements of the environment: the cultural commitment to an economic order in which market mechanisms and private enterprise are key characteristics, and the federal political arrangement. The former helps to account for the idea of a partnership between the public and the private sectors, and it also explains the emphasis on capital rather than labor subsidies and the suspicion of central planning. The decentralization of responsibility for policy in this domain is attributable to the nature of American federalism.

All these features create a market milieu for economic development policy-making in which competition for private investment among states and local governments has been the driving force. A great deal is at stake in this competition, and success and failure seem to be easily measured and assiduously monitored by the public.[9] Competitive pressures are

---

9. The success or failure of governors' economic development policies was an issue in a number of state elections in 1986, according to *State Policy Reports* (Nov. 27, 1986, p. 21). *State Policy Reports* does not cite extensive data to back this contention, but it does report a Connecticut survey that found that 49 percent of the respondents thought state

such, then, that the main test of policy initiatives in economic development is a pragmatic one rather than whether they fit with ideological or theoretical precepts.

Major changes began to occur in the environment at some point during the 1970s, as we shall see in Chapter 4. These changes appear to have had only modest effects on the basic framework elements of the policy domain. Yet these effects, combined with changes that we have yet to examine in other structural elements, were sufficient to bring about design changes, namely the advent of entrepreneurial policies. What is striking, however, about the framework characteristics that we have just reviewed is that they have created a domain both stable and capacious enough to accommodate the supply-side tradition as well as the demand-oriented entrepreneurial policies of recent origin.

Yet these very characteristics that suggest the capacity for accommodation on the one hand also make clear the limits of policy invention in this domain on the other. Exclusive state and municipal ownership of enterprises and industries (the subnational equivalent of nationalization), national central economic planning, and extensive public employment programs are all foreclosed as approaches to economic development by the partnership principle, decentralization, and the commitment to capital-based solutions. Thus, the decentralized economic interventions pursued by states and cities fall short of the strong state models familiar to students of comparative political economy and therefore constitute a distinctive American adaptation.

---

government should get the credit for the state's healthy economy; only 19 percent believed that the federal government was responsible.

CHAPTER 3

Justifying Economic Development

IN popular discourse economic development is understood principally and quite simply as the creation of more jobs. Sometimes the term is qualified with the words "in the private sector"—the locus of "real" or productive work—but this is generally a needless qualifier in a society where large-scale public employment is not a genuine alternative. New jobs are generated locally, it is assumed, when new business enterprises are established, when existing concerns expand in place, or when distant firms in-migrate. Each of these processes is made possible by private investment.

In the mind of the politician or development official the benefits that flow from such investment are quite clear. Investment generates jobs. Jobs mean fewer unemployed people, more income, greater tax revenues, fewer social expenditures, lower-cost government, and a more robust employment multiplier. As Mario Cuomo, governor of New York, put it, "[W]hile there are no panaceas, nothing comes closer than one simple word: jobs" (*State Policy Reports,* Feb. 27, 1984).

The various links between private investment and its private and public benefits constitute the justifications for economic development policy in the minds of economic development practitioners, for it is policy that helps to generate the dynamism in this causal chain. The progression from investment to benefits can be expressed schematically in terms of two models—the private benefit model and the public benefit model—disaggregated for theoretical, though not practical, purposes (see Figure 3-1).

Political rhetoric and statements in public documents often come remarkably close to a merged version of these models. For example, in his state-of-the-state speech in 1984 Mario Cuomo proclaimed:

[G]rowth in private sector jobs is our very best hope for the future. . . . At this moment . . . in this state, nearly 600,000 men and women are out of work. Imag-

I. The Private Benefit Model

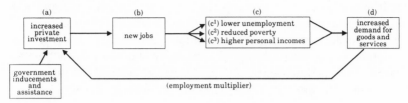

II. The Public Benefit Model

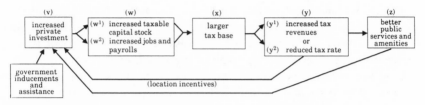

Figure 3-1. Economic Development Models

ine, if you will—and it needs imagining—a state where all of those people were working, receiving salaries, paying taxes, where none of them would need the unemployment benefits or welfare benefits or job-training benefits paid for by the rest of us. In such a state, the cost of government could go down and revenues up, allowing us to invest in what we needed for the disadvantaged, for education, for infrastructure, for the arts and housing, while at the same time reducing the rate of taxes. (*State Policy Reports,* Feb. 27, 1984, p. 5)

Or consider the following testimony by Detroit's Mayor Coleman Young in response to the question of whether jobs for city residents serve a "public purpose": "To the degree that it is in the public interest to provide adequate services to our people . . . it is necessary to have a tax base, and the basic ingredient of a tax base is jobs and manufacturing" (quoted in Jones and Bachelor, 1986, p. 119).

Another variant is provided by the city of San Francisco's strategic planning document: "Not only does [economic] growth provide business opportunities, but it also provides the jobs and employment base that are absolutely necessary for the City's residents. . . . This economic base provides the public works infrastructure to support job and business growth . . ." (Arthur Andersen and Co., 1983, p. 4).

Both models require a continuous flow of private investment to fuel the development cycles, but for a variety of reasons that flow is uncertain. From a national macroeconomic point of view the flow may be dependent on a sustained rate of personal savings and high demand levels. It may also be dependent on the vision and courage of those who control capital, a function of the ability to see opportunities in the market and a willingness to bear risks. From the perspective of states or cities there may simply be problems of slippage in the two models. For example, in the private benefit model, increased demand for goods and services may be directed at producers beyond a state's or city's borders, thereby producing no new local investment. In the public benefit model there may be information slippage: potential investors may not know about an area's reduced tax rate or its better services and infrastructure and thus will not be attracted to the locale as an investment site. In both models factors in the local environment seen as inimical to further investment—high energy costs, an unproductive labor force, poor transportation infrastructure—may lead to the withdrawal of capital or disinvestment from a particular place. The role of the state and local government in economic development is to ensure continuous private investment in local enterprises and undertakings by whatever actions or inducements seem acceptable and effective.[1]

How subnational governments might intervene most effectively raises the issue of supply-side versus demand-oriented strategies. But before confronting the problem of the nature and evolution of government intervention in the development cycle, let us consider the validity of the public and private benefit models from the point of private investment onward.

Growth versus Development

There exist among policy-makers in the economic development domain certain ambiguities about how the models relate to one another and what precisely they signify. For example, public officials normally treat employment and tax-base growth as compatible objectives. But as Gerweck and Epp (1974) have argued, employment (the private benefit goal) and an increase in disposable local tax revenues (the public benefit objective) are to some extent in mutual conflict: the in-migrants that tend to be attracted by new employment will usually more than absorb addi-

---

1. Kurihara has written that "models of laissez-faire growth have the negative virtue of demonstrating how precarious and unfruitful it is to leave the secular growth of an economy to the vagaries of private saving and investment, to the accident of profit-motivated inventions and innovations, and to the working of unguided market forces. All these growth models have this positive lesson for underdeveloped economies, that the State should be allowed to play not only a stabilizing role but also a developmental role, if those economies are to industrialize more effectively and rapidly . . ." (1959, p. 185).

tional revenues. Gerweck and Epp contend that the most effective way to maximize tax revenue growth is to encourage new industries that are highly automated, that use a high percentage of nonresident workers, or that hire a large number of second-income workers from local families, all features that limit added municipal service responsibilities.

Another ambiguity has to do with the private benefit model, and it inheres not so much in the contradictions between the ultimate goals of economic development as in the evolving complexity of its justifications. These are in the process of shifting from a largely quantitative formulation to a qualitative one. Historically, the private benefit model seemed to function simply as a series of quantitative relationships in which the stated goal was employment growth. Within this framework economic developers and politicians made no effort to specify what sorts of jobs constituted desirable additions to a local economy and what sorts did not. Nor was there an explicit acknowledgement of distinctions among jobs and the attendant implications for community well-being. In the urgency that often surrounded the search for an industrial employer, distinguishing between union scale versus minimum-wage jobs, employment in growing versus dying industries, and permanent versus seasonal work could be dismissed not only as an indulgence but as potentially self-defeating, at least in the short run. Growth, pure and simple, was the limit of the developer's aspiration.

The booster campaigns in vogue in the industrializing southern states between 1935 and the 1960s exemplify this pattern. These efforts built on the appeal of "an abundance of docile workers willing to work for wages well below the national average" (Cobb, 1982, p. 92). Moes (1962, pp. 37–38) has argued in fact that southern states deliberately sought low-wage industries in order to stretch their industrial subsidies. Low-wage firms tend to be labor intensive, that is, with a low ratio of capital to labor. A small amount of capital generates a comparatively large number of jobs. Economic development subsidies, of course, subsidize capital, not labor. Thus, in low-wage, labor-intensive industries there is less capital to subsidize, and the subsidy creates a greater number of jobs than in capital-intensive industries.

Whether it was the existence of a low-wage workforce or the deliberate recruiting efforts of state governments, the strategy drew a range of low-wage labor-intensive operations to the region, from apparel firms to Mississippi and Alabama in the depression to microchip production firms to North Carolina and Texas in the 1970s.

The indiscriminate quest for employers of local labor may have brought temporary relief to many communities; as Wildavsky and Pressman once pointed out, in depressed areas, "any job is the right job" (1973, p. 154). But labor-intensive industries that hire low-wage workers are notoriously footloose in search of cheaper labor markets. The entire history of such development efforts has been plagued by plant departures or shutdowns as manufacturers of everything from hosiery to silicon chips have moved abroad or gone bankrupt in the face of foreign-wage competition (*New York Times,* Dec. 8, 1984, and Mar. 21, 1985). In addition, many states that relied heavily on low-wage industries for industrial employment have experienced slightly lower-than-average levels of personal-income growth. For example, a majority of the states that have had long-standing right-to-work laws, the most explicit legislative measure designed to preserve a low-wage climate, maintained this pattern even into the 1980s. Between 1979 and 1984 the average per capita income growth rate for all 50 states was 72 percent. Thirteen of the 20 states that had right-to-work laws in 1980 fell below that figure. For all 20 right-to-work states the average income growth rate for that period was 70.2 percent (based on data in *State Policy Reports,* June 1985, p. 6).

Michael Conroy has argued that an emphasis on employment growth alone is a form of "naive boosterism" in which "more" is equated with "better" (1975, p. 63). He and others (e.g., Thompson, 1965) suggest that development properly refers to a process of *qualitative* change to which the mere addition of jobs may make little contribution. Employment ought to be conceived of less as an end in itself than as a means to well-being. As Thompson puts it, "The fundamental normative assumption here is that the local growth rate is a lever through which desirable changes in the level, distribution, and stability of income may be achieved" (p. 2; see also p. 181).

Sensitivity to the impact of new jobs on income distribution and growth rate or on cyclical unemployment patterns makes it clear that purely seasonal work, minimum-wage jobs, and part-time employment for primary breadwinners are less likely to alter significantly a locality's aggregate level of well-being than are jobs in, say, a defense contractor's plant or the workshop of a manufacturer of specialty commodities for the international industrial market. Those who stress employment as a satisfactory goal in itself point out that more jobs are almost always better than fewer jobs by any standard. The qualitative perspective concedes this point but maintains that certain types of jobs are far more productive means than others to improve aggregate economic status.

A number of state and local economic development strategists began in the 1980s to recognize and articulate the qualitative perspective, contrasting this approach to the older simple growth efforts. In hearings conducted by Congress on the subject of federal and state roles in economic development, the director of policy of the Council of State Planning Agencies commented: "We have decided to define economic development as the process of creating wealth. . . . Development is more than the creation of jobs . . ." (U.S. Congress, House, 1985, p. 262). And consider the following passage in Indiana's strategic development planning document:

Many states have adopted economic development strategies which are geared to protecting and generating the largest number of jobs possible. In Indiana, however, the economic development community believes strongly that growth for growth's sake will not best serve the needs of Indiana residents. Furthermore, because of changing demographic and employment characteristics, only a relatively modest increase in the total number of jobs is required to meet the needs of Indiana residents. . . . Thus, rather than emphasizing the quantity of jobs, Indiana is pursuing an economic goal that focuses on the quality of jobs and the development of more rewarding prosperous employment and business opportunities. . . . (Indiana Dept. of Commerce, n.d., p. 43)

Similarly, the Minnesota Department of Energy and Economic Development writes in its strategic plan prospectus: "It is not enough to create any job; the concentration must be on creating employment which pays a living wage and has potential for growth" (1985a, p. 3).

The embrace of the notion that economic development involves a qualitative increase in collective well-being, a perspective long articulated by the field of international development economics,[2] was late in coming. From the American point of view *development* was always considered a process by which "underdeveloped" societies caught up to nations which had long since traversed the path to economic modernity. By contrast, growth was simply a process by which a society augmented an already abundant economy (Potter, 1954); growth, therefore, rather than development constituted a legitimate American objective.

It is only since Americans have begun to appreciate that steady

---

2. Development economics began as an effort to address problems of societies with low per capita incomes, stagnant growth rates, great income disparities, unskilled labor, and insufficient capital to exploit whatever natural advantages there might be (Kurihara, 1959, pp. 26–31). The goal of development economics has been to identify strategies for increasing per capita incomes, achieving a more equitable income distribution, and improving "quality of life" factors (see, for example, Hirschman, 1958; Todaro, 1977; and Kindleberger and Herrick, 1977).

growth and unending abundance are vulnerable to international market trends, shifting technologies, and domestic migration patterns that economic development policy has turned from the task of simply creating more jobs to one that evinces a concern for creating long-term, stable, remunerative employment in the industries of the future.

In practice the essence of the new qualitative perspective is a selective approach to stimulating employment growth. Strategic economic development planning has emerged as the most sophisticated vehicle for identifying those industries in a particular state's economy that appear to offer growing and remunerative employment opportunities. Rhode Island's strategic planning effort provides one of the clearest examples of such an exercise.

The goal of the Rhode Island Strategic Development Commission (n.d.) was to generate recommendations for programs by which "to improve the standard of living of [the state's] citizens" (p. 1). This, it argued, could best be done by increasing the value added per work hour for goods and services produced in the state rather than fostering the growth of low-wage industries that must compete with cheap labor markets in foreign countries or other states (pp. 5, 7, 9). "There will always be another region where wages are lower," the commission warns. "The southern states that adopted this strategy during the 1950s and the 1960s are victims of it today" (p. 186). The key to development is "encouraging industries already here to expand; encouraging the formation of new businesses within the state; encouraging the exploration of new technologies that can lead to new businesses within the state . . ." (p. 833). The focus on a home-based strategy is contrasted with development as a form of "piracy": Rhode Island "is not interested in providing incentives to steal an established industry from some other state" (ibid.).

The commission then points out that "while this report contains many potentially exciting recommendations for creating new industries and new companies in the state of Rhode Island, this process will take a long time. . . . The major industries and companies that are now based in the state . . . are going to be the most significant employers in the state for the next 10 to 15 years. A major focus of any economic development effort must therefore be to ensure that these businesses remain as competitive as possible" (p. 834). The report proceeds to identify specific industries—boat building, tourism, jewelry, fishing, and wholesale trade—on which to target development assistance. Only then does the commission go on to recommend policies for the nurturance of new firms and industries that might flourish in Rhode Island's particular economic environment.

Targeting selected industries is a central element in the strategic plans of other states. Thus, Wisconsin identifies food processing, printing, and forest products as key industries deserving attention. Illinois targets drugs and plastics; Nevada identifies high-tech industries and agriculture; North Dakota, agribusiness and energy firms; Pennsylvania, high-tech companies and the coal industry. Even some states that have not undertaken a formal strategic-planning exercise target selected industries: Massachusetts, which concentrates state development assistance on high tech and certain traditional "mature" industries such as fishing, is a prime example.

The Empirical Basis of the Development Models

New business investments do not always result in new jobs. They may instead be used to up-grade or augment a firm's capital stock in such a way that productivity may either be increased without a concomitant increase in labor or held constant while the labor force contracts. From the investor's point of view the absence of positive employment effects may be of little concern: what is of primary interest is the cost or gain to the firm from the trade-off of labor for capital.

For political leaders and economic development officials, however, investments that lead to the capital intensification of production are problematic. This is particularly so when the investment is subsidized by public funds, at which point the failure to create new employment may become a public issue (Wildavsky and Pressman, 1973, p. 155). It is true that some kinds of capital investments—particularly those for real estate improvements—produce added local tax revenues, but many do not. Indeed, in cases where property taxes are abated for new construction or building rehabilitations (33 states allowed their local governments to offer partial property tax abatements for industrial or commercial real estate investments in 1985), the costs of servicing the new development may outweigh any tax revenues it generates. Even if the new investments do enhance the local tax base, however, revenues are distinctly secondary to employment goals in the economic developer's hierarchy.[3]

How common is the situation in which new investments fail to generate new jobs? Or to put the question in another way, how valid is the expectation in the economic development arena that private-sector investment will set into motion a chain of beneficial effects beginning with

3. For example, in transmitting Illinois' economic Action Plan to the governor, the director of the state Department of Commerce and Community Affairs writes, "Jobs are the top priority of the Department . . ." (Illinois Dept. of Commerce and Community Affairs, 1985, letter of transmittal from Michael Woelffer). A 1973 survey of directors of state

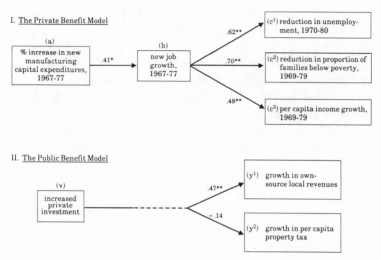

Figure 3-2. Bivariate Relationships (Pearson's *r*) among Model Links for the 50 Largest U.S. Cities

Note: Different time periods reflect differences in data collecting conventions of various federal government agencies.

** p < .001
* p < .01

the creation of new employment? Data to illustrate the relationship between investment and employment exist for the manufacturing sector on a city-by-city basis.[4] Simple bivariate correlations (Pearson's *r*) were run between the magnitude of change in various measures of new capital investment in manufacturing and the level of change in both total civilian job growth and manufacturing employment for the 50 largest cities in the United States. Figure 3-2 shows a modest relationship of .41 between the percentage increase in new capital manufacturing expenditures and total civilian job growth during the 10-year period beginning in 1967. (The use of total civilian employment growth, rather than simply manufacturing growth, as the dependent variable here is designed to catch the employment multiplier effect of manufacturing jobs, a phenomenon dis-

economic development agencies found that the primary problems that engaged their energies were unemployment and low per capita income (ACIR, 1981, p. 27). A more general discussion of employment as an economic development priority is found in Levy (1981, p. 2).

4. All data are drawn from the U.S. Bureau of the Census, *County and City Data Book* (Washington, DC: GPO, 1972, 1977, 1983).

cussed later on.) The relationship between the percentage increase in manufacturing investment and growth in the more limited employment category of manufacturing jobs is, as one would expect, somewhat stronger at .62. These coefficients suggest that increases in capital investment do tend to be accompanied by employment growth.

Once new jobs are created, economic development planners and politicians expect specific beneficial effects to follow: lower unemployment, less poverty, and higher per capita income. Figure 3-2 shows relatively strong relationships in the expected direction between new job growth (b) and all three measures of personal well-being (c1, c2, and c3).

The statistical relationship in these data between local job growth and decreasing local unemployment rates is noteworthy. It is a standard finding in demographic research that new local employment opportunities tend to attract migrants or commuters from outside the city to fill the new jobs (Pack, 1973; Fields, 1976; Clark and Ferguson, 1983). The indigenous unemployment pool may in many instances remain unaffected or even grow. For example, during 1984 the number of jobs in New York City rose by approximately 80,000. At the same time, however, the number of jobless also increased from 229,000 to about 300,000, driving the unemployment rate up by 2.4 percentage points. The new jobs, mainly in the high-skill service sector, attracted new commuters to the city, who account for a constantly increasing proportion of New York's workforce (*New York Times,* July 8, 1984). But the New York case may not be entirely typical: the 50-city data suggest that in the modal case enough locally unemployed workers benefit from job growth to lower the unemployment rate. A multiple regression analysis in which unemployment rate change is the dependent variable allows us to determine the specific degree of change in the two variables, controlling for others. Among the 50 cities a 1 percent increase in jobs is associated with a 0.6 percent decrease in unemployment, controlling for local population increase, capital investment, and growth in the number of manufacturing jobs and establishments.[5]

---

5. The full regression results follow. The coefficients are unstandardized Betas. The dependent variable is the local unemployment rate increase. The independent variables include:

Increase in total jobs	−.634	(p<.001)
Population increase	.293	(p<.10)
Increase in number of manufacturing establishments	−.099	(NS)
Increase in number of manufacturing jobs	.163	(NS)
New capital investment increase	−.167	(NS)

A strong link between employment growth and positive measures of economic well-being is generally supported by other research. Muller (1975b) has shown for a sample of 30 cities that job growth and income growth are positively related. As for distributional patterns, Wilbur Thompson (1965, p. 182) argues that "affluence and egalitarianism go hand-in-hand," a variation of the original argument by Kuznets (1955). More recently, Hilary Silver has shown that income inequality among families in 79 metropolitan areas actually rose in all regions between 1970 and 1980, but areas that experienced job growth had significantly lower rates of increase in levels of inequality than those undergoing deindustrialization. "Economic growth," she writes, "be it in manufacturing or services, tempered the rise in inequality . . ." (n.d., p. 18).

The assumed series of relationships depicted in Figure 3-2, beginning with increased investment and ending with personal economic well-being, constitute the heart of the private benefit economic development model. With the various exceptions noted, the assumptions are generally supported empirically. In short, a valid expectation underlies the economic developer's effort to increase personal well-being by encouraging private investment.

The public benefit model, whose fiscal goals tend to be secondary to the private benefit goals, enjoys less substantial empirical support. Economic growth, measured alternatively by an increase in new manufacturing capital expenditures (as in box v in Figure 3-2), the increase in number of new manufacturing establishments, or new employment, is related to growth in local tax revenues.[6] The hope that economic growth will reduce property tax rates or retard their growth finds little support, although the small coefficient in Figure 3-2 (− .14) is in the anticipated direction. Trends in property tax rates per capita are unrelated to employment shifts or changes in the number of manufacturing establishments. This finding suggests that while economic development is indeed likely to enhance the local treasury, additional revenues will not be devoted to property tax relief. Instead, they are probably absorbed by the increased service demands associated with an increase in the number of business establishments and their larger workforces.

------

6. Growth in own-source tax revenues is related to new capital expenditures (as shown in Figure 3-2) at the .47 level, to the increase in number of new manufacturing establishments at .51, and to job growth at .60. The two latter variables are not shown in Figure 3-2. All are significant at the .001 level.

The Costs of Economic Development

When Princeton University lured the first tenant to its Forestal Center "corporate campus" in 1977, it set into play an explosive process of growth along the 26-mile stretch between Trenton and New Brunswick known as the Princeton Corridor. By 1985 more than 50 companies with nearly 7000 employees had located in the industrial park itself, and construction of an additional 14 million square feet of office space was scheduled for the entire area. Planners estimate that by the turn of the century the population of the corridor will rise from 250,000 to 450,000, the number of homes will more than double, and the number of jobs will more than triple. Already the costs of such growth are apparent: land and housing prices have risen precipitously, roads are crowded with commuters, and municipal service departments are overburdened (*New York Times,* Apr. 21, 1985).

The Princeton development offers an example of a normal, though usually less dramatic, concomitant of economic development: there are costs as well as benefits associated with such growth. This assertion would come as no surprise to environmental activists or to members of the planning profession, whose sequential development timetables, impact analyses, and green-space preservation plans are all efforts to minimize those costs. Among economic development officials, however, costs are seldom calculated or even acknowledged.[7] This is so for several reasons. For one thing, costs are difficult to predict and quantify with precision. Furthermore, benefits often outweigh costs, insofar as they can be determined. This is particularly true in the short term. Finally, it scarcely needs saying that it is easier to mobilize political support for development projects by emphasizing benefits and pushing costs into the background.

The costs of economic development may be gauged by such indicators as the depletion of water resources by industrial users or rising housing prices or the consumption of farmland. Most of these costs are a function in one way or another of the population growth that tends to accompany expanding business activity. Population growth in American cities is associated with positive as well as negative factors: growing cities, for example, exhibit above-average gains in personal income[8] and

7. One exception is Levy (1981, pp. 6–8). Costs of growth are well known among suburban town officials and underlie fiscal and exclusionary zoning.

8. The explanation is that employment in growing cities often increases faster than the working population. Competition for workers tends to drive wages up; widespread job opportunities also mean lower unemployment.

higher per capita property values (Muller, 1975b). But it is also associated with higher public-service costs, housing shortages, service short-falls, traffic congestion, and environmental damage.

Population increase appears to be a virtually unavoidable accompaniment to employment growth. In the 50-city data set, population and job growth covary in an almost perfect relationship ($r = .98$). There is no doubt that much of the observed population increase is a function of in-migration, but whether the predominant pattern is for migrants to follow job opportunities or for firms to form or move to exploit a growing labor force and expanding market is a matter of debate in demography. The most obvious instance in which migrants move to a community to take jobs concerns "boomtowns" that spring up at the site of new mines or energy construction projects or military installations (Finster-busch, 1980, Ch. 6). Stories of displaced Michigan auto workers who moved to Houston to find work in the oil economy in the late 1970s provide another often-cited example.

A number of aggregate analyses offer a broader basis for the notion that people follow jobs. Gary Fields, for example, finds in his study of 20 metropolitan areas that the rate of in-migration is positively related to new hiring and negatively related to layoffs and concludes that "it may be the availability of jobs . . . which is the primary determinant of labor force migration" (1976, p. 413). Katherine Bradbury and her associates confirm this finding, using a much more extensive data set. Analyzing changes in 121 cities and their metropolitan areas between 1970 and 1975, they conclude that "SMSA [Standard Metropolitan Statistical Area] employment growth was a critical determinant of city population growth" (1982, p. 138). Survey data bolster these conclusions: most interstate moves by people of working age are explained by the desire to look for new work or a job transfer (Finsterbusch, 1980, pp. 49–51).

Donald Steinnes (1977) finds, however, that intrametropolitan residential movement *precedes* jobs, and Clark and Ferguson (1983, p. 211) supply evidence to show that jobs may follow people even on an interregional basis. Service-sector firms in particular form or expand to meet the demands of a growing population of retirees as well as younger people whose migration may be explained less by job considerations than by the search for amenities, cultural stimulation, or favorable climatic conditions. Clark and Ferguson, along with Muth (1971), conclude that both processes are no doubt at work in explaining simultaneous job and population growth: that is, people follow jobs, and vice versa, with the causal direction and the relative magnitude of influence varying from moment to moment and even from city to city.

Whether or not all or most in-migration is a function of employment opportunities is not finally of critical importance: some substantial population increase is certainly associated with certain types of economic expansion, and it tends to impose costs on communities along with the dividends of growth. One of the principal concerns has to do with the fiscal effects of rapid population growth. One problem is that the tax contribution of each additional household to a community often falls short of the marginal costs of providing services to that household. The problem is particularly severe in school financing. In one typical New Jersey suburb in the 1970s, for example, the average new single-family house produced $675 in school taxes, but the cost of educating a child in such a house was $955 (Danielson and Doig, 1982, p. 89). Imbalances such as these between revenues and service costs have led many suburban communities to adopt growth-control zoning ordinances that establish a large minimum lot size as a means to limit the number of families with children in the community (Windsor, 1979).

A negative fiscal balance is a common though not invariable result of population growth: both the production of tax revenues and the demand for services vary with the demographic characteristics of the in-migrants (Hardie, 1985; Finsterbusch, 1980, p. 42). Thus, working-class families with children will tend to pay lower taxes and make heavier use of public services than childless young professionals. It is therefore proper to conclude that economic development is neither an unmitigated good nor is it inevitably an imposition on the community. As Muller concludes, "Industrial developments are found to have a mixed effect when secondary impacts, particularly in-migration, are considered" (1975a, p. 42).

If population growth in association with employment increase tends in some circumstances to create revenue problems, it also may generate public expenditure problems. A rapidly growing population poses an unpleasant choice for the local public sector: either local officials must allow demand to outstrip available public services or they must increase public spending (and therefore taxes) at a higher-than-customary pace. The latter course may be characteristic of only a few very rapidly growing cities. Helen Ladd's analysis of 103 Massachusetts communities in the mid-1970s showed that per capita local expenditures described a U-shaped curve when arrayed along the population growth dimension (1981, p. 351). Expenditures were highest in both rapidly declining cities (where fixed service costs were hard to adjust downward even as population decreased) and the most rapidly growing cities. Only in these booming places are service shortfalls dramatic enough to generate pressure on the public sector to boost spending. Communities in Ladd's sample with moderate levels of population growth did not tend to adjust spending upward at an unusual rate.

Officials in some growing cities, intent on maintaining a low tax rate, have seemed deaf to growing service demands (Lupsha and Siembieda, 1977). Houston during its great growth period provided a dramatic case in point. In 1980 this fourth largest city in the United States ranked 146th in park acreage and maintained one of the lowest ratios of police officers to population of any large city in the country. Severe inadequacies plagued the mass transit, sewer and waste-water treatment systems, and the road network. Seventy percent of the city was subject to a sewer hookup moratorium in the 1980s that limited new service to five units per acre (Kaplan, 1983; Feagin, 1984). Houston's number of miles of limited access freeways per 100 square miles (9.6) compared unfavorably with New York (32), Dallas (18.5), and Los Angeles (25) (*New York Times*, Sept. 2, 1984). When a city like Houston finally does adjust services to meet demands, the costs are unusually high. Muller found in comparing a sample of growing and declining cities that per capita municipal debt increased in the former group by 48 percent between 1972 and 1977, while in declining cities it increased by only 18 percent. Per capita outlays for police saw increases of 74 percent and 54 percent, respectively, in growing and declining cities, while highway expenditures grew by 75 percent and 56 percent in the two categories. In Houston in particular the increase in per capita spending for the police in this period was 126 percent, while in Phoenix, another rapidly growing city, the increase for fire services was 123 percent, compared with an all-city gain of 53 percent (Muller, 1981, p. 291). Finally, even without taking into account the extraordinary expense of suddenly attempting to overcome a tradition of low taxes and minimal services, the costs of public services are subject to increasing diseconomies of scale as cities grow in size (Muller, 1975a, pp. 22–23). Thus, the per unit price of everything from protective services to parks may be as much as two or three times higher in cities over half a million as in places with fewer people. Muller's data (1975b, p. 23) suggest that during the 1970s every additional 50,000 people in a city drove up the per capita costs of common municipal services by about 9.5 percent.

The economic development community has not been especially attentive to the costs of economic development, particularly those associated with population growth. It is noteworthy that the frenetic competition among states in 1985 for the General Motors Saturn plant, projected at that time to create 6000 permanent manufacturing jobs, never generated any widely acknowledged public discussion about the potential impact on land prices, housing, public services, and the environment of building such a facility. It was only when the little town of Spring Hill, Tennessee, was finally chosen as the Saturn site that that the enormity of the disruption of the real estate market and the nature of the burden faced by the public sector began to take on specific form (*New York Times,* July 31, 1985; see also Corrigan, 1985a).

The Decline-Distress Model

If there has been only a rudimentary sense of the costs of economic development—or a politically motivated reluctance to acknowledge their existence—there is no such lack of awareness concerning the consequences of disinvestment and population decline. The links between capital flight and business failure, population and job loss, and personal and fiscal distress are as clearly assumed in the economic development domain as the causal chain in the benefit models. Economic development is therefore conceived not only as a strategy for prosperity but as a means to forestall, or counteract, the process of deterioration.

Variants of the decline-distress model tend to serve, along with the public and private benefit justifications, as key premises in strategic planning prospectuses. Thus, even as it acknowledges that some industrial contraction is natural in a healthy economy, the *Greenhouse Compact* declares that "layoffs and plant closings cause great hardships. . . . [T]he public pays the bill in the form of welfare payments, unemployment compensation, tax losses. . . ." (Rhode Island Strategic Development Commission, n.d., p. 77). Other states begin their strategic planning reports not by extolling the fruits of growth but by analyzing job and population losses over time and the threat or hardship they pose (see, for example, Wisconsin Strategic Development Commission, 1985, pp. 16–18); Minnesota Department of Energy and Economic Development, 1985a, p. 2). Even states without a commitment to strategic planning often tend to justify development policy as much on the grounds of the threat of the decline-distress syndrome as on the benefits of economic expansion. Thus at a meeting of the southern governors, a major item on the agenda was the growing threat to the emergent regional prosperity posed by import competition. The governors called for action to stem job losses in mainstay industries of the South, including textiles, shoes, sawmills, and food processing, as cheaper foreign goods captured the consumer market (*New York Times,* Sept. 15, 1985).

THE PRIVATE IMPACTS OF DECLINE

Just as the benefit models focus on the anticipated returns to both private and public beneficiaries, so too does the decline-distress model stress the vulnerabilities of both domains to economic deterioration. On the private side the personal effects of unemployment have been the central concern. The first systematic documentation in the United States of the range of social effects, economic privations and adjustments, psychological reactions, and health costs of unemployment dates back to depression-era studies. Alienation, resignation, family disintegration, malnutrition, and so on, are among the consequences explored by Komarovsky (1940), Bakke (1940), and others in that period.

A hiatus of two or three decades separates this early research from contemporary investigations. Modern studies of unemployment have been stimulated, however, not so much by the phenomenon of joblessness as a widely shared condition as by the experience of *dislocation* or *displacement*.[9] Although unemployment in general is an abiding concern of economic development officials, the displaced or dislocated worker (the two terms are used interchangeably) poses a somewhat different set of problems from the cyclically or chronically unemployed. Displacement—defined as structural unemployment caused by international competition, new technology, or industrial capital mobility to other locales or other uses—is less a function of economic cycles or personal or ascriptive disabilities than it is of great economic transformations.[10] The relative decline of heavy industry as the domestic economic backbone, the rise of the service and technical sectors, and the emergence of foreign industrial competition all mean that the displaced can no longer expect to use the skills and experience with which they once earned their livelihood. Cyclical recoveries do not suffice to reemploy the displaced in their

---

9. The notion of displacement did in fact stimulate one of the earlier studies of unemployment effects, an investigation of the shutdown of the L. Candee rubber shoe company in New Haven just prior to the depression. Although the phenomenon of displacement is not carefully developed in this study, the authors are clearly struck by the sudden calamity of unemployment for long-time, skilled workers, victims not of cyclical economic fluctuations but of the reorganization of the business through a reallocation of capital to a reduced number of plants. See Clague and Cooper, 1934.

10. Analysts disagree on the scope of the displacement problem. Estimates range from an annual displacement of about 100,000 workers—less than 1 percent of the nation's unemployed in the mid-1980s—to over 3 million (Bendick, 1983; Corrigan and Stanfield, 1984). Furthermore, some economists doubt that displaced workers constitute a class distinct from those thrown out of work by prolonged recessions. Many states, however, have initiated dislocated-worker programs (Balderston, 1986; see also Chapter 13).

former jobs because their industries constitute an irrevocably diminishing part of the domestic economy. Thus, the displaced are not merely without work; they are, at least in their accustomed economic roles, superfluous.

Displacement, unlike the chronic unemployment of the permanent underclass or depression-level cyclical unemployment, tends more to be concentrated in certain industries in certain regions. Thus it threatens local or regional economies in particular, making it a special concern of the economic development community (Balderston, 1986). How to retrain and reemploy displaced workers who have well-defined but obsolete skills and a history of steady work and how to deal with the psychological and health aftereffects of sudden plant shutdowns are key issues.

One of the most thorough summaries of the personal impacts of displacement is contained in Bluestone and Harrison's *The Deindustrialization of America* (1982, Ch. 3). Although the authors clearly suggest a distinction between displacement and other forms of unemployment (pp. 51, 65), they do not attempt a systematic investigation of whether the personal consequences of different sorts of unemployment vary. Nevertheless, much of the discussion alludes to or implies differences both in kind and magnitude. Long-term unemployment tends to affect about a third of all workers displaced, and most of those thrown out of work by plant closings who later find jobs experience a decline in status and income (p. 51). Such losses, less common apparently for people who are thrown out of work for other reasons (p. 55), tend to be particularly acute for workers in the better-paying unionized industries such as steel, meat-packing, glass-making, and automobiles. Another difference is that people who fall victim to brief periods of unemployment may survive on unemployment insurance and savings, but displaced workers often suffer losses of all their accumulated assets, including savings, health and life insurance, and home equity.

A substantial body of medical research summarized by Bluestone and Harrison indicates that "acute economic distress associated with job loss causes a range of physical and mental health problems," ranging from ulcers and headaches to depression, anxiety, and alcohol abuse (pp. 63–64). It is not clear that such problems are more prevalent among displaced workers than among people thrown out of work for other reasons. These effects may be mitigated if workers are rehired or find other work, as a study of displaced steel workers in Youngstown by Buss and Redburn (1983, pp. 73, 87) shows, but no matter how physical health and mental health are measured, "the unemployed were worse off on each scale" than was the case for those who had found work or were continuously employed (p. 71).

Any sort of unemployment, structural or otherwise, is a cause for concern for those responsible for economic development policy. But it is the sudden plant closing or the departure of a major employer to another locale that is a special nightmare. It is true that the legions of jobless minority teenagers constitute a drag on the local economy and a special burden on its public agencies every bit as severe as the assemblers of small appliances displaced by Japanese competition. But large communities are accustomed, politically, to the chronically unemployed, and in small communities they often do not exist at all. Even cyclical unemployment is less threatening, for in a recession at least there is a prospect that conditions will eventually improve. Displacement, however, has a certain finality about it. Crafting policy to forestall displacement or mitigate its effects thus takes on a special urgency.

PUBLIC IMPACTS OF DECLINE

State and local officials must concern themselves with the personal effects of structural unemployment not only for compassionate reasons but because they pose sudden and potentially long-term burdens on government. These burdens, as well as those associated with more generic population and employment loss, constitute the public impact of economic decline. On the one hand government must respond to the deprivations of joblessness; thus, spending for welfare, relief, health care, housing assistance, school lunches, and other social services tends to increase. At the same time, however, fewer employed workers and a smaller population base in the community mean a diminution of tax revenues. Bluestone and Harrison cite a U.S. Bureau of Economic Analysis study that estimates that in 1980 each percentage point rise in unemployment nationally increased federal social spending by $4.1 billion and cut federal tax revenues by $20.2 billion. Displacement in particular accounted for three additional percentage points in the unemployment rate in 1980 (1982, p. 77). At the local level Clark and Ferguson show that between 1960 and 1974 cities losing population not only experienced declines in own-source revenues but also increases in total spending. These increases occurred at a higher rate in these years than for those cities gaining population (1983, pp. 80–81, 83).

A similar analysis of revenue and spending in northern and southern states finds essentially the same pattern (Bahl and Schroeder, 1981). The gross comparison between regions is justified on the grounds of differential rates of population, employment, and income growth in the 1960s and 1970s. The research shows for selected time periods in those decades that northern states generally had to increase revenue effort—the proportion of income taxed—at a more rapid rate than states in the southern regions in order to maintain a revenue growth rate roughly equal to that in the southern states (pp. 318, 320). At the same time per capita government expenditures grew at about the same rate in both regions, despite slower growth in northern fiscal capacity as measured by employment and income growth rates (p. 315).

For the economic development community the implications of such analyses are clear: in declining states and cities, the strategy is to boost investment, create jobs, and expand the tax base. In growing communities the emphasis is on maintaining and diversifying patterns of private investment as a hedge against disinvestment and its attendant problems.

Conclusions

The economic development community justifies policy intervention on the grounds that it will encourage private investment. The importance of private investment in commercial and industrial undertakings is expressed through both positive and negative modes of reasoning or models of justification. In the positive model, private investment initiates a chain of occurrences that lead to private and public well-being. In the negative, or decline-distress, model the absence of investment leads eventually to personal and fiscal deterioration.

There is considerable empirical support for the proposition that private investment is a condition of private and public well-being and that the absence of investment leads to personal and fiscal distress. Whether or not policy intervention can induce investment or keep it at a level sufficient to produce or maintain prosperity is a different matter. But the link between investment and personal income and a healthy state and local fisc is reasonably well-established, as a review of the literature has shown.

One important feature of these models is that the path to well-being lies exclusively through the private sector. As one politician, a recent candidate for the statehouse in North Carolina, put it: "First, we recognize that business, not government, creates jobs and that *healthy* business creates and preserves jobs. Government's proper role is to enhance resources, promote a healthy and fair climate for business, and assist business in doing what business does best . . ." (*State Policy Reports*, Oct. 31, 1984). Neither the creation of public employment nor the socialization of industry are considered debatable alternative models to well-being. The issue, then, is how best to encourage private-sector invest-ment. Traditional theories suggested that government performed that task best by keeping supply-side factor costs low to create a hospitable business climate. The advent of the entrepreneurial state, however, has meant that policy is increasingly focused on demand forces to keep in-vestments flowing.

CHAPTER 4

The Context of Economic Development Policy

THE structure, design, and transformation of economic development policy are to a large extent products of their political and economic context. In a federal political system in which substantial powers and responsibilities are decentralized to subnational governments, it is not entirely surprising to witness a bidding war among states for private industry; such governmental competition would be unlikely to occur among administrative jurisdictions in a unitary state—say, among the *départements* of France. Nor is it out of character for government in a capitalist system to appeal to a firm's profit motive in an effort to influence its behavior, though the use of business incentives designed to enhance the profit margin would be unusual in other sorts of economic systems. The shape of economic development policy in America not only reflects the influence of its federal and capitalist matrix, but it is also responsive dynamically to transformations in these and other contextual phenomena. Both the federal system and the scope and nature of the market have changed in recent years, and so have other critical forces, including the geographic distribution of people and industry and the role of heavy manufacturing in the national economy. These transformations have influenced the intensity of the search for effective development policy and wrought changes in policy design. Thus, to understand the growing ascendance of demand-based growth models that underlie the emergence of the entrepreneurial state it is necessary to examine these recent currents in American life.

The Decentralization of People and Industry

The evidence of the scope and recency of southern and western growth can hardly escape the long-distance automobile traveler. Mobile homes and new tract housing cover once-barren Wyoming and Nevada hillsides; pink and white suburban cities have obliterated all memory of the cherry and apricot orchards that dotted California's Silicon Valley as late as the 1950s; a skyline of new glass office towers dominates Charlotte, where only 1 out of 10 houses was built before World War II; and in Florida miles of coastline present an unbroken aspect of condominia to the sea.

Population statistics confirm these easily accessible impressions (Greenwood, 1981). Although the story of the postwar Sun Belt[1] surge has been recounted many times (Sale, 1975; Perry and Watkins, 1977; Weinstein and Firestine, 1978), its dimensions are important to review. Between 1950 and 1984 the western census region grew by nearly 27 million people, while the South added more than 43 million. The combined growth of the Northeast and Midwest came to roughly 25 million by comparison (U.S. Bureau of the Census, 1985a). In that 34-year period California alone gained 15 million people, while Texas more than doubled its 1950 population of 7.7 million to 16 million. Florida grew from 2.8 million to almost 11 million. By 1984 the two Sun Belt regions as a whole accounted for 54 percent of the American population.

Much of the Sun Belt growth is a product of interregional migration. Until the 1960s the South was a net exporter of population to other regions, but the flow was reversed in that decade. Between 1970 and 1984 the South gained a net of more than 8.7 million people through in-migration, the bulk of it to Florida and Texas. Retirees, young professionals in the burgeoning aerospace industries, people who had grown up in the South and left years before, both black and white, flocked to cities like Atlanta, Charlotte, Lexington, Jackson, and Austin. In percentage terms the most dramatic population in-migration occurred in the western states. Migrants swelled Nevada's population by nearly 60 percent in those 14 years (U.S. Bureau of the Census, 1985a). Altogether the western states gained a net of 5.7 million people through migration alone. Meanwhile, the two northern census regions experienced a net

---

1. It is safe to say that there is absolutely no agreement among scholars about which states or cities constitute, respectively, the "Sun Belt" or "Frost Belt." For my purposes "Sun Belt" refers to what the U.S. Census Bureau has designated the western and southern census regions, while the "Frost Belt," or northern regions, refers to the midwestern (formerly called the North Central) and northeastern census regions. The four regions and their respective subregions are shown in Figure 4.1. I use the terms here simply because they connote very broad regional differences in growth rates and culture. No imputation of homogeneity within these regions should be inferred. For discussions of definitional problems see Bernard and Rice (1983) and Abbott (1981).

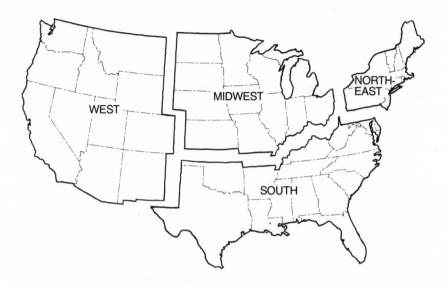

Figure 4-1. Major U.S. Census Regions
    Note: In addition to the four main census regions shown in the figure above, the Census Bureau also designates eight subregions. I refer to these occasionally in this volume. The subregions and the states they contain are:

New England: CT, ME, MA, NH, RI, VT
Mideast: DE, MD, NJ, NY, PA

Great Lakes: IL, IN, MI, OH, WI
Plains: IA, KS, MN, MO, NE, ND, SD

Southeast: AL, AR, FL, GA, KY, LA, MS, NC, SC, TN, VA, WV
Southwest: AZ, NM, OK, TX

Rocky Mountain: CO, ID, MT, UT, WY
Far West: CA, NV, OR, WA, AK, HI

loss in migration exchanges of nearly 7.3 million people in these years. In the first half of the 1980s, migration losses were so severe in Michigan, Iowa, and Ohio that those three states actually recorded population decreases.

The national dispersion of population since the war overlies a simultaneous intraregional deconcentration typically marked by suburban growth and central city loss. Suburban growth has been great enough in most cases to produce net metropolitan growth, even in areas with rap-

Table 4-1.   Regional Population Share and Growth, 1950–84

	1950		1984		
	Population (in thousands)	Regional Share of Total (%)	Population (in thousands)	Regional Share of Total (%)	Percent Increase
Northeast	39,478	26	49,728	21	26
Midwest	44,461	29	59,117	25	33
South	47,197	31	80,576	34	71
West	20,190	13	46,738	20	131

Sources: U.S. Bureau of the Census, 1985a, b.

Table 4-2.   Interregional Net Migration, 1970–84 (in thousands)

Northeast	−3134
Midwest	−4162
South	8744
West	5705

Sources: U.S. Bureau of the Census, 1985b, p. 14; U.S. Bureau of the Census, 1985a, p. 7.

idly declining core cities like St. Louis or Gary. A somewhat different pattern characterizes some of the newer urban areas of the Sun Belt, though it too is consistent with metropolitan population dispersion; in these cases both the central city and the surrounding suburbs have gained population, but the growth rates of the suburbs typically far surpass those of the central cities. For example, while Phoenix grew by nearly 36 percent between 1970 and 1980, its suburbs grew by 86 percent. The population of San Diego increased by almost 26 percent in that decade, but the suburbs grew by more than 49 percent. Los Angeles, Miami, St. Petersburg, Dallas, Houston, and Oklahoma City are other examples of cities that conform to this pattern (Bernard and Rice, 1983, pp. 10–11).

In the mid-1970s yet a different intraregional diffusion pattern appeared. Interim census figures, confirmed in 1980, show that by 1975 one out of every six metropolitan areas was actually losing population. Many people who were leaving the central city were heading for small town and rural destinations beyond the metropolis. Although by the mid-1980s rural growth rates had moderated, there was a brief moment during which nonmetropolitan areas were growing at a faster rate— though on a small population base—than either suburbs or metropolitan areas as a whole (U.S. Dept. of HUD, 1980b, pp. 1–19).

Table 4-3.   Regional Share of Employment and
Employment Growth, 1950–85

	1950 (%)	1985 (%)	Percent Change in Number of Jobs
Northeast	27	21	40
Midwest	31	25	48
South	29	34	104
West	13	20	186

Sources: U.S. Bureau of the Census, 1953, p. 189; U.S.
Bureau of the Census, 1987, p. 377.

Table 4-4.   Regional Share of Manufacturing
Employment and Manufacturing
Employment Growth, 1950–85

	1950 (%)	1985 (%)	Percent Change in Number of Jobs
Northeast	36	24	− 17
Midwest	35	28	− 2
South	20	31	90
West	8	16	141

Sources: U.S. Bureau of the Census, 1953, p. 189; U.S.
Bureau of the Census, 1987, pp. 730–31.

These population shifts have been accompanied by a decentralization
of employment. Although each of the four major census regions gained
jobs in the postwar period, the rates of growth in the South and West far
outstripped those of the northern regions. The Sun Belt states were the
locus of 54 percent of all jobs in the United States by 1985, up from their
42 percent combined share in 1950.

More striking than these figures are the data on manufacturing employment. Between 1950 and 1985 the nation's economy as a whole
added roughly 3.5 million manufacturing jobs; in the same period the
southern and western census regions added over 4.4 million jobs in this
broad sector, reflecting net manufacturing losses in the two northern regions. As recently as 1970 the South's share of national manufacturing
employment was 26 percent, third behind the Midwest (33 percent) and
the Northeast (29 percent). By the mid-1980s, as Table 4.4 shows, the
South commanded a larger share of manufacturing jobs than any other
region. The West and the South combined contained 47 percent of all
manufacturing jobs, up from 28 percent in 1950. Consistent with the
population migration to nonmetropolitan areas, much of the South's factory employment is located in small towns. Nationally, only 20.5 percent

Table 4-5. New Plants and Expansions, 1961
and 1984, by State Ranking

Rank	1961	1984
1	New York	California
2	Ohio	Texas
3	Florida	Florida
4	Illinois	Alabama
5	Massachusetts	New York
6	Texas	Kentucky
7	Pennsylvania	North Carolina
8	California	Tennessee
9	North Carolina	Georgia
10	Puerto Rico	Kansas

Sources: *Industrial Development and Manufacturers Record* (Dec. 1961), p. 58; *State Policy Reports* (Jan. 1985), p. 25.

of such jobs are situated in rural locations, but in the South the percentages in 1984 ranged between 29 in Mississippi to 39 in Tennessee (*New York Times,* Mar. 21, 1985; see also Noyelle and Stanback, 1984, p. 100).

Data on the location of new plants and expansions offer another way of observing the deconcentration of manufacturing activity. Table 4.5 shows the leading states in 1961 (along with Puerto Rico), the last year during the 1960s that such data were collected on a systematic basis by the *Industrial Development and Manufacturers Record,* and in 1984. Of the five states in the two northern census regions in 1961, only New York, the most popular site in that year, remained on the list 23 years later. Sun Belt locations dominate the later compilation. Most new plants in southern and western states, incidentally, are found in suburbs, though some central cities in the Sun Belt also experienced manufacturing expansion in recent years (Greenwood, 1981, pp. 124–25).

How has this population and employment dispersion contributed to the emergence of economic development as a policy concern of subnational government? It seems clear that as states in the Northeast and Midwest began to come to terms with low or negative growth rates, they embraced economic development incentives as a defensive response to perceived Sun Belt success in a bidding competition for private industry. Indeed, Governor Raymond Shafer of Pennsylvania said as much as he signed a tax-exempt bond financing law in 1967: "[I am] committing an act of self-defense" (Liston, 1967, p. 22). A Wisconsin development official in the same year expressed the hope that his state's new set of in-

Table 4-6. Economic Development Policy Penetration, 1966–85

	1966		1976		1985	
	Penetration Score (%)	Programs per State	Penetration Score (%)	Programs per State	Penetration Score (%)	Programs per State
Northeast	46.9	21.0	56.6	30.0	69.8	38.4
Midwest	45.1	19.8	45.6	21.7	61.4	33.8
South	39.3	17.3	47.3	23.7	57.6	31.7
West	24.3	10.7	36.6	19.4	52.4	28.8

Sources: Calculated from data in *Industrial Development and Manufacturers Record* (Dec. 1966), pp. 26–27; *Site Selection Handbook* (Dec. 1976), pp. 106–8; and *Industrial Development and Site Selection Handbook* (Jan., Feb. 1985), pp. 52–54.

Note: The penetration scores represent the percentage of actual programs in place of all possible programs. The number of all possible programs is calculated for each census region by multiplying the number of states in that region by 44 different program types in 1966, 53 in 1976, and 55 in 1985.

centives would "neutralize offers by other states" (ibid.). No sense of regional loyalty constrained this competition. As New Jersey's commissioner of industry and labor commented in 1976, "What the South has been doing to New Jersey for 15 years, I'm now doing to New York. It's cutthroat, regrettably, but it's every state for itself" (*Business Week*, June 21, 1976, p. 71).

The diagnosis of decline, in other words, appears to have focused in the 1960s and 1970s on the relative attractiveness of the states as locations for industry, a comparison in which northern states were found wanting. Thus, an influential series of articles in Rhode Island's *Providence Journal-Bulletin* in 1972, which began with the question "What's Wrong with Rhode Island Today?," elicited a response by a business commission that noted, among other problems, too few fully serviced industrial sites, an antiquated tax structure, and a lack of financial incentives to encourage capital investment (Rhode Island Strategic Development Commission, n.d., p. 2).

If the problem of northern decline did possibly lie in the lack of public incentives and services to support industry, this could be remedied in the state legislature. Thus, as Table 4.6 and Figure 4.2 show, the growth of policy initiatives was particularly thorough among states in the two northern regions. Both the table and the graph are based on data from the annual survey reported in the *Industrial Development and Site Selection Handbook*. About three-fifths of the incentive programs tracked involved some sort of capital subsidy or tax exemption. Most of the remaining programs offer technical assistance, land write-downs, and job

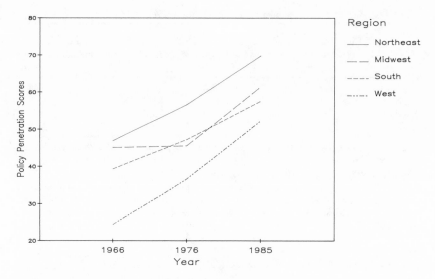

Figure 4-2. Policy Penetration Scores, by Region, 1966–85

training. The table shows that by the baseline year of 1966, northeastern and midwestern states already had in place a greater number of programs than the Sun Belt states, even though subsidy programs and tax incentives had originated in the South. The average northeastern state had implemented 21 programs out of a possible 44, and the typical midwestern state had 19.8. By contrast the southern average was 17.3, and western states had only 10.7 programs apiece.

Since the baseline magnitudes are different for each region (it is impossible to begin at an earlier date, since no systematic data were collected prior to 1966), it makes little sense to compare regional rates of change over time. Nevertheless, graphing the penetration scores is instructive: note in Figure 4.2 that the slopes for all the regions but the South become much steeper after 1976, reflecting the intensification of economic development competition.

The thoroughness of the search for locational incentives in the northern states is striking, but it is also noteworthy that the same sort of activity went on at a high level in the Sun Belt regions as well. That the Sun Belt states themselves continued to adopt development incentives may be explained in several ways. States in which incentives had originally appeared—Mississippi, Alabama, Louisiana—attributed their industrialization in large measure to the success of these programs and continued to trust in their effectiveness (Cobb, 1982; Liston, 1967). These particular states still tend to offer an array of incentives as diverse as their northern competitors. Not coincidentally, these three states exhibit lower rates of population, employment, and income growth than some of their comparatively better-off regional neighbors, such as Texas and North Carolina. Although a low growth rate does not perfectly predict a large number of programs, there is a rough inverse relationship even within regions.

Another reason that states in the Sun Belt census region have continued to adopt development policies is to diversify single-industry economies in order to protect continued growth prospects from cyclical downturns or international threats to their critical industries. Houston's experience provides a local illustration. When world oil prices fell in the 1980s, the city lost nearly 100,000 jobs in 1983 alone. The shock spurred business leaders, with city backing, to launch an elaborate effort aimed at diversifying the city's oil-dependent economy (*New York Times,* Sept. 2, 1984, and Nov. 2, 1985).

The state of Nevada's strategic development report of 1985 provides another example. "[E]conomic growth based on the fortunes of one industry [tourism and gambling] is not only risky," the report declares, "but significantly affects the characteristics and quality of growth" (Nevada Commission on Economic Development, 1985, pp. 9–10). Thus, the commission warns, the state must seek to diversify its economic base to reduce its vulnerability to national changes in personal income that affect, among other things, vacation habits. The report goes on to identify areas of economic activity, such as agribusiness and high technology, that would broaden the state's base and to recommend a series of policy steps to ensure diversification (see also Hawaii Governor's Committee, 1985, pp. 8, 22).

Yet another reason for Sun Belt states' continued adoption of development policies is that competition from other states is perceived as a threat even to robust Sun Belt economies and must be challenged. Thus, even in California, whose "gross national product" would make it the eighth most productive nation in the world if it were an independent country (California Department of Economic and Business Development, 1984, p. 11), there is concern about the prospects for continued growth and prosperity. According to the director of the state's Department of Economic Development: "We assumed for too long that California was always the obvious place to locate. Then other states got aggressive and took the momentum away from us" (*Business Week,* June 10, 1985). The state offered only 14 of the 44 surveyed programs in 1966 and only 16 of 53 possible programs in 1976. But by 1985 it had 38 of the 55 types of programs in place, as well as a host of new ones not tracked by the *Industrial Development and the Site Selection Handbook* survey.

To summarize, I have argued that population and employment deconcentration after World War II resulted in serious enough economic deterioration in northern states to elicit a policy response. Since the interpretation of the causes of out-migration focused on the locational advantages for industry in the Sun Belt states, the policy prescription was to offer a set of business subsidies and tax concessions that would at least equalize business locational costs among states or create comparative locational advantages. States with favorable growth rates felt compelled to respond to this competitive challenge with their own programs. The continual efforts of northern states to establish a competitive advantage and of Sun Belt states to meet competitive challenges drove the policy penetration scores steadily upward through the 1970s and into the 1980s.

Federalism

The deconcentration of people and economic activity is best understood as a spur in the competition among states. Deconcentration helped to establish the competition and continues to drive it by generating a sense of lost prosperity in regions losing jobs and a sense of precarious advantage in those regions that have grown. The crucial factor that established the *states* as the primary combatants in this competition for private investment is American federalism. Furthermore, changes in the relationship between states and nation that began in the late 1970s have ushered in an era of greater state and local fiscal self-reliance. The consequence has been to heighten the urgency of the economic development enterprise.

Federalism is a mode of political organization in which power and responsibilities are allocated to both national and subnational governments, with the latter retaining a certain autonomy of action. Such a capability is important for fulfilling one of the principal responsibilities of state government: namely, the nurturance of the state's economy. The idea of a "state economy" is neither a constitutional nor a statutory artifact. Nor in the contemporary era does the concept have great economic validity. Trade and labor flows, the development of the interstate commerce clause, capital mobility, and the assumption of vast economic power by the government in Washington have long since rendered state economies especially permeable and relatively unbounded. From a national perspective we might think of subnational parts of the general economy to the extent that we are interested in regional or subregional patterns of prosperity and deprivation or in the geographical distribution of productive activity. But from this larger vantage point subnational economic activity is part of the whole.

But if the concept of a state economy may be challenged on economic grounds, it may nevertheless by justified politically. The political rationale for the idea of a state economy rests on the states' inherent responsibility to provide for the common safety, health, and welfare of all who live within their respective boundaries and their power and need to tax to finance those services for the common good.

Each state's ability to perform those various commonweal functions depends in large part upon its revenue-raising capacity. This in turn is a product of the personal incomes of the state's residents and the sorts of economic activities in which they are employed. From the state's perspective, then, what goes on in the productive life within its borders and what comes into or goes out of the state—goods, workers, taxpayers, capital, tourists—produces a balance sheet that is distinct from the national account. Additionally, the dimensions of the obligation to foster the general welfare are delineated by the patterns of work in the state. Specifically, the scope of poverty and unemployment, job-training needs, educational demands, and public health problems reflect the level and character of labor-force participation and the opportunities for work. It follows, therefore, that a state will be interested as a matter of policy in maintaining or expanding its tax base and in ensuring adequate and remunerative employment for its citizens. In short, the state has a political interest in the concept of a state economy.

In a society in which most of the productive resources are privately controlled, a state's tax base and labor market are dependent on a multitude of independent private investment decisions. Since the private owners of capital are relatively free to invest when and where they wish and in whatever sort of enterprise they believe will deliver a return, states must compete with one another to attract enough capital to their jurisdiction to provide jobs for their citizens and taxes for their coffers. Thus, by devolving or reserving major public welfare responsibilities and tax powers to subnational governments, federalism in a capitalist society validates the notion of a state economy in political terms and further makes necessary the competition among states for private investment.

But there is another element in American federalism that works to thrust the states into a mutual competition, and that is the policy vacuum created by the reluctance of the government in Washington to embrace a coherent national policy of even regional development.[2] Although grants-in-aid to state and local governments are partly justified in federal theory on the grounds that they redistribute resources to needy regions and places, much evidence suggests that the aggregate effects of federal aid are not markedly redistributive among states and cities (Richardson and Turek, 1984). One analysis of the pattern of intergovernmental grants to cities found, for example, that

declining cities received proportionately the same as fast-growing cities, high unemployment cities the same as low unemployment cities, and low income cities the same as high income cities. . . . There is no noticeable change in this pattern between 1970 and 1976, except for a slight increase in concentration of total federal outlays in growing cities relative to declining ones. (Vernez, 1980, p. 81)

Some particular federal programs, such as Community Development Block Grants (CDBG), Economic Development Administration (EDA) assistance, and Urban Development Action Grants (UDAG), do attempt to target economic aid to the most depressed localities. In each of these instances the national government provides resources to state and local governments to permit them to offer location incentives or provide amenities to stimulate local development. As we shall see in the next chapter, however, targeting criteria are broad enough in practice to allow extremely wide geographical distribution. Furthermore, such programs are not part of a conscious, carefully constructed national development plan. As a matter of general policy the preference in Washington has been to eschew the more rigorous redistributive efforts that characterize European national growth policies (Rodwin, 1970; Sundquist, 1975).

Although the Carter administration did enunciate a short-lived national urban policy based on the principle of targeting aid to distressed places, the president's own Commission on a National Agenda for the Eighties later rejected this approach. The deconcentration of industry, the commission report declared, is beneficial: it is a sign that capital is being put to its most productive uses. "Firms must be reasonably free to invest, disinvest, and reinvest in a manner that gives them maximum ability to

---

2. This is not to say that the federal government ignores regional considerations. Public power and irrigation projects, for example, have been aimed at underdeveloped regions. But as Harry Richardson and Joseph Turek write, "Compared with other mixed economies, *explicit* regional policies in the United States have been extremely weak (some would say nonexistent)" (1984, p. 211).

function and thrive" (President's Commission for a National Agenda for the Eighties, 1980, p. 41). The commission argued that the federal government should not squander resources in a futile attempt to counter the market's strain toward efficiency by pouring aid into declining areas or creating a national system of targeted incentives and disincentives (pp. 37, 43, 104–5). Although the modestly countermarket CDBG, EDA, and UDAG programs survived the Reagan administration's efforts to eliminate them, the Reagan perspective was fully sympathetic to the Carter commission commitment to an unimpeded market. "Urban growth in a free society," according to President Reagan's 1982 National Urban Policy Report, "is the result of decisions by many individuals, households, and firms acting independently to cluster together in particular places" (U.S. Dept. of HUD, 1982c, p. 11; see also p. 57). The role of the federal government is to accommodate rather than resist the market forces that distribute people and industry across the land and to help declining communities adjust to their new, diminished circumstances (U.S. Dept. of HUD, 1984b, p. 5).

The Contraction of the Federal System

For much of the postwar period the urgency of the search for effective economic development policies was mitigated by the growing flow of intergovernmental fiscal assistance from Washington. Between 1955 and 1978 federal grants-in-aid to states and localities rose from 0.8 percent of the GNP to 3.7 percent. In constant (1972) dollars the amount of assistance in this period increased from $5.6 billion to $49.4 billion, and the number of separate programs soared from 132 in 1960 to 492 in 1978 (ACIR, 1985a, p. 21). Table 4.7 shows the steady rise in federal spending for fiscal assistance and the growth of state and local reliance on funds from Washington. By the midpoint of the Carter administration the federal government was supplying funds not only for major capital projects such as highways, housing, and waste-water treatment facilities, but for the most intimate traditional functions of local government such as fire protection, education, personnel administration, and parks.

Matters changed abruptly in 1978. No single factor appears to be responsible; rather a combination of forces simply came to a head and reversed the long-term increase of intergovernmental aid. The Congress was clearly concerned about record peacetime deficits in each of the fiscal years from 1975 to 1978. These ranged between $45 billion and $66 billion, at least twice as great as the largest postwar deficit up to that time (ACIR, 1985a, p. 20). Furthermore, the public seemed unwilling to

Table 4-7. Federal Grants-in-Aid to State and Local Government

Fiscal Year	Amount in Current Dollars (in billions)	Percent of State-Local Own-Source Receipts	Amount in Constant (1972) Dollars (in billions)	Percent of Real Increase or Decrease from Previous Year
1955	3.5	11.8	5.6	3.7
1960	7.0	16.8	10.8	8.0
1965	10.9	17.7	15.5	5.4
1970	24.0	22.9	27.0	11.6
1975	49.8	29.1	39.2	3.4
1976	59.1	31.1	43.5	11.0
1977	68.4	31.0	46.7	7.4
1978	77.9	31.7	49.4	5.8
1979	82.9	31.3	48.1	-2.6
1980	91.5	31.7	48.2	0.2
1981	94.8	30.1	46.1	-4.4
1982	88.8	25.6	40.4	-12.4
1983	92.5	24.7	40.7	0.7
1984	97.6	23.7	41.3	1.5
1985[a]	106.0	23.7	43.5	5.3
1986[a]	102.6	21.4	40.1	-7.0
1987[a]	100.4	19.5	37.7	-6.0

Source: ACIR, 1986, p. 19.
[a]Entries are estimates.

support ever-increasing domestic spending, a sentiment symbolized at the state level by California's Proposition 13 property tax limitation measure passed by referendum in 1978. The lessons of the "tax revolt" were apparently taken to heart in Washington, where Congress eliminated countercyclical revenue-sharing and job-training programs in the second half of Carter's term. Growing concern over the state of American military preparedness, apparently stimulated in part by the pro-Soviet coup in Afghanistan in 1978 (Howard, 1984), led to a reversal of the steady proportional decline in defense spending dating from the peak years of the Vietnam War.[3] Combined with rising inflation and a sluggish economy, these diverse factors converged to brake the growth of federal aid to state and local governments, a trend that had scarcely wavered since the depression. The process was accelerated during the first Reagan administration, so that by 1983 the real value of intergovernmental dollars had fallen by 25 percent, the number of aid programs had declined to

---

3. In 1969 defense spending accounted for 40.5 percent of the total budget. By 1978 it had fallen to 21.7 percent, a modern low point (ACIR, 1985a, p. 19).

405, and federal grants had fallen from 17 percent of all federal outlays to 11.4 percent (Roberts, 1984, p. 19; ACIR, 1985a, p. 21).

Until the Reagan years, tax-base enhancement seldom figured prominently among state and local officials as a consideration in economic development policy. With the recession of 1981 and the articulation of the Reagan version of the "new federalism," however, the realization that a new era of state and local fiscal self-reliance was in the offing began to crystallize (see, for example, Shannon, 1985, p. 75; U.S. Congress, House, 1985, pp. 8, 139). As federal aid decreased, the Reagan administration sought to encourage states and cities to "make the most of [their own] existing resources" (U.S. Dept. of HUD, 1984b, p. 1). By 1985 the nation's mayors at their annual meeting were speaking of the "new localism," a strategy based on building coalitions with the private sector "to fill the resource gap left by dismantling the Federal programs" (*New York Times,* June 18, 1985). At the annual meeting of the Council of State Governments, former governor of Mississippi, William Winter, noted that "we can no longer depend on Federal largesse. What we do now is based on our own devices and our own resources" (*New York Times,* Dec. 9, 1985). Interestingly, scholarly evidence had begun to emerge showing that those states with high levels of tax effort—that is, those that were already maximizing use of their taxable resources—were more likely to adopt more economic development policies designed to broaden their tax bases than those states with slack capacity (Ambrosius, 1985, p. 9).

The United States in a Changing Economy

For economic development policy actors the shifting distribution of people and industry and the contraction of federal aid to state and local governments represent contextual phenomena in a state of flux. The impact of these transformations in this policy domain has been to heighten the urgency of the search for effective measures and to increase the incentives for policy innovation. Changes of an even more fundamental nature have been taking place in the economic context of development policy, providing not only a stimulus to innovate but in a broad sense some substantive guidance. Since the design of traditional locational subsidies is responsive to characteristics of an economic order that no longer exists as it once did, it is not surprising that as those characteristics have changed, new policy designs have begun to emerge.

In the formative period of economic development policy, roughly from the depression era to about 1970, the American economic context could be characterized as "domestic industrial capitalism." That is to say first of all that in these decades manufacturing was regarded as the economic backbone of the nation, and the domestic market loomed as the key point of reference for both producers and consumers. Though not the activity of a majority of workers, manufacturing nevertheless still occupied 31 percent of the workforce as late as 1960 and contributed 28.7 percent to the gross national product (U.S. Bureau of the Census, 1970, p. 218). Employment in most industrial sectors—apparel, chemicals, automobiles, glass and cement, primary metals, and papermaking—was still expanding in the 1960s. Not once in these years did the United States import more goods than it exported. In fact, one had to go back to 1889 to find the last foreign trade deficit. The combined value of imports and exports in 1970 amounted to only 12.6 percent of the GNP (U.S. Bureau of the Census, 1985b, p. 432).

Things changed in the 1970s. In 1971 the country experienced the first of a series of annual trade deficits, unbroken save for two years, that reached record proportions in the 1980s (ibid., p. 813). Much of this imbalance was a function of oil imports, but even excluding oil and non-manufactured commodities, the nation still suffered a deficit in the trade of manufactured goods in 5 of the 13 years between 1971 and 1983, including a record level $31 billion in 1983 (President's Commission on Industrial Competitiveness, 1985, p. 14). Imported televisions, radios, automobiles, steel, clothing, and shoes captured steadily increasing shares of the domestic consumer market in these years (ibid., p. 181). According to the U.S. Department of Commerce, 70 percent of all American products were competing with imports by the mid-1970s. On the export market, American producers found they were being undersold by foreign manufacturers, some of them from countries that barely a decade before had only a negligible industrial capacity. Between 1960 and 1980 the U.S. share in world trade of manufactured goods, measured in terms of value, declined steadily from around 24 percent to about 17 percent (ibid., p. 15). This was true not only for industrial products such as steel and chemicals, but also for high technology goods and engineering, financing, and insurance services (ibid., p. 174). The increasing involvement of the American economy in the world market brought the combined value of imports and exports to 20.6 percent of the GNP by 1983.

At the same time that the United States was becoming more reliant on imports and less competitive on the export market, manufacturing employment began to decline swiftly relative to the service-producing occupations. This shift is a function in part of the emergence of foreign industrial competitors who can undersell American producers, thus displacing American manufacturing workers, and of the saturation of the domestic market for durable goods, such as small appliances. Between 1940 and 1960 manufacturing held a fairly steady share of U.S. employment, dropping only from 33.9 to 31 percent of all workers. But in 1970, manufacturing occupied only 27.4 percent of the workforce, and by 1983 the figure had dropped to 19.8 percent (U.S. Bureau of the Census, 1975, p. 137; and U.S. Bureau of the Census, 1985b, p. 404). During the 1970s, 13 of the 20 standard industrial groups lost employment in absolute terms, including papermaking, shoemaking, glass and clay production, and primary metal fabrication (U.S. Bureau of the Census, 1985b, pp. 750–55). By 1983 manufacturing was contributing only 20.7 percent to the GNP, down 8 percentage points from 1960 (p. 433).

What has emerged in place of the economy of the postwar decades is a pattern of productive activity based increasingly on services. Bureau of Labor Statistics projections indicate, for example, that of the 20 occupations expected to produce the greatest number of new jobs between 1980 and 1990, all but 3 (construction workers, blue-collar supervisors, and carpenters) are in service occupations. The corps of office secretaries is expected to grow by 700,000, while nurses' aides and janitors will each add over half a million workers to their ranks. Sales clerks, cashiers, nurses, truck drivers, fast food workers, and elementary school teachers are also among the ranks of the occupations expected to produce the most jobs (*National Journal*, Feb. 26, 1983, p. 428).

The service sector covers a wide range of occupations whose chief common characteristic is that they do not involve the production of tangible goods for sale in the market. Social services (including government, education, and health), personal services (such as repairs, restaurants, tourism), distributive services (retail, wholesale, communications, and utilities), and producer services (banking, law, advertising) are standard categories (Nelson and Lorence, 1985). Not all of these are expected to grow. Personal service jobs, for example, are declining in number, and so are many occupations in the distributive category (Stanback and Noyelle, 1982, p. 11). Other service occupations will continue to grow, but at a slower rate than in previous decades. For example, a Bureau of Labor Statistics study finds that the growth in clerical occupations peaked in the mid-1980s, leading some labor analysts to predict that office automation will eventually actually decrease the number of such jobs (*New York Times*, Oct. 4, 1985). Among the fastest-growing occupations are paralegal personnel, engineers, data processing and office machine mechanics, and fast food workers.

Several characteristics of the growing service sector have implications for economic development policy. One is that the growth of service employment does not always offset the loss of manufacturing jobs. Norton's analysis of cities in the 1948–72 period finds impressive service-job growth rates in cities like Cleveland (48 percent) and Philadelphia (62 percent); however, in all but two cases among northeastern and midwestern cities there were net employment losses in these years (1979, p. 96). While a few cities, such as New York, appear to have gained net employment since that period, the pattern of substantial manufacturing loss and modest service gains is still occurring in many places. In Erie and Niagara counties in New York, for example, manufacturing employment declined between 1979 and 1984 by 40,000 jobs, while service jobs grew by only 16,000 (Corrigan, 1985a, p. 1733).

Service growth is also uneven geographically, both among and within regions. Thus, not only has such employment increased faster in the cities of the southern and western census regions, but it has also concentrated within all regions in certain "nodal" centers (Noyelle and Stanback, 1984, pp. 53–58). In northern states, smaller production cities—Peoria, Flint, Evansville—suffered manufacturing losses without sharing in the service growth occurring in regional centers.

A second characteristic of the service sector is that its earnings structure is bifurcated. Few service jobs pay middle-level incomes, that is, wages equivalent to the union-scale earnings of factory workers in heavy industry. Some analysts argue that the greatest increase in service employment has come at the high end of the earnings scale, reflecting swift growth among high-skill occupations, while low-paying jobs are stable or slowly declining. The consequence of this pattern has been to increase income inequality, particularly in metropolitan areas with high concentrations of producer services (Nelson and Lorence, 1985; Kasarda, 1985).

The general decline of manufacturing and the rise of services is accompanied by a proportional decrease in the ranks of middle-income earners in the United States. There is some disagreement about the degree to which this pattern is a product of changes in the occupational structure (Rosenthal, 1985), but the direction of the earnings trend is incontrovertible, as the data in Table 4.8 show. Both the high and the low groups have grown proportionally, but the relative size of the middle group has shrunk dramatically.

A third feature of service jobs at the lower end of the occupation scale is their marginality. Many are part-time: for example, 85.5 percent of fast food workers do not work a full 40-hour week (*New York Times,*

Table 4-8. Percentage Distribution of All U.S.
Households, by Income (in constant 1983
dollars), 1967–83

	1967	1983
Households below $15,000	33.5	35.9
Households between $15,000 and $35,000	49.4	39.8
Households above $35,000	17.0	24.3
Total	99.9	100.0

Source: U.S. Bureau of the Census, 1985b, p. 442.

June 10, 1985), nor do many retail clerks. Few lower-end service jobs offer opportunities for occupational mobility, and few provide generous, if any, fringe benefits. Service jobs are far less likely to be unionized than are manufacturing jobs. In 1984 only 10.5 percent of all service workers were union members compared with 24 percent of workers in manufacturing (*New York Times,* Feb. 8, 1985).

The Capitalist Context of Economic Development

As long as the basis of steady American economic growth remained in place, it was entirely predictable that economic development policy-makers would pursue initiatives consistent with the assumptions of domestic industrial capitalism. These assumptions are the roots of the supply-side policy tradition: they led policy-makers to embrace a theory of economic growth that deferred to capital and relegated government to a subsidiary role. The result in practice was the location incentive in the form of tax concessions, land write-downs, and capital subsidies. In the next section we shall examine the supply-side theory of economic growth. Here we turn to the assumptions which made that theory attractive.

The most important of these assumptions is the idea that private business possesses a special claim to efficiency, effectiveness, and vision, though it must be induced by government to exercise these in the public interest. A second is the proposition that it is optimally efficient for the private sector, acting without government direction or constraint, to allocate resources functionally and geographically; furthermore, whatever modest negative externalities might result from these decisions can effectively be countered or mitigated by government policy. A third is the conviction that competition in the marketplace is a valid testing and winnowing process for firms and entrepreneurs which will in the long run produce economic growth. This competition should, therefore, be allowed to run its course.

The notion that the private sector possesses a special claim vis-à-vis government to efficiency, vision, and know-how—traits that may be traced to the profit motive—has been one of the crucial presumptions of domestic industrial capitalism. The idea is that, in order to maximize the return to capital, business is constantly driven to increase the efficiency of its undertakings through the application of technology, ingenuity, and adaptive organizational principles. The public sector operates without an incentive as compelling as profits and without the flexibility to pursue adaptive strategies (see, for example, Savas, 1982). It follows, therefore, that the performance of many discrete public tasks as well as general public responsibilities can be more efficiently and effectively accomplished by the private sector. The role of government is to induce and guide private performance in the public interest by making it profitable. The task of war mobilization in the 1940s provides an apt example:

In order to speed procurement, the War and Navy departments turned naturally to big business. . . . Big business had much of the plant and most of the experience to handle enormous orders for military materiel, and big business had the stock of executives and engineers capable of undertaking the management of new, technologically difficult programs. . . . The inducements [for cooperation] for established firms were precisely those from which newcomers like the Higgins and Kaiser enterprises also profited: subsidies or low-interest federal loans to enlarge plants and build new machinery, fast tax write-offs for expansion and retooling, generous contracts negotiated on the basis of costs plus a fixed fee, the assurance that facilities for war production financed by government funds would be available at bargain-basement prices for postwar use. Those and other devices guaranteed large profits without risk. That was [Secretary of War Henry] Stimson's intention. "If you are going to . . . go to war . . . in a capitalist country," he wrote, "you have to let business make money out of the process or business won't work." (Blum, 1976, pp. 121–22)

Perhaps the most critical function performed by the private sector in a capitalist system is to determine the character of the economic life of the society. Thus, Charles Lindblom argues that corporations decide a nation's industrial technology, the pattern of work organization, market structure, and resource allocation. Jobs, prices, production, and growth are all a function of business decisions. All of these, of course, have crucial public implications (Lindblom, 1977, pp. 172–77). To make sure that business does its job—that is, that it fosters general growth and prosperity—government, in Lindblom's view, must offer inducements in the form of market benefits and political considerations, but it may not properly assume full responsibility itself for economic growth:

Every government in [a pluralist free market system] accepts a responsibility to do what is necessary to assure profits high enough to maintain at a minimum employment and growth. If businessmen say, as they do, that they need tax offsets to induce investment, governments in all these systems seriously weigh the request, acknowledging that the tax concessions may indeed be necessary. (p. 174)

Economic development tasks are simply a subset of these broader economic responsibilities. From the perspective of domestic industrial capitalism they are best performed by the vigorous private sector, supported by public-sector subsidies that lower the costs of major production factors.

A second assumption that could be sustained in an expanding, largely domestic economy has been that national economic efficiency is served when business is left to allocate its resources geographically and functionally as it thinks best. Businesses choose geographical locations, it is assumed, by determining those particular places where they can minimize their production costs and maximize their profits. There are, of course, some problems that arise when capital migrates from high-cost to low-cost regions: some workers are displaced and some communities and states experience fiscal hardship. But the idea behind supply-side location incentives is to counter the free-market forces that drain capital from some regions by subsidizing business costs in those disadvantaged places and thus equalizing costs. In theory enough businesses would be induced to stay put or move from other locations to offset job and tax-base losses.

Business is also thought to be the best judge of the kinds of undertakings in which to invest. These decisions are made on the basis of calculations that take into account market opportunities, existing expertise, and the ratio of initial investment and on-going operating costs to profits over time. Government may need to offer incentives to offset high initial costs or low profits to ensure the development and production of a certain limited range of goods, such as military hardware, but for the most part the decisions about what to produce are left to the private sector.

A third assumption has involved the idea that business formation, survival, and death are all natural outcomes of the competitive market and ought not be tampered with by government. Ultimately, the competitive process produces a strong, growing economic base, for the vigorous and efficient survive; the weak and superfluous and wasteful do not. Competition sorts these out. Much is made here of the entrepreneurial spirit, a trait of individual visionaries and risk-takers. These are the engineers of growth and progress in American history. Though the casualties among them are high, "it would be a terrible mistake," according to a witness at a Joint Economic Committee hearing on the entrepreneurial climate in the United States, "for our government to attempt to save the 95 percent that fail" (Premus et al., 1985, p. viii). If conditions are right—favorable tax laws, no red tape, a flexible regulatory climate—there will be enough entrepreneurs who will survive the scrutiny of the marketplace to drive economic growth.

The Supply-Side Theory of Urban and Regional Economic Growth

Although two broad theoretical explanations of how urban and regional economies grow have coexisted for most of this century, the one that stresses supply rather than demand factors was the more attractive to policy-makers during the era of domestic industrial capitalism. The supply-side explanation asserts that growth is a function of resources attracted to a particular locale. Here the critical idea is comparative locational advantage. The demand-side model stresses the need to attract or develop industries that export beyond local borders as a condition of growth. Although this model was for many years the "more fashionable" among urban economists (Thompson, 1965, p. 37; see also Conroy, 1975, p. 41), its influence on actual policy design was substantially less in the old economic order than that of the supply-side model.

The policy implications of the demand-side export-base model require that planners encourage the development of only certain selected industries, namely those that serve external, preferably growing, markets and produce income-elastic goods. This necessitates a detailed level of market analysis and selectivity for which state and local development agencies have been politically and administratively ill-equipped. In the era of domestic industrial capitalism the concept of an "industrial policy"—which involves government efforts to discriminate between growing and declining industries in order to nurture the former—had few, if any, partisans. Such a vigorous government role in economic affairs commanded scant legitimacy. A practical handbook written in 1960 for industrial development practitioners, for example, advised that "although industrial development analysis is important, the government should seek to make the fullest possible use of the market as a means to direct industrial investment to various industries . . ." (Bryce, 1960, pp. 64–65).

Not only were development agencies ruled in these years by the conviction that *any* industrial or commercial growth was desirable, but most were too poorly staffed to carry out selective market analyses: in 1966 the average number of professionals and administrators in the typical state development agency was only 31, a figure that nearly tripled by the early 1980s (Thomas, 1975, p. 42; Reinshuttle, n.d., p. 5). If the export-base model made sense in theory, translating it into policy promised to outstrip government capabilities, to say nothing of stretching the acceptable limits of public intervention in the economy.

Supply-side theory in contrast offers an administratively simple, politically congenial option. Application of the term "supply side" to urban and regional economic growth models can be traced to Wilbur Thompson (1965). Button (1976) also writes of "supply orientated" models in this context. But the roots of supply-side theory lie in classical location economics developed in the first half of the century by Von Thunen, Alfred Weber, Edgar Hoover, and Walter Isard, among others (Watkins, 1980, Ch. 2). Location theory initially posited that firms would position themselves in space in such a way as to minimize transportation costs incurred in shipping raw materials to the point of production and finished goods to their markets. Once location economists recognized geographical differences in the costs of production factors—land, labor, capital—these too were entered into the site decision. In its modern form, then, location theory asserts that, all things being equal, firms will seek those sites where their combined production and transport costs are minimized (Webber, 1984).

The costs of production are said to enter the economic process on the supply rather than the demand side. Variations among factor costs exist among cities, metropolitan areas, states, and regions and are products of the relative availability of land, the abundance of capital, the size and skill of the labor force, the proximity of energy sources, and a variety of other factors. In a free market the prices of most of these factors are influenced by government only tangentially, if at all, a problem we shall consider in detail later on. The prices of a few factors, however, are set by government—especially processing costs such as taxes and administrative regulations—and the costs of others may be subsidized by government. The object of economic development policy in the old economic order was to establish an advantageous price structure insofar as possible, thereby creating a comparative location advantage. The assumption was that growth (in the form of investment) would occur in those locales that offered the lowest factor prices.

Supply-side development policies tend to be administratively simple. Among the most popular are various sorts of tax exemptions that may be enjoyed by all firms nonselectively and are administered routinely through the established tax system. An example is the widespread sales tax exemption on the purchase of industrial equipment and machinery. Even for those location incentives for which individual applications are normally required, such as tax-exempt bond financing or tax abatements, administrative costs are held down by the use of simple decision rules. For example, if virtually all applications receive a tax abatement, as is the case in many cities that offer such location incentives, then the decision costs to the city will be very low.

Such policies also had political virtues in the old economic order. Even though subsidizing capital or providing industrial land discounts with public funds represented departures from a completely free market, at least government was not in the business of making investment decisions or charting industrial development patterns over the long term by subsidizing those firms it deemed potential "winners." As the subsidizer of location costs, government could operate in the background, deferring to the investment decisions and preferences of private capital. Supply-side incentives were, of course, regarded as *inducements* to elicit investment that might not otherwise have occurred in a particular place. But state and local government had no guide or rationale for initiating and nurturing economic activity; it could capitalize or play upon only those impulses already present in the private sphere. If a low-wage hosiery factory wished to move to town, the city would write down the cost of the land, just as it would if the firm were instead a high-wage manufacturing operation producing for the international market. Supply-side policy offered no guide as to where public support might be most effectively applied. Location inducements fitted nicely into the framework of assumptions that underlay domestic industrial capitalism, marking out a modest and deferential position between an entreprenurial government role and complete disengagement from the market.

The Erosion of the Old Economic Order

The emergence of the global marketplace and the service-based domestic economy strained public officials' commitment to the notion that private capital, gently guided by location incentives, would produce local prosperity. The short-comings of the assumptions on which the old order was based could hardly be ignored. For one thing the private sector's performance of what Lindblom called its "public functions"—the maintenance of growth and the generation of jobs—arguably failed to sustain its claim to great efficiency and effectiveness. Rather, the record projected a pattern of inconsistency at best and, in some areas, helplessness. Unemployment, for example, which hovered around 5 percent during the entire period from 1950 to 1974, suddenly rose to 8.5 percent in 1975 and then averaged 7.7 percent annually through 1984 (U.S. Bureau of the Census, 1985b, p. 391). Although the service sector was generating vast numbers of new jobs, many were dead-end positions that offered few prospects for mobility or economic security. And business had virtually nothing to contribute to the solution of rampant minority unemployment in central cities, particularly among young people.

Although actual numbers of manufacturing jobs grew during the 1970s, many of the new jobs, particularly those in high-technology manufacturing, paid far less than the old heavy industrial jobs that were in decline. Indeed, the rate of annual personal income growth in the United States in the two decades leading up to 1983 was lower than that of all of the major nations of Western Europe and Japan save Great Britain (President's Commission on Industrial Competitiveness, 1985, p. 109). On another front the United States lagged through the 1970s and early 1980s behind most European and Asian nations in its rates of capital formation and productivity measured in terms of gross domestic product (ibid., pp. 110–12).

Another problem concerned the movement of capital to more efficient locations. Free capital mobility has always been regarded as essential to economic efficiency, and it has been a constant in American economic history. Though an industry's or firm's departure from one region for another inflicted hardship on places and workers left behind, there appeared to be mitigating responses available to government and individuals. Workers could migrate to where the new jobs went, and states and cities could, it was thought, replace those lost industries by offering other firms location incentives. Regions on the receiving end of capital migration naturally regarded the process of mobility in favorable terms, for it provided the basis for industrialization of those largely agrarian economies. In short, unimpeded capital movement was tolerated in some regions because its effects could, it was assumed, be offset; and it was welcomed in other regions because it brought employment. Economic development policy focused on capturing some portion of this mobile capital.

Policy-makers gradually realized, however, that all through the period in which state legislatures and city councils of declining regions were passing lavish economic development blandishments, businesses continued to move out, and the toll of job losses mounted. At the same time the pace of capital flight abroad accelerated. Direct foreign investment by American firms increased at a faster rate than domestic investment all through the period from 1950 to 1980, and particularly so after the late 1960s (Bluestone and Harrison, 1982, pp. 42, 142). Localities that had gained industrial employers by attracting mobile firms now began to lose the same firms to low-wage countries in Latin America and Asia. The lesson in these movements was not only that capital mobility caused problems that could not be easily mitigated by public policy based on location incentives, but also that the efficient solution for business was not necessarily the efficient solution for American society.[4] Unimpeded capital mobility cost American jobs and created extraordinary fiscal burdens for states and communities left behind.

A third problem arose in regard to the assumption that growth would emerge from unrestricted competition in the marketplace. A critical requirement of this assumption is that there be many entrants in the competition, for the failure rate of firms is high in their early years. The rate of entry of business into the market is a product in some measure of the climate for entrepreneurship. If the promise of returns is in doubt and if the necessary financial, intellectual, and organizational support for entrepreneurial activities is lacking, the rate of new business births and the process of innovation and product development slows down. The implication of this may not be very severe in aggregate economic terms when applied to small service or retail business: most bars and restaurants, dry cleaning establishments, specialty shops, and so on are started with personal savings, provide little employment, and, if they survive, add little, in any given case, to a local or state economy. But it is a more serious problem where the manufacturing and research sectors are concerned. Fewer new products find their way on to the market, and the ability of the nation to compete with countries with a high level of innovative activity declines.

---

4. Carter's National Urban Policy Report of 1980 took direct issue with the "free market" notion. "[C]urrent job losses in central cites simply cannot be regarded as an efficient response to economic forces," the report argues (U.S. Dept. of HUD, 1980b, pp. 3–12). The costs of adjusting urban infrastructure and land use to both decline and growth and the burdens imposed by unemployment, migration, and job retraining are borne largely by individuals and the public sector and are not included in the efficiency calculations of private businesses.

Many observers became convinced in the late 1970s and early 1980s that the American climate for entrepreneurship was discouraging innovation and market entry (Premus et al., 1985). The private market, left to its own devices, was not generating the incentives or the support for more vigorous competition. The indicators were numerous. Less venture capital was available after the increase in the federal capital gains tax in 1969 (ibid., p. vii). Spending by the private sector on research and development as a percentage of GNP remained virtually unchanged at slightly over 1.4 percent from 1966 to 1979. During this period civilian R&D expenditures were increasing sharply in such countries as West Germany and Japan, substantially outpacing the United States in effort (President's Commission on Industrial Competitiveness, 1985, p. 100). The number of patents granted in the United States fell by 31 percent between 1971 and 1984 (Premus et al., 1985, pp. 24–25). In declining states and cities the absence of new business births was particularly acute: although rates of business failure were evenly distributed across the country, the rate of new business formation was much lower in the northern census regions (Birch, 1979).

Drawing Lessons for Economic Development Policy

The old economic order, operating within a framework of political federalism, provided a supportive context for a generation of supply-side location incentives. In that system government played a subordinate role to capital. Policy initiatives were launched from the sidelines as businesses moved up and down the market field of play. Government seldom joined the action. Policy was designed not to create roles for government as an actor in the market but rather to influence the movement of others on the field.

The transformation of domestic industrial capitalism and the obsolescence of its critical assumptions has not led to a new economic ideology. Rhetorical commitment to the free market does not appear to have flagged. The assumptions about the primacy and reliability of private capital have not been self-consciously abandoned as much as they are in the process of being recast in the crucible of the policy process by the entrepreneurial state with policies that call for a more vigorous economic role for state and local government. The specific lessons that states and communities have drawn from the challenge to the assumptions of domestic industrial capitalism involve paying greater attention to the possibilities of foreign trade, placing far more emphasis on building and expanding business and entrepreneurial activity within state borders than on competing for mobile capital, and targeting industries with a potential to tap or create expanding demands in the market. In pursuing these and other strategies, which we shall explore later on, subnational governments have not entirely abandoned supply-side theory and location incentives. But they have turned increasingly to a theory of growth that stresses accommodation and attentiveness to the demand side of the economic process. This has meant in short that state and local governments are now entering the field of play, assuming more central, entrepreneurial roles in the market than they have ever contemplated before.

Part II

THE SUPPLY-SIDE

TRADITION

CHAPTER 5

The Federal Role in State and Local Economic Development

THERE is a risk that the intensity and variety of state and local economic development efforts will obscure the rich history of federal policy in this domain. This is not, perhaps, surprising, for the rapid ascent and transformation of subnational policy contrasts with the recently troubled course of many federal development programs. Even as the efforts to attract business and stimulate capital formation on home grounds were becoming more solidly entrenched functions of state and local government in the 1980s, the survival of several federal efforts in this field, including the Small Business Administration programs, Economic Development Administration assistance, and Urban Development Action Grants, were under challenge by the Reagan administration each year at budget time. Although all of these survived the first half of the decade, often by dint of last minute compromises, they emerged for the most part with greatly diminished resources.[1]

Since the depression various federal programs have provided important assistance and guidance to states and cities in their efforts to en-

1. As the data below show, funding for each of the major federal economic development programs declined during the Reagan years.

Appropriations for Federal Economic Development Programs (in millions of dollars)

	1980	1981	1982	1983	1984	1985	1986
SBA	1996.1	1189.9	569.9	1017.3	597.8	1253.7	714.4
EDA	553.4	476.5	223.5	293.9	293.7	230.7	190.9
CDBG	3752	3695	3456	3456[a]	3468	3472	n.a.
UDAG	675	675	435	440	440	440	440

Source: Executive Office of the President, Office of Management and Budget, *Budget of the United States Government,* for the years shown.

[a] Does not include a one-time add-on $1 billion Emergency Jobs appropriation.

courage business growth, and they have continued to do so even in the 1980s. A study by the Congressional Budget Office calculated that in 1983 federal grants to state and local governments for economic development amounted to slightly more than $5.6 billion, a sum that dwarfs the states' comparable direct expenditures of $280 million in that year (CBO, 1984, p. 2). The federal figure as it is presented by the CBO is somewhat misleading, for it neglects to note that only a portion of the $3.5 billion of Community Development Block Grant money is used for strictly economic development purposes. On the other hand the total does not include other federal monies that support, sometimes indirectly, state and local development efforts, such as research grants to public universities ($2.8 billion), foregone tax revenues in the amount of $4 billion that result from industrial revenue bonds issued by subnational governments, and a host of loan guarantees and direct loans, mostly to private small businesses and U.S. export firms, that came to nearly $15 billion in 1983 (ibid., pp. 3–4). By any account federal support for economic development activities at the state and local level has been and still is substantial.

The gross budget figures give little sense of the variety on the menu of federal programs that bear on subnational economic development. Focusing first on those efforts explicitly aimed at enhancing state or local economies—a place-oriented criterion—one can distinguish two main groups of federal programs. The first, which includes nearly a dozen programs administered by six different agencies (top panel of Chart 5-1), embraces a series of initiatives that provide resources to state or local governments to be used for the purposes of attracting or stimulating business investment. These programs offer funds for the acquisition of land to be sold or leased to firms at submarket rates, for the construction of public works to support a particular business concern, for the purchase and preparation of industrial park real estate, for the establishment of business loan programs, and for the preparation of economic development plans, among other uses. At least another half dozen programs in the second group (middle panel) target loans, loan guarantees, and special assistance directly to particular types of high-risk businesses in particular places experiencing some sort of economic need or distress. These latter programs do not directly enhance state or local government capabilities for undertaking economic development projects, but they are designed to improve local economies.

A third group of federal programs (bottom panel of Chart 5-1) involves loans and other assistance to various sorts of small and minority-

Chart 5-1.   Federal Assistance for Subnational Economic Development

Grant and Loan Programs for Subnational Governments		
Community Facility Loans	Insured loans to rural communities and nonprofit corporations for construction or improvement of industrial parks	Department of Agriculture (USDA)
Water and Waste Disposal Grants and Loans	Grants to rural governments for water and water-treatment-facility construction or improvement	USDA
Public Works and Development Grants (Title I)	Grants for construction of infrastructure to attract industry	Economic Development Administration (EDA)
Technical Assistance (Title III)	Grants for the design of local economic development programs	EDA
Special Adjustment Assistance (Title IX)	Flexible planning and program grants to help localities overcome sudden and severe job losses	EDA
Minority Business Development Assistance	Grants to states and localities and business development organizations to provide technical assistance to minority-owned businesses	Department of Commerce
Community Development Block Grants (CDBG)	Grants to cities for a wide range of development and revitalization uses, including land acquisition, public facility construction, financing industrial facilities, funding local development corporations	Department of Housing and Urban Development (HUD)
Section 108	Loan guarantees to cities for land acquisition and development for commercial or industrial uses	HUD
Urban Development Action Grants	Competitive grants to cities to support commercial industrial projects through financing subsidies and construction of public works	HUD

(continued on following page)

Chart 5-1.   Federal Assistance for Subnational Economic Development (*continued*)

Grant and Loan Programs for Subnational Governments (*continued*)		
Historic Preservation Assistance	Grants to states, to be passed through to individuals and public or private organizations for acquisition or preservation of historic properties	Department of the Interior
Appalachian Regional Commission	Promotion of regional economic development by funding infrastructure projects	Appalachian Regional Commission
Assistance for Businesses in Distressed Places		
Development Assistance Program	Management and technical assistance for small businesses owned by disadvantaged persons or located in areas of high unemployment	Small Business Administration (SBA)
Section 503: Certified Development Company[a]	SBA-guaranteed debentures sold by business development companies to raise funds to provide long-term loans to small businesses	SBA
Farmer's Home Administration Loans	Loan guarantees for business firms in rural areas to finance land, equipment, and building purchases or provide working capital	USDA
Business Loans and Loan Guarantees (Title II)	Assistance for businesses locating in distressed areas	EDA
Labor Surplus Area Program	Federal procurement targeted to firms in areas with high unemployment	All federal agencies
Defense Logistics Agency Test Program	Procurement targeted to firms in areas with high unemployment	Department of Defense
Assistance for Targeted Businesses		
Trade Adjustment Assistance	Technical-assistance grants, loans, and loan guarantees for construction, modernization, or acquisition of land or capital to firms demonstrating adverse impacts from imports	Department of Commerce
Section 7(a) Regular Small Business Loans	Loans and loan guarantees to small businesses for construction, acquisition or expansion	SBA

(*continued on following page*)

Chart 5-1. Federal Assistance for Subnational Economic Development (*continued*)

Section 8(a) Business Development Program	SBA-arranged procurement contracts between companies owned by disadvantaged persons and federal agencies	SBA
Small Business Investment Companies	Loans and guarantees to SBICs to enable them to provide equity and venture capital to small and minority-owned firms	SBA
Pollution Control Financing Guarantees	Loan guarantees to small businesses to meet pollution control requirements	SBA
Service Corps of Retired Executives and Active Corps Executives	Mobilization of management skills of executives to help small businesses	SBA
Minority Small Business and Capital Ownership Program	Technical assistance to minority-owned businesses for market development	SBA
Export Credit Program	Loan guarantees for small businesses for export financing and development of foreign markets.	SBA
Small Business Research Innovation Program[b]	Federal agency set-aside of R&D funds to be spent on contracts with small businesses	SBA
Office of Private Sector Initiatives	Assistance in arranging public-private partnerships to benefit small businesses	SBA
Small Business Set-Aside Program	Federal procurement set-asides for small business	All federal agencies
U.S. Export-Import Bank	Loans and credit insurance to U.S. exporters and foreign firms importing U.S. goods	Export-Import Bank
Technical Assistance and Marketing Information	Provision of technical assistance to exporting firms, including market information, analytic support, and promotional assistance	Department of Commerce
National Consumer Cooperative Bank	Market-rate loans for consumer and worker-owned producer cooperatives	NCCB

[a]SBA's 503 program became SBA 504 in September 1986.
[b]Small Business Research Innovation grants were subject to a 1987 sunset provision.

owned businesses *regardless of their location*. Strictly speaking, these initiatives do not seek to enhance subnational economies, although many may in fact have that effect. Their policy purpose is primarily to foster the development of certain types of businesses rather than certain subnational economies. Nevertheless, they play a role of some importance for state and local governments as economic development actors by providing programmatic models and guidance for public action in this policy domain, particularly with regard to small business development and export trade.

In addition to these 30-odd programs listed in Chart 5-1 there are numerous other federal actions and programs that clearly affect particular state and local economies. But because they do not deliberately set out to strengthen subnational economic .development capabilities, or seek primarily to increase private investment in distressed places, or serve as program models for state and local development efforts, they cannot be considered federal economic *development* programs. These include defense spending; the siting of military bases, space exploration centers, and federal research facilities; highway and transportation programs; and national park and recreation-area development, among others. Federal tax and tariff policies may also have particular regional economic effects. These actions and programs notwithstanding, the efforts important for understanding the purposive contributions of the federal government to subnational economic development capabilities fall into the first group in Chart 5-1. A few programs from the second and third groups also merit discussion, either for the ways in which they have been self-consciously incorporated in subnational economic development strategies or for their didactic effects.

Washington has rarely administered any program for economic development, either in the past or present period, according to a national growth plan. As a Congressional Budget Office study observes, "With the exception of aid to distressed regions, the location of economic activity is not a matter of explicit national policy" (CBO, 1984, p. 8; see also Vaughan, 1977, p. 127). Neither has the federal government sought vigorously to control the content or administration of its intergovernmental programs. Indeed, an important feature of several programs is their flexibility, a characteristic that has permitted local recipients, in particular, great creativity in their use. Some programs were never intended primarily for economic development assistance, but the latitude built into the decentralized American federal system has allowed local government to transform such programs as urban renewal and CDBG into mainstays of their economic development efforts.

Traditionally, most federal programs in this policy field supported the interstate competition for mobile, existing capital. Federal assistance allowed communities to offer subsidies to private firms as inducements to relocate. More recently, however, cities in particular have begun to use federal monies to help underwrite the new activities of the entrepreneurial state such as stimulating new business births and providing expansion capital to local firms.

By the 1980s the torch of economic development policy had clearly passed from Washington to the states and local governments. In the current period it is the inventiveness, energy, and sense of urgency of officials at these lower levels that animate this policy field. But state and local efforts have been neither entirely self-sustaining nor self-generated. They derive much of their inspiration from patterns laid out by federal policymakers. In short, subnational economic development policies cannot be fully understood without full knowledge of comparable and complementary federal efforts.

Federal Aid for Subnational Development before World War II

The roughly 160 years between the end of the Revolution and the close of World War II are rife with examples of federal actions and policies that selectively affected subnational economic development. Nineteenth-century tariffs that boosted the New England economy, railroad land grants and homesteading that opened the western lands, the Morrill Act of 1862 that established the land grant college system, the Highway Act of 1916 that "got the farmers out of the mud," the great public works projects of the depression, and the establishment of military bases and defense plants throughout the Sun Belt in the 1940s all come to mind. Yet few of these efforts were designed with subnational economic development goals as a prime objective, and fewer still were intended to help state and local governments in their pursuit of development ends. By this latter standard only a few instances of federal involvement qualify. One of the most notable is the intergovernmental campaign to create an internal transportation network in the early years of the nineteenth century.

Unlike modern federal economic development initiatives, federal assistance to states and localities in the canal era did not represent an attempt to implement a congressional program or to articulate and promote national objectives. Gallatin's plan of 1808 for a nationally financed, nationally planned network of roads and canals had been rejected by a Congress concerned with states' rights issues. Yet the federal government did for a brief time make available its considerable resources for state and locally initiated projects. Thus, Elazar (1962) has documented early federal involvement in the construction of the Dismal Swamp Canal through both the provision of technical assistance and the purchase of stock issued by the canal company, even though the canal was entirely a Virginia scheme. Later, the federal government agreed to grant the state of Ohio a half million acres of land, proceeds from the state's sale of which could then be used to support its ambitious canal building (Scheiber, 1969). As in Virginia, the idea for the canal and the mobilization of support for its financing and construction originated within the state and not in Washington. Other federal land grants followed in Indiana and Illinois to assist state-initiated road and canal projects. The principal sources of capital in these later projects were private money and state bond issues. In addition, as Scheiber has observed, "the states were the locus of planning and the arena in which the formative policy decisions were made" (1975, p. 93; see also Goodrich, 1961, pp. 252–53). Any expectations that the federal role in transportation development would grow from these beginnings were ended with President Jackson's veto in 1830 on states' rights grounds of the Maysville Road Bill, which called for federal support for a Kentucky turnpike project. Significant federal assistance to states for transportation facilities did not appear again until the Highway Act of 1916.

That the canals and roads of the period before the Civil War contributed to local economic development there can be little doubt. Though a number of canals did not handle sufficient tonnage to produce returns on the investment in them, property values along the waterways nevertheless rose steadily, vast tracts of land were turned to agricultural production as access to markets become possible, and new towns sprang up (Hacker, 1970, p. 114). Such gains were ultimately in the national economic interest, but the federal role in their achievement was largely a supporting one. And certainly the impact of transportation facilities was selective: areas close to canals in the prerailroad era tended to prosper, while other places languished.

Another example of deliberate federal efforts to facilitate local economic development involves the authorization of waterworks on the Colorado River and the construction of the Hoover Dam in the two decades prior to World War II. Undertaken at the urging of Los Angeles leaders, who foresaw the economic effects that additional water would have on the city, these massive projects were crucial to the extraordinary growth in the postwar period of this naturally arid region (see, for example, Ostrom, 1953).

Two important features of these federal development activities in the century and a half before World War II set them apart from the pattern of federal involvement after 1945. One is that these activities were episodic. Unlike the various postwar renewal and redevelopment programs, which represent sustained commitments of national scope, federal canal and water assistance for economic development purposes was short-lived and limited to only a few locales. Washington's aid in the early period has a certain accidental quality. The second feature is that those federal activities represented responses to projects initiated entirely at the state or local level. In both these respects the involvement of the national government was consistent with the decentralized nature of the federal arrangement before its radical transformation in the postdepression era. Yet at least two additional features of these early episodes provide a thread of continuity to the modern period. First, assistance for the purpose of constructing public works infrastructure to facilitate local industrial and commercial growth remains an important development strategy. And second, even though the federal government initiated the postwar development programs to which it has been a party, the principle of decentralized participation in spending federal resources is still a vital part of contemporary economic development programs.

A survey of the key programs follows, including Urban Renewal, selected programs of the Small Business Administration, the efforts of the Economic Development Administration, Community Development Block Grants and the Urban Development Action Grants, and the proposed national urban enterprise zones.

Urban Renewal: 1949–1974

Urban renewal began life as a housing program but turned progressively, both by law and by practice, into a major tool for subsidizing and assisting private-sector commercial and industrial projects in American cities. The mechanics of the program were simple. Title I of the 1949 Housing Act authorized federal grants to local redevelopment agencies to cover two-thirds of the net cost of acquiring and clearing "a slum area or a deteriorated or deteriorating area" for the purpose of leasing or reselling to a private developer who agreed to implement the provisions of the locality's redevelopment plan (Foard and Fefferman, 1966). Local governments, which were required to put up a third of the net cost of the project, either in cash or by providing public works and facilities to serve the project, assembled the land parcels by exercising their right of eminent domain. The subsidy to private interests came in the form of a write-down on the cost of land resold or leased to the developer: although the law stipulated that a fair market price be established for the land, this was inevitably less than what urban renewal agencies had in fact paid for acquisition and clearance (ibid., p. 95; Weicher, 1972, p. 6; and Slayton, 1966, pp. 191–92). More important, perhaps, was that public power was used to acquire land that in many cases would never have been available to private developers, at least not at a reasonable price. Thus, urban renewal created potentially lucrative opportunities for private investors, and this was justified on the grounds that such development produced public benefits.

Implementation of the entire program was consistent with a decentralized federal structure. Before local governments could establish urban redevelopment agencies, state legislatures had to pass enabling legislation. Renewal projects themselves were planned and administered at the local level. Each urban renewal agency decided in conjunction with other officials in the local government which areas qualified as "slums" to be cleared, how the cleared land was to be used, and which private developer would implement the plan. Although roughly half of the acreage cleared was ultimately devoted to public uses (U.S. Dept. of HUD, 1975, p. 22), the main impact of urban renewal was to transfer federal funds to local hands for the purpose of encouraging and supporting private development.

At its inception urban redevelopment (it did not acquire the name "urban renewal" until 1954) was conceived as an integral part of the federal response to the postwar housing shortage. The 1949 Housing Act was, after all, the fulfillment of President Truman's promise to see comprehensive housing legislation through Congress. The preamble of the bill promised "a decent home and a suitable living environment" for every American family, and Title II authorized a major commitment to public housing. Title I, the redevelopment provision, limited clearance to "predominantly residential" areas or to those which were "to be developed or redeveloped for predominantly residential uses." Although no definition of "predominantly residential" appears in the law, a rule of thumb emerged that more than half the land use of an area had to be devoted to housing to qualify as "predominantly residential" (Foard and Fefferman, 1966, pp. 105–6). To its congressional proponents in particular, therefore, Title I was very much part of a broad housing initiative in which slum dwellings would be demolished and new housing, both public and private, would rise in their place.

But there was a loophole in the law that made it possible for cities to raze dilapidated residential structures and redevelop the land for commercial purposes: Title I did not specify that redevelopment areas had to be predominantly residential both before *and* after redevelopment, only one or the other. What is important from an economic development perspective is that many cities from the outset seized upon this loophole as the way to demolish decaying inner city slums that abutted the downtown and lure major investors to the cleared land with the promise of the write-down as well as new public facilities such as parking garages and "vest pocket" parks. Residential property of little value would be replaced on the tax rolls by commercial structures of higher value, and cities would demonstrate their revival through the construction of dramatic new city centers. Mere housing projects could not produce equivalent visual, psychological, or fiscal impacts.

Cities were still not allowed under the law to demolish predominantly commercial areas for commercial redevelopment. To permit limited activity of this type Congress, yielding to pressure, amended the program in 1954 to allow up to 10 percent of the federal funds to be spent on projects involving areas that were not predominantly residential in character either before demolition or after redevelopment. The exception was increased to 20 percent in the 1959 Housing Act, to 30 percent in 1961, and finally to 35 percent in 1965. As the commissioner of the Urban Renewal Administration, William Slayton, put it in 1963: "This increase in the authority to undertake nonresidential projects [reflects] a growing awareness of the importance of using renewal to revitalize the economic base and the taxable resources of cities, large and small. It recognize[s] the contribution of urban renewal in creating better job opportunities . . ." (Slayton, 1966, p. 194).

In the end, it is true, urban renewal did not entirely abandon its housing purposes. When the program was terminated in 1974 through consolidation into the Community Development Block Grant in the Housing and Community Development Act of that year, some 411,000 housing units had been planned in renewal areas, of which about 240,000 had already been completed (U.S. Dept. of HUD, 1975, p. 21). But these housing accomplishments should not be exaggerated. Urban renewal agencies oversaw the demolition of over 100,000 housing units *more* than the planned final total (Weicher, 1972, p. 6). Furthermore, of all projects approved though 1966, the point at which land acquisition and demolition began to give way to an emphasis on neighborhood preservation, 67 percent had involved land that was originally predominantly residential but only 43 percent involved residential development (ibid., p. 11). At that date 10,700 acres of the total 27,000 acquired by renewal agencies had been shifted from residential to nonresidential uses (Abrams, 1966, p. 579; Weicher, 1972, p. 10).

In retrospect the program is associated with downtown revitalization: New Haven's Oak and Church Street developments near the Puritan town green, New York's Columbus Circle, San Francisco's Yerba Buena Center, Boston's Government Center, and so on. Its housing accomplishments pale in comparison, particularly in a society that manages to produce privately between a million and 1.5 million housing units *every year*. Some critics at the time argued that much of the development on prime downtown land would have taken place without the intervention of the public sector (Anderson, 1964). There is no entirely convincing way to test this assertion, but it seems reasonable to counter with the argument that private developers would not have been able in many cases to piece together enough land parcels held by different owners in timely enough fashion to make large-scale development projects feasible or attractive.

In any event the outcomes of the program, whether or not induced by the support provided by public power and resources, were consistent with economic development goals. No data on employment effects of the program were published by the Urban Renewal Administration, but evidence regarding the stimulation of investment and the production of tax revenues shows what may be interpreted as strong development impacts. The program exhibited a relatively high leveraging ratio throughout its history, eliciting between four and six dollars of private investment for every one dollar of federal funds (Groberg, 1966, p. 521). When urban renewal ended in 1974 the federal government had committed over $13.2 billion to 3284 projects in 1258 towns and cities (U.S. Dept. of HUD, 1974). At the minimum leveraging ratio of federal to private dollars, the program stimulated more than $50 billion in private investment.

The property tax effects were also substantial. Although taxable land in urban renewal areas declined from 76 percent of the acreage before redevelopment to 47 percent afterwards, total assessed valuation of property in renewal projects rose 203 percent over the course of the program (U.S. Dept. of HUD, 1975, p. 22).

The Small Business Administration

Most of the programs of the Small Business Administration, an independent federal agency established in 1953, provide various sorts of assistance directly to small business concerns or private development corporations (Parris, 1968; U.S. SBA, 1984a). The bulk of this assistance is in the form of loan guarantees, but there are also direct loans, assistance in procuring federal contracts, technical help, and venture-capital funding. Unlike most other federal economic development programs, those of the SBA are not administered intergovernmentally, nor is the intent to provide state and local governments resources with which to compete for or develop private businesses. Distinctly national interests are said to be at stake: as the 1953 Small Business Act (Section 2) put it, "It is the declared policy of Congress that Government should aid, counsel, assist, and protect . . . the interests of small-business concerns . . . to maintain and strengthen the overall economy of the Nation." Nothing is said in the act about the economies of older inner cities or depressed areas or regions. With only a few exceptions, which we shall examine, the programs of the SBA are neutral with respect to location in the sense that they are designed primarily to aid particular enterprises no matter where they reside rather than strengthen the economies of particular places.

If the SBA programs are not specifically designed to strengthen state and local economic development capabilities, neither do they serve well, in the view of many observers, as carefully crafted national development tools. They are too scattered; they serve a broad and extremely diverse constituency; and they are not responsive to any well-defined underlying principle save some general sense that "small business" is important to promote. As one position paper at the 1980 White House Conference on Small Business acknowledged: "A cursory survey of federal agencies reveals numerous small business assistance programs, few of which appear to be tied to any central policy objective. For example, five different federal agencies . . . currently administer eleven major programs offering business loans to small and medium businesses across the States" (U.S. SBA, 1980b, p. 76). In arguing for the complete abolition of the SBA and most of its major programs, Office of Management and Budget Director David Stockman suggested in budget hearings in 1985 that the programs had a scattershot character: "SBA conducts a $3–4 billion annual lending program which indiscriminately sprays a faint mist of subsidized credit into the weakest and most prosaic nooks and crannies of the nation's $4 trillion economy" (Rausch, 1985, p. 1846).

In essence, then, most of the various SBA programs—Section 7(a) loans and loan guarantees, the Small Business Investment Companies program, the Minority Small Business Program—cannot be regarded as a major part of the federal contribution to state and local economic development capabilities. SBA programs are best characterized as serving diffusely defined national economic objectives by directly supporting small business firms wherever they exist.

This is not to say, however, that the SBA serves no subnational economic development functions. First of all, there are several minor, though growing, programs of recent origin whose purpose is either to serve the economic interest of specifically defined places or to support directly and complement particular state and local economic development initiatives. Second, the SBA serves leadership and clearinghouse functions for state and local economic development officials through conference sponsorship and publications.

Three "place-oriented" programs of the SBA are noteworthy. The first is the Small Business Development Center program, begun in 1976 as a pilot project in eight locations and greatly expanded in the 1980s. In this program the SBA arranges directly with public and private universities for the establishment of business counseling and training centers where the resources of the universities, the federal government, and the private sector can be brought to bear to teach sales promotion techniques, market research, financial analysis, and accounting to people who operate small businesses. The explicit purpose of the SBDC program is to help develop the economic area served by the university by enhancing small business opportunities and capabilities (U.S. SBA, 1979a, pp. 1-1, 1-5). By the end of the 1984 fiscal year the program had grown from the original 8 centers to 35. Although the Reagan administration eventually sought to phase out the program, funding had steadily increased through the early 1980s and stood at $22 million by 1984 (U.S. SBA, 1984a, pp. 30, 51–52).

The second SBA device with a specific place orientation is the 503 Certified Development Company program enacted in 1980.[2] This permits the organization of nonprofit development companies to provide long-term financing to small business concerns for land or capital acquisition or improvement. These companies must operate within a defined geographical territory, ranging from an entire state to purely local areas. Certified Development companies raise lending capital by selling SBA-guaranteed debentures to the Federal Financing Bank. By 1984 there were nearly 500 such entities, all but a few of which were organized on a community or county basis (CBO, 1984, p. 22). In the 1985 budget

---

2. The 503 CDC program resembles two earlier programs, both still in existence but both receding in importance in deference to 503. One is the 501 State Development Company Program, which creates for-profit corporations eligible for loans from the SBA to foster small business growth within a particular state. The other is the 502 Local Development Company, which operates on a substate basis. It too may receive direct loans from the SBA. Companies under the 501 program have received no loans in recent years; only 92 LDC loans were made in fiscal year 1983, amounting to $26.2 million (U.S. SBA, 1984a, p. 47).

503 funding grew more than that of any other program in the Small Business Administration.

More than any other SBA program, the 503 CDC provides a setting for close involvement between the SBA and state and local authorities. Indeed, the program in practice resembles in some measure conventional intergovernmental arrangements in which federal resources are administered by subnational public officials for uses that are worked out through the local political process. By law a CDC board of directors must include representatives not only from the business and lending communities and community organizations but also from the appropriate levels of government. Although there are no studies of the decision-making process on these boards, the Congressional Budget Office reports that "in general, the state or local government representatives on CDCs are heavily involved with the administration and allocation of funds" (ibid., p. 25).

A third program involves performing coordinating and consulting functions for selected public-private partnership arrangements through the SBA's Office of Private Sector Initiatives. Established only in 1983, OPSI has worked with several existing state and local economic development programs to identify public- or corporate-funding sources, to establish demonstration programs, and to provide technical assistance. For example, this SBA office has worked with the state of Ohio to create a new equity-capital pool for small businesses; it has sought to broker corporate resources for Pennsylvania's Ben Franklin Partnership, which sponsors joint public-private research and product development in advanced technological industries; and it has worked with county supervisors in California to establish a series of small business incubators where SBA, state, and corporate resources can be used to nurture small business growth (U.S. SBA, 1984a, pp. 61–62).

Each of these place-oriented programs is extremely modest by comparison with the major lending programs of the Small Business Administration, and by virtue of their geographical focus none is perfectly typical of the small-enterprise emphasis of the agency. These programs, however, serve as genuine resources for state and local development efforts, and two of the programs—the 503 Certified Development Company and the Office of Private Sector Initiatives—actually function in ways similar to traditional intergovernmental arrangements.

The Small Business Administration serves subnational economic development interests not only programmatically but as a clearinghouse for information and as a stimulus to action. Early in 1979 the Office of Advocacy in the SBA undertook a survey of state small business programs whose chief finding was that most states were interested in beginning or expanding such programs but had no information or models to guide their efforts (U.S. SBA, 1979b). This "startling absence of communication" among the states prompted the SBA to organize a national conference on state small business programs. It was held in Denver in September 1979, and more than 200 state officials and owners of small businesses came. The conference has now become an annual affair, and it has acquired the cosponsorship of the National Conference of State Legislatures, the U.S. Conference of Mayors, and the National Council for Urban Economic Development.

If the object of these conferences has been, in the language of the Office of Advocacy, "to sensitize state and local officials to small business needs, problems, and priorities" (U.S. SBA, 1984a, p. 25), then by all indications they have been successful. For example, the National Governors' Association, at its first opportunity after the initial national small business conference, adopted a resolution declaring the importance of small business to state and local economic development prospects and pledging state government support for such enterprises (Padda, 1981, p. 93). And an early SBA *Directory of State Small Business Programs* reported that one year after the first national small business conference the number of state offices, advisory boards, and ombudsmen concerned with small business had more than doubled (U.S. SBA, 1980a). By 1983 more than 30 states had held their own small business conferences and several others were planning such meetings (CBO, 1984, pp. 16–17). Between 1979 and 1985 the number of state legislative committees dealing with small business issues rose from only 4 to 27 (telephone interview, National Council of State Legislatures, Dec. 16, 1985; and Margolis, 1985, p. 93). Finally, there has been a surge in the number and variety of new programs aimed at small business support and creation.

The Economic Development Administration

The first sustained set of federal programs that sought explicitly to promote economic development in distressed areas of the country was established by the Public Works and Economic Development Act of 1965.[3] By providing federal resources for public works construction,

3. The Public Works and Economic Development Act succeeded a similar, though smaller and less elaborate, program established in 1961 by the Area Redevelopment Act. Appropriations under this program of loans and public works grants amounted to about half of what Congress appropriated for the PWEDA, and most of this in fact was never

economic development planning at the local level, and capital subsidies for industry, Congress hoped to encourage job-producing private investment in areas with lagging growth rates and high levels of structural unemployment. The object was to address poverty and joblessness in particular communities through economic rather than welfare means (Cameron, 1970, p. 59). Unlike urban renewal, which focused on the physical revitalization of cities, and the early programs of the Small Business Administration, which addressed the needs of small firms, the programs of the PWEDA were designed principally to support the capacity of local governments to deal with unemployment by attracting industry.

To administer the new programs contained in the PWEDA, Congress created a new agency, the Economic Development Administration. Its initial orientation was on structural unemployment in rural communities. As the first annual report of the agency noted:

There are coal miners in eastern Kentucky who have not had a steady job or regular paycheck in years. Many men in northern Minnesota are unemployed because the rich iron ore deposits have been depleted. President Johnson had these people in mind when he requested Congress to approve the Public Works and Economic Development Act of 1965. (U.S. EDA, 1966, p. 3)

Congressional debate prior to passage of the PWEDA also assumed a rural focus (Wildavsky and Pressman, 1973, p. 10). When, indeed, the specific areas eligible to apply for EDA assistance were first announced, only eight large cities were included along with more than 1300 largely rural counties and labor market areas. Several urban members of Congress, as well as the head of EDA, however, believed that structural unemployment was at least as much a city problem as a rural one (ibid.). In response to these views Congress amended the PWEDA in 1967 and 1969 to permit the broadening of eligibility criteria to make it possible for cities to compete. After the mid-1970s the business assistance and public works programs of the EDA were as often directed to urban areas as to rural ones. Statutory and administrative changes in the definition of "economic distress" also occurred in the 1970s, so that by the middle of the decade distress in an area could be measured by a large number of different standards, including substantial or persistent unemployment, low family income, sudden rises in unemployment due to natural disaster or plant shutdown, major structural changes in the local economy, job

---

spent. The ARA covered about a quarter of the population that the later EDA programs did (see Levitan, 1964, pp. 48–50, 66).

Table 5-1.   Economic Development Administration Assistance: The
Cumulative Distribution of Spending, by Program, 1966–84

	Number of Projects	Dollar Amount (in thousands)
Public works loans and grants (Title I)	6,517	3,472,074
Business loans and loan guarantees (Title II and Trade Act of 1974)[a]	1,308	1,682,089[b]
Technical assistance and planning grants (Title III)	11,101	601,198
Economic adjustment (Title IX)[c]	730	604,303

Source: U.S. EDA, 1984, p. 13.
[a]Between 1975 and 1981 businesses adversely affected by foreign imports could apply under the Trade Act of 1974 for EDA loans and loan guarantees.
[b]Loan guarantees account for 53 percent of this total.
[c]Title IX was passed in 1974; the figures are for 1975–84.

loss due to foreign competition, or simply status as an Indian reservation. By the peak years of the program during the Carter administration 84.5 percent of the nation's population lived in cities, labor market areas, or counties eligible to apply for EDA assistance (Stanfield, 1979, p. 1034). Although the most distressed of the qualified areas tended to receive a disproportionate share of the grants, EDA programs covered an extremely broad segment of the nation.

The EDA administers four main programs that bear on state and local economic development. The most important in dollar terms has been the public works program (Title I), which provides matching grants and long-term loans to communities and counties for a variety of fixed-capital projects. Title I accounted for 54.5 percent of all EDA funding through 1984 (see Table 5-1). The central object of this program has been to create jobs by supporting local efforts to develop public works infrastructure or other facilities that would attract industry or allow it to expand. Specific projects include water and sewer systems, access roads to industrial sites, industrial park development, and warehouses. More than 70 small communities have constructed airports with EDA grants. Port and harbor improvements, health care facilities, exposition centers, and public recreation developments are among other Title I uses.

An early evaluation by the EDA of the impact of public works projects, based on a survey of 125 of the then 326 projects in existence, found mixed results. Nearly 10,000 jobs in the private sector had been generated or saved, according to the study, an average of about 80 per project (U.S. EDA, 1970). An additional 3700 jobs had been created indirectly as a result of the infusion of new payroll money into local economies. These direct and indirect job effects were produced by only 61 percent of the funded projects, however. Thirty-nine percent of the projects studied produced no jobs at all. Of the 10,000 jobs created or saved, the EDA judged 58 percent to be stable rather than seasonal positions that contributed to local economic diversification. The Reagan administration considered the entire EDA record of job production an unimpressive one and sought largely on this basis to terminate the entire agency (Ellwood, 1982, pp. 180–82; *New York Times,* Feb. 6, 1986).

Later evaluations by independent consulting firms focused on the "leveraging" ability of EDA grants, that is, the degree to which the expenditure of public funds elicits private investments. A review of these studies found that leveraging ratios for all projects ranged from $2.41 to $2.94 of private money for every federal EDA dollar (Bingham and Blair, 1983). The studies found higher ratios, however, specifically for road projects ($5.18) and water ($4.62) and sewer ($4.53) undertakings. Such ratios tend to be lower than in other federal economic development programs.

The second largest EDA program in aggregate terms has been the business loan and loan guarantee program, though after the Carter years it dwindled to the merest symbolic presence. From 1966 to 1984 business assistance accounted for 26 percent of all EDA expenditures, but year-to-year spending in this program has exhibited wide swings. Business loans and guarantees were designed to allow the EDA to help firms whose establishment in or relocation to severely depressed areas would be judged such a liability by the private lending industry that they could not get conventional financing. Title II permitted long-term loans for up to 65 percent of fixed-asset costs of a newly located or expanding business with an interest rate based on the government's borrowing costs, a figure that falls beneath the rate attached to private securities. In the first 10 months of the program the EDA made over $43 million worth of loans to 62 firms.

This activity declined sharply during the Nixon and Ford administrations. By 1974 only 10 loans were made for about $9.7 million. In the Carter years, however, the notion that business could be induced through various incentives to stay or relocate in distressed central cities became a crucial part of the president's urban policy. Initially, the administration pushed for the establishment of a National Development Bank to make loans and grants to private firms (Stanfield, 1978). When this proposal met with skepticism in Congress, the business loan program of the EDA, already in place, was revived with a vengeance. It appeared to be the perfect vehicle for implementing the "new partnership" between government and business proclaimed by the president.

In 1977 the business loan and loan guarantee program represented only 18.9 percent of the EDA budget. In 1978, the year in which the "new partnership" was announced, Title II rose to 37.9 percent of EDA's spending, and in 1979 it rose further to 59.6 percent. In that year the EDA committed over $600 million to this program, not including an additional one-time loan guarantee to the steel industry of half a billion dollars funneled through Title II.

Reagan's election in 1980, however, resulted in massive reductions in the business loan program. Arguing that general economic recovery was a more effective way to create jobs than business subsidies, the new administration reduced Title II to 11.3 percent of the EDA budget in 1982 (down from 30.8 percent in 1981) and then to only 4.2 percent in 1984. In the latter year the only activity under Title II was one loan guarantee for $11 million.

Besides administering the vastly expanded business loan program in service to the new partnership, the EDA was given other urban-oriented responsibilities in the Carter years. The agency served as the overseer of two short-lived demonstration projects designed to show how a concentration of resources could spur business growth in decaying cities. The Comprehensive Economic Development Strategy of 1978 was launched in 37 cities to help those places design strategic economic development plans. The cities involved were helped, according to the EDA, to identify needs, establish priorities, and work out the means to achieve them. The EDA described this two-year experimental program as an attempt to link planning with the effort to leverage private investment (U.S. EDA, 1979, p. 16). Another program, this one in 10 cities, provided Community Economic Development grants in a pilot attempt to demonstrate the stimulus effects of downtown physical revitalization. After the Carter years little was heard again of either of these programs.

The EDA took on a more intensive urban cast in the late 1970s in one other way. In the waning days of the Ford administration the agency had been given the responsibility for administering a countercyclical program called Local Public Works. Round I in 1974 called for an expenditure of $2 billion to stimulate employment in the construction industry, whereas Round II in 1977 amounted to $4 billion. Under Ford, 65 percent of the nation's largest cities received Local Public Works grants, but under Carter the percentage rose to 93 as the administration sought in a more concerted way to attack urban unemployment.

The third major program of the EDA is its technical and planning-assistance grants, mainly to smaller communities, as provided by Title III of the PWEDA. These grants cover up to 75 percent of a particular project, with the local government or planning entity supplying the other 25 percent. The grants tend to be small—around $55,000 on average. They are designed to permit the solution of narrowly focused problems or help a small community write an economic development plan. Grant awards tend to reflect prevailing local concerns of the moment: in 1983 about a third of the 92 technical grants went to support studies designed to develop local export capacities and to study technology transfer (U.S. EDA, 1983, p. 2). In earlier years technical grants went for industrial park feasibility studies and projects involving inner city and minority economic development (U.S. EDA, 1966, p. 20; and U.S. EDA, 1975, p. 9).

The fourth and most flexible of all EDA programs in statutory terms is Special Adjustment Assistance (Title IX), passed as part of the 1974 amendments to the PWEDA. Its purpose is to help communities develop and implement plans to deal with "sudden and severe economic dislocation." A wide range of economic catastrophes and changes are included under this rubric: natural disasters, the shutdown of a major private employer, the long-term deterioration of an industry in the face of foreign competition, the closing of a major military facility, and even the sudden changes in a local economy associated with "boomtown" development in response to the establishment of a new military or resource extraction installation.

In applying for Title IX assistance state and local officials have virtually unlimited discretion in proposing how to use their grants. Eligible activities include, but are not limited to, construction of public facilities, public services, business development, planning, the provision of unemployment compensation, rent supplements, mortgage payment assistance for workers about to lose their homes to foreclosure, job training, relocation of individuals and businesses, as well as any other assistance that furthers adjustment. Among the most innovative uses of Title IX funds are programs to capitalize revolving loan and venture capital funds to foster small business development, mainly in high-technology fields. Some of these programs include New York's Corporation for Innovation Development, the Massachusetts Technology Development Corporation, Oregon's Business Development Fund, and the California Innovation Development Program. Several of these are discussed in more detail in Chapter 10.

One of the largest early grants under Title IX, $8.2 million, went to the state of Rhode Island following the closing of the Newport Navy Yard to convert its facilities into a shipbuilding and repair center (U.S. EDA 1966, p. 10). Other grants have gone to cities and counties dependent on automobile manufacturing and suffering from import competition, to communities devastated by floods and earthquakes, and to towns faced with the closure of a major industrial employer.

The statutory promise of Title IX and the scope of the projects funded under that program are deceptive, however. Title IX has always been one of the smaller EDA programs, and during the Reagan presidency it withered to the level of the modest planning and technical grants. By 1984 it had fallen to $35.5 million for the fiscal year, down from its high point of $100 million in 1978. Even in that peak year, however, the allocation represented only 17.8 percent of the EDA budget, despite mounting public concern over plant closings and foreign import competition. Nevertheless, state and local officials never seriously agitated for an expansion of Title IX, nor did Congress ever view it as a major vehicle for a federal response to the unemployment and community hardship induced by structural economic shifts and capital migration. The Sudden and Severe Dislocation Program thus remains a very modest program in the federal repertoire.

Community Development Block Grants

Community Development Block Grants were not initially designed to aid local economic development, but the discretionary nature of the program, combined with several facilitating statutory changes, has resulted in rapid growth in the proportion of these funds used for such purposes. CDBG, funded on average at about $3.5 billion per year, is a legacy of the Nixon administration's efforts to persuade Congress in the name of the "new federalism" to consolidate related categorical grants-in-aid into more flexible block grants. The idea behind the Nixon agenda was to reduce the influence of the federal government in domestic matters by devolving major responsibility to state and local officials for the establishment of program priorities and program design (Nathan et al., 1977).

The Housing and Community Development Act, actually signed into law by President Ford shortly after Nixon's resignation, consolidated seven categorical programs, the two most important of which were Urban Renewal and Model Cities. Funds were to be distributed as entitlements to cities over 50,000, to smaller cities that were the central cities of their metropolitan area, and to urban counties by means of a formula that targeted disproportionate shares to places with high poverty levels, large populations, and overcrowded housing. To rectify a bias in the original formula in favor of growing southern and western cities, a second formula was established in 1977 to include population-growth lag and age of housing stock along with poverty, a modification that greatly increased the entitlements of northeastern and midwestern cities. Recipients were permitted to choose the more advantageous of the two formulas. The formula system does serve the interest of the most needy cities: in 1984 the top 10 percent of the most distressed cities were projected to receive 3.7 times more per capita in CDBG funds than the 10 percent that were least distressed (U.S. Dept. of HUD, 1984a, p. 6). Although needy cities clearly receive more money under this program, the entitlement pool includes many communities, some of them affluent suburbs, with high average incomes and low tax rates, a feature of CDBG that diminishes its targeting effects.

Smaller cities not included as entitlement jurisdictions were originally permitted to compete for an earmarked pool of funds by submitting applications to the Department of Housing and Urban Development. Congress amended this program in the 1981 Omnibus Budget and Reconciliation Act to allow states instead of HUD to administer the Small Cities program, and by 1985 all but three states were deciding how to allocate small city CDBG funds among competing communities within their respective borders.

In establishing the new block grant Congress invoked as its primary goal the same national objective that prefaced the 1949 Housing Act, namely a commitment to "a decent home and a suitable living environment." In place of the phrase "for every American family," however, Congress substituted the words "principally for persons of low and moderate income," thereby evincing a strong concern for social targeting. In addition Congress listed a number of specific objectives to be achieved by the program. Most of these are based on the purposes served by the categorical programs consolidated into the block grant. They include the elimination of slums and blight, code enforcement, the conservation and expansion of the nation's housing stock, historic preservation, improvement of community services, and the spatial deconcentration of housing opportunities for low-income people. As if the list of objectives were not enough, Congress also provided a long and often redundant list of eligible activities on which grant recipients could, at their discretion, spend their money. Section 105 of the act enumerates 13 different eligible uses of these federal grants, including land acquisition, demolition and site preparation, the construction of public works, the removal of architectural barriers to the handicapped, and relocation payments to people and businesses displaced by redevelopment. In addition a variety of administrative regulations sought, among other things, to ensure that communities planned in advance how to spend their allotment, that projects were neighborhood-oriented rather than citywide facilities, and that "maximum feasible priority" be given to projects that benefited low- and moderate-income people. Federal oversight of the program reached its zenith during the Carter administration, partly in response to findings by early studies of the program that the proportion of benefits to low- and moderate-income persons had declined steadily in the first three years (U.S. Dept. of HUD, 1979a, p. VI-1). A series of new program regulations issued by HUD in 1978 sought to ensure greater attention to the social-targeting goal and greater citizen participation in planning the use of CDBG funds.

Despite the various congressional strictures on how the block grants might be spent and the managerial impulses of the Carter administration, CDBG has not been part of any coherent national development plan. For one thing the geographical reach of the program is so broad that no region significantly benefits in relation to any other. Just under 600 local jurisdictions were initially included as entitlement recipients (the figure rose to 814 by 1985), nearly a third of which had never competed previously for any federal funds under the old categorical programs. Most of this latter group of communities were in fact suburban towns (Dommel and Associates, 1982, pp. 36–37). In addition, the lists of objectives and specific activities are extremely broad. Nor did Congress establish any priorities among the items on the lists. Thus, the specific uses to which funds are put have been determined by local officials and citizens groups. HUD reviews of local planned-use documents and performance reports have tended to be limited and uncritical. Therefore, the essential nature of the program, even as federal involvement peaked in the late 1970s, has been to assist communities financially in the pursuit of local development projects worked out entirely through the local political process.

During the early years of the Reagan presidency federal oversight was greatly reduced. Detailed local applications, heretofore necessary to gain release of the entitlement, were eliminated, and most citizen participation requirements were ended. HUD also ceased to monitor the degree to which projects benefited low- and moderate-income groups (Dommel et al., 1983, pp. 17–20).

Given the high degree of local discretion throughout the life of the program, it is not surprising to find that the uses to which communities have put their CDBG allotments have reflected shifting local concerns. One of the most rapidly growing of these has been economic development, and indeed the proportion of CDBG funds devoted to this purpose, though small in absolute terms, rose more swiftly than for any other purpose in the early 1980s (U.S. Dept. of HUD, 1984a, pp. 18, 41; and Dommel, 1984, p. 105).

Economic development was not one of the original specific objectives or eligible uses of the block grant. Communities had used CDBG funds from the beginning to support projects that may have helped to facilitate industrial or commercial development or to create jobs, but the explicit application of these grants to economic development purposes or their inclusion in a local economic development strategy was not common. Early allocations to economic development are difficult to track, in part because it is hard to distinguish specific development activities from others, such as construction of public infrastructure, which may in itself stimulate, support, or attract private investment. Furthermore, there was no separate budget line for economic development expenditures in the CDBG application form until 1979. Nevertheless, HUD analysts estimate that at least half of all grant recipients spent some of their allocation in these early years for projects that directly supported a specific, private, commercial or industrial undertaking (U.S. Dept. of HUD, 1979a, p. VIII-1). Activities of this sort accounted for approximately 5 percent of all CDBG expenditures from 1975 to 1978 (U.S. Dept. of HUD, 1981, p. 68). Dommel's detailed case studies of spending patterns in 10 cities found that even relatively distressed cities, such as Cleveland and St. Louis, were spending only 2 or 3 percent of their annual entitlement on this sort of economic development prior to 1978 (Dommel et al., 1983, p. 88).

Then in the 1977 amendments to the Housing and Community Development Act, Congress added economic development to the list of specific objectives. Since then, communities have been explicitly permitted to use CDBG funds for "the alleviation of physical and economic distress through the stimulation of private investment and community revitalization in areas with population out-migration or a stagnating or declining tax base" (P.L. 95–128 [1977] Sec. 101[c]8). Specifically, it became possible for local governments to make grants out of their CDBG allocation to neighborhood-based nonprofit corporations, local development corporations, or small business investment corporations, which in turn can use the money to make loans, acquire real property, construct public facilities or industrial buildings, and make site improvements, among other uses, when these promise to attract private capital or create jobs.

In further amendments to the law in 1981, Congress broadened the range of eligible recipients of CDBG economic development funding by allowing communities to "provide assistance to private, for-profit entities, when the assistance is necessary or appropriate to carry out an economic development project" (Sec. 303[a]; Sec. 105[a][17] as amended 1981). This addition to the law has made it possible for local governments to use these general monies to make direct loans to businesses and to write down the cost of land for private firms. Of the $306 million devoted by entitlement jurisdictions to economic development in 1985, 50 percent went for loans to businesses (U.S. Dept. of HUD, 1986, p. 13).

Two other amendments to the Housing and Community Development Act in 1977 created two devices by which grants can be used to leverage private investment for economic development purposes. Since 1977 cities have been able to "draw down" or receive their entire annual allotment in a single lump sum with which they can then establish a revolving loan fund in a private financial institution (Sec. 104[i]1). These funds may be loaned over the short-term to private firms at below-market interest rates as a way of providing cheap start-up financing. As the loans are paid back, the principal and interest are used to finance the community development projects for which the funds were originally allocated. Dommel and his associates cite several examples of such "float" financing, including a case in which the city of Seattle loaned its entire $12.5 million allotment in one year to a private developer at a below-market rate and gained nearly $1 million in interest to add to its community development budget (Dommel et al., 1983, p. 91).

A second leveraging device is a provision that allows HUD to guarantee notes or other obligations issued by a local government that may amount to as much as three times the sum of the recipient's CDBG allotment. The revenues from these notes may be used mainly to finance property acquisition and improvement for redevelopment purposes (Sec. 108[a] and [b]). Almost 250 cities had borrowed money through this arrangement through 1985, their numbers increasing virtually every year (U.S. Dept. of HUD, 1986, p. 27).

The combination of these various facilitating statutory changes and growing local interest in economic development has led to an increase in spending for such purposes. Data compiled by HUD show that the proportion of CDBG funds devoted to economic development in 1985 by entitlement jurisdictions had risen to 11.1 percent (ibid., pp. 35–36). Among the cities in this group, spending on economic development rose from 3.6 percent of total CDBG expenditures in 1979 to 11.5 percent in 1985, a 195 percent increase in dollar terms. This compares with a dollar increase of only 24 percent for housing-related activities, the dominant purpose for which CDBG funds are used. Only one other program category showed a dollar increase in this period: funding for public services rose 26 percent. At the same time allocations for public works, land acquisition and clearance, and various miscellaneous purposes all declined. What is particularly striking about the large percentage increase in economic development spending is that, during much of the period in which a greater and greater proportion of funds was being used for this purpose (1979–83), overall CDBG funding for entitlement cities was decreasing from $2.47 billion to $2.15 billion.

Spending on economic development in entitlement counties increased at an even faster rate than among cities, going from $8.2 million in 1979 (2 percent of CDBG allocations) to $62.2 million in 1984 (13.1 percent), a change of 675 percent, before dropping to $42.2 million in 1985.

The most dramatic upward movement in economic development spending by entitlement jurisdictions occurred after 1981. This suggests that such spending patterns were not stimulated so much by the statutory changes of 1977 as by the deregulation of the CDBG process by the Reagan administration. This assumption is supported by the shift in priorities in the Small Cities CDBG program from the period in which it was entirely administered by HUD (through 1981) to that in which it was largely taken over by the states as part of the devolution of federal power orchestrated by the White House. In 1981, the last year of HUD administration of this competition among smaller cities, only 4 percent of the funds was devoted to economic development. In the first year of state administration (34 states elected in 1982 to take over the program) the proportion of dollars committed to economic development rose to 22 percent. By 1985, when 47 states were participating, the proportion declined slightly to 21 percent (ibid., p. 49), but the point is that spending on economic development was substantially higher when states rather than HUD could choose which projects to fund.

Compared with some of the other functions on which CDBG funds

Table 5-2.   The Functional Allocation of CDBG Funds (in millions of dollars) and Their Percentage Distribution among Entitlement Cities and Urban Counties, 1979–85

	1979	1980	1981	1982	1983	1984	1985[a]
				Cities			
Economic development	89.2 (3.6%)	119.4 (5.1%)	121.5 (5.1%)	174.1 (8.2%)	204.7 (9.5%)	293.1 (13.3%)	263.3 (11.5%)
Public facilities[b]	712.4 (28.8%)	632.6 (26.9%)	569.4 (24.0%)	423.0 (20.0%)	431.0 (19.2%)	421.8 (19.1%)	433 (19.0%)
Housing[c]	702.6 (28.4%)	752.8 (32.0%)	816.0 (34.4%)	768.1 (36.3%)	802.5 (37.3%)	837.8 (37.9%)	871.2 (38.2%)
Land acquisition and clearance	324.7 (13.1%)	278.7 (11.9%)	260.4 (11.0%)	176.0 (8.3%)	99.9 (4.6%)	85.3 (3.9%)	96.2 (4.2%)
Public services[d]	191.2 (7.7%)	180.1 (7.7%)	180.3 (7.6%)	195.1 (9.2%)	254.1 (11.8%)	217.9 (9.9%)	241.2 (10.6%)
Miscellaneous[e]	449.7 (18.1%)	387.1 (16.5%)	426.8 (18.0%)	382.3 (18.0%)	377.8 (17.5%)	351.8 (15.9%)	377.3 (16.4%)
				Urban Counties			
Economic development	8.2 (2.0%)	10.3 (2.4%)	11.5 (2.6%)	31.2 (7.6%)	58.1 (12.3%)	62.2 (13.1%)	42.2 (9.0%)
Public facilities	185.6 (45.7%)	178.5 (42.3%)	171.1 (39.3%)	155.6 (37.7%)	161.2 (34.1%)	164.7 (34.7%)	165.6 (35.6%)
Housing	94.4 (23.2%)	109.6 (26.0%)	135.7 (31.2%)	117.4 (28.5)%	119.1 (25.2%)	132.5 (27.9%)	125.5 (26.8%)
Land acquisition and clearance	37.0 (9.1%)	37.2 (8.8%)	32.9 (7.6%)	18.9 (4.6%)	7.1 (1.5%)	5.5 (1.2%)	15.9 (3.4%)
Public services	8.0 (2.0%)	7.3 (1.7%)	7.6 (1.7%)	18.4 (4.5%)	22.0 (4.7%)	22.3 (4.7%)	23.4 (5.0%)
Miscellaneous	75.2 (18.5%)	78.8 (18.9%)	76.9 (17.7%)	71.8 (17.5%)	104.9 (22.2%)	85.2 (17.9%)	94.5 (20.2%)

Source: U.S. Dept. of HUD, 1984a, pp. 41, 43; and U.S. Dept. of HUD, 1986, pp. 35–38.

Note: Column percentages do not always total 100 because of rounding.

[a]Figures for 1985 are estimates.

[b]For example, streets, water and sewer works, parks, flood control.

[c]For example, rehabilitation of private and public housing, code enforcement, historic preservation.

[d]For example, day-care, shelter for women, assistance for the elderly, drug counseling.

[e]For example, administration, closeout of categorical programs.

are spent, economic development is certainly not a central focus of the program, at least measured in terms of national spending aggregates. But a number of cities and states exploit CDBG more heavily for economic development purposes than is the national norm. Dommel's study of this block grant in 10 cities shows, for example, that Rochester, Chicago, and Atlanta spent, respectively, 27, 26, and 22 percent of their CDBG allocations on economic development in 1982 (Dommel et al., 1983, p. 88). Some cities have spent even higher proportions. An early HUD evaluation found that Gary, Indiana, and Racine, Wisconsin, spent 44 and 42 percent, respectively, of their grants on economic development in 1979 (U.S. Dept. of HUD, 1980b, p. X-9). Some cities deliberately target a high proportion to such projects: Madison, Wisconsin, for example, seeks as a matter of policy to allocate 30 percent of its entitlement to economic development (City of Madison, 1985). Four states allocated 40 percent or more of their Small Cities grants to economic development in 1985, including Michigan (47 percent) and Wyoming (50 percent) (U.S. Dept. of HUD, 1986, p. 49).

The impact of CDBG spending on private investment patterns and job generation has been difficult to determine. CDBG funds are often used in economic development projects in conjunction with other federal monies, serving as either a catalyst or "filler" in undertakings funded primarily from other public sources (U.S. Dept. of HUD, 1980b, p. X-10). Thus, the fiscal contribution of CDBG to many individual projects may in proportional terms be relatively minor. The real leveraging impact vis-à-vis the private investors in such cases is more a product of the other, more substantial, government expenditures. The Department of Housing and Urban Development attempted in 1979 to measure the ability of CDBG funds to elicit private investment by surveying a sample of 25 cities. Analysts found only 12 cities willing or able to provide data on the subject. Among these cities the range of leveraging ratios was so great—the CDBG contribution ranged from 2 to 73 percent of the total project costs—that the summary measures for so few cities were not very meaningful (ibid.). Only 5 of the 25 cities in this HUD study were willing to estimate job-generation effects of CDBG expenditures (p. X-8).

The Urban Development Action Grant Program

Shortly after his inauguration in 1977 President Carter sent his chief domestic policy advisor to a meeting of the U.S. Conference of Mayors to promise that his administration would make a major commitment to America's cities (Goldsmith and Derian, 1979). The legislative centerpiece of this commitment, which eventually blossomed into an elaborate enunciation of a "national urban policy" (Eisinger, 1985), was the Urban Development Action Grant program of 1977. Passed into law that October as part of the act renewing the CDBG program, UDAG was designed to permit a wide range of public investments in major development projects in a way that the comparatively modest CDBG entitlements could not manage (U.S. Dept. of HUD, 1979b, p. 72). The funding of this versatile program, the explicitness of its mission, and the expectations that have surrounded it have made UDAG the single most important federal contribution to subnational economic development policy in the modern period.

The Urban Development Action Grant section of the 1977 Housing and Community Development Act authorized the secretary of HUD to make grants "to severely distressed cities and urban countries to help alleviate physical and economic deterioration" (P.L. 95–128, Sec. 119 [a] [1977]). Although the act mentions neighborhood reclamation and community revitalization and development, the words "economic development" do not appear in the law at this time, except in passing reference to a planning requirement contained in the 1965 Public Works and Economic Development Act. Yet it is evident that economic development, understood as the stimulation of private investment, was one of the more clearly defined strategies Congress had in mind to address severe urban distress: communities were required to develop proposals to use the action grants "to take advantage of unique opportunities to attract private investment, stimulate investment in restoration of deteriorated or abandoned housing stock, or solve critical problems resulting from population out-migration or a stagnating or declining tax base."

The importance of private investment is indicated by another provision of the act and by the administrative regulations promulgated to implement it. Grant applicants must "indicate public and private resources which are expected to be made available toward achieving the action plan." This provision quickly came to be regarded by HUD officials as a critical feature of the UDAG program (U.S. Dept. of HUD, 1979b, p. 4). HUD did not interpret the passage as an injunction merely to indicate the degree of *probable* ("expected") private participation. Instead, the department established regulations pursuant to this section that require local officials to elicit a firm, legally binding, private-sector financial commitment to a project before any UDAG funds may be released. The insistence on a prior guarantee of private-sector investment distinguishes UDAG from all previous federal economic development programs.

The economic development focus of the program was clarified and elaborated in the Housing and Community Development Amendments of 1981 (P.L. 97-35 [1981]). References to neighborhood reclamation and revitalization and community development were dropped. The secretary of HUD was now authorized simply to make grants to distressed places "to help stimulate economic development activity needed to aid in economic recovery." Grant proposals must now focus exclusively on taking "advantage of unique opportunities to attract private investment." The option to offer solutions to distress based on investment in housing rehabilitation, though not prohibited, is no longer explicitly suggested. Furthermore, the 1981 amendments establish a set of expected economic development impacts as criteria to be considered by HUD in awarding grants. These include the degree to which private investment is leveraged, the number of permanent jobs created, and the impact of the project on the local tax base. None of these appears in the 1977 law.

As one student of the UDAG program has observed, Congress provided quite specific instructions in the law about how action grants were to be allocated, but it said almost nothing specific about how they might be spent (Webman, 1980, p. 87). Distribution is left to the central authority, but implementation is the responsibility of the subnational units in this intergovernmental program. Only cities and urban counties that meet minimum levels of economic distress are eligible to apply for these competitive grants. The secretary of HUD is responsible for establishing particular criteria but is instructed to take into account such factors as age of housing, extent of poverty, unemployment, population and employment lag (indicated by a rate of change below the national mean), and per capita income. At the beginning of the program only about half of the 605 cities with more than 50,000 people were eligible to apply, according to the set of standards established by HUD (Nathan and Webman, 1980, p. 42). Since a number of growing Sun Belt cities did not qualify, despite the presence in their midst of severely depressed neighborhoods, Congress added the so-called pockets-of-poverty provision in 1979: communities that otherwise were not eligible for UDAGs nevertheless could apply if they contained one or more contiguous census tracts with specified high levels of poverty and whose residents represented a certain proportion of the community's total population.

In addition to establishing eligibility criteria, Congress also provided guidelines for allocating grants among eligible jurisdictions. The primary criterion is the relative degree of economic distress, measured in terms of poverty and so on, but other factors are also mentioned, such as the jurisdiction's demonstrated performance in housing or community development programs, the extent to which state and local funds have been committed to the planned project, the feasibility of the project, minority and low-income job effects, and the economic development impacts already discussed. Congress also forbids the award of a grant unless there is a determination that the project could not go forward but for the federal money. This is known in economic development parlance as the "but-for" provision.

The original act in 1977 had required the secretary of HUD to achieve a "reasonable balance" in the distribution of grants among projects devoted to industrial, commercial, and neighborhood (or housing) projects. As part of an effort to shift the focus of the program more toward industrial and commercial projects (on the grounds that housing development is a poor way to generate jobs), the balance provision was dropped in 1981.[4]

In the first eight years of the program (1978–85) appropriations amounted to nearly $3.9 billion, a sum which has funded 2550 separate projects. Funding reached a peak in the 1980 and 1981 fiscal years and declined thereafter. Congress authorized $440 million for the program in 1985. About half of all applications are rejected out of hand for failure to demonstrate a firm private-sector financial commitment, failure to show that the project would not go forward without UDAG funds, or incomplete applications (U.S. Dept. of HUD, 1984a, p. 82). Among the remaining eligible applicants, nearly all of which were awarded grants until demand outstripped resources in 1983, the dollar distribution was reasonably faithful to the targeting principle enunciated in the law. HUD data indicate that the top third of the most distressed, eligible large cities received 62 percent of the dollars awarded between 1978 and 1983, whereas the third that were least distressed received only 13 percent of the funds (ibid., p. 106). By 1985, 89 percent of UDAG dollars were going to the top third of the most distressed cities. Among cities under 50,000, which compete in a separate competition for an earmarked 25 percent of the annual UDAG appropriation, targeting has been less evident. Fifty-six percent of the funds went to the top third of the most distressed small cities, whereas 13 percent went to the third that were least distressed in 1985 (U.S. Dept. of HUD, 1986, pp. 70–71).

In contrast to its interest in the distributional principles of the UDAG

---

4. A good summary of the mechanics of UDAG administration is to be found in Gatons and Brintnall, 1984.

program, Congress offered little guidance as to how the funds might actually be spent. In the section of the law that deals with uses of the money, Congress simply refers recipients back to the passage in the Housing and Community Development Act of 1974 that makes a long list of activities eligible for Community Development Block Grant funding. The UDAG law then adds that eligibility also extends to "such activities . . . as the Secretary determines to be consistent with the purposes" of the program.

Projects are planned at the local level, most often by city development departments, special task forces, or economic development commissions. Private developers, according to an early study of project origination by HUD, initiated undertakings in just 18.4 percent of all cases (U.S. Dept. of HUD, 1979b, p. 31).

The only significant indication of congressional concern over the specific uses of UDAG funds is contained in the "reasonable balance" directive to the secretary of HUD. During the years when this provision was in effect, however, 60 percent of the funds awarded went to commercial projects, creating a marked imbalance. Larger cities in particular used UDAG money in the early funding rounds to launch downtown projects involving hotels, convention centers, and office towers, often constructed on land that had been acquired and cleared years before in the urban renewal program. Only 25 percent of UDAG funds in that period went to industrial projects; the remaining 15 percent was devoted to neighborhood revitalization, primarily housing and local commercial strips (U.S. Dept. of HUD, 1984a, p. 85). Curiously, after the elimination of the balance requirement in 1981, a more even distribution between industrial and commercial projects emerged, though the housing share declined. Forty percent of the combined 1982 and 1983 funding went to industrial projects, 48 percent to commercial ones, and only 12 percent to housing. One reason for this more recent pattern is that HUD issued regulations in 1982 designed to favor funding projects that promised substantial job creation and tax impacts (U.S. Dept. of HUD, 1983, p. 79). Although housing projects generate temporary construction jobs, the permanent employment impact is negligible.

The specific uses to which UDAG funds are put seem limited primarily by the imagination of local recipients. HUD has classified these uses into two major general categories: direct incentives to private firms and infrastructure development. Direct incentives lower the costs that a private firm or investor must bear in undertaking any business development project. These incentives include below-market-rate loans, loan guarantees, interest-rate subsidies, and land write-downs. Some direct incentives involve the assumption by the public sector of the private sector's share of the costs of new infrastructure to serve a new development, such as sidewalks, street lighting, mass transit stops or stations, access roads, and so on. The proportion of funds devoted to direct incentives rose rapidly from the early years of the program. Slightly over half (53 percent) of UDAG funds were devoted to loans and other direct incentives in 1978–79, but by 1985 the proportion had risen to 87 percent (U.S. Dept. of HUD, 1984a, p. 103; and U.S. Dept. of HUD, 1986, p. 81).

These latter subsidies can be distinguished from the second major category of UDAG uses, in which the public sector spends its grant for infrastructure development for which the private sector has no legal obligation to share the cost. Thus, a UDAG grant can be used to construct a highway interchange to provide access from an industrial site to an interstate road; or it can finance downtown parking facilities to accommodate a new office tower. The proportion of grants devoted to infrastructure costs declined from 43 percent to 12 percent between 1978 and 1985.

Both forms of assistance—direct aid and infrastructure development—are classic supply-side incentives. That is, they represent, by and large, subsidies designed to influence the location decisions of potentially mobile capital by reducing land, borrowing, and transportation costs rather than attempts to stimulate growth by encouraging capital formation and expansion to respond to market demands for particular goods and services. But UDAG is a program versatile enough to have been shaped in its implementation by the emerging entrepreneurial impulses among subnational governments. The two most striking manifestations of these more aggressive modes of economic intervention are the growth of revolving-loan-fund mechanisms, which may significantly expand local governments' commercial and industrial banking capabilities, and the establishment of public-sector equity positions in UDAG-funded projects. Both of these program variants permit entrepreneurial local governments to share the risk burden with private actors, thus creating greater leverage in steering private investment decisions toward undertakings that promise high public benefits in terms of jobs and tax revenues.

Once a city receives an action grant, there is no federal requirement to return any recoverable portion of that grant to HUD, nor is there any provision in the law that prevents a city from retaining any earnings that may accrue from the investment of UDAG monies. City officials realized quickly that they could both provide attractive incentives to private developers by offering below-market-rate loans and at the same time recycle the loan when the principal is paid back along with modest interest payments. In the early years of the program the use of UDAG funds for repayable incentives accounted for less than a quarter of all funds allocated. In 1978 cities devoted 20.5 percent of their UDAG monies to repayable loans, which represented less than half of the funds devoted to direct incentives. By 1985 all but a negligible proportion of the 87 percent devoted to direct incentives was paid back to cities. Over the first eight years of the program approximately $128 million was paid back to cities by private borrowers.

There are two virtues of payback arrangements from the cities' point of view. First of all, they may recycle the sums granted by the federal government and even augment them by lending the money for a price. Second, the projects funded by the repaid loans need not be approved by HUD or any other agency of the federal government. Once the original UDAG has been spent for the purpose for which it was granted, cities are free to recycle the grant for development undertakings of their own choosing.

Cities also pursue an entrepreneurial course when they take an equity position in a private-sector project in return for UDAG assistance. Approximately 33 percent of all grants in 1985 involved some provision permitting cities to share in the profits of a project. Federal law does not explicitly authorize such arrangements, but it does not prohibit them either. A case study of UDAG implementation in Newark during the early years offers an illustration of how an equity arrangement works. The city used a $10 million action grant to help finance a $35 million office building on the edge of the central business district. The loan, in the form of a second mortgage supplied by the Newark Economic Development Corporation, was to be paid off over 30 years at 4 percent interest per year. As a condition of this heavily subsidized loan, the city demanded and received a right to 50 percent of any profits shown by the project (Nathan and Webman, 1980, pp. 27–28).

In the administration's annual search during the Reagan years for programs to eliminate in order to reduce the federal deficit, UDAG was a perennial candidate. That it has managed to survive concerted termination efforts by the Office of Management and Budget is testimony not only to its popularity among local officials of both major political parties but also to its perceived effectiveness. UDAG has been subject from the beginning to varied and detailed scrutiny. HUD has collected performance data each year of the program and has commissioned at least one major evaluation study (U.S. Dept. of HUD, 1982a). By all indications the program has been successful in leveraging private investment, creating jobs, and enhancing local tax bases.

Although HUD regulations set a minimum leveraging ratio of 2.5 private dollars to every 1 UDAG dollar, the actual ratio has been much higher. Through 1985 the aggregate leveraging ratio was about 5.9:1, reflecting a commitment to $22.9 billion in private investment and $3.9 billion in UDAG funds. Most UDAG projects also involve expenditures of state and local funds as well as money from other federal programs such as CDBG or those administered by EDA. These other public sources accounted for about $1.9 billion during the first eight years of the program or roughly 7 percent of all public and private funds committed to UDAG projects (U.S. Dept. of HUD, 1986, pp. 72, 67). If the leveraging ratio were calculated using the sum of all public money to private investment, the overall program ratio would come to approximately 3.9:1.

Federal officials anticipated that UDAG projects initiated during the first eight years of the program would eventually generate 503,254 permanent new jobs. In addition, over 414,000 temporary construction jobs would be created by these undertakings. Finally about 123,000 jobs were saved that would otherwise have been lost altogether through firm failure or lost to a particular community through plant out-migration, according to the reports of local officials.

HUD calculates that the UDAG program creates one permanent job at an average cost of $7700 in federal funds. Comparisons with other job-creating programs are not entirely reliable, for modes of calculating costs and estimating job creation vary from program to program. UDAG appears to be slightly less efficient than the one-time 1983 Emergency Jobs Appropriation of $1 billion, administered through the CDBG program, where the average cost per job was approximately $5800 (U.S. Dept. of HUD, 1984a, p. 39). By Economic Development Administration standards, however, UDAG is the less expensive program: EDA uses a $10,000 per job cost as its guideline.

The UDAG job data themselves are probably overstated, however. The total number of anticipated jobs is based on local expectations, and these tend to be optimistic. Among projects that had been *completed* through 1985, only 77 percent of previously anticipated jobs were actually created (ibid., pp. 90–91). If this actual performance rate were extrapolated to the entire UDAG program, the cost per job would rise to around $10,000.

Detailed data on the occupational distribution of UDAG-generated jobs are not available. Jacobs and Roistacher (1980, pp. 354–55) point out, however, that office, hotel, and retail jobs created by UDAG projects (which account for nearly half of all projects in the program) tend to be low-paid, often part-time, and in some businesses seasonal. Remuneration in these service-sector jobs runs on average between 50 and 75 percent of wages in manufacturing. At the beginning of the program over 70 percent of all jobs created by UDAG were in commercial projects. As greater emphasis has been placed on industrial projects, the proportion of service jobs has dropped. In 1983 about 61 percent of new UDAG jobs were created in service occupations in commercial and neighborhood projects (U.S. Dept. of HUD, 1979b, p. 64; and U.S. Dept. of HUD, 1984a, p. 91). Nearly 4 out of 10 new jobs were in manufacturing. Since only about 2 out of 10 new jobs nationally are created in the manufacturing sector (*New York Times,* Dec. 6, 1985), the UDAG program appears to generate twice as many jobs in the better-paid goods-producing industries than the economy at large manages.

One of the problems in making impact comparisons between UDAG and other federal economic development programs is that no other program has been subjected to the same degree of systematic scrutiny by its parent agency. This is not only the case where job creation and costs are concerned but also in regard to the local fiscal effects of UDAG projects. In some absolute sense UDAG undertakings have enhanced local tax bases. In the old urban renewal program the long time span between acquisition and clearance of the renewal site (which meant its removal from the tax rolls) and the beginning of new construction usually produced short-term property tax losses. But UDAG projects have often been constructed on land already vacant and in the hands of public authorities. In addition UDAG, in contrast to the urban renewal program, requires the prior commitment of a private developer before any project goes forward. Federal approval of a UDAG project, therefore, produces almost immediate implementation and accompanying tax benefits.

Approximately 70 percent of commercial projects and 43 percent of industrial projects involve brand new construction. Historic preservation, expansion of existing facilities, and rehabilitation account for the remainder. At least half the industrial firms participating in the program are new to the community (although by law UDAG funds may not be used to "facilitate the relocation of . . . plants or facilities from one area to another" unless it is determined that there is no adverse effect on the area suffering the loss). Many of the industrial firms new to a community—about a third—are new start-ups or new branch plants of parent organizations (U.S. Dept. of HUD, 1984a, pp. 97–99).

For every UDAG dollar spent, local taxes are expected to increase annually by 14¢. As with anticipated job effects, such projections may be optimistic. Among UDAG projects actually completed through 1985, only 37 percent of anticipated tax revenues had been received (U.S. Dept. of HUD, 1986, p. 75). But just as the anticipated revenues are misleadingly inflated, so too is the shortfall exaggerated: about a quarter of all UDAG projects receive local tax abatements for periods ranging up to 20 years. When the abatements expire, tax revenues will be calculated on property constructed under UDAG on the same basis as property elsewhere in the city. Revenues will rise sharply as abatements end, making up much of the current shortfall.

As with other incentive programs, it is virtually impossible to conclude with confidence that UDAG stimulates investment that would not otherwise occur. To the degree that comparisons with other federal programs are possible, UDAG appears to be productive and reasonably efficient. It is regarded by local officials as a critical element of their economic development efforts. Two HUD officials in that agency's Office of Policy Development and Research conclude an analysis of the program with the judgment that "there is no question that UDAG funding has made the difference for many urban development initiatives in distressed areas . . ." (Gatons and Brintnall, 1984, p. 137). But the real test, they continue, is whether UDAG projects will stimulate or sustain spinoff development to produce measurable economic recovery.

Conclusions

In surveying the welter of federal economic development programs, it would not be difficult to forget that this activity neither adds up to a coherent national policy nor evinces an enduring or carefully articulated commitment to an aggressive federal role in stimulating investment and encouraging business formation. There is, of course, much evidence of federal concern, but the evidence is full of paradox and contradiction. Congress has passed many programs to assist state and local governments in attracting private investment, but in fact the motives behind each program differ significantly. Some, indeed, acquired their economic development purpose only after the fact. Furthermore, the coalitions that led to passage of each of these programs differed, suggesting the absence of any stable development constituency of organized dimensions. The provision of federal resources to subnational governments in this policy domain has been marked by the same mounting degree of policy invention and diversification evident among states and communities, yet suddenly the federal commitment all but evaporated at the moment of peak programmatic capacity. Job creation remains the primary goal of most federal development programs today, yet the means always involve some form of capital rather than labor subsidization. A number of programs are designed in principle to channel assistance to distressed areas, but in fact resources in most programs have been thinly spread and widely distributed.

The motives of each of these programs included under the rubric of federal economic development policy cannot in fact be traced to a single impulse to encourage private investment as the means to well-being or to any single set of political actors and interest groups. Rather the concerns and justifications out of which each of the programs grew are distinctive in character and were articulated by different champions. Urban renewal, the child of an unusual union between public housing liberals and the real estate industry, emerged from the conviction that slum clearance and housing construction were appropriate ways to absorb the energies freed by conversion to a peacetime economy (Gelfand, 1975, Ch. 4).

The Small Business Administration was created to foster the interests of small business, an icon in the culture of individual liberty.[5] The origins of its programs date to the depression-era Reconstruction Finance Corporation. The forces that created the SBA itself in 1953 lay within Congress and were mobilized not by outside interest groups but by internal reaction to scandal and improprieties in the postwar RFC (Parris, 1968, Ch. 1). In contrast, the roots of the Economic Development Administration lie first in the virtually single-handed efforts of Senator Paul Douglas (D.-IL) during the 1950s to push depressed-areas legislation. Douglas was able to win modest support from organized labor in his unsuccessful campaign (Levitan, 1964, Ch. 1). In the 1960 presidential primaries John Kennedy's pledge in West Virginia to make aid to depressed areas a major priority of his administration won wider public support for such a program and, indeed, after Kennedy's election Congress passed the Appalachian-oriented Area Redevelopment Act of 1961. The programs of the EDA, established in 1965, were the direct successors of those of the Area Redevelopment Administration. Put into place just as the Area Redevelopment Act expired by a coalition of senators and representatives from states with lagging growth rates, the EDA was designed initially to ad-

---

5. Addison Parris' history of the SBA begins with the following quote from Judge Learned Hand: "It is possible, because of its indirect social or moral effect, to prefer a system of small producers, each dependent for his success upon his own skill and character, to one in which the great mass of those engaged must accept the direction of a few" (Parris, 1968, p. vi).

dress the problems of largely rural areas cut off from the prosperous national economy. The original EDA programs represent the first explicit federal economic development initiatives, but their approach to encouraging private investment and job creation was a narrow one based on infrastructure development, modest business loans, and planning assistance.

The Community Development Block Grant program had an entirely different genesis. Its importance at its inception lay less in its programmatic purposes than in its role as a vanguard of the new federal disengagement. By consolidating specific categorical programs the Nixon "new federalists" hoped not only to reduce the total amount of federal funds devoted to intergovernmental assistance but also to diminish federal influence in program planning and implementation. CDBG, then, was the creation of those who wished to cut back the scope of federal power; economic development objectives did not enter the picture at all until the amendments of 1977.

In the same bill that renewed and amended the CDBG program Congress also created the Urban Development Action Grant. UDAG is a broad and flexible program explicitly devoted to economic development purposes, and it was so from its initial passage. Supported by the nation's mayors, development officials, and major business interests, UDAG was an important gesture to middle-class urban interests awaiting action on the Carter administration's pledge to assign a high priority to the problems of the cities.

This summary account of motives, origins, and actors suggests that federal action in this realm has never been an effort to elaborate or fill out a predetermined economic development policy framework. Federal policy is rather a collection of uncoordinated programs, some of which were turned to economic development purposes by the recipients of assistance rather than by the federal grantors. At best it may be said that the federal government has responded in the postwar years to unemployment, particularly that which is structural in origin, and to urban and rural infrastructure deficits and deterioration with a set of piecemeal programs that take little cognizance of one another. Their common themes have been capital rather than wage subsidies and, at least since the EDA was established, a commitment to targeting resources to the most needy areas that has varied from extremely modest in the case of the EDA programs and CDBG to moderate in the UDAG program. Furthermore, they have all been designed to stimulate growth by manipulating the supply side. Lowering land acquisition and site preparation costs, providing good transportation and other infrastructure facilities, and reducing the cost of capital for firms willing to locate in less than optimal sites are the chief devices to encourage growth. But for all these common features these federal programs cannot be said to constitute a consistent or coherent policy for economic development: there is overlap and duplication among the programs, little if any coordination, an absence of goals and timetables, and no explicit theory of development that provides a common base.

As economic development became an increasingly visible public issue in the 1970s, the federal government's responses showed a similar, though less adventurous, mounting degree of invention and diversification to that which is evident at the subnational level. Between 1974 and 1983 Washington either put into place or sharpened the economic development emphasis of most of its programs in this policy domain. CDBG was signed into law in 1974, followed almost immediately by Title IX of EDA. Then came the SBA's Small Business Development Centers (1976), UDAG (1977), the CDBG amendments of 1977 and 1981, the SBA's 503 program (1980), and its Office of Private Sector Initiatives (1983).

Yet this intensification of effort was accompanied by a certain ambivalence about the maintenance of a federal role in economic development. Although some of the government's programs were in fact created during the Reagan administration, the president and his Office of Management and Budget sought regularly to eliminate the SBA and the EDA and to cut and even terminate the UDAG program. The orthodox position in Republican Washington in the 1980s was that the best economic development policy lay not in government subsidies but in economic recovery from the inflation and high interest rates of the latter year of the 1970s. Recovery could be achieved, according to the president's economists, through tax cuts to free up capital, the elimination of burdensome regulations, and reductions in government spending to cool inflationary pressures.

One logical implication of this economic strategy is to divest the government of all authority to intervene in market processes on a microeconomic level, that is, essentially to end firm subsidies and other location incentives. But even as it did indeed seek to terminate the major economic development programs, the Reagan administration offered a new proposal for federal location incentives called the Urban Enterprise Zone.

Based on the notion that complete deregulation of economic activity within a particular geographical area, combined with a variety of tax credits and abatements, is the most efficient and productive way to stimulate latent entrepreneurial energies, the enterprise zone idea was introduced repeatedly, though unsuccessfully, in Congress though the first half of the 1980s.[6] The idea in its contemporary form was first proposed in 1977 by a British urban planner, Peter Hall, who intended, in his words, "to recreate the Hong Kong of the 1950s and 1960s inside inner Liverpool or inner Glasgow" (quoted in Butler, 1981, p. 26). The enterprise zone concept was introduced in the United States in 1979 by the Heritage Foundation, a conservative policy institute.

In its original form the plan called not only for offering tax reductions to businesses, investors, and workers who located in designated zones but also for the suspension of "burdensome" regulations such as the minimum wage, pollution standards, and perhaps even occupational safety and health requirements. Later proposals sent to Congress by the president stepped back from the effort to deregulate enterprise zones in the face of negative reactions from organized labor and environmental groups. Under later versions of the plan, state and local governments would be permitted to request relief for their enterprise zones from any federal regulation unless it would directly violate a requirement imposed by statute such as nondiscriminatory hiring, pollution controls, and the minimum wage (*Congressional Quarterly*, 1983, pp. 634–35). Although the legislation attracted bipartisan sponsorship and support each time it was introduced—indeed a number of similar bills have been introduced by members of both parties independent of White House efforts—the proposal to stimulate business formation in part by foregoing federal taxes during a period of record federal deficits did not seem compelling to a majority in Congress (*New York Times*, June 27, 1984).[7] In any event, more than half the states now have enterprise zone programs of their own.

Although the federal government has not managed to pass a nationally sponsored enterprise zone program, the continued presence of this proposal on the congressional agenda suggests that at some level Washington's historic interest in fostering subnational economic development

---

6. The first urban enterprise zone bill was introduced in Congress in May 1980. Through 1985 at least 21 other bills providing in one way or another for enterprise zones were introduced. All died in committee before ever coming to the floor, except for one bill that made it to the House-Senate Conference Committee as part of the Deficit Reduction Act of 1984. Here it was deleted, however.

7. A Treasury Department analysis of President Reagan's enterprise zone proposal to Congress for fiscal year 1986 indicates that it would cost the United States $4.4 billion in foregone taxes between 1986 and 1990 (Roth, 1985, p. 2).

nevertheless persists. Even in a period marked by a commitment in national politics to free-market doctrines, the enterprise zone campaigns demonstrate an abiding interest in helping state and local governments to attract private investment. Yet the enterprise zone story is a sign of the times: the only new idea in economic development policy to originate in the 1980s at the federal government level, it was quickly, perhaps preemptively, adopted by the states. In the economic policy domain in the 1980s, it has been the states, not Washington, that seem to deliver the goods.

CHAPTER 6

Supply-Side Incentives to Development: Business Climate Policies

IMPRESSED with the vigorous efforts that southern states were making to attract industry and concerned at the same time about northern fears that southern growth was coming mainly at New England's expense, the nonprofit National Planning Association commissioned a study in the 1940s to discover "why industry moves South" (McLaughlin and Robock, 1949).[1] This early investigation, based on a survey of 88 new plants across the South, concluded that by far the most important factors had to do with the expansion of the regional market in the postwar years and the abundance of untapped raw materials. New farm machinery plants, rubber manufacturing, synthetic fiber mills, and forest-product concerns, among others, moved south to exploit a market in which consumer-spending power had increased faster during the war than anywhere else in the nation. Other firms moved to be near vast supplies of pulpwood, phosphorus, cotton, and sulphur. The availability of a large and docile labor force was also a consideration, though only about a quarter of the plants studied considered labor a primary factor (ibid., pp. 32, 52–64, 76–83). The overall impact of low tax rates, tax incentives, capital subsidies, and other such elements designed to sway plant location decisions was minimized in the study: "Manufacturers,"

---

1. Economic growth is not simply a function of plant relocations to an area, of course. But development officials' tendency up until the 1970s to focus on this limited aspect of the growth process, to the exclusion of other forces making for growth, was unmistakable. In his survey of various sorts of economic development organizations, both public and private, Donald Gilmore found that attracting new industry to a particular place was a far more important objective than assisting firms already present to expand (Gilmore, 1960, p. 17).

the authors reported, "were usually not impressed by local concessions" (p. 112).

Although the role of labor later came to be regarded as more important than this early study had found, numerous subsequent investigations of location criteria confirmed the distinctly secondary role of general state tax policy and the more particular concessions and inducements. But several factors nevertheless encouraged the states, not only in the South but also in New England and then elsewhere, to continue to offer such lures. For one thing state and local governments in the South particularly would have been hard-pressed to believe that their postwar growth was purely coincidental to the recent introduction of such devices as low-interest tax-exempt bond financing and tax abatements and the assiduous maintenance of low business and personal taxes. Not only had the introduction of certain of these policies and the increase at least in manufacturing employment occurred more or less simultaneously, but also everyone in every region who was involved in business promotional efforts could cite stories of firms that had demanded concessions before they would move, as well as tales of companies that had jilted communities that could not or would not satisfy their desires. Besides, even if public officials harbored private doubts about the necessity or generosity of government inducements to industrial growth, once one state promoted itself with such devices, there was little choice among neighboring states but to follow suit (Cobb, 1982, p. 228). Furthermore, there was scattered evidence, not only in the National Planning Association study of the 1940s but also in later investigations, that tax rates and various location incentives influenced *some* site choices after all, especially when all other factors of primary importance were equal (McLaughlin and Robock, 1949, p. 107).

What is striking for the contemporary observer is that the maintenance of the traditional supply-side policies pioneered (or perpetuated, as in the case of low taxes) in the two decades surrounding World War II has still been a matter of concern in the 1980s, despite the "discovery" of the new, more aggressive policies of the entrepreneurial state and the surge in their implementation. The old policies based on efforts to reduce factor costs for potentially mobile capital in order to lure it to a new location have not been displaced by efforts to stimulate new capital formation or to nurture new markets and industries of the future. Even though the old policies have receded in relative importance, it is nevertheless the case that the two approaches to economic development coexist in nearly every state.

In this and the following chapter we shall examine the origins and form of the major supply-side location incentives. Then in Chapter 8 we shall look at the evidence regarding their success in stimulating investment and influencing location decisions.

Comparative Business Climates

The phenomenon that particularly sustains the maintenance of location incentives designed to lower the factor costs of existing mobile industries is the notion of comparative business climates. Though business climate is an old idea, it has taken on new force by the introduction in recent years of ranked lists of states as places to do business.

These rankings have become an activity in which a wide range of arbiters, both self-appointed and under contract, now indulge (Hagstrom and Guskind, 1984). Such scales provide business people with a simple comparative gauge by which to judge the lengths to which a state government and its people are willing to go to accommodate business interests. States regard these scorecards—even those that produce what many believe to be spurious results—in deadly serious terms. Among the most important indicators on which the various scales are based are state and local tax policies and the presence of certain incentive programs. Thus, the compulsion to maintain a battery of supply-side policies is clear: they are essential in order to rank well on business climate surveys.

Business climate, as an official of the Fantus Company, a major plant-location consulting firm, notes, is a "slippery concept" (Harding, 1983). One meaning of the term is that it refers simply to an assessment of "all the factors taken into account when siting a plant" (ibid., p. 22). These include everything from the costs of the major factors of production to the availability of necessary resources and transportation facilities to the "quality of life." A narrower definition of business climate is that it represents a composite measure of the attitudes of a state's population and government officials toward business (ibid.). These attitudes are gauged largely by legislative and regulatory provisions that affect tax rates, the availability of special incentives, technical and financing assistance for special businesses, environmental regulations, and labor laws. The object of business climate surveys, however they are defined, is to identify in a selective fashion a variety of factors thought to affect business costs of most firms located within a state, to measure these, to assign relative weights to each set of factors that correspond to their relative importance in the site-selection decision of most firms, and finally to rank the states on a composite index.

The historian James Cobb indicates that efforts to advertise the southern business climate surfaced as early as the "New South" cam-paigns to industrialize the region in the late nineteenth century (1982, p. 224). Here the central theme of the promotions was the abundance of cheap labor and natural bounty. Most southern and border states estab-lished formal programs in the 1920s and 1930s—some under the juris-diction of industrial development boards or departments and others in cooperation with state chambers of commerce—in which advertising and out-of-state trips to prospect among northern firms were used to publicize their respective virtues (Lepawsky, 1949, pp. 57–70)

But if "business climate" has been a long-standing staple of southern boosterism, it was not until 1975 that the first effort to measure the con-cept across states appeared. When the Illinois General Assembly dramat-ically increased workers' compensation and unemployment benefits in that year, the president of the Illinois Manufacturers' Association, con-vinced that the legislature had put the state at a severe disadvantage in the competition for industry, hit upon the idea of commissioning a com-parative business climate study as a way of persuading the lawmakers to reconsider what they had done (Biermann, 1984). The Fantus Company was engaged for the job, and it produced a ranking of the 48 contiguous states that relied heavily on different state and local tax burdens. Illinois ranked, as the state's manufacturers' association feared, near the bottom of the list. California also ranked low—indeed, next to last—prompting the implementation of an elaborate business-climate-rating study by that state's Department of Finance. Based on 88 variables, rather than the mere 15 of the Fantus study, the final result showed California ranked 6th in the country rather than 47th.

When Fantus was asked to undertake a second ranking exercise the following year, the company declined on the grounds that a single com-posite list failed to serve the widely varying needs of different companies (Hagstrom and Guskind, 1984). But the Alexander Grant Company, an accounting firm, agreed to compile and publish a business climate survey in 1979 aimed at manufacturing firms, and it has been doing so each year since. The Grant survey, conducted with the support of the Confer-ence of State Manufacturers' Associations, and a more recent effort by *Inc.* magazine geared especially to the small business community, have become the two major annual rankings in the 1980s.[2] Table 6-1 offers a list of the key variables on which each is based.

---

2. In 1986 *Inc.* forsook what it called "the controversial notion of business climate" rankings and instead ranked the states according to how they were actually doing in stim-ulating entrepreneurial activity and economic expansion. The rankings take into account

In both surveys factors are weighted. Grant Thornton weights according to the judgments of state manufacturers' associations about which factors are critical in site decisions, while *Inc.*'s rankings are based on its own judgment as to their relative importance to small businesses. Labor costs and state-regulated employment costs carry slightly more weight in the Grant rankings, while capital availability, a persistent concern of small enterprises, and state support services for small business are the most important factors for *Inc.* Taxes rank lower in both surveys relative to most other factors. Nevertheless, both surveys tend to reward states with low taxes.

Rankings tend to vary considerably from one company's survey to another, as Table 6-2 clearly shows. For example, South Dakota was ranked number 2 in the 1984 Grant survey but 26 in the *Inc.* survey of 1985. Massachusetts was 33 in the former, 4 in the latter; Illinois 44 and 10. Even in the same survey, rankings might swing sharply from year to year. South Carolina and Idaho, for example, both rose substantially in the *Inc.* rankings between 1983 and 1985, while North Dakota and Oregon dropped. The volatility of the rankings, which are established in some cases on the basis of very minor differences in scores on any particular variable, suggests the pitfalls of using such scales as serious location guides. The small business entrepreneurs who might have sought a Texas location in 1983 on the basis of that state's number 1 *Inc.* ranking, found themselves located in the number 18 state in 1985. Similarly, those who shunned South Carolina in 1983 no doubt regret their hasty decision: although in 1983 *Inc.* ranked the state 50, by 1985 the magazine rated it number 14. Other states seesaw from year to year. In the 1982 *Inc.* rankings (not shown in Table 6-2), Montana was 27. It rose to 14 in 1983, but then dropped to 24 in 1985. Pennsylvania traced a three-year pattern as follows: 37, 15, 39. What people who operate small businesses ought to make of such fluctuations is not readily apparent.

According to the president of the Corporation for Enterprise Development, a nonprofit economic development organization, business concerns take the rankings seriously, particularly when searching for a branch plant site (Hagstrom and Guskind, 1984). Several statistical analyses have attempted to explore the effects of business climate rankings on various measures of economic growth. The results, most of which

---

job growth over the prior four years, new business births, and the presence of high-growth young companies (Kahn, 1986).

The Alexander Grant Company has changed its name to Grant Thornton.

Table 6-1.   Variables Employed in Business Climate Surveys

Alexander Grant and Company	*Inc.* Magazine
Taxes and Fiscal Policies (17.8%) State and local taxes per $1000 of personal income Change in taxes Expenditure growth vs. revenue growth State and local debt per capita Welfare expenditure per capita	**Capital Resources (25%)** Bank loans as a percentage of assets Commercial/industrial loans per capita Small Business Investment Companies financing per capita State programs: direct loans, loan guarantees, bond guarantees, venture capital programs
State-regulated employment costs (21%) Average unemployment compensation benefits per year Net worth of unemployment compensation fund per worker Maximum weekly disability insurance payment Workers' compensation insurance rate	**Labor (25%)** Average weekly wage Percentage of unionized workers Percentage of high school graduates Value added per worker
Labor costs (22.8%) Average hourly manufacturing wage Percentage of change in wages Percentage of unionized nonagricultural workers Change in unionization	**Taxes (10%)** State and local taxes per $1000 of personal income
Availability and Productivity of Labor Force (20.1%) Vocational education enrollment as a percentage of population Percentage of high-school graduates Percentage of working time lost to work stoppages Value added per dollar of production payroll Average hours worked per week	**State Support (20%)** Advisory office, ombudsman, advisory council Legislative small business committee State small business conference Percentage of change in wages
Other (18.3%) Fuel costs per million BTUs State expenditures on environmental control as a percentage of state and local expenditures Population density per square mile Percentage of population change	**Business Activity (20%)** Percentage of population change Percentage of employment gain Percentage of change in personal income Business units per 1000 population Number of *Inc.* top 100 fastest-growing companies in the state

Sources: Margolis, 1985; and Alexander Grant and Co., 1982.

Note: Figures in parentheses are the relative weights assigned to each set of factors in determining the composite scores by which states are ranked.

Table 6-2.   State Rankings on Different Business Climate Surveys, Selected Years

	Fantus 1975	California 1977	Grant 1979	Grant 1982	Grant 1984	Inc. 1983	Inc. 1985
Alabama	2	19	17	23	19	41	37
Arizona	16	5	29	7	5	38	15
Arkansas	8	39	6	18	9	36	30
California	47	6	36	26	30	2	1
Colorado	18	10	20	15	18	3	3
Connecticut	43	45	38	38	34	9	2
Delaware	44	26	42	41	36	16	16
Florida	7	8	12	1	1	6	6
Georgia	13	47	7	6	13	23	12
Idaho	25	16	19	11	17	47	28
Illinois	35	17	41	42	44	11	10
Indiana	9	23	27	29	25	18	11
Iowa	14	21	25	35	31	34	38
Kansas	20	20	16	10	11	25	23
Kentucky	22	46	26	30	24	22	36
Louisiana	26.5	30	24	12	16	27	29
Maine	30	13	15	40	37	45	34
Maryland	36	42	35	27	27	35	45
Massachusetts	46	43	37	33	33	7	4
Michigan	45	40	48	48	48	28	40
Minnesota	41	41	32	32	43	5	7
Mississippi	12	9	1	9	7	40	42
Missouri	19	15	14	19	22	32	41
Montana	31	35	33	25	20	14	24
Nebraska	17	34	18	8	4	39	49
Nevada	32	3	31	16	23	42	44
New Hampshire	28	37	21	21	26	17	22
New Jersey	37	44	47	34	29	10	8
New Mexico	23.5	15	5	31	28	8	17
New York	48	22	46	45	39	4	9
North Carolina	6	29	2	3	10	30	13
North Dakota	11	18	12	4	3	19	33
Ohio	26.5	31	45	44	46	29	25
Oklahoma	21	12	8	24	21	33	43
Oregon	40	32	39	43	47	21	47
Pennsylvania	42	24	44	46	41	15	39
Rhode Island	33	48	34	47	45	20	27
South Carolina	5	38	3	5	15	50	14
South Dakota	4	4	9	14	2	43	26
Tennessee	15	36	11	13	14	24	46
Texas	1	1	22	2	6	1	18
Utah	10	2	4	20	8	37	19
Vermont	38	25	23	28	35	26	32
Virginia	3	33	10	17	12	13	5
Washington	39	11	43	37	38	12	21
West Virginia	29	28	40	39	40	48	50
Wisconsin	34	27	30	36	42	49	31
Wyoming	23.5	7	28	22	32	44	48

Sources: Margolis, 1985, for the *Inc.* 1985 survey; Biermann, 1984, p. 18, for all others except the Grant 1984 survey.

derive from simple correlation techniques, provide modest support for the notion that business is somewhat sensitive to the business climate rankings in making investment decisions. Cobb, for example, found a statistically significant relationship (Spearman's rank order correlation = .568) between rank on the 1975 Fantus study and rank in terms of the percentage of growth in manufacturing employment from 1970 to 1978 (1982, p. 224). But Biermann's zero-order correlations between business climate ranks and percentage of growth in manufacturing employment for a variety of selected time periods found nothing higher (and most much smaller) than a .26 Pearson r coefficient.[3] The analysis produced only a .06 correlation between rank on the Grant survey of 1982 and the number of new plants established in the state in that year (Biermann, 1984).

The strongest evidence that business climate rank might make a difference is contained in an analysis by Plaut and Pluta (1983). They found significant Spearman rank-order correlations averaging about .51 between ranks on both the Fantus study and the 1979 Grant study on the one hand and three measures of business growth on the other. These latter included change in real value-added, change in manufacturing employment, and change in manufacturing capital stock between 1967 and 1977. The greater the magnitude of change, the higher the business climate rank. Furthermore, business climate, measured by a principal-components index that explained 90 percent of the variance in each of the rankings, emerged as a significant predictor of manufacturing employment growth and growth in real capital stock (but not value-added) in a regression equation that controlled for a number of other factors. Despite the relatively robust coefficients in the regression, however, Plaut and Pluta conclude that business climate variables are less important in explaining regional differences in growth than traditional market factors, such as labor costs and the cost of energy.

Whatever the empirical reality, state development officials and politicians worry extensively about poor rankings and, conversely, work hard to advertise favorable ones. One indication of the level of concern is that of the 17 states that had released strategic economic development plans by the end of 1985, 12 discussed their state's business climate ranking at some length (see Table 6-3) Nine of these were concerned specifically with their low ranking. For example, the Iowa report recounts a 1984 meeting sponsored by the Iowa Development Commission at which state

---

3. Biermann does not report significance levels.

Table 6-3.   Incidence of States Mentioning Business Climate
Rankings in Strategic Economic Development
Planning Documents, 1985

Mention of High Rankings or Improvement	Mention of Concern over Poor Rankings	No Mention
Arizona	California	Illinois
Indiana	Hawaii	Michigan
Montana	Iowa	Ohio
	Minnesota	Rhode Island
	Nevada	Utah
	New York	
	North Dakota	
	Pennsylvania	
	Wisconsin	

and local officials were told that "business climate was without doubt the main reason for the South's outstanding growth record." The report then goes on to note that Iowa had ranked 33, 35, and 31 on the Grant surveys from 1981 to 1983, a status achieved in the view of the development commission because of high taxes and the absence of certain business tax exemptions. The commission offered a series of policy recommendations designed to bring Iowa's tax burden into line with its midwestern neighbors (Committee for Iowa's Future Growth, 1984, pp. 27–29).

The Governor's Office of Montana has attempted to offset the state's mediocre business climate by observing that its rankings on both the Grant and *Inc.* surveys have improved steadily. The jump from 27 to 14 on the successive *Inc.* rankings of 1982 and 1983 is attributed to the implementation of a number of business-assistance programs (Montana Office of the Governor, 1985, p. 20.

The Wisconsin Department of Development was sufficiently distressed by the state's consistently low rankings in the business climate surveys and by the adverse publicity that this engendered in the national business press that it commissioned its own survey to find out whether local business people in fact agreed that Wisconsin was a poor place to do business. The study design involved interviews with business people not only in Wisconsin but also in two neighboring midwestern states and two fast-growing states for contrasting purposes (Yankelovich, 1984). To the dismay of state officials it was found that by comparison with Wisconsin business people, respondents in other states were far more willing to rate their respective home states as good places to do business. Wisconsin respondents complained about the "unfavorable" attitudes of the state government (65 percent reported that they had actually "suffered" at the hands of state government, particularly its Department of Natural Resources with its stringent environmental regulations) and the tax system. The survey analysis concluded that the business climate in Wisconsin was marked by "an unusually negative atmosphere." Although Wisconsin officials contended that business perceptions were not always supported by the facts (for example, the state's business tax burden was not particularly high, especially within the region), the governor's Strategic Development Commission concluded that "the Yankelovich survey of 1984 provided evidence that strong steps are needed" to improve the Wisconsin business climate (Wisconsin Strategic Development Commission, 1985, p. 88).

States that rank well on the business climate surveys may feature their good fortune prominently in their economic development planning documents. Arizona's plan, for example, explains the state's current growth "in part because of a good business climate" and cites the state's high ranking (seventh) in the 1983 Grant survey (Arizona Governor's Office of Economic Planning and Development, n.d., p. 11). The high standing is attributed to the state's "overall tax and spending policies."

States without strategic plans often cite their favorable rank in promotional literature. Mississippi, for example, is proud that it ranks consistently in Grant's top 10 states (Mississippi Ad Hoc Committee, n.d.). And North Carolina's Department of Commerce buttresses its own claims about the state by referring to the higher authority of external judges:

North Carolina offers one of the most favorable business climates in the nation and is internationally known for its progressive policies toward business and industry. In a survey by *Business Week* magazine, corporate decisionmakers ranked North Carolina one of the two states they would most likely consider first in the search for new sites. A similar study by *Fortune* magazine ranked North Carolina second in the nation as the state most likely considered for new research and development laboratories. (North Carolina Department of Commerce, n.d.-b., S-2)

Whether or not business climate surveys actually play a serious role in influencing location decisions of private firms, such rankings clearly loom large in the vision of state politicians and development officials. The business climate surveys may neither encourage nor discourage a particular firm, but they do carry considerable political symbolic weight. No political leader wishes to be accused of acting in such a way as to lower a state's business climate ranking. In state politics this is tantamount to the presidential sin of losing Central America to the Communists. Conversely, there is much good will to be gained from the business community at home and in the national business press from taking measures that may improve the state's ranking.

State governments cannot, of course, control all of the elements that go into the assessment of their respective business climates. Labor costs, value added, and population and income growth are beyond the reach of the legislature. But taxing and spending policies and the provision of incentives and assistance, all of which play a role in establishing a state's ranking, are under the state's control..It is important to realize that no credit is given in the manufacturing business climate survey for demand-side policies that stress export-trade assistance programs or business formation efforts, and programs such as these played only a modest role in the small business (*Inc.*) survey. Some state officials may doubt the efficacy of taxes and incentives in influencing location decisions or stimulating measurable growth, but this is in many ways beside the point: their symbolic importance, exemplified by the idea of a business climate, is a sufficiently powerful incentive.

Tax Policy

Although tax policy accounts for a relatively small fraction of the composite Grant and *Inc.* scores, state and local government officials tend to regard their jurisdictional tax profiles as the central characteristic of their business climates. The tax profile is composed of two elements: the general tax structure and tax incentives. The former includes the types of taxes imposed on individuals and businesses, rates, and burden, a function of the relationship between rates and income. These elements of the tax system affect all businesses and business people in the state. Tax incentives are particularistic in application and work in various ways to limit or mitigate the effects of the general tax structure. Thus, for example, the comparatively high tax rates of a state such as Louisiana may be offset by the generous tax abatements available to firms that move or expand there. Tax incentives include various exemptions, tax credits, and abatements. Table 6-4 lists the common sorts of incentives and shows their spread among the states over a 20-year period.

The perceived importance of taxes, particularly the general tax structure, is a perspective imposed upon public officials partly by chamber of

Table 6-4.   Number of States Employing State and Local Tax
Incentives for Industry, 1966–85

	1966	1985
Excise tax exemption	5	16
Tax exemption or moratorium (tax abatements) on land or capital improvements	11	32
Tax exemption or moratorium on machinery and equipment	15	32
Inventory tax exemption on goods in transit	32	46
Tax exemption on manufacturers' inventories	19	43
Sales tax exemption on new equipment	16	38
Tax exemption on raw materials used in manufacturing	32	46
Tax credits for use of specified state products	2	6
Tax exemption to encourage research and development	3	19
Accelerated depreciation of industrial equipment	9	36
Tax incentive for creation of jobs	0	27
Tax incentive for industrial investment	0	24

commerce and other booster advertisements that tout low taxes as a desirable location criterion and by business association lobbyists who make the case at budget time in the state capitals for the stimulus effects of tax reductions on investment behavior. Partly it is a function of the universal embrace of the general tax system: other policies and programs that may affect economic development prospects and thus influence the business climate—venture capital funds, for example, or particular tax credits or industrial revenue bond financing—are of interest to much smaller constituencies. And finally tax reductions in particular offer a certain economy of effort to lawmakers seeking to signal their friendly and flexible attitudes to the business community at large. According to the director of the New York Office of Economic Development, "[T]ax and fiscal policies have more to do with shaping a positive business perception of the state's environment for growth than any other factor" (New York Office of Economic Development, 1985, p. 51).

Many state development planners are convinced that lowering taxes does not in fact offer a rapid route to economic prosperity but nevertheless argue for doing so anyway. Thus a Michigan task force report concludes that state-controlled costs of doing business in that state— particularly local property tax rates as well as workers' compensation insurance—are unusually high. The report continues:

Our analysis revealed that lowering these state-imposed business costs will not alone restore vitality to Michigan's imperiled economic base industries. Even so, bringing the aggregate of these costs into line with the average of our Great Lakes neighbors is a prudent and important part of our strategy to restore the competitive position of our own industries and to let the rest of our nation know that Michigan is a good place to do business. (Michigan Task Force, 1984, p. 96)

This passage, typical of much thinking in state and local economic development circles, illustrates two persistent themes in this policy field. One is the desire to resemble one's geographical neighbors, the regional competitors for investment, rather than attempt to hit some national mean or compete with states with unusually low taxes. Thus, the Iowa economic development body points out that "Iowa does not have to be a South Dakota or a Texas with few business taxes, but at least it should strive to be competitive within our immediate geographic region" (Committee for Iowa's Future Growth, 1984, p. 28)). Similar concerns and recommendations may be found in the planning documents of many other states (see, for example, California Department of Economic and Business Development, 1984, p. 18; Wisconsin Strategic Development Commission, 1985, pp. 87–93). A second theme in the passage from the Michigan report is that tax policy plays an important symbolic role in the competition for investment. Whether or not lowering taxes makes a sufficient difference in factor costs to induce additional investment or influence a business location decision is in fact secondary. What is important is the message of the act itself. "Despite the inability to show a strong link between Wisconsin taxes and economic growth," the Wisconsin Strategic Development Commission writes, "there is still reason to view taxes as an important element in state policy. . . . [I]f business leaders 'perceive' that a legislative change is pro-business, it becomes a successful tool for economic growth. Perhaps perception is more important than reality" (Wisconsin Strategic Development Commission, 1985, pp. 88–89). The supply-side location-inducement strategy in this context is less related to economic theory than it is to the craft of advertising.

The federal Advisory Commission on Intergovernmental Relations once evinced a concern that "tax-based competition for people, capital, and jobs [would] reach the point where many state policymakers [would] feel obliged to pursue a 'beggar thy neighbor' strategy" (ACIR, 1981, p. 1). But the state and local conviction that tax cuts and low tax rates send a salutary message to the business community has not in fact resulted in a downward spiral of unremitting tax reductions. State and local tax policy is far more complex, for though economic development needs would appear to dictate tax cuts in competitive response to other states, other state responsibilities require significant public outlays. Thus, Minnesota officials write: "The hidden costs of both tax cuts and tax increases must be understood. A delicate balance must be achieved, ensuring quality public services while at the same time maintaining the lowest possible level of taxation" (Minnesota Department of Energy and Economic Development, 1985a, p. 24).

The following summary of broad developments in state and local taxation over the last several decades makes evident the dimensions of the struggle to reconcile the competing incentives to cut and to spend.

As was true at the national level of government, state and local real per capita spending increased steadily after World War II. In constant (1972) dollars state government outlays per capita rose from $111 in 1954 to around $346 in 1982. Local government spending increases were slightly less dramatic, rising from $200 to $498 in the same period (ACIR, 1985b, p. 194). These trends represent a clear response to increased demands for higher education, modern transportation infrastructure, prisons, welfare, recreation facilities, and so on at the state level, and for public school improvements, social services, urban redevelopment, law enforcement, and so on at the local level. State and local public employment per 10,000 people rose in these years from 256.5 workers to 465.2 (ACIR, 1985a, p. 134.)

Naturally, states and local governments had to finance their enlarged responsibilities. Thus, a substantial number of states were compelled to adopt one or more additional major types of taxes in the postwar period. In 1950 only 17 states were levying both a sales tax and an individual income tax. By 1985, 37 states had both types of taxes. The number of states with neither had declined from 7 to only 1, Alaska. In 18 states (14 of them in northern regions) the top marginal personal income tax rate was higher in 1984 than it had been in 1976. Only four states had cut their tax rates in this period.

A total of 44 states also imposed corporate income taxes by 1985. Nine of them began to do so only after 1963, and counter to expectation, most of these were states vulnerable to the perceived southern manufacturing challenge: Illinois, Indiana, Michigan,[4] Maine, New Hampshire, and Ohio. Corporate income tax rates rose steadily in every region in these years. States in the midwestern census region—that is, the traditional manufacturing belt around the Great Lakes and the Plains states— had the lowest average top marginal corporate income tax rate of any

---

4. Michigan repealed its corporate income tax after only seven years and replaced it with a modified value-added tax.

region in the country (5.97 percent), followed closely by states in the South (6.1 percent). Northeastern states continued to impose the highest top marginal rate at 9.14 percent, while the West was second highest in 1984 at 7.5 (ibid., pp. 99–102). Several states, however, have levied no corporate income tax at all, including Texas, South Dakota, Nevada, Washington, and Wyoming.

At the local level a similar process of tax-system diversification was under way. The number of towns and cities levying a sales tax rose by 33 percent in the decade after 1976, while the number of local governments employing income taxation increased by 8 percent. (If Pennsylvania units of government are excluded—they accounted for 2644 of the 3332 governments with local income taxes in 1984—then the rise is a more impressive 28 percent) (ibid., pp. 81, 90). In general the Advisory Commission on Intergovernmental Relations characterizes the period between 1959 and 1977 as a time of "steady strengthening of state tax systems to underwrite real expenditure growth" (ibid., p. 71). Although the brief "tax revolt" period of 1978–80 saw tax cuts and the introduction in 15 states of constitutional and statutory restrictions on state taxing and expenditure powers, the years that followed saw new tax increases to offset recession-induced revenue shortfalls.

The dominant impression of steadily increasing state and local taxation—a surprising trend in the context of the competition for investment—must be tempered by several developments. For one thing, although state and local governments were diversifying their tax structures and raising tax rates to keep up with real increases in expenditures, those expenditures as a percentage of the GNP reached a high point in the mid-1970s and then began to decline. State outlays of own-source revenues equalled 6.2 percent of the GNP in 1975 but fell steadily to an estimated 5.7 percent in 1982. Local government expenditures went from 5.2 percent of the GNP in 1974 to 4.8 percent in 1982 and fell as low as 4.5 percent in 1981 (ACIR, 1985b, p. 194). In other words, the rate of economic growth in these years exceeded the rate of state and local expenditure growth.

It is also the case that the weight of increasing taxation in the postwar decades has been falling more and more on individuals and less and less on businesses. The ratio of business taxes to total state and local tax receipts fell from 36.8 percent in 1957 to 30.6 percent in 1977 (ACIR, 1981, p. 62). Most of this decrease involved property taxes on business. Although the property tax is overwhelmingly a local levy, the state may influence the administration and burden of property taxes by enacting

Table 6-5.   Taxes on Business as a Percentage of Total State
and Local Taxes, by Region, 1967–77

	1967	1977	Percent change
New England	29.6	26.8	− 9.5
Mideast	32.8	29.6	− 9.8
Great Lakes	32.4	28.6	− 11.7
Plains	27.0	26.7	− 1.1
Southeast	32.6	32.2	− 1.2
Southwest	39.0	40.7	+ 4.4
Rocky Mountains	33.7	32.6	− 3.3
Far West	33.8	31.3	− 7.4

Source: ACIR, 1981, pp. 66–67

levy limits, providing property tax relief through state shared revenues, and by passing enabling legislation to permit various types of tax concessions administered at the local level such as tax abatements. Property taxes on business as a proportion of state and local revenues fell from 20.3 percent in 1957 to 12.3 percent in 1977 (ibid.; for slightly different figures see Gold, 1979, p. 129). Corporate income and sales taxes increased moderately in these years as a proportion of total state and local receipts. At the same time, however, the proportion of revenues raised from individuals rose from 63.2 percent to 69.4 percent in those two decades, with rising sales and income taxes—particularly the latter—accounting for most of the increase.

It is entirely reasonable to interpret these trends of greater state and local fiscal reliance on personal income and diminishing reliance on business as part of the supply-side business climate enhancement to compete with other places. This interpretation is bolstered by an examination of the regional patterns involved. The shift is especially evident in the decade 1967–77, as Table 6-5 shows. The greatest decreases in reliance on business as a source of tax revenue occurred in New England and the Great Lakes. More than two-thirds of the states that showed decreases in this period are located in the Frost Belt region.

There appears in fact to have been some degree of tax burden convergence among regions and subregions during this period. Other data provide support for that conclusion: for example, the annual rate of increase in tax revenue as a percentage of personal income from 1965 to 1978 declined in the Frost Belt states, but it rose in those years in every part of the Sun Belt except the Southwest. According to ACIR data the average annual rate of increase in the 23 northeastern and North Central states was 1.5 percent from 1965 to 1975 and 0.86 percent from 1975 to 1978. In the states of the South and West (excluding Alaska, which greatly exaggerates the trend) the corresponding increases were 0.97 percent per year in the decade after 1965 and 1.23 percent per year from 1975 to 1978 (calculated from data in ACIR, 1981, pp. 16–17). It is important to note here, however, that the percentage of personal income exacted by state and local governments reached a peak in 1978 in 32 states. Only two states imposed a heavier burden in 1983 than in 1978. No region appears to stand out in its annual average rate of decline since 1978.

It may be said in summary that the course of postwar state and local tax policy does not permit a clear conclusion that states sought to outbid one another for industry through manipulation of their general tax structure. The pattern rather is one of alternating increases and decreases, where action is governed more by growing state responsibilities, local and national economic conditions, and taxpayer pressure than by any single-minded effort to lure capital to the state by offering minimal taxes. Thus, though 8 states cut their individual income taxes in 1981–82, 19 raised them in the following two years (including 13 in New England and the Midwest). Six states cut various business taxes in 1981–82, but 22 increased them in 1983–84 (ACIR, 1985a, pp. 69–70).

Two dominant trends in postwar state and local fiscal policy seem to stand out. One is the rise in real expenditure levels. The other is the steady increase until the late 1970s of the percentage of personal income that went to taxes. As individuals and businesses have been taxed in more and more creative ways to finance these higher expenditures, state and local governments have sought to mitigate the impact of heavier taxes by reducing the most visible taxes, by selective relief, or by redistributing the burden. Both individual and business property owners have been granted relief from high rates of property tax increase by statutory and constitutional property tax limitations, by so-called circuit breaker laws that exempt low-income and elderly property owners from the tax, by tax abatements for commercial, industrial, and rental-housing investment, and by the use of federal and state shared revenues to forestall or slow the rate of local property tax increases. Ten states provided relief from inflation-induced income tax increases through indexation between 1978 and 1985. And for businesses in particular, states have reduced the proportion of the costs of government borne by the business sector and shifted it increasingly to individuals.

Through all of this the spectre of the business climate comparisons looms. But it is evident that tax behavior has not been and cannot be perfectly responsive to business climate considerations, at least in regard to general tax structure. The solution that states appear to have hit upon is first to advertise vigorously on those occasions when they are able to cut taxes (as in New York in 1985, for example, where personal income tax marginal rates were cut and in Wisconsin in 1980 when indexing was passed). Tax increases on the other hand occur only under duress and are often said to be temporary.[5] And finally, states and cities have used various tax incentives to mitigate otherwise high tax rates.

Tax incentives refer to various exemptions, abatements, and credits that may be made available to all businesses as a matter of right or to some through selective negotiation. Incentives are designed to encourage or protect certain activities. Some states, for example, give tax credits to firms that spend money on research and development; others provide tax credits for the installation of pollution-control devices and energy-efficient heating and cooling systems. The widespread exemption from inventory taxes on goods in transit is designed to protect and create employment in shipping, wholesale trade, and warehousing. Some states— Oklahoma is an example—do not tax parts or raw materials in transit through the state even when they remain in the state for assembly, fabrication, or processing and thereby seek to encourage the creation of jobs in the manufacture of goods for export beyond the state borders. Some credits and exemptions provide protection for certain industries important to a state: Wisconsin provides sales or property tax exemptions for equipment used to produce maple syrup, for materials used in packaging meat, and for natural cheese-aging in storage.

For economic development purposes the most important incentives are those designed specifically to encourage industrial or commercial investment in real property or equipment. Accelerated depreciation of industrial equipment and the exemption from sales taxes of equipment and machinery used in manufacturing are common devices to reduce the costs of new investment. About half the states also offer job-creation and investment tax credits. These may take the form, for example, of a one-time credit of $100 per new job created or $100 per $100,000 invested in depreciable capital stock for a certain number of years.

Most of these incentives have extremely low visibility, not only among the general public but apparently also among potential recipients.

---

5. Many tax increases are in fact temporary. At least five states have allowed temporary tax increases to expire in 1984. But three states in that year made temporary increases permanent.

Through 1980, for example, only one Maine corporation had ever claimed the investment tax credit available in the state (Rhode Island Strategic Development Commission, n.d., p. 648). Michael Kieschnick surveyed 337 firms that had made a manufacturing investment in any one of 10 selected states that offer a range of tax incentives. Among other questions, he asked the following: "Some states offer special tax incentives—such as investment tax credits—for new and expanding firms. Did the state tax code of your final choice include a special tax incentive?" Only 19.6 percent of new firms knew that such incentives existed, while 36 percent of expanding firms and 50 percent of branch operations were aware (Kieschnick, 1983, pp. 225, 256). It is interesting to note that only 3.3 percent of the new firms surveyed, 6.3 percent of the branch plants, and none of the expansion firms said that they would have located in another state in the absence of any tax incentives. Yet states believe they must continue to offer such inducements, if for no other reason than to cancel the appearance of advantage by another state.

A particular tax incentive may become widely known locally, either for its imputed effects or for its absence. Indiana officials are convinced that the state's practice of taxing business inventories detracts from its business climate reputation (Indiana Dept. of Commerce, n.d., p. 36). Wisconsin business leaders in contrast regard the machinery and equipment sales tax exemption as the single piece of legislation most identified with economic growth in the state (Wisconsin Strategic Development Commission, 1985, p. 88). For the most part, however, tax incentives occupy a seldom-explored margin of the tax system.

One exception to this generalization is the property tax abatement. Not only is it one of the oldest location inducements of the modern period, but it has been the subject of heated public controversy in such cities as New York, Cleveland, and St. Louis. Perhaps for these reasons its various forms have been the subject of more systematic study than any of the other tax incentive devices.

A tax abatement can be defined as a partial reduction of the property tax liability of a given piece of real estate for a specified number of years. Occasionally, when tax forgiveness is complete rather than partial, the abatement is called a property tax exemption. Generally, however, the terms are used interchangeably. Eligible local governments may offer abatements, pursuant to state enabling legislation, to property owners for new construction or for rehabilitation of commercial, industrial, or multiunit residential property, all depending on the particular nature of the law. Chart 6-1 provides a summary of the standard components of state abatement-enabling laws and the variations among them.

Chart 6-1. Range of Variations among Tax Abatement Programs[a]

Type and size of jurisdiction	New York: cities over 1 million Connecticut: cities over 35,000	Alabama: any county or municipality
Type of eligible real estate	Georgia: firms engaged in manufacturing or processing cotton, wool, rubber, clay, wood, and other specified products Colorado: commercial and small residential property over 30 years old Oklahoma: new manufacturing facilities	New Jersey: commercial or industrial properties
Time period of the abatement[b]	Indiana: 5 years Louisiana: 5 years, renewable Missouri: up to 25 years	
New construction or rehabilitation	New York: rehabilitation of housing Pennsylvania: improvements to commercial or industrial property	Rhode Island: new or remodeled manufacturing or commercial properties
Area targeting[c]	New York: economically underprivileged areas Missouri: blighted areas	
Minimum value of improvements or construction[d]	Connecticut: at least $5 million South Carolina: additions to existing establishments costing at least $50,000	
Payments in lieu of property taxes[e]	New Jersey: 2% of the cost of the project annually or 15% of annual gross revenue or a tax phase-in from 0% in the first years increasing 20 percentage points per year	

[a]States may have more than one abatement program (e.g., New York). Examples provided in the chart may refer to only one of these and do not necessarily characterize all such programs in that state.

[b]No laws offer indefinite abatements.

[c]Targeting abatements only to particular areas is not common. Many state enterprise zone programs, to be discussed in Chapter 7, specifically exempt zone businesses from local taxes, but abatements in those states are not limited to property within enterprise zones.

[d]Most programs do not specify minimum values.

[e]Most programs do not require payments in lieu of taxes.

Abatements are classic location incentives: the provision of the Oklahoma constitution authorizing abatements, for example, permits voters "to exempt manufacturing establishments . . . from municipal taxation for a period not exceeding five years as an inducement to their location" (Oklahoma Dept. of Economic Development, 1985, Appendix XXIX). Michigan's Department of Commerce describes the state's abatement program "as a significant incentive to expand and locate in Michigan" (1982, p. v).

The practice of granting tax abatements emerged at the municipal level in the South during the depression, often in direct defiance of state constitutional prohibitions against industrial subsidies or preferential tax treatment of particular property owners (Cobb, 1982, pp. 6–7). The earliest state provisions of the modern period for tax abatements appear to be a law passed by the Delaware legislature in 1935 allowing the city of Dover to exempt new manufacturing plants from municipal taxes for up to 10 years (International Association of Assessing Officers, 1978, p. 4) and a 1936 amendment to the Louisiana constitution exempting new and expanded plants from state and local taxes (Ross, 1953).[6] The use of tax abatements was limited primarily to the South for 40 years, where every state in the region except North Carolina and Texas experimented with this tax incentive at one time or another. By 1953 Moes (1962, p. 85) was able to identify nine states that offered abatements, all in the South except Rhode Island and Vermont. The number of states with abatement programs fluctuated moderately in these years but settled back to nine in 1975, according to Swanstrom's survey (Swanstrom, 1982). Suddenly, as with so many economic development programs, the number of tax abatement laws burgeoned. The sudden growth in such devices can probably best be explained by the general forces that intensified interstate competition in these years, but it is notable that tax abatements were regarded as the number-one, most important incentive in a 1977 survey of member firms of the Industrial Development Research Council. Abatements outranked right-to-work laws, industrial bond financing, and a host of other tax concessions, including exemptions of sales taxes on raw materials and manufacturers' inventory taxes (Industrial Development Re-

---

6. Oscar and Mary Handlin report tax exemptions granted to particular industries— glassmaking, salt and sugar works, breweries—by the Massachusetts General Court (the legislature) beginning in 1785 and running at least through 1806 (Handlin and Handlin, 1969, p. 79). These were clearly intended to subsidize important fledgling industries rather than to induce location decisions. The practice appears to have died out early in the nineteenth century.

search Council, 1977). In any event, by 1985 the *Industrial Development and Site Selection Handbook* survey found 32 states offering some form of abatement to real estate developers and investors.

To get a fuller understanding of how abatement programs work, it is useful to examine the operations of several in more detail. Missouri's Chapter 353 program is among the oldest programs outside the deep South and is regarded as having played a crucial role in the growth of metropolitan St. Louis. The abatement feature of this development incentive program was made possible by Article X of the Missouri constitution of 1945, which states, "For the purpose of encouraging . . . the reconstruction, redevelopment and rehabilitation of obsolete or blighted areas, the General Assembly may provide for partial relief from taxation of the lands devoted to any such purpose, and of improvements thereon, . . . for such periods of time, not exceeding 25 years . . ." (see Mandelker, 1980, Ch. 1). State enabling legislation (Chapter 353) was passed in 1945, permitting St. Louis alone among Missouri cities to offer tax abatements. St. Louis waited, however, until 1959 to implement the program.

Under the current version of the law, any city in Missouri over 20,000 in population may grant a tax abatement to a private developer whose development plans for a project in an officially designated "blighted" area have been approved by the city. For an initial period of 10 years the developer must pay taxes equivalent to those paid on the purchased land, exclusive of improvements, in the calendar year prior to acquisition of the property. This freeze on the tax assessment is lifted after a decade, but for the next 15 years the developer is liable only for taxes based on half of the assessed valuation of both land and improvements. At the end of the total 25-year period taxes on land and improvements are assessed at full value (St. Louis Community Development Agency, 1980).

Between 1960 and 1984 the city approved approximately 70 development plans involving more than 300 projects. City development officials estimated that $4.2 billion has been invested in office buildings, industrial projects, hotels, and residential projects under Chapter 353. For fiscal year 1984 alone the cost of abatements to St. Louis was $38 million in foregone taxes (Pomeroy, 1984). Proponents of the tax abatement argue that such costs must be set against the eventual return. Mandelker's estimate is that the tax gains to St. Louis will amount to more than twice the foregone revenues by the turn of the century (Mandelker, 1980, p. 45).

The Mandelker study, however, does not take into account the increased cost to the city of servicing the new buildings. Investigations of the net fiscal effects of tax abatements in other places, taking service costs into account, are inconclusive, however. A study by the Michigan Department of Commerce found in three Michigan cities that additional services to tax-abated properties cost less than 35 percent of the net revenues generated, resulting in a net fiscal gain (1982, p. 23). But a study of San Francisco found quite different results. Although California does not permit tax abatements, a comparison of the revenues generated by new construction and the additional costs of services is nevertheless suggestive. In that city service costs substantially outweighed new tax revenues when downtown construction was at issue (Swanstrom, 1982, p. 28).

Although Missouri law now permits all communities over 20,000 in population to offer tax abatements, the program has been exploited primarily by two cities, St. Louis and Kansas City. By contrast nearly 500 Michigan towns and cities offer abatements under that state's Plant Rehabilitation and Industrial Development Districts Law of 1974. Any city, village, or township may exempt an industrial firm from all property taxes for a period of 12 years in return for new construction or rehabilitation. In lieu of the property tax the firm pays an Industrial Facility Tax equal either to the amount assessed against the obsolete plant immediately prior to renovation or to half the property tax which would otherwise be payable for a new plant (Michigan Department of Commerce, 1976). Between 1974 and 1984 over $13.7 billion worth of industrial construction and rehabilitation was subsidized by this program; net foregone property tax revenues among Michigan communities amounted to $350 million in fiscal year 1984.

The state of New York initially entered the abatement field as a means of upgrading New York City housing stock. The 1946 New York Tax Law conferred "broad and flexible powers" on local governments to enact laws to encourage housing rehabilitation, including abatement incentives. New York City adopted such a program, eventually called J-51 (Vorsanger, 1983–84, p. 120), which offers developers two different tax breaks: a 12 to 32-year exemption from *increases* in property taxes as a result of rehabilitation or conversion of a structure to residential use; and an annual abatement of the frozen tax assessment for no more than 20 years equal to a prorated portion of 25 percent of the cost of the project (ibid., pp. 117–18, 121–22). The cost to the city of this abatement program in fiscal year 1982 alone was $280 million (Avens et al., n.d., p. 16).

A second abatement program for private developers of housing is designed to encourage construction of new middle- and moderate-income dwellings. This program was authorized by the state legislature in 1971 and is known as 421a. Developers of new housing are exempted from a decreasing portion of their property tax liability on the new building until the abatement reaches zero after 10 years. Between 1971 and 1984, 50,000 new apartments, few of them for middle- or moderate-income tenants, were built with 421a subsidies (Achtentuch et al., 1984, p. 10).

The city did not offer tax abatements for nonhousing projects until 1977. Pursuant to state enabling legislation passed the previous year, the city created an Industrial and Commercial Incentive Board to offer abatements that range in the first year from 50 to 95 percent of the taxes on the increase in assessed value resulting from improvements. The abatements decline at a prorated pace over periods of 5, 10, or 19 years, depending on the project. Annual foregone taxes range currently between $40 million and $65 million (Finch, 1981).

Although some public officials believe that tax abatements are effective devices to encourage investment,[7] these programs are one of the few economic development tools to have engendered significant controversy. Dennis Kucinich first won the mayoralty of Cleveland in the 1970s by running in part on a populist antiabatement platform. His argument was that abatements, available only to commercial and industrial investors, shift the property tax burden from capital to homeowners and small businesses (Swanstrom, 1982).

All three of New York City's abatement programs have been vocally opposed by public interest groups, and indeed the city itself sought unsuccessfully in the state courts to uphold its decision to deny a $20 million 421a abatement to the Trump Tower on Fifth Avenue on the grounds that luxury dwellings need no special investment incentives (Achtentuch et al., 1984, p. 14). As in St. Louis, Detroit, and Cleveland, tax-abated projects in New York City are overwhelmingly located on prime downtown real estate. Furthermore, the tax benefits are concentrated in the

---

7. Consider the conclusions of the Michigan study of abatements in the communities of Battle Creek, Romulus, and Cadillac: "There is general agreement that offering tax incentives to industry is a positive if not always determinative factor in selecting a location for a new plant. Local officials interviewed for the study were not able to identify any specific projects for which the availability of Act 198 [the abatement] was a direct inducement to locate a new plant within their community, although they strongly felt that the Act has benefitted their communities by providing them with a competitive edge over alternative locations. . . ." (Michigan Dept. of Commerce, 1982, p. 11)

hands of a few large investors. According to figures prepared for city council opponents of the New York abatements, 92.3 percent of the foregone taxes in the industrial and commercial program have involved projects built in Manhattan (Finch, 1981). A similarly high concentration of housing rehabilitation and new construction abatements is found in Manhattan, particularly in the most vibrant high-value neighborhoods south of 96th Street (Avens et al., n.d.; Vorsanger, 1983–84). So pronounced was this pattern that the use of abatements for high-income housing rehabilitation in this part of Manhattan was barred by city officials in 1983.

Opponents of abatements regard such incentives for projects constructed in high-rent neighborhoods as "public handouts for the wealthy" (Avens et al., n.d., p. ii). No incentive is ordinarily needed to induce development in prime locations. Yet the selective awarding of abatements has been fought successfully by developers in the courts, leading to a pattern in most places of granting abatements to all applicants who meet threshold eligibility criteria (Wolkoff, 1983). After the luxury Palace Hotel in New York received an abatement worth more than $2 million, a city council member commented: "Where else could Harry Helmsley build such a hotel? Certainly not in Hoboken" (*New York Times,* July 26, 1981, p. 6-E).

Abatements tend to be awarded to corporations or developers capable of undertaking large-scale projects with potentially dramatic development impacts. In most such cases a tax subsidy is a small consideration in the financial package put together, for development on this scale is normally well-capitalized to begin with. Thus it is not surprising that abatements are awarded disproportionately to a few developers and probably to those who need them least.

The most careful studies of the concentration of benefits have been conducted in New York City. Public interest group researchers found that, between 1981 and 1984, 10 real estate developers in that city accounted for over 75 percent of the citywide tax reductions in the 421a program to encourage housing construction (Achtentuch et al., 1984, p. 25). In the industrial and commercial incentive program, according to data gathered by New York City Council staff researchers, three firms had received over a third of the benefits awarded by the city by 1981. Ninety percent of the beneficiaries accounted for only 9 percent of the abated taxes.

Even in the geographically dispersed abatement program in Michigan the names of major firms—Kellogg's, General Motors, Ralston Purina,

St. Regis Paper—are among the principal beneficiaries. Indeed, these four firms or their subsidiaries accounted for 76 percent of the capital investment subsidized by tax abatements in the three-community study by the Michigan Department of Commerce. Forty-one smaller firms accounted for the remaining 24 percent of capital invested and the commensurate tax relief (calculated from data in Michigan Dept. of Commerce, 1982, pp. 8–13).

Despite these problems, tax abatements remain attractive to some development officials. Because future taxes are foregone, there is no need to appropriate current funds to provide benefits to business. Furthermore, abatements are administratively simple to operate, particularly if they are made available to all applicants with eligible projects. And finally, the existence of an abatement provides an unambiguous signal to the private sector that local government will be responsive to its needs. To business people, abatements may seem more important as a symbolic measure of the esteem that business interests command in a community than as a financial benefit of significant proportions (see Mandelker, 1980, p. 33).

Debt Financing

Subsidized capital has been the companion location incentive to tax concessions since the depression. Although examples of state and municipal loans to private firms at little or no interest can be found in the immediate postcolonial period, there is no evidence that these early efforts at public financing of private ventures were designed to influence investment location choices. Such efforts were intended more to nurture crucial, but economically immature, existing industries (Handlin and Handlin, 1969, p. 79). Beginning in the depression, however, individual communities and then states offered cheap capital to companies as an inducement to relocate from out of state. Such was the concern for drawing in new industry across the state line that Mississippi's Balance Agriculture With Industry program of raising capital for firms through the sale of municipally backed bonds ruled out such arrangements for new local enterprises (Moes, 1962, pp. 76–77).

Two basic types of public capital are made available to private enterprise: debt financing and equity investments. Debt financing, currently more widespread than equity arrangements, is the traditional supply-side incentive. Under debt-financing programs, a public entity makes or guarantees loans backed by collateral which are paid back according to a preestablished schedule. Equity investments, in contrast, place government in a higher-risk position as part owner of an enterprise: recovery of the investment is dependent on the success of the firm or a particular product. Such financing, which includes certain types of venture capital programs, is usually employed to foster particular types of industry or commerce thought to provide high potential for job creation. As such, it is not primarily used to influence location choices of existing firms or well-capitalized investors but rather functions as one of the several tools of the entrepreneurial state as it seeks to create a stable growth economy. In this section we shall explore debt-financing arrangements only, through which states or communities hope to attract investment by reducing the cost of capital.

Debt-financing arrangements are the subject of virtually infinite invention. William Hamilton and his colleagues list and describe 23 different ways in which state and local governments subsidize capital for private firms (Hamilton et al., 1984, pp. 31ff.). These include at least 10 kinds of direct public loans where the subsidy takes the form of low or no interest or one of several types of favorable payback arrangements. Other modes of public subsidy include at least five types of loan guarantees, public/private pooled capital funds to spread risk, subordinated debt arrangements, and secondary market activity. Most of these individual variants are quite limited both in dollar terms and in the number of jurisdictions that employ them. The details of each are of more interest to the practitioner than to students interested in policy considerations. The most useful way of understanding public debt financing as a policy tool is to examine four major categories: direct loans, publicly chartered but privately financed pooled development funds, loan guarantees, and revenue bond financing.

By 1985, 22 states were offering direct loans of public money to private firms, beginning with New Hampshire in 1955. Some states maintain only one direct-loan program, while others administer as many as three separate ones. Typically, direct-loan programs are run by the state department of economic development or a separate industrial development authority. States capitalize their own programs in several ways. California, for example, employed a one-time legislative appropriation to establish a revolving-loan fund. Ohio permits its Department of Development to sell tax-exempt bonds to raise loan money. In addition, Ohio sets aside a fixed amount ($25 million per year, beginning in 1983) of the state's profits from state-owned liquor stores to handle debt service on the bonds. Pennsylvania and Kentucky both use legislative appropriations and bond issues.

Several states account for the bulk of direct-loan activity in the country. Pennsylvania, whose Industrial Development Authority was established only a year after New Hampshire's initiative, accounted in 1983–84 for 64 percent of all the dollars loaned by all the states involved in such programs (CBO, 1984, p. 66). Other states with significant programs included West Virginia (9.9 percent of all funds loaned), New Jersey (6.2 percent), and Kentucky (4.7 percent).

By any measure state direct loans represent a minor effort. In the fiscal year 1983–84, the Congressional Budget Office calculates, 21 states loaned a total of $114.77 million for 552 projects. This small sum is even less impressive when the two-thirds that Pennsylvania accounts for is taken out. On the other hand, there is clear evidence that direct-loan programs are growing in size. No aggregate data exist on a year-by-year basis, but Bridges' work establishes a baseline. He found that between 1955 and 1963 the 10 states with active loan programs had lent out a total of $56 million to 416 projects (Bridges, 1965a). Since then the number of states offering such assistance has more than doubled. Several programs were only recently established: South Dakota, Missouri, Michigan (all in 1982), and Arkansas (1985) are among newcomers to direct-loan programs. Several states increased their loan pools dramatically in the 1980s. Between 1956 and 1979, for example, the Pennsylvania IDA had loaned a total of $65.4 million. But from 1979 to 1985 it loaned an additional $296.9 million to 623 projects, accelerating the pace of its efforts at the governor's request (Pennsylvania Office of the Governor, 1985, p. 12). In 1983 the Ohio General Assembly doubled the bonding limit of the Department of Development to make more money available for loans (Ohio Office of the Governor, 1983, p. 22). West Virginia, whose direct-loan program began in 1962, committed nearly $18 million in loans to 31 projects in 1984–85, the largest loan outlay in the history of the program (West Virginia Economic Development Authority, 1984–85, p. 2).

States that operate such programs generally require that businesses receiving subsidized loans attempt first to get reasonable financing in the private lending market. Furthermore, most states target their lending to firms that meet certain specifications. Kentucky will provide loans for small firms with high growth potential in the areas of tourism, agriculture, or manufacturing, a strategy more akin to an entrepreneurial demand-based approach than to traditional supply-side subsidies. New Jersey and Pennsylvania are among the states that target aid to firms that locate in communities or rural areas with high unemployment and low income. (These are examples of spatially targeted programs, discussed in the next chapter.) The Pennsylvania program also seeks to loan 25 percent of its funds to "advanced technology" firms, a proportion that has risen since 1979. Ohio aims at businesses already operating in the state; Hawaii and Alaska both offer loans to owners of fishing vessels unable to find conventional financing. Seven states target at least one of their programs at small businesses, and six states maintain direct-loan programs for minority-owned entrepreneurs (Hamilton et al., 1984, pp. 32–36).

Direct loans by a state agency or special authority represent only one of several devices by which subnational governments seek to make inexpensive capital available on favorable terms to private firms. Another arrangement is the business development corporation, first tried in Maine in 1949. These organizations are chartered by their respective states (30 states had them in 1986), but they are capitalized entirely by private investors. Their purpose is to provide debt financing, and in some cases equity financing, usually to high-risk emerging companies, on a long-term basis (U.S. SBA, 1984c, pp. 1–2). The virtue of such corporations is that they allow investors to pool capital and share risks. Under such conditions investors are more willing to provide capital for small business ventures. From the beginning, the bulk of the firms assisted in these programs have been in-state companies (Bridges, 1965a), a requirement enshrined in the by-laws of the more recently established corporations.

Investors, normally financial institutions and other corporations, are attracted by the possibility of profit[8] and by the tax credits that at least 10 states make available for investments in a business development corporation. In Montana, for example, investors can take a 25 percent tax credit on their state income tax liability for investments in Montana Capital Companies; West Virginia and Maine permit a credit equal to 50 percent of the investment.

The size and particular structure of these corporations vary considerably. Indiana's Corporation for Innovation Development, chartered by the state in 1982, went into operation with $10 million to invest in emerging, expanding, and mature businesses located in the state. The Massachusetts Capital Resource Company was capitalized at $100 million over a five-year period beginning in 1977 by a consortium of eight

---

8. Bridges (1965a) reports that, through 1964 at least, "all development corporations have made profits," ranging from a cumulative return on equity of 20 percent to 1 percent.

insurance companies in exchange for a reduction in state taxes. In some states the development corporations augment their lending pool with loans from the U.S. Small Business Administration through its Small Business Investment Companies program. Most business development corporation portfolios are quite small: typical activity involves four or five loans per year and less than $5 million in total loan commitments. The interest of state governments in these arrangements is to encourage financing of new small businesses. As we shall see in Chapter 9 a high rate of business formation is regarded as a key factor in the creation of new jobs. Yet it is just this sort of business venture that conventional lenders regard as too risky to support.

Loan guarantees represent another slightly less common device for lowering the cost of credit. In 1984, 17 states maintained loan guarantee programs, an increase over the 11 with such programs at the beginning of the 1980s. Details of each program vary, but the basic element is a guarantee by the state to a private lender that some portion of a loan to an industrial or commercial firm will be paid back in case of default. With the risk to the private lender reduced, the interest charge on the loan can be lowered. States establish reserve funds at a fraction of the amount guaranteed to cover their potential obligation.

The Rhode Island program provides one example. The state's Industrial Building Authority will guarantee up to 90 percent of the cost of loans for buildings and land and up to 80 percent of equipment and machinery. The maximum commitment to any one project is $5 million. The state charges a small premium each year on the guaranteed portion of the loan (Rhode Island Strategic Development Commission, n.d., p. 651). Indiana has introduced a novel provision in its loan guarantee program: a minimum of 15 new jobs must be created within a year if the guarantee exceeds $100,000 (ibid.). As with the direct-loan programs, the aggregated loan guarantees do not amount to very much money. Congressional Budget Office figures for 11 states in 1983–84 indicate that the states backed only $23 million in loans, of which 42 percent was accounted for by Indiana alone (CBO, 1984, p. 67).

By far the most important economic development tool for generating low-cost capital for private firms has been tax-exempt bond financing, which far outstrips the other three debt-subsidy programs. In 1984 alone state and local governments issued $17.4 billion worth of such bonds (U.S. Congress, 1985b, p. 60). With Idaho's passage in 1982 of enabling legislation permitting the issuance bonds for private businesses, the offer of such subsidies became a universal feature of state and local economic development policy. Because the interest on bonds sold by state or local governments has historically been exempt from federal taxation, purchasers are typically willing to accept a lower interest rate on their investment. This means that the cost of borrowing through tax-exempt securities is lower than it is through commercial banks, where the interest rate must be adjusted upward to compensate the lender for the federal tax liability. Thus, the use of tax-exempt bonds to finance plant and equipment purchases by businesses enables state and local governments to pass on these savings in the cost of capital to the private sector.

The first tax-exempt bonds used for private industry—those issued by Mississippi in 1936—were general obligation bonds, that is, backed by the full faith and credit of the state. If the firm that used bond revenues had gone bankrupt, the taxpayers of Mississippi would have been responsible for paying off the bond-holders. Although several states, particularly Tennessee and Missouri, still permit the use of general obligation bonds for general financing, the practice never became widespread. The far more common device is the industrial revenue bond (IRB), for which the state or local government issuing authority bears no liability. The bonds are backed instead by the revenues and collateral of the beneficiary firm.

Bonds may be issued by a state agency or authority, by local governments, or by both levels of government, depending on the state. In the mid-1980s, 5 states (Alaska, Connecticut, Hawaii, New Jersey, and Rhode Island) prohibited local governments from issuing IRBs, and 11 states allowed both levels of government—state and local—to issue such bonds (Hamilton et al., 1984, p. 84).

Tax-exempt bond financing began as an incentive to draw companies to a particular location with the inducement of low-cost capital. States that came late to such programs adopted revenue bond financing as a defensive measure to keep local business at home. Thus the Wisconsin Industrial Revenue Bond Act of 1969 declares:

> It is found and declared that industries located in this state have been induced to move their operations in whole or in part to, or to expand their operations in, other states. . . . It is therefore the declared policy of this state to promote the right of gainful employment . . . and to preserve and enhance the tax base by authorizing municipalities to acquire industrial buildings and to finance such acquisition through the issuance of revenue bonds. . . .

With every state able to offer such capital subsidies in the 1980s, many public officials came to regard IRBs as most crucial not so much for the purpose of attracting footloose firms but rather for the purpose of encouraging local business expansion (U.S. Congress, Senate, 1985, pp. 130, 141, 154–55). Nevertheless, the wide variance among states in the vigor with which they and their communities actually use tax-exempt bonds for industrial financing and the manipulation of the bonds as bargaining chips in competitions between otherwise comparable locales still endow IRBs with the practical qualities of a classic location inducement. There is another sense as well in which tax-exempt financing may be viewed as a major device of the traditional economic development strategy: such bonds are normally available only to established firms with good credit histories. IRBs are generally not employed to nurture new business formation, a preoccupation of the entrepreneurial state, because bond buyers are wary of purchasing obligations backed only by the future business performance of companies without a track record in the marketplace.

The savings in interest payments on capital for firms with access to tax-exempt financing are considerable. Data compiled by the staff of the Joint Congressional Committee on Taxation show that the ratio of the average municipal bond interest rate to the average corporate (taxable) security interest rate never rose above 0.78 between 1950 and 1982 and fell as low as 0.644 in one year (U.S. Congress, Joint Committee on Taxation, 1983, p. 15).

The growth of tax-exempt financing was relatively slow until the 1970s. When Gilmore conducted his survey of economic development programs in 1957, he found only eight states that authorized the issuance of tax-exempt bonds for the purchase of plants for lease or sale to industrial concerns (1960, p. 57). Five of these states were in the South, and over half the total bond activity was accounted for by Mississippi alone. In light of the opposition at the time from such groups as the Municipal Finance Officers Association, the U.S. Chamber of Commerce, and the American Federation of Labor, as well as the fact that the bonds were so difficult to sell on the open market that most bond dealers would not handle them, the device seemed destined to retain its predominantly regional focus and modest dimensions (ibid., p. 61). Indeed, a decade after Gilmore's survey, only 10 states and their local governments were actively pursuing such financing arrangements (Marlin, 1985, p. 30), although 13 states had laws on the books permitting a state authority to issue such bonds and 39 states had passed enabling legislation to allow cities or counties to do so.

The trend picked up momentum in the 1970s. By 1977, 44 states had

Table 6-6.   Trends in Tax-Exempt Industrial Bond
Financing, 1975–85[a]

	Dollar Value (in billions)	Percent of All Tax-Exempt Bonds
1975	1.3	4.2
1976	1.5	4.3
1977	2.4	5.1
1978	3.6	7.3
1979	7.5	15.5
1980	9.7	17.8
1981	13.3	24.1
1982	14.7	17.3
1983	14.6	15.6
1984	17.4	15.2
1985	11.2[b]	—

Source: U.S. Congress, Joint Committee on Taxation, 1985, pp. 60, 88.

[a]The data pertain to so-called small issue IRBs, defined by congressional legislation in 1968. Details
are discussed in the text.

[b]The dollar volume for 1985 is an estimate.

active programs at the state or local level; and the dollar volume went
from $1.3 billion worth of bonds issued in 1975 to $7.5 billion in 1979.
Table 6-6 shows the year-by-year trend line. Note that although the volume of industrial revenue bond financing continued to rise during the
early 1980s, such bonds as a proportion of all tax exempt bonds began
to fall after 1981. Bonds of this particular type are called small-issue
industrial development or industrial revenue bonds. They compete in the
tax-exempt bond market with general obligation bonds issued by state
and local governments for traditional public purposes, such as school
and road construction, and with pollution-control bonds, various sorts
of housing-mortgage subsidy bonds, and others. One of the concerns of
municipal finance analysts has been that the increasing use of IRBs will
oversaturate the tax-exempt bond market and drive the interest rates up
as various sorts of such bonds compete with one another for a finite
number of buyers (U.S. Congress, Joint Committee on Taxation, 1983,
p. 26). The declining percentages in the right-hand column indicate,
however, that industrial revenue bonds are not the major contributors to
the rise in total tax-exempt bond activity.[9]

---

9. In fact the fastest rate of growth among tax exempts in the 1980s has been in housing bonds. Volume increased from $4.8 billion in 1981 to $20 billion in 1984. Bonds for
docks, airports, and sewage disposal facilities to serve private industry also rose in this

The use of IRBs may be universal, but volume varies sharply from state to state. Pennsylvania witnessed the most activity in the early 1980s, with its local governments issuing an average of $1.58 billion each year from 1980 through 1984. Hawaii issued no IRBs in these years, and Idaho communities issued only $18 million worth in 1984. Other states where there was heavy activity in 1984 included, in order of magnitude, New York, New Jersey, Virginia, and Texas. Although northeastern states accounted for a plurality of all IRB issues in 1980, the South had overtaken the lead by 1982 with 38 percent of the volume (Rhode Island Strategic Development Commission, n.d., p. 649).

From the state and local point of view IRB financing was a nearly ideal program until the 1980s. The entire cost of the program was borne by the federal treasury in the form of foregone tax revenues. Decisions about the volume of bond activity, however, lay entirely with state and local officials. Even the administrative costs incurred by the issuing authority could be recovered through fees levied against the beneficiary firms. IRBs, therefore, offered subnational officials an essentially cost-free inducement to hold out to industry. But Congress eventually became concerned over the mounting size of a federal subsidy over whose volume it had no control.

The first statutory regulation of IRBs was passed in the Revenue Adjustment Act of 1968,[10] an attempt to delineate the purposes for which all sorts of tax-exempt bonds would be permitted. These included financing of housing, sport and convention facilities, airports, docks, parking facilities, sewage and waste disposal plants, as well as private industry. Bonds for this latter purpose were designated as small issues. They were initially limited to issues of no more than $1 million, but almost immediately the limit was raised to $5 million. Their purpose was to allow on a small scale the continued subsidy of industrial-site and plant investments. The $5 million limitation was doubled under the Carter administration in the Revenue Act of 1978, and a provision was included that permitted IRB financing up to $20 million for projects that were funded in part by Urban Development Action Grants. Data on the volume of small-issue IRBs in Table 6-6 suggest that these liberalized

---

period from $2.7 billion to $14 billion (U.S. Congress, Joint Committee on Taxation, 1985, p. 60).

10. The Internal Revenue Service had ruled favorably in 1954 on the use of tax-exempt revenue bonds to provide financing for private business. For a discussion of this ruling and subsequent congressional restrictions, see U.S. Congress, Joint Committee on Taxation, 1983, and Hamilton et al., 1984.

rules of 1978 had a strong effect, for both the dollar amount of bond financing and the ratio of IRBs as a proportion of all tax-exempt issues more than doubled in 1979.

At this point the size of the federal subsidy was becoming substantial. Economists on the staff of the House-Senate Joint Committee on Taxation later projected a revenue loss to the U.S. Treasury due to the tax exemption on IRBs at an annual average of $4.8 billion between 1984 and 1988. The cumulative tax loss over time from bonds issued in any single year is, of course, greater: projections indicated that the IRBs issued in 1984 alone would eventually cost the United States $7.9 billion in foregone taxes (U.S. Congress, Joint Committee on Taxation, 1983, pp. 19–20).[11] With the emergence of the federal deficit as a persistent issue on the Washington political agenda, Congress was no longer willing to countenance the unlimited growth of these tax expenditures.

In the Tax Equity and Fiscal Responsibility Act of 1982 (TEFRA), issuers of IRBs were required to make quarterly information reports to the Internal Revenue Service concerning bonds issued by them. Furthermore, Congress required more stringent public-approval procedures at the local level and banned the use of IRBs to finance facilities whose purpose was automobile sales or service, food or beverage service, or recreation or entertainment. Most important of all, it terminated the tax exemption of all small-issue IRBs, effective at the end of 1986. This so-called sunset provision was modified in 1984, postponing termination of the tax exemption on IRBs used to finance manufacturing facilities until the end of 1988.

Further restrictions were imposed in 1984 in the Deficit Reduction Act of that year. The most important of these is a state volume cap on the issuance of tax-exempt bonds, including not only small-issue IRBs, but also student loan bonds, financing of private health care facilities, and bonds for pollution control, the construction of sewer and solid-waste facilities, water supply and distribution works, parking structures, and stadiums. For 1985 each state was allowed to issue no more than $150 per capita worth of bonds for the various purposes or a total of $200 million per state, whichever was greater. Thirteen states qualified for the $200 million cap. The initial cap was in fact relatively generous: only seven states were exceeding the $150 per capita ceiling when the

---

11. These figures differ from those issued by the same congressional committee staff two years later. By 1985 the loss of revenues for any given year was projected at $2 billion less than had been estimated in 1983 (U.S. Congress, Joint Committee on Taxation, 1985, p. 87).

law went into effect, and three of these were small states covered by the $200 million total. In the Tax Reform Act of 1986 the per capita figure was reduced to $75 to take account of the termination of small-issue IRBs for other than manufacturing facilities. Congress also limited the amount of IRB financing available to any one company and its branches to $40 million in outstanding bonds.

Patterns of administration and usage indicate how IRB financing has been integrated with and adapted to state and local economic development strategies. First of all it is regarded as a predominantly local tool: 80 percent of the volume of IRBs has been issued by municipal and county governments, where, according to TEFRA, new issues must be the subject of a public hearing and must be approved by an elected official or a voter referendum. States establish the basic limitations on such financing, however. About a dozen states require the targeting of IRB projects to high unemployment or distressed areas, for example. Some states may also establish—or permit their local governments to establish—explicit employment goals for firms aided by IRBs. Projects financed by such devices in Massachusetts were required in 1985 to generate at least one new job for each 1000 square feet of new space constructed (U.S. Congress, Senate, 1985, p. 142). The city council of Madison, Wisconsin, requires seven new jobs for each $1 million in IRB financing for new firms moving to the city (City of Madison, 1981). North Carolina requires that at least 10 jobs be created for each $1 million of bonds issued and that the company pay a higher-than-average manufacturing wage for the county (North Carolina Department of Commerce, n.d.-a).

All but 11 states also make specific provisions for the property tax treatment for IRB-financed projects. Since the typical arrangement involves public ownership of the industrial or commercial facility and its lease to the private beneficiaries until the bonds are paid off, the property is technically tax exempt. Nevertheless, at least 30 states require the full payment of property taxes or equivalent payments-in-lieu of taxes. A 1981 survey found that 17 states permit the coupling of IRB financing and full or partial tax abatement (Pollock, 1982).

Industrial revenue bond financing has always aided mainly smaller companies, and it has also been restricted almost entirely to existing companies rather than new ones. Data on early recipients are not widely available, but both Gilmore (1960, p. 58) and Bridges (1965a) claim that the preponderance of firms receiving such assistance have been small operations. Nevertheless, there are early examples of extremely large companies that took advantage of such benefits. In the years before any limitation on the size of any single IRB issue, Harvey Aluminum received $50 million in financing; this company was joined by such national firms as Westinghouse, Olin Mathieson, and Armstrong Tire and Rubber (Bridges, 1965a; Cobb, 1982, pp. 58–59). More systematic data from recent surveys indicate the continuing small business emphasis. In Massachusetts, for example, 68 percent of the firms receiving IRBs between 1978 and 1985 had fewer than 100 employees, and 77 percent had annual sales under $20 million (U.S. Congress, Senate, 1985, p. 146). A national survey conducted by the Council of Industrial Development Bond Issuers found similar patterns: 70 percent had fewer than 100 employees and 80 percent had sales below $20 million per year (ibid., p. 147). A council official argues that the small business focus has intensified in response to congressional restrictions on IRBs: state and local governments have been forced by the congressional cap on such bonds to permit such financing only in the most dynamic job-creating segment of the economy, namely the small business sector (ibid., p. 145).

The emphasis on small business assistance has stimulated the spread of two developments in IRB financing: IRB guarantees and umbrella bonds. At least a dozen states will guarantee IRBs by committing the state, through a reserve fund, to pay the outstanding principal and interest on a bond if the beneficiary firm defaults. One of the oldest such programs has been administered by the Arkansas Industrial Development Commission since 1967. The purpose of the guarantee is to give bonds destined for small companies more market allure. Ordinarily, investors will avoid bonds intended to assist very small firms, because such instruments are backed only by the revenues and collateral of the firm, and small businesses are extremely risky propositions. By guaranteeing such bonds—the Arkansas program is limited to bond issues of $1 million or less—very small businesses are provided access to the tax-exempt market. The record of the program in that state is a good one: through mid-1985 Arkansas had guaranteed 130 issues for a total of $62 million. There had been only six defaults (Patrick, 1985). Nationally, fewer than 1 percent of all IRBs are guaranteed by states (Rhode Island Strategic Development Commission, n.d., p. 650).

Umbrella bonds represent another innovative device to provide tax-exempt financing for small firms whose credit needs might be too small to attract investors. A few states were already using umbrella bonds in 1981 when they were declared illegal by the U.S. Treasury Department. They were, however, formally authorized by Congress in TEFRA in

1982, leading to their adoption by nearly a dozen more states. An umbrella bond is a single tax-exempt bond issue that provides loan funds for several small companies. Small businesses are able to share the modest administrative costs associated with a typical bond issue. For investors the risk of backing very small businesses is divided among several companies. Connecticut has been the most aggressive user of umbrella bonds, accounting for nearly a third of all issues in this category (ibid.).

Labor Incentives

In the study of industrial location decisions, as we shall see in Chapter 8, labor considerations generally emerge as one of the most important factors on the supply-side, particularly for branch plants and mobile firms (Webber, 1984, p. 67). State governments have thus developed an array of tools designed to create a competitive labor climate. Since the most important labor factors—wage rates, labor availability, worker productivity and reliability—are by and large beyond the direct control of the state, labor policy designed to attract industry often operates on the margins of the labor factor, directly affecting only minor cost elements. Efforts to influence key factors, such as wage rates, are indirect and may carry more psychological than economic weight.

Labor policy is pursued on a broad front, along which there are three main concentrations: right-to-work laws, job-training programs, and policies regarding worker compensation and unemployment insurance. Right-to-work laws originated in Florida and Arkansas in 1944 and spread throughout the South in the following decade. By the mid-1980s, 21 states had passed such legislation: besides the solid South, the other strongholds are the central plains states and those just east of the Sierras (see Chart 6-2).

Right-to-work laws prohibit the closed union shop; that is, no worker can be compelled to join a union as a condition of employment, even if his or her co-workers have decided by majority vote to engage in collective bargaining. By removing the obligation to abide by majority preferences—and conversely by encouraging free ridership—right-to-work laws weaken the bargaining power and legitimacy of union organization under such circumstances.

The absence of unions is thought to reduce labor costs in two main ways: not only do nonunionized workers tend to earn less, but they are also less able to complicate and prolong the management process by bargaining for a role for workers in matters ranging from personnel administration to production practices. At least with regard to the first point,

Chart 6-2.   States with Right-to-Work Laws, 1985

West	South	Midwest
Arizona	Alabama	Iowa
Idaho	Arkansas	Kansas
Nevada	Florida	Nebraska
Utah	Georgia	North Dakota
Wyoming	Louisiana	South Dakota
	Mississippi	
	North Carolina	
	South Carolina	
	Tennessee	
	Texas	
	Virginia	

there is much supporting evidence. Figures reported in the *New York Times* based on data gathered by the U.S. Bureau of Labor Statistics show that in 1984 the median weekly wage of unionized workers age 16 and over, controlling for industry, was $405 compared with $303 for nonunion members (*New York Times*, Feb. 8, 1985). Differences were particularly striking in construction, manufacturing, and wholesale and retail trade.

Levels of unionization are substantially lower in right-to-work states than elsewhere. In states with right-to-work laws an average of only 16.2 percent of all nonagricultural workers belonged to unions in 1984 compared with an average of 26.6 percent among the other 30 states.[12] Wages in right-to-work states are also lower: in 1983 the average hourly manufacturing wage for production workers in right-to-work states was $8.10 compared with $9.14 in the other 30 states (calculated from data in U.S. Department of Commerce, 1985, p. 418). These differences are not, of course, entirely attributable to right-to-work laws: regional variations in types of manufacturing, cultural predispositions toward union membership, educational and skill levels of the workforce, its racial composition, and cost of living are also important factors in explaining earnings differences and rates of union membership. But even if right-to-work is not responsible for these variations, it is nevertheless regarded as a good proxy for the docility of a state's workforce. It is noteworthy that the top 16 states in the Grant survey of 1984 all had right-to-work laws on their books.

12. Figures are based on the 20 states that had right-to-work laws prior to 1985. Data for Idaho, which passed such a law in 1985, are not included. Figures for union membership and right-to-work were calculated from data in the *Statistical Abstract of the United States*, 1985 (U.S. Bureau of the Census, 1985b, p. 424).

Right-to-work is nevertheless a blunt instrument and no guarantee that a state will maintain a wage advantage over its competitors. In fact, average hourly manufacturing wages in 10 of the 21 right-to-work states (mainly in the West) now exceed the national average. In 1975 this was true for only 3 of the 17 right-to-work states, so regional wage disparities are likely to continue to diminish as workers migrate to the South and Rocky Mountain states from other regions and as the manufacturing base in those places diversifies. States interested in attracting industry through the offer of labor incentives need complementary policies of more precise application and calculable value. One of these is customized job training.

The Congressional Budget Office reports that 39 states maintain job-training programs (although the *Industrial Development and Site Selection Handbook* survey indicates that all 50 states do so) (CBO, 1984, p. 36). All but 6 of these 39 programs are designed as an incentive to businesses seeking to relocate or expand (National Governors' Association, 1983, p. 17); the remaining minority are intended mainly to serve the needs of the unemployed themselves. As part of an inducement package a state will offer funds to screen and train workers for a particular firm. In 29 of the 39 programs the costs of training are borne entirely by the state; in the remainder they are shared with the firm, which typically contributes any special equipment necessary for the training course.

An example of the way in which a state will make the offer of training and the mechanisms for it is contained in the proposal submitted by the state of Wisconsin to the General Motors Corporation as part of a bid for that firm's new Saturn auto plant. The state proposed to train the new GM workforce at the worksite as well as in the classroom through its 42-unit vocational, technical, and adult-education system (Wisconsin Office of the Governor, 1985). At its full capacity Saturn was expected to employ 6000 production workers, but the state believed that the burden of training this labor force would absorb only 4 percent of the capacity of the vocational training system. The proposal promised customized training in quality control, spectrometry, orthographics, electro-mechanical fuel injection systems, and other specific skills. The state pledged that "the entire resources of the statewide VTAE system will be made available to the Saturn Corporation through assignment of an educational coordinator on-site at the Saturn plant on a permanent basis" (pp. 12–13).

Wisconsin's bid for Saturn was not successful, but state officials there believe that job-training programs do provide the critical edge in many cases. The same customized job-training arrangement was regarded as the key to winning a modern printing plant that weighed sites in Tennessee and Wisconsin. The company chose Wisconsin when the state made a $225,000 training program commitment (Madison *Capital Times,* Apr. 6, 1984). Both the inclusion of customized job training as part of an incentive package and its administration through the state's vocational college system are typical (Levy, 1981, p. 124; see also *New York Times,* Oct. 8, 1985).

If the promise of job training is often made for new or expanding firms, the budget commitment from state to state has nevertheless been relatively small. In 1984 the states spent only $122 million on such programs, training approximately 200,000 workers (CBO, 1984, p. 37). Southern states train the largest number of workers, according to data gathered by the Urban Institute, while at the same time maintaining the lowest cost per trainee (Rhode Island Strategic Development Commission, n.d., pp. 698–99). North Carolina, with a budget of $12 million in the 1983–85 biennium, was one of the best funded customized job-training programs in the country in the mid-1980s (North Carolina Dept. of Commerce, n.d.-b, p. S-16).

State policy regarding unemployment and disability insurance represents a third area for manipulating labor costs. All states require employer payments to an unemployment insurance trust fund and for workers' compensation insurance. Burdens vary from state to state, with the traditional union states of the Northeast and Midwest exacting more from employers than states in the South. In 1983, for example, the annual unemployment insurance tax liability per employee was three times greater in Pennsylvania ($371) than it was in Texas ($119). The average workers' compensation tax as a percentage of payroll in manufacturing varied even more sharply, ranging in 1984 from 4.73 in California to 0.057 in North Dakota (*State Policy Reports,* Sept. 1985, p. 20).

Although business climate surveys consider these quasi-tax burdens important in the determination of rankings, states are constrained in what they can do by economic fluctuations (a number of heavily industrialized states, hurt by the recession in the early 1980s, ran negative balances in their unemployment compensation trust funds in those years) and by the strength of organized labor. Nevertheless, the Grant survey reports that 25 states had lower average workers' compensation insurance rates in 1982 than in 1981 (Alexander Grant and Co., 1982, p. 14). Drastic changes are uncommon, however. Most high-cost states seek in-

stead to adjust rates marginally downward nearer the mean of their regional neighbors. As with tax policy, this is the relevant reference group.

Regulatory Policy: Growth versus the Environment?

States are involved in the regulation of utility rates, minimum wages,
professional licensing, the issuance of corporate securities, banking practices, and a host of other functions that bear on the costs of doing business. But it is the protection of the natural environment and related
limitations on land use that seem most central to debates over the relationship between regulation and economic growth. There is an abiding
suspicion among many in the development community that those states
that make minimal efforts to protect their natural environment from the
ravages of industrial activity are particularly attractive to business firms.
Conversely, these observers worry that particularly stringent laws, such
as New Jersey's model 1983 Environmental Cleanup Responsibility Act,
will discourage industries from locating in the state (Lyne, 1985). And
commonly, in the search for scapegoats to blame for a state's lagging
economic fortunes, the targets are departments of the environment and
natural resources, often responsible for the issuance of plant-siting permits. Certainly the impression that the enforcement of environmental
standards is negotiable in some states reinforces the conviction that the
character of regulatory policy is an important aspect of the state's business climate. It is noteworthy in this regard that after General Motors
announced its decision to build the much sought-after Saturn plant in a
small town in Tennessee, state and company officials began a series of
discussions in which the new facility's impact on the environment was
one of several issues yet to be worked out (*New York Times,* July 31,
1985).

One thing at least is certain in this debate, and that is that regulation
is costly to business. Installing pollution-control equipment, disposing of
hazardous wastes, and cleaning up after industrial accidents are sources
of obvious expense that derive from regulatory policies, but federal environmental laws and the spread of state efforts to control polluters have
reduced interstate differences in such costs. In some respects a greater
problem for many businesses has been the existence in a number of states
of a labyrinthine permit process necessary to begin new construction,
expand a business, or enter the market in the first place. Although individual firms and entrepreneurs disagree about how important the burdens imposed by regulations are in affecting growth prospects or the abil-

ity to begin a business (majority opinion seems to be that regulation is a significant barrier for a small number only), regulatory requirements can be imposing. To start a grocery store in the state of Washington, for example, the proprietor must obtain over two dozen permits. In some states a firm proposing to build a new manufacturing facility may need to acquire more than 60 separate permits and approvals, involving variances for rezoning from agricultural to industrial land use, cancellation of open-space designation, registration of environmental-impact statements, air-emission permits, permission to withdraw water from rivers, dredge and fill permits, waste-disposal plans, and so on. A case study of a major SOHIO project in California in the mid-1970s, never built, found that to obtain the necessary permits the company had to deal with 10 federal agencies, 22 state agencies, and 6 special districts (Duerksen, 1983, p. 28). The costs both of delay and of filling out required forms and record keeping for new and ongoing businesses can obviously be substantial.

In the debate over the relationship between regulation and growth there is a question whether differences actually exist from state to state in the enforcement of environmental regulations and in the character of the regulatory climate. A survey of directors of the air and water quality program in six midwestern states found that most respondents saw little evidence of variable or lax enforcement of environmental regulations. Only 29 percent agreed with the statement that "increased state responsibility in implementation [of federal environmental standards] will result in adjacent states reducing the level of enforcement in order to attract new industries or retain existing ones" (Kraft et al., 1986).

However, an attempt to rank all 50 states according to their effort to protect the natural environment suggests deep differences in regulatory climates. Christopher Duerksen and his associates at the Washington-based Conservation Foundation devised a simple additive scale based on 23 indicators of concern for the environment (Duerksen, 1983, pp. 218–23). These include, for example:

- the voting record of each state's congressional delegation on environmental and energy issues
- existence of a state environmental-impact process
- per capita environmental quality-control expenditures
- existence of wetlands protection
- existence of state law with an environmental review process for the siting of power plants

- existence of a law regulating development in floodplains
- existence of a federally approved solid-waste management plan

States could score a maximum of 63 points. Actual scores range from Minnesota's 47 and California's 46 to Alabama's 10 and Missouri's 14. The low-scoring states—there are six that scored under 20—tended not to require environmental-impact statements from firms proposing new plants, maintained modest hazardous-waste programs or had none at all, had no historic preservation programs, no floodplain restrictions, and so on.

Given these genuine differences in environmental-regulation effort, the next question is whether the regulatory climate serves as a significant location factor for industry. Such laws are seldom cited as major negative considerations in surveys of company officials. *Fortune* magazine, for example, asked executives of the 1000 largest U.S. corporations to pick the decisive location factors for a specific plant, and only 11 percent mentioned environmental laws among the top several considerations (ibid., p. 59). Duerksen treated certain employment growth measures as dependent variables over the 1970–76 and 1976–80 periods and ran these in a regression against the state scores on the environmental effort index. He found that manufacturing employment grew at a slightly higher rate in states with lax effort than in states with a rigorous regulatory climate, but the difference was not statistically significant. Differences between lax and rigorous states' growth of employment in those industries that are particularly pollution-intensive were even less visible. Duerksen concludes: "The right to pollute is not an important determinant. No evidence of a migration of industry from one state to another in search of 'pollution havens' was unearthed . . ." (p. xxi).

If the "right to pollute" is not a particular attraction, there is some evidence that efficient regulatory administration is important to firms. A 1983 University of Cincinnati study concluded that companies do not explicitly search for areas with lower environmental control costs, but they do seem to be attracted to states that offer streamlined permitting procedures (ibid., pp. 60–61).

The movement to reform environmental-permitting administration was pursued most aggressively at first by Georgia. During Jimmy Carter's governorship of the state, all state environmental-permit programs were placed under the direction of the newly created Environmental Protection Division of the Department of Natural Resources. Georgia's "one-stop" permit system allows a business to acquire both state and federal permits through this single agency (Georgia Governor's Office of Planning and Budget, 1984, p. 13). The state then began to run full-page advertisements in national magazines, promoting its new permit system (*Business Week*, Sept. 11, 1978, pp. 55–56). "One-stop" permitting caught on quickly: by the time the Council on State Governments surveyed state development efforts in 1982, 33 states had adopted these streamlined procedures (Reinshuttle, n.d., pp. 10–11).

One other regulatory reform has attracted notice and that is state programs modeled after the federal Regulatory Act of 1980. By 1984, 21 states required all state agencies to perform an impact analysis of all types of proposed and existing regulations to consider their effect on small business. In addition, state agencies are instructed to take measures, including less stringent compliance and reporting requirements and more flexible deadlines, to relieve small businesses of the regulatory burden (U.S. SBA, 1984e, p. 17).

215

CHAPTER 7

Geographically Targeted Policies on the Supply Side

BY and large the benefits of state tax laws, capital subsidies, labor policies, and regulatory streamlining are made available to eligible firms no matter where they are located within a state. Though there are a few exceptions,[1] these so-called business climate policies do not have a particular or selective substate spatial focus. Theirs is what might be called a threshold concern: the object is simply to lure outside firms across the state's doorstep and to keep existing firms within it. But in addition to these various inducements that blanket states geographically, there also exist increasing numbers and a growing use of economic development tools on the supply side designed to distribute firms to particular locales within a state. The major geographically selective devices include site-development programs, financial assistance to firms in distressed areas, tax-increment financing, and state enterprise zones. While programs in each of these categories have in common the intention of stimulating economic development in particular geographical places, they vary considerably in the criteria they use to target those places. All but a few of the site-development programs, for example, seek simply to attract industry to preselected, prepared land parcels chosen for their availability, access to transportation facilities, or underutilization. In contrast each of the other types, as well as several of the site-development arrangements, uses some measure of economic distress as a criterion in selecting geographic areas in which to encourage development.

Policy tools of this latter sort represent one pole of a fundamental

---

1. The major exceptions involve programs in several states that provide financial assistance to firms that locate, expand, or start up in distressed areas. In 1983, 20 states offered some sort of grant, loan, loan guarantee, or interest subsidy on this basis (ACIR, 1985b, p. 90).

Chart 7-1.   Geographically Targeted Financial Assistance, 1983

Alaska	Revolving loan fund for native American fishing in western Alaska
California	Job-training grants and other services for communities experiencing a plant closing
Connecticut	Grants to distressed communities and loans to firms in areas of high unemployment
Illinois	Loans to business in labor-surplus areas
Indiana	Tax abatements for business in blighted areas
Iowa	Tax abatements for business in revitalization areas
Maine	Tax abatements for property development in dilapidated areas
Massachusetts	Tax incentives to business in UDAG-eligible cities
Michigan	Loans to firms in UDAG-eligible cities
Minnesota	Loans to business in distressed areas
Nebraska	Loans to business in blighted areas
New Hampshire	Loans to high-risk business in high-unemployment areas
New Jersey	Loans, grants, loan guarantees, and tax abatements to business in distressed communities
New York	Loans to business in distressed rural areas and public-improvement grants to distressed communities
Ohio	Loans and loan guarantees to business in distressed areas
Oregon	Corporate excise-tax credit for new investments in distressed areas
Pennsylvania	Loans to business in distressed areas
South Carolina	Loans to business in distressed areas
Texas	Loans to projects that expand industry in rural areas
Vermont	Grants to nonprofit development corporations in distressed areas
Wisconsin	Venture capital for business in blighted or impoverished areas

Source: ACIR, 1985a, pp. 119–38.

strategic debate that greatly exercised practitioners in economic development policy during the 1970s. Though the intensity of the dialogue has dissipated to a large degree, the question of whether to emphasize what was then called a balanced-growth approach to development or a targeted approach is still germane, because policy-makers worry about distributing scarce resources in the most effective way.

The term "balanced growth" has a checkered history. It was originally conceived in the late 1960s as the objective of a vigorous federal growth policy involving, among other things, public support for new town development as a way of relieving "excessive population concentrations" in deteriorating urban centers (ACIR, 1968). In the Nixon years it took on a quite different meaning, serving not as the basis for federal intervention but rather as the justification for allowing private market forces to disperse population and industry to the suburbs and countryside (Executive Office of the President, 1972). Market forces, left to themselves, would produce "balance," that is, growth that permitted nonindustrialized nonurban areas to "catch up." The term emerged again at the 1978 White House Conference on Balanced National Growth and

Economic Development as an alternative to the Carter administration's preference for targeting aid to distressed places. In this incarnation balanced growth meant the even-handed distribution of public assistance for development to all communities. As the ACIR observed at the time, assumption of the balanced-growth theme means that "state aid funds for local development tend to be made available to *every* community in the state, rather than limited to the neediest jurisdictions" (ACIR, 1979, p. 4).

For many state officials, particularly those in the legislature, such a strategy often has a great deal more political appeal than any selectivity principle. Inclusiveness avoids favoring one substate region over another. The pursuit of economic development may proceed more or less unencumbered by the downstate-upstate, urban-rural, or upland-lowland animosities that typically cleave state politics. Some proponents of "balanced growth" even go so far as to argue that communities in distress are less likely than economically stable or fiscally healthy places to use development assistance effectively (ACIR, 1981, p. 10). By strengthening the advantaged jurisdictions, it is possible, according to this view, to set in motion a trickle-down process that will ultimately benefit needy places. But this is a minority perspective among opponents of targeted distribution, not only for the extremity of the position but also because it implicitly accepts the targeting distinction between distressed and healthy communities. For the majority of balanced-growth advocates, this distinction is in itself problematic. As the ACIR notes, "State officials appear to shy away from the possibility of offending local sensibilities by designating individual communities as 'declining' or 'distressed,' a delicacy of approach which militates against targeting" (ACIR, 1979, p. 4).

The most important obstacle to the wholesale embrace of an economic distress targeting principle in state economic development, however, is that many business firms simply believe that needy communities or distressed zones within otherwise healthy jurisdictions are particularly unattractive locations for investment. While a firm may be persuaded one way or another to invest in a state if there are well-equipped and commodious sites to consider, no inducement will be sufficient to make it locate within that state in a place characterized by such severe handicaps as above-average unemployment, blighted real estate, rapid population and industrial out-migration, deteriorating infrastructure, declining public services, and above-average poverty.[2] Such typical indicators of dis-

---

2. According to the president of the National Federation of Independent Business, "[D]epressed areas offer companies nothing short of a hostile environment" (*Wall Street Journal,* Mar. 26, 1985, p. 30).

Table 7-1.   Growth of State Programs Targeted to
Economically Distressed Areas, 1980–85

	Number of States Offering Program		
	1980	1983	1985
Targeted grants, loans, loan guarantees, tax incentives	12	21	—
Targeted IRB financing	10	11	—
Tax increment financing	20	31	32
State enterprise zones	0	19	26

Source: ACIR, 1985c, d.

tress (ACIR, 1981, p. 8) may impose costs on a business that cannot be offset by any sort of development incentive.

Nevertheless, despite the persuasiveness for many state officials of the arguments in favor of maintaining a balanced-growth approach to economic development assistance, there has been a distinct growth in the adoption of a limited number of programs that target assistance on the basis of economic distress.[3] (See Table 7-1.)

In 1979, when the ACIR first began to explore the extent to which states targeted aid and program capability to distressed areas, it concluded that targeting on the basis of economic need was in its "formative stage" and could only be described as "modest at best" (ibid., p. 6). No state had yet implemented an enterprise zone program, and only a handful of others, mostly located in the Northeast and Midwest, were experimenting with targeting in other areas. As federal intergovernmental aid began to decline during the Reagan years, however, state and local governments found that the incentives to use their remaining resources in the most effective way had greatly increased. Spending scarce program funds broadly or permitting every community in the state to make tax expenditures against future state revenues became in some places an untenable strategy. It is noteworthy that, of the four categories of targeted programs shown in Table 7-1, the one that has not spread among the states significantly since 1980 is targeted industrial revenue bond financing. This is the only type of program in this table in which neither state nor local governments bear any costs. Thus, at least prior to the federal imposition in 1984 of a cap on IRB issues, the states had no particular

3. Geographically targeted policies can be distinguished from those that target particular social groups (minority or female entrepreneurs, for example) or small businesses.

incentive to limit the use of these programs by selective targeting to the neediest areas.

Industrial and Commercial Site Development

The simplest geographically targeted economic development programs involve public efforts to acquire and improve sites for industrial or commercial use. The object is to offer land to private firms at a reduced cost by subsidizing acquisition, preparation, infrastructure provision, and even landscaping. The location of sites in most programs is determined without reference to the economic condition of the particular locale. Such programs must be distinguished from the various debt-financing arrangements discussed in Chapter 6, which often permit the use of subsidized capital for land acquisition and improvements. The difference is that in site-development programs a public agency selects and acquires particular sites for subsequent disposition to private firms, whereas in the financing programs discussed in the previous chapter, it loans or subsidizes capital with which a firm may purchase or lease land that the firm itself has chosen. Site-development efforts should also be distinguished from location assistance provided by state and city departments of development. At least 48 states either provide catalogues of available industrial sites within their respective borders or seek to match relocating or new firms with appropriate sites.

There are two major types of site-development programs: subsidized industrial parks and land banks. An industrial park is a planned tract, zoned and subdivided for industrial use by what the Dartmouth College Conference on Industrial Parks has called "a community of industries" (Flores y Garcia, 1969, p. 9). Such parks or districts offer prepared sites served by transportation facilities and utilities; some offer buildings as well. A land bank, whose holdings may be used either to create an industrial park or for individual sites, involves the acquisition by a public agency of undeveloped land to hold in reserve for future private development (Kamm, 1970, pp. 6–7). Site-development programs that seek sites in distressed areas are a small subset of these more general efforts.

Most industrial parks, whose origins in the United States date back to the Clearing Industrial District in Chicago in 1899, are developed entirely by private interests (often railroads in the early days) without public subsidies. The principal public entities involved in industrial park development are cities and counties, and such arrangements exist in every state. State participation is uncommon: only a dozen states maintained industrial park programs in 1985. All but four of the states limited their involvement to planning and development, relinquishing ownership and operation of the parks to the private sector or to municipalities. Typical examples include Connecticut's program of grants to municipalities to help develop and support 52 publicly owned industrial parks across the state (Connecticut Dept. of Economic Development, 1985, p. 9). And under the Maryland Industrial Land Act, that state provides loans to local governments for the purchase of land, the planning of industrial parks, and the construction of shell buildings (New York Legislative Commission, 1985, p. 38). New Hampshire, Rhode Island, New Jersey, and Hawaii actually operate industrial parks.

New Hampshire was the first state to create an Industrial Park Authority, and it did so in 1955 as a companion to its pioneering direct-loan program. New Hampshire's action was a classic example of response to perceived market failure: the decision to establish state industrial parks came after private park developers had spurned New Hampshire as a rural backwater unlikely to attract industry (Gilmore, 1960, p. 50).

Parks developed and operated by local governments actually appeared in the 1940s. Some involved turning federal wartime facilities into industrial districts under municipal control (as in Chico, California), and others were developed as components of an urban renewal project. Indeed, one of the very first urban renewal projects undertaken in the country, under the sponsorship of the Norfolk Redevelopment and Housing Authority, involved the demolition of 123 acres of slum housing, of which 35 acres were turned into an industrial park. Another early urban renewal project, this one in Chicago, became the first such federally assisted redevelopment undertaking in which essentially all the salable land made available through clearance was earmarked for industrial use (Boley, 1962, pp. 51, 183, 189).

Unfortunately, no current data exist on how many of the nation's approximately 5800 industrial parks are publicly sponsored or owned. Neither the National Association of Industrial and Office Parks nor the Urban Land Institute collects such data. In the mid-1960s an Urban Land Institute survey of 259 parks found that just over 20 percent had been developed with public assistance (Flores y Garcia, 1969, p. 71), but these figures provide no basis for making current estimates. Interjurisdictional competition for investment has intensified greatly since that time, and it is likely that a substantial portion of the roughly 7 percent annual growth in the number of industrial parks (O'Connor, 1985) is fueled by public subsidies. One consequence of this rapid growth, incidentally, is a very high vacancy rate in such parks: nationally, 59 percent of the land in such reserves is without tenants (*State Policy Reports,* Jan. 1985, p. 4).

There are several advantages of public development that result in potential cost savings for tenant firms. Publicly owned industrial parks do not levy property taxes on their lessees (though they may require payments-in-lieu of taxes), and the initial cost of roads, utility lines, land grading, and other facilities is borne mainly by the public entity, which typically finances these developments by general obligation bonds, a one-time appropriation, or with federal EDA or CDBG monies. Other advantages to private firms include saving land-assembly costs, which the state or local government may have to bear in eminent domain settlements.

Industrial parks represent geographically targeted efforts, but they seldom involve attempts to induce industry to locate in systematically defined areas of high distress. It is true that some urban industrial parks were created in "blighted areas," as defined by the standards of the old federal urban renewal program; and some parks, such as those in the early New Hampshire program, were designed to attract industry to remote locations lacking industrial employment. Only three state programs, however, target assistance for industrial parks to urban areas, and three others target "blighted" areas (ACIR, 1985c, p. 81). Most industrial park programs, in short, simply represent attempts to attract businesses to particular jurisdictions in situations where distress, even measured in such terms as "blight," is not at issue.

Land bank programs are another means of assembling parcels of land suitable for private industrial development. These are far less common than public industrial parks. Perhaps no more than half a dozen genuine land banks are in operation, though, again, no organization collects data on the matter.[4] Since these programs almost always involve the acquisition of undeveloped land, purchase on the open market rather than eminent domain condemnation is the typical mode of operation. The idea of local land banks as a tool to limit and direct urban growth was promoted for more than 30 years by various federal bodies. The first proposal for such an arrangement appeared in the 1937 report of the National Resources Committee entitled *Our Cities: Their Role in the National Economy.* It was suggested again, this time in some detail, in 1968 by the National Commission on Urban Problems (the so-called Douglas Commission, after Senator Paul Douglas, its chairman) (Kamm,

---

4. Interviews with officials of the Urban Land Institute and the National Council for Economic Development turned up no data.

1970, p. 2, 60). During the early 1970s, when interest in the possibility of a national urban growth policy was at its peak, there were additional calls from federal task forces and national advisory groups (e.g., the President's Council on Recreation and Natural Beauty, the National Urban Coalition) for state enactment of land bank programs (Francis, 1975).

For the cities that actually pioneered land banking, however, economic development rather than urban planning has always been paramount. The oldest municipal land bank is located in Philadelphia. Begun in the late 1950s, it was designed explicitly to provide a reserve of improved industrial sites to compete with suburban locations that were attracting jobs and tax revenues from the city (Hamilton et al., 1984, p. 13). Much of the land that ultimately went into the land bank was already publicly owned, though undeveloped; other parcels were in private hands but were unimproved or inaccessible for industrial purposes.

To acquire, develop, and market this land, the city sold general obligation bonds to establish a capital revolving fund, and it set up the nonprofit Philadelphia Industrial Development Corporation (PIDC) as the titleholder to the land. PIDC is responsible for further land acquisition through negotiated purchases; it does not have powers of eminent domain. Land is then prepared by the city's redevelopment authority for industrial use and offered for sale by the PIDC at competitive market prices. However, PIDC also administers a program of land-purchase subsidies available to businesses that agree to meet certain employment goals. These subsidies can reduce the per acre cost of land by as much as 90 percent. By 1984 the city had over 1300 acres of improved sites in its land bank inventory, and over 250 firms were located on land purchased from the land bank.

The second oldest municipal land bank, begun in 1963, is run by the city of Milwaukee. It is smaller in scale than the Philadelphia bank, involving in 1984 about 950 improved acres, of which approximately 40 percent is occupied. The program is administered by the Department of City Development, and it is financed by the proceeds of land sales that go into a revolving fund initially established by a city council appropriation. Land is offered at the cost of acquisition (the city buys land; it has never used eminent domain proceedings for the land bank) plus improvements. Since the land bank fund carries no holding costs and pays no real estate taxes, the sites are competitively priced (Hamilton et al., 1984, pp. 14–15; *Nation's Business,* Oct. 1972, pp. 67–68). According to the Milwaukee Department of City Development, firms located on bank sites have generated 2400 jobs and more than $2.5 million annually in property taxes for the city. The total cost of the bank to the city at the point of this reckoning was $5.4 million (Milwaukee Department of City Development, 1979, p. 4).

The only state land bank program for economic development purposes was established by the Massachusetts state legislature in 1975. Originally designed to help communities turn surplus state and federal property to private use, it was expanded in 1980 to permit the acquisition of blighted developed land. The Massachusetts land bank will sell to developers who propose industrial, commercial, or residential projects in deteriorating neighborhoods and in downtown commercial districts.

As with industrial parks, land banks represent an effort to attract firms to particular geographic sites that, left undeveloped, might otherwise be rejected by industrial investors as too costly to acquire or develop, too inconvenient, or too encumbered by the problems that plague central-city locations. Although the extant banks employ "blight" as one criterion for the acquisition of land, the targeting of distressed areas for development is not a primary purpose of such programs.

Targeted Financial Assistance for Capital and Infrastructure

Programs that make economic distress a condition of economic development financial assistance for capital investment take two basic forms. The more common is to make tax abatements and various capital subsidies—loans, loan guarantees, IRB financing—available only to firms that locate in areas of high unemployment or areas characterized by blight.[5] A second form is to make public works grants to local governments on the basis of economic distress as a way of helping the neediest jurisdictions to attract industry. Most of these targeted financial aid programs are found in the Northeast and Midwest. Many of the states that offer incentives targeted to distressed areas also make more general assistance available too.

A few examples of targeted programs illustrate their nature. The Pennsylvania Industrial Development Authority, whose loan program was discussed in the previous chapter, will make loans only to firms in "critical economic areas," determined by unemployment level. In 1986 the PIDA listed 75 eligible jurisdictions, most of them counties, in which

---

5. Indiana's 1973 tax abatement law, for example, limits this device to "blighted" areas, that is, those "undesirable for normal development and occupancy because of lack of development, cessation of growth, deterioration of infrastructure, age, obsolescence, substandard buildings, or other factors which have impaired values or prevented normal development or use of property" (quoted in ACIR, 1985a, p. 122).

firms qualified for assistance (Pennsylvania Industrial Development Authority, 1986). New Jersey targets its extensive loan guarantee and limited direct-loan programs more broadly to firms in 122 cities and townships that meet one of several distress criteria: high population density, more than 250 children on Aid to Families with Dependent Children, below-average per capita property value, or high unemployment, among others (New Jersey Economic Development Authority, 1985). Massachusetts permits every one of its 351 towns and cities to apply for Massachusetts Community Development Action Grants, but these must be spent for publicly owned infrastructure improvements in "economically distressed areas" within those municipalities in order to attract industry (ACIR, 1985c, p. 84). Of the 21 states that maintained targeted financial assistance or tax incentives in 1983, only one state had conducted any sort of program evaluation through that year, and that single study (in Massachusetts) focused only on internal management concerns (ibid., p. 91).

In the absence of careful studies of these programs, two observations can nevertheless be made. Targeted financial aid represents an approach in which rigorous distress criteria are employed to distribute available funds. Even when there are many eligible jurisdictions, as in New Jersey and Massachusetts, efforts are made to allocate resources to firms locating in the most distressed communities or in distressed neighborhoods. The second point is that the number of states offering such assistance on the basis of economic need has greatly increased in the 1980s, evincing a growing state concern with focusing resources for development.

Tax Increment Financing

That land banking for economic development is not widely used in the United States, despite the success of such programs in Canada and Sweden, is due in part to the ease with which such acquisitions are open to challenge in the courts when eminent domain powers are used. Courts have generally held that such seizure of property must be for immediate and specific public purposes rather than held for future use (Kamm, 1970; Francis, 1975). For land acquired through purchase on the open market and for surplus public property improved at public expense, the uncertainty of demand for industrial sites in older central cities has been sufficient to discourage many cities from making the initial investment in a revolving land acquisition and development fund. The few cases for which employment and tax revenue data exist suggest that the payoffs for cities are not inconsequential, and for private firms a land subsidy, which reduces the cost of a nondepreciable asset, should in theory constitute an attractive location incentive. But a number of states have chosen a different device to provide land subsidies in blighted areas—tax increment financing—which offers a greater degree of geographical flexibility and perhaps a higher probability of initial investment recovery than land banking.

State and local officials have increasingly come to regard tax increment financing, or TIF, as a highly efficient, versatile, and cost-effective development tool (ACIR, 1985c, p. 184–93). Yet of all the spatially targeted economic development policy devices that originate at the subnational level, TIF is encumbered by both its perceived complexity and its controversial reliance on interlocal subsidies. Tax increment financing is poorly understood, and the lack of comprehension is no mere public failure to assimilate the technicalities of this financing arrangement. It extends even to many of the local officials who oversee TIF projects. In 1981 the Wisconsin legislature's Audit Committee conducted a survey of local officials to see how this widely used device was working in the state. To the surprise of the committee the survey revealed that "representatives of [all] municipalities had misconceptions and uncertainties about their own tax districts [i.e., TIF districts]. Representatives in seven municipalities that created districts before 1980 could not answer basic questions about their tax districts or refer us to anyone in the municipality who could" (quoted in *Milwaukee Journal,* Feb. 4, 1981, Accent Section, p. 4).

The controversy that attends tax increment financing goes beyond the usual debates in the economic development policy domain over whether investment would take place without public assistance. It comes to rest instead on the fact that TIF requires diversion to the municipality of new property tax revenues that, under normal circumstances, would belong to other local jurisdictions, such as the county, school district, and special districts, that share the same tax base as the town or city. Simply put, nonmunicipal local governments must to some degree subsidize development that occurs within a municipality. One study found that in Wisconsin 70.3 percent of the eligible costs of development in TIF districts were in effect borne by nonmunicipal governments as a result of foregoing their share of the tax increment from new investment in real property (Huddleston, 1984). There are, of course, mitigating features of TIF that enable state and local officials to justify these interlocal subsidies, but there is a pervasive sense that tax increment financing arrangements permit municipalities to take advantage of other governments in some way.

Tax increment financing allows a municipality to earmark all of the anticipated *increased* property tax revenue that will result from a new development project to back bonds that go to help finance certain elements of that project. It works in the following way: the municipal government, usually by city council action, designates an area within its borders as "blighted" and suitable for development involving new construction or rehabilitation. Of all the various meanings of "economic distress," blight is perhaps the broadest, thus making tax increment financing the most geographically versatile of the tools targeted to areas in economic straits. Dilapidated real estate is, of course, one indicator of blight, but areas with sound buildings may also qualify as blighted if the real estate is obsolescent or underutilized. Even vacant areas may qualify in some states if they have been unable to attract development for some specified period.

Once a city designates an area a tax increment financing district, it calculates the value of the existing property within the borders of the district and the resulting property tax revenues that derive from it. This sum is frozen; it constitutes the baseline on which the tax increment is calculated. The new project, it is assumed, will increase the aggregate value of property within the district, thereby generating additional tax revenues. The amount of this increment is estimated before the development project begins, and that sum is used to back tax increment bonds issued by the municipality.

Property taxes are typically shared among several overlying jurisdictions, of which the school district usually takes the largest share, and this division of the baseline property tax remains unaffected by the establishment of the TIF district. Under a tax increment financing arrangement, however, the municipality is permitted to reserve for itself the entire tax increment for a designated period of years to pay off the bonds. When those bonds are fully paid off, the TIF district is dissolved, and the overlying governments begin to receive their full share of the new taxes generated by the development project.

Among the virtues of TIF is that the revenues received by overlying local jurisdictions do not diminish: while the TIF bonds are being paid off, those governments continue to receive the same revenues they would have collected before the TIF district was established. Eventually, these jurisdictions are able to share in the benefits generated by the new development. Although some states permit the period of bond indebtedness to run as long as 30 years, municipal officials seek to pay off the TIF bonds in much shorter periods of time in order to appease the overlying jurisdictions temporarily denied a share of increased taxes.

Interlocal subsidies in TIF arrangements are justified on the grounds that individual municipalities ordinarily tend to bear the costs of development alone, although overlying tax jurisdictions benefit from the increased tax base (Huddleston, 1984). Nevertheless, the use of TIF districts rose so quickly in some states that school districts and counties found themselves denied access to the fruits of growth on a substantial portion of property in their tax base. As a consequence, several states now require that new TIF districts be approved by a fiscal review committee consisting of representatives of each affected tax jurisdiction. California, the state in which TIF is most widely used, began to require this procedure in 1977. Wisconsin, the second heaviest user of TIF, made such reviews mandatory in 1983. Wisconsin also limits the value of property within all TIF districts in a community to no more than 5 percent of the total assessed valuation. Both states also protect school districts from deleterious effects of TIF. California law guarantees school districts an amount of revenue annually equal to a state-established revenue limit. The state then provides the difference between what school districts raise locally through the property tax and the amount of the revenue limit. Thus, freezing a portion of a school district's tax base may affect the source but not the amount of its revenue. Wisconsin provides less state aid normally to school districts in which the value of property rises. Under TIF as it was initially instituted in the state, school districts where TIF was used found that state school aid declined as property values rose from the new development, but the school district could not capture its share of the tax increment. Now Wisconsin provides supplemental school aid to such districts to alleviate this problem.

Tax increment financing was begun in California in 1952, but it did not spread to other states in any significant degree until the early 1970s, when it came to be seen as a way to replace the federal urban renewal program, then in the process of closing down (Hegg, 1973). Urban renewal greatly influenced TIF administration. Like in the federal program TIF is generally limited to blighted areas, and consistent with the downtown redevelopment emphasis of many local urban renewal agencies, most TIF projects in the early days involved commercial revitalization. A study commissioned for the California state treasurer in 1976 found in fact that only 21 of 226 projects surveyed involved the development of industrial areas (Sherrod, 1978). Similarly, in Wisconsin, which authorized the use of TIF in 1975, commercial redevelopment projects predominated during the first three years of the program (Wisconsin Dept. of Development, 1985b, p. 17).

By the early 1980s the preparation of industrial sites had assumed nearly equal if not greater importance in some states. In California, for example, through 1983, 42 percent of the total square footage of TIF projects that did not involve housing was devoted to industrial space (Ralph Andersen and Associates, 1984, p. 60), and in Wisconsin industrial projects and mixed use (industrial, commercial, and housing) far outstripped commercial development. Of the 327 projects in Wisconsin initiated through 1984, 16 percent were devoted solely to commercial development, whereas 38 percent were industrial and 42 percent were mixed use (Wisconsin Department of Development, 1985b, p. 19).

TIF bonds may be used to finance land acquisition and clearance, the construction of various public facilities, and landscaping. They are not used to finance construction of private buildings or the purchase of equipment. The savings for any particular firm can be considerable, however. The following case illustrates the purposes, applications, and value of this supply-side inducement.

When Rayovac, a battery maker, was sold by its parent holding company in 1982, the new owners announced that they would consolidate their scattered operations in the Madison, Wisconsin, area into a single world headquarters complex. Immediately, they began to receive unsolicited offers from around the country to relocate. These offers invariably included land and improvement subsidies. As a defensive measure, the city of Madison decided to establish a TIF district on some unused land[6] zoned for industrial use "intended as an inducement for Rayovac to commit capital investment to a headquarters facility in the City of Madison" (City of Madison, Dept. of Planning and Development, n.d., p. 4).

The city calculated that the cost of acquiring the land and preparing it for an industrial tenant would come to $3.7 million. A private firm setting out to purchase and prepare such a site would have to contemplate a cost at least as great. But under the TIF arrangement Rayovac was asked to pay only $530,350. For this price it received a 15–20-acre site, graded for construction and eventually landscaped, fully equipped with storm and sanitary sewers, sidewalks, streets, curbs, gutters, access roads to nearby highways, and a large parking lot. The city proposed to finance the project by selling $3.2 million worth of TIF bonds, for which over $6 million of the tax increment accruing from the planned construction of the headquarters complex was necessary to pay off the bond prin-

---

6. The major—and in most states the only—criterion for designating an area as a tax increment financing district is that it must be blighted. Wisconsin, however, also permits areas to be designated TIF districts if they have been vacant for a specified number of years and are suitable for industrial development.

cipal plus interest. As city economic development planners noted: "The proceeds available from the land writedown will be reinvested in the project. . . . The use of tax incremental financing . . . will allow the company to direct its more limited capital to production facilities, product development, marketing and employment, all of which are intended to enhance its position in the marketplace and continue its recent growth" (ibid.).

The ability of local governments to finance land acquisition and public infrastructure to support development with bonds backed by future tax gains has made TIF an increasingly attractive tool. From modest use by California, Minnesota, and Oregon in the 1970s, the device had spread by 1985 to 32 different states, and several others were contemplating passage of enabling legislation. In California alone the number of municipalities and counties with TIF districts rose from 113 in 1975 to 221 in 1984; the number of individual districts rose from 229 to 467; and the revenue generated by what California calls tax allocation bonds backed by the tax increment increased from $50 million to $378 million, a considerable development fund. In the mid-1970s less that 1 percent of the total assessed value in the California counties using TIF was frozen in TIF districts, but by 1984 the proportion had risen to 3.6 percent (Ralph Andersen and Associates, 1984, pp. 64–65, 79). What is particularly notable about this explosive growth in the use of TIF in California is that the device had been available for over 20 years before it was so heavily exploited.

In Wisconsin the mid-1970s constitute the baseline: TIF enabling legislation was passed only in 1975. By 1976, 0.3 percent of the aggregate value of property in Wisconsin municipalities was contained in newly established TIF districts, a figure that rose at roughly the same pace as that in California to 3.3 by 1983 (Wisconsin Department of Development, 1985b, p. 9). Over 200 Wisconsin communities, large and small, were administering TIF projects in the mid-1980s. The Minnesota experience is virtually identical: property in TIF districts constituted 0.2 percent of the value of all real estate in 1975 but rose to 2.2 percent in 1985 (Minnesota Dept. of Revenue, 1985, pp. 29, 51).

Evaluations of the development impacts of tax increment financing are rare, as the Advisory Commission on Intergovernmental Relations observes (ACIR, 1985c, p. 189). Data from Minnesota and Wisconsin indicate, not surprisingly, that the increase in property values within TIF districts tends to occur at a significantly faster rate than on property located in other parts of the community (Hulkonen, 1974; Wisconsin

Dept. of Development, 1985b, p. 24). And both California and Wisconsin publish data on job creation within TIF districts that suggest major impacts. Those monitoring TIF in California estimate that nearly 25,000 jobs have been generated annually in such redevelopment projects, including direct construction employment, jobs in the businesses that locate in TIF areas, and secondary employment associated with TIF development (Ralph Andersen and Associates, 1984, p. 72). Wisconsin job estimates are less dramatic: the state's Department of Development attributes a total of 24,000 new jobs to TIF development between 1976 and 1984. Thirty-six percent of the TIF districts, however, produced no new jobs at all (Wisconsin Dept. of Development, 1985b, p. 26).

From the point of view of local development officials, TIF has much to recommend it. This financing device is entirely locally derived; it seldom requires voter approval to sell TIF bonds; it permits interlocal subsidies of construction of substantial public facilities in TIF districts; and it does not diminish the property tax revenues flowing into the general municipal accounts. By relieving private firms of much or all of the cost of public facilities, such as paved roads and storm sewers, normally assessed to property owners, and by providing generous land write-downs on sites that might be difficult to assemble on the open market, TIF offers a valuable location incentive in selected cases. There was certainly little reason to doubt the Rayovac Corporation's assertion that, without the TIF subsidies, the consolidated headquarters project in Madison would not have gone forth. As construction began on the new complex, it would have been difficult to persuade local officials that the TIF benefits were not decisive.

State Enterprise Zones

No recent economic development innovation better illustrates the prairie-fire spread of what state officials and politicians consider a good idea than enterprise zones. When the notion was first broached in domestic politics in 1979, the intention was for Washington to implement it as a limited federal experiment to demonstrate the generative powers of deregulation on the entrepreneurial spirit. But congressional concerns, heightened by doubts about the wisdom of suspending hard-won labor and environmental protections and by visions of the resulting surge of sweatshop operations, prevented its passage as a national program. At the state level, emphasis shifted almost immediately from deregulation to coordinated tax incentives as the key to enterprise zones, and the idea quickly emerged as a major initiative promoted by Democrats and Republicans alike in every region of the country.

The first state enterprise zone bill was passed by the Illinois legislature in 1979, but it was vetoed by the governor. Two years later, however, the Connecticut legislature passed a similar program, and it was placed in operation in October 1982. By the end of 1985, 26 states had enacted enterprise zone programs, of which all but three had been implemented, and bills had been introduced in several other states. By one count there were 1281 zones in over 500 local jurisdictions (New York Legislative Commission, 1985, p. 4).

Aside from the broader interstate competitive forces at work in the economic development field, at least two additional factors fueled the shift from federal to state initiative in the enterprise zone program. One is that the federal version of the program was simply too limited. Seventy-five zones were to be established all around the country as a demonstration program. There was concern that such a limited number would place nondesignated depressed areas at a disadvantage. In addition, federal policy-makers were reluctant to begin a program based on tax expenditures in a period in which the federal deficit was rising sharply. In contrast, state fiscal fortunes looked brighter in the early 1980s, even among the struggling industrial states around the Great Lakes. At the state level the tax incentives involved in an enterprise zone seemed increasingly affordable.

State enterprise zones represent the solidification and refinement of targeting as an acceptable approach to state and urban economic development. Distress standards in enterprise zone programs tend to be more rigorous than the vague blight criterion used in tax increment financing. Thus, zone designation tends to be more selective. Of the 26 states with enterprise zone programs in 1985, 20 limited the number of zones that could be established, and most of these required a competitive rather than automatic designation process to select eligible contenders. At least 19 states used either unemployment or a poverty measure as distress standards, and several states used population loss as well.[7] The spread of enterprise zones does not mean that states are abandoning their traditional practice of offering incentives to firms wherever they choose to locate within state borders, but they are making careful targeting an important complementary strategy.

Enterprise zones at the state level are also important because they represent a bridge between the traditional supply-side approaches to

---

7. Connecticut's targeting criteria are typical: to qualify for a zone, a city must have a census tract with 25 percent of its population dependent on welfare or earning incomes below the official poverty line. Alternatively, a city qualifies if one census tract exhibits an unemployment rate 200 percent higher than the state average.

stimulating economic development and the strategies of the entrepreneurial state. On the one hand enterprise zones are geographical areas whose presumed locational attraction to firms is based on the standard inducements states and communities have historically offered: lower costs of doing business through tax incentives, job-creation grants, and in some cases cheap capital and land. No effort is typically made by zone administrators to target growth industries, to take investment risks with public funds, or to market goods produced in the zones, all key activities of the entrepreneurial state. On the other hand, however, the emphasis in enterprise zones is not on encouraging existing businesses to relocate to the zones or to expand there but rather on creating the conditions that foster new business formation. The zones are settings for the state in its midwife role. To this extent, then, the enterprise zone may be regarded more as a contribution to the state's *entrepreneurial climate* than to its *business climate*. A reasonable distinction may be made between these: entrepreneurial climate, the concern of the state as entrepreneur, refers to conditions that encourage new business formation, the risk-taking that leads to capital creation. Business climate, as we have seen, refers to those elements that attract mobile firms and capital seeking a business site. Former New York governor Hugh Carey expressed the idea behind the notion of an entrepreneurial climate in a typical way:

The key to sustained economic progress is the continued development of new business enterprise. The range of new business enterprise is as broad and as diverse as the economy itself. . . . What all of these [new business people] have in common is a willingness to invest, to innovate, to take risks. The State cannot by itself create this entrepreneurial spirit—but it can help create the conditions that allow it to flourish. (Carey, 1981, p. 301)

The point of enterprise zones is to remove the barriers to private entrepreneurial impulses, such as disincentives to invest contained in the tax codes or regulatory structure or shortages of capital or a skilled workforce.

The Illinois enterprise zone bill introduced (but vetoed) in 1979 focused on the putative regulatory impediments to new business formation. It proposed to eliminate the minimum wage, institute right-to-work provisions within the zones, temper health and safety codes, and reduce zoning restrictions (Mier and Gelzer, 1982). Subsequent federal proposals contained similar provisions, along with a variety of tax incentives. The emphasis on deregulation began to weaken, however, in the face of opposition from organized labor and environmental and civil rights groups.

In addition, evidence began to appear that indicated that regulation per se was not the burden to small business that some enterprise zone proponents had assumed. A survey conducted by the National Federation of Independent Business is illustrative (reported in U.S. Congress, House, 1983, pp. 59–65). A sample of small-business owners was asked, presumably in an open-ended survey, to rank, in order of severity, the problems they faced in trying to do business. Seventy-two problems were mentioned. "Unreasonable government regulation" ranked 14th, "state and local paperwork" ranked 20th, "finding out about regulatory requirements" was 27th, and "cost of government required equipment or procedures" ranked 39th. In short, regulatory matters as a group fell into the middle range of small entrepreneur concerns, well behind interest rates, the cost of liability and property insurance, utility rates, getting qualified workers, and various federal taxes.

Another survey, this one of people registered with a Small Business Devolopment Center in Wisconsin who chose *not* to initiate a business venture, found that "too many rules and regulations" was cited by only 7 percent of the respondents as a reason for deciding not to go into business. This placed regulation in a tie for fifth place among the 13 barriers to business entry cited in the survey (Wisconsin Strategic Development Commission, 1985, p. 63).

The Connecticut enterprise zone program, the first in the country to be implemented, abandoned the deregulation strategy and focused instead entirely on an assortment of tax incentives. As Chart 7-2 shows,[8] that was the common pattern by 1985: most enterprise zone programs offered tax incentives or job-creation tax credits. Only nine states offered any form of regulatory relief, and most of these provisions involved the modification of zoning restrictions. Subsequent federal proposals, incidentally, followed the states' suit by deemphasizing regulatory relief. For example, President Reagan's 1985 version of the enterprise zone program would have allowed state and local governments to request relief for their zones from certain federal regulations, unless such relief had directly violated a requirement imposed by statute. Thus, the minimum wage, environmental pollution laws, and civil rights guarantees, among others, would be protected.

---

8. Details on the states' respective enterprise zone incentives are drawn from descriptive materials sent from each state. However, a useful summary of programs in several states—Florida, Kentucky, Illinois, Louisiana, Missouri, Connecticut, Pennsylvania, and Maryland—is contained in a report by the New York Legislative Commission on Public-Private Cooperation (1985).

Chart 7-2. State Enterprise Zone Incentives, 1985

	AL[a]	AR	CA	CT	DE	FL	GA	IL	IN	KS	KY	LA	MD	MI	MN	MO	NV	NJ	OH	OK	OR	PA	RI	TN	TX	VA
State tax incentives																										
Investment tax credit		•	•																	•						
Sales tax exemption for construction materials, machinery	•		•	•				•		•	•	•		•	•	•		•		•					•	•
Dividend deduction from state income tax					•			•																		
Exemption of interest from loans to zone businesses			•					•			•													•		
Unemployment compensation offset																		•								•
Corporate income tax deduction or exemption				•	•	•			•							•				•			•			•
New-job tax credits or grants	•	•	•	•	•	•			•	•	•	•	•	•	•	•		•					•			
Other					•	•			•		•				•											
Local tax incentives																										
Property tax abatement	•			•		•		•	•	•	•		•		•	•			•		•		•	•		•
Local sales tax exemption												•														
Other							•	•		•	•															
Capital programs																										
Low-interest loans, venture capital				•	•			•			•[b]		•					•		•		•		•		•[b]
Targeted IRBs				•	•																					
Other										•																
Miscellaneous																										
State/local regulatory relief		•	•					•		•						•	•	•			•			•	•	
Shopsteading								•										•								
Job-training grants				•	•			•								•		•		•		•		•		
Public service improvements		•	•																			•		•		•
Tax credit for zone employees									•																	

[a] Alabama does not have a state program. Two local zones were established by 1986.
[b] Provision of venture capital is a local option only.

Various tax incentives, both state and local, remain at the heart of most enterprise zone programs. The most popular types are the new-job credits or grants and local property tax abatements. Details of job credits vary from state to state, but the basic notion is the same: a set-dollar tax credit is available to a firm for each qualifying person it hires to fill an existing or new job. For example, Kansas provides a $350 tax credit for each Kansas resident hired. Minnesota offers firms an annual $3000 tax credit for every new employee hired, while Maryland provides a credit worth $3000 over a three-year period for new, disadvantaged employees. Property tax abatements for zone businesses may be more generous or of longer duration than those available to real estate investors in other parts of the city, but they take the same basic form as standard abatements.

The third most common incentive is exemption from the state sales tax on materials purchased for new construction. Three states permit local governments to exempt zone firms from local sales taxes as well. Many of the pioneering zone programs also provide for corporate income tax exemptions, though the idea was not picked up by most of the later states. Missouri, for example, will exempt half the business income of a zone enterprise from state income tax, and Connecticut offers a similar deduction for 10 years, provided that 30 percent of the firm's employees are zone residents or eligible for federal Job Training Partnership Act benefits.

Among the inducements that do not rely on tax exemptions and credits, 10 programs offer special access to low-cost capital, 9 provide some regulatory relief, and 7 mandate special public service improvements to enterprise zones, primarily infrastructure improvements.

As a number of critics have pointed out, exemptions from or credits against corporate income liability presuppose profits subject to tax (Sternlieb, 1981, p. 54; Walton, 1982). A sales tax exemption on construction materials presumes that the entrepreneur has been able to raise the necessary funds to finance new building. And a property tax abatement is useful to property owners rather than businesses that must rent space. These sorts of incentives are more useful to established and reasonably successful business enterprises than to the sorts of start-up operations enterprise zones are intended to encourage. To remedy this problem, several state enterprise zone programs provide venture capital or favorable loans to new businesses in addition to or instead of tax incentives. The Pennsylvania program, for example, does not offer tax incentives. Its focus is on the provision of low-cost capital to firms that cannot obtain financing on the private market. Firms are eligible for Pennsylvania Industrial Development Authority loans and for money in a special revolving fund capitalized by state appropriations and federal Small Communities Block Grants. Connecticut led the way in including a venture capital pool, set at $1.5 million, and a small business loan fund in its enterprise zone program; several other states—Maryland and Illinois, for example—followed. It is the provision of start-up and early-stage capital that most distinguishes these state enterprise zones from the federal versions promoted in Washington in the early 1980s.

Some early evaluations of state enterprise zones have offered generally positive assessments, although all of them recognize the extremely modest dimensions of these programs. Late in 1983 a private research organization in Washington, the Sabre Foundation, surveyed enterprise zone officials in the nine states that had programs in operation at that time. A majority of the zones had existed for less than a year. Sabre researchers tallied local reports of jobs created, saved, and planned (these totaled over 20,000) and aggregated the total value of new investment in the zones ($450 million). The report, though it acknowledged the small numbers of jobs relative to the national workforce, nevertheless concluded that "job creation is particularly dramatic in light of both the short time that most of the zones have been in operation. . . . It is particularly significant that the long-term unemployed appear to have received a large proportion of the positions . . ." (quoted in New York Legislative Commission, 1985, p. 3).

A more sophisticated effort to explore the impact of enterprise zones on the rate of employment growth was conducted by Cambridge Systematics under contract to the U.S. Small Business Administration (Jones et al., 1985). The authors studied eight enterprise zones, each in a different state, that had been in operation for at least two years. Rates of employment change in the enterprise zones were compared with rates of change in the city in which the zone is located and with the area of the zone in the two years prior to its designation. As Table 7-2 shows, all but two zones showed faster rates of employment growth or lower rates of loss than the cities as a whole. Only two zones—the same two in St. Louis and Norwalk—lost jobs after their establishment as special areas.

This record is tempered to some degree by the actual figures involved in some cases. The extraordinary performance in Baltimore is based on an increase in the zone from 167 jobs to 439 in the two years, for example. A separate evaluation of the Maryland enterprise zone program by two economists, one of whom was the state's enterprise zone administrator, put this performance in perspective:

Table 7-2. Comparative Rates of Employment Change: Enterprise Zones versus the City, 1980–84

Enterprise Zone Location	Enterprise Zone Alone, 1982–84 (%)	Entire City, 1982–84 (%)	Enterprise Zones Area Prior to Zone Designation, 1980–82 (%)
Baltimore, MD	163.0	9.0	28
Dayton, OH	−1.0	−10.4	−11
Decatur, IL	1.7	−14.0	−16
Louisville, KY	2.3	−6.9	−22
Norwalk, CT	−8.6	40.0	5
Philadelphia, PA	0.1	−4.6	−1
St. Louis, MO	−1.7	−1.0	5
Topeka, KS	11.2	−1.9	9

Source: Calculated from data in Jones et al., 1985.

The relatively modest absolute levels of new private investment and employment which have occurred in the initial two years of zone operation in Maryland strongly suggest that the differential impact of the zones on economic activity is as yet unobservable, if it exists at all. For example, the total number of new employees in all [Maryland] zones in 1983 and 1984 was 1964 persons. (Funkhouser and Wise, 1985, p. 7)

In absolute terms the largest employment increase observed by Cambridge Systematics occurred in the Louisville zone, amounting to 1062 jobs. The Topeka zone's gain of 11.2 percent translates into 643 additional jobs. The Decatur zone, which encompasses 61 percent of all jobs in that city, expanded by 450 jobs. Other states report similarly small job results: Minnesota, for example, tallied 116 new jobs in the first year of its zone operation, although 517 businesses had been awarded tax credits at a cost to the state of $1.4 million (Minnesota Dept. of Energy and Economic Development, 1985b). Illinois reported 3555 new jobs created in 21 zones with a combined total population of 668,000 between 1983 and 1985 (Illinois Dept. of Commerce and Community Affairs, 1985). All states report much higher numbers of "retained jobs" in the zones, but as Jones and her Cambridge Systematics colleagues note, "There is no way of knowing how many of the jobs 'retained' were ever really in threat of being lost" (1985, p. 11–19).

Another thorough evaluation of enterprise zones was conducted by the state of Connecticut two and a half years after the program had gone into operation (Connecticut Dept. of Economic Development, 1985). Despite a generally positive tone, the report offers finally a curiously mixed picture that raises questions about the power of enterprise zone incentives: on the one hand the six Connecticut zones exhibited high levels of economic activity measured in terms of jobs created, businesses started, vacant buildings recycled, and investments made. On the other hand the number of zone firms that actually used the various incentives or that were even eligible for them is surprisingly low. Much activity appears to have been stimulated less by the inducements offered by the state than by the psychological stimulus created by the excitement of a new program.

The Connecticut enterprise zones provide a battery of different incentives: low-interest loans and venture capital, a 50 percent reduction in corporate business taxes for 10 years, property tax abatements, a sales tax exemption on replacement parts for manufacturing machinery, a grant of $1000 for manufacturing firms for each new job created, and a special job-training program for zone workers. In the first 30 months of the program 309 businesses started or expanded in the six zones, investing over $113 million. More than 4300 new jobs were created, and a nearly equal number were reported saved. Three-quarters of the new jobs and the same proportion of new investment was in commercial, service, or retail concerns. Almost 300 empty or "underutilized" buildings were rehabilitated and returned to active use in the zones, some of which had been idle for years (ibid., p. 5).

Leaving aside the problem that the true rate of growth in the Connecticut zones cannot be gauged because there are no comparisons with growth rates anywhere outside the zones, several features of this apparent activity necessarily moderate any positive judgments about the program. First of all most of the businesses that started or expanded in the zones—242 out of the total 309—were commercial, retail, or service concerns. Grocery stores, a firm that retrieves and distributes bibliographical information in medical research, several market research firms, a wholesale bakery, an automobile dealership, firms offering various engineering services, and warehouses are examples. These nonmanufacturing businesses were responsible for generating 77 percent of all the new jobs in the six zones. Jobs in this broad service sector, as we saw in Chapter 4, tend either to be lower-paid, less stable, and more poorly sheltered than manufacturing jobs or they tend to be high-skilled jobs whose requirements cannot be met by people with minimal education and training skills, that is, by typical residents of distressed urban areas. In fact, although several Connecticut zone incentives are contingent upon a firm's employment of zone residents, only 68 new jobs (out of 4304) appear to have gone to such people. The Connecticut report concludes that

the data gathered by the Department [of Economic Development] suggest that there may not be a clear match between jobs generated by private investment and the Zones' unemployed residents, contrary to the hopes and expectations of residents and local and state officials. While Zone residents have likely gained positions in the retail sector, there is concern that the more high-tech career-oriented positions are not being filled by Zone residents. (p. 10).

Among the industrial enterprises that located in the Connecticut zones, the record of job generation has not been impressive. Over 70 percent of the 3431 industrial jobs were retained rather than new positions. Furthermore, the preponderance of manufacturing operations were small in size: 9 firms accounted for 2665 of the total jobs, while 58 firms accounted for the remaining 766. A majority of these businesses had fewer than nine employes, and among the new ones, most had four or fewer workers. These tiny firms are subject to all of the risks and disabilities that plague the small business sector in general: difficulty in gaining access to capital, undercapitalization, inadequate resources to provide good worker benefits, limited marketing and distribution skills and networks, and a high failure rate. No data exist on the survival rate of Connecticut zone businesses, but the prognosis for these concerns and others like them in other states' programs is not good.

The paucity of manufacturing firms in the Connecticut zones is a puzzle to state development officials because most of the incentives are limited in fact to manufacturing enterprises. But a more troubling aspect of this program from the point of view of its designers is the low rate of use of the incentives offered. Much activity seems to have occurred without benefit of any or many incentives. Usage rates reported in the 1985 evaluation for certain of the incentives are incomplete, since there is a lag between application for the benefit and certification by the state or local tax administrators. Nevertheless, the evaluation found the following patterns:

- Of the 242 eligible commercial and retail projects, only 38 had received or even applied for a graduated deferral of any increase in property taxes due to new construction or rehabilitation. The report concludes: "Participation in the seven-year tax abatement program is lower than expected" (p. 14).
- Only 14 of 43 manufacturing firms reported in the first 18 months that they had applied for or received the 80 percent tax abatement.

Most could not meet the requirement that they have a five-year renewable lease.

- Only 9 of 67 manufacturing firms had applied for the $1000 new-job incentive grants. "It would appear," the report notes, "that participation in the program should be higher since there are 67 industrial projects" (p. 13).
- Only 34 businesses had applied for low-interest loans; only 5 of the manufacturing businesses had requested sales tax exemptions for replacement manufacturing parts; and only 3 businesses had sought to take part in the special job-training program for zone workers.

Plausible explanations exist for some of the nonparticipation: many firms could not show that 30 percent of their new employees were zone residents, which made the firms ineligible to claim some of the benefits. Many were lessees and could not take advantage of the property tax abatements; most firms were in services and could not therefore capitalize on the manufacturing incentives. But there is a clear sense in the evaluation that incentives were for the most part tangential to the investment decision made by zone firms, and that what drove much economic activity was essentially a psychological dynamic of the same sort that impels certain neutral observers to want to join someone else's celebration or picnic. Here is the conclusion of the Connecticut report:

A certain psychology of investment was generated on a large scale here. The fact that the Connecticut Zones were neighborhoods frequently kindles a kind of confidence in the Zones across the financial community, across layers of government, and across residents of the Zones. . . . In varying degrees, city officials, businessmen and residents attached a fair amount of prestige to their own Zone areas. This prestige generated a kind of psychological boost encouraging the investments that occurred. (p. 14)

A study by the U.S. Department of Housing and Urban Development of 10 enterprise zones in nine different states found similar results: "The zone designation process appears to produce a positive and tangible impact on business investments; however, zone designation itself may have more impact than the specific package of incentives offered" (Battle and Underhill, 1986).

If this is an accurate description of what is happening in state enterprise zones, then it recalls the point that Michael Kieschnick, former director of the state of California Office of Economic Policy, once made in regard to the broader tax incentives that states offer: such inducements, he speculated, may be primarily important in a symbolic sense. Except for a very few firms on the margins, the various tax benefits do not seem to have major economic significance, either the general incentives or those offered in the enterprise zones only. But their *existence* constitutes an important and inexpensive way to signal entrepreneurs and investors of a state's and community's interest in development (Kieschnick, 1983, p. 182). Enterprise zones, considered in this light, represent the distillation of such interest. As the focus of particular official interest, such areas may serve as particularly attractive magnets to certain classes of investors and business people, irrespective of the actual value of the associated inducements.

CHAPTER 8

The Determinants of Economic Growth and Industrial Location Decisions: A Critique of Supply-Side Strategies

THE rationale for supply-side investment incentives grew out of the assumptions of classical location theory in urban economics. Location theory, in seeking to understand the spatial distribution of economic activity, begins from the premise that firms will tend to observe a rationality principle that dictates locating at those sites where costs of production are minimized in proportion to revenues (Watkins, 1980; Webber, 1984). Profitability at alternative locations, as Wasylenko puts it, depends on a vector of market and cost characteristics that vary from place to place (Wasylenko, 1985). Although early location theory focused almost exclusively on finding the point for any given producer where the costs of transporting raw materials to the point of manufacture and of shipping finished goods to market were minimized, later efforts reflected the realization that the costs of other factors—mainly labor, land, capital, energy, and taxes—might also vary geographically. Optimal siting now became an exceedingly complex multivariate problem. Furthermore, the logic of the least-cost principle that was seen to guide location choices was extended to the analysis of investors not necessarily seeking to site a new plant but simply searching for those locales where the return on capital invested might be maximized because of site-specific characteristics.

Industrial revenue bonds, specific tax concessions, land write-downs, capital subsidies, low tax rates, and so on, all represent efforts by states to establish a comparative cost advantage. They are designed to reduce the costs of production and to increase the rate of return on a given investment. Almost as soon as states and local governments began to employ such inducements, analysts began to wonder if, in the search for optimal sites, investors and firms were actually decisively influenced by these inducements or whether they considered them essentially marginal in the face of differences in more significant factors over whose cost governments have little or no control. In short, the question has been whether or not supply-side inducements are important enough in the calculus of investment to make a difference in drawing firms and capital to a particular place.

The question has been of such substantial importance for public policy and at the same time so intractably difficult to answer that it has generated an enormous but finally inconclusive literature. It may nevertheless be shown, however, that the distribution of scholarly opinion has shifted only recently from what was once a nearly unanimous conviction that such policies had virtually no effect on investment behavior to a more balanced division in which a considerable group now argues that there are discernible effects. Although there are, perhaps, several lessons to draw from this body of research taken in the aggregate, the issue is not likely to be resolved definitively one way or the other. As one economist conceded in apparent frustration, "Perhaps one of the most important conclusions to be drawn is that location of investment is a complex process in which intangible factors and historic accident figure prominently" (Browne, 1980).

Several issues establish the framework for the exploration of the question of whether or not state and local supply-side policies influence investment behavior. There is first of all a need to distinguish between two forms of investment behavior, each of which serves as a dependent variable in various investigations of the impact of economic development policies. One is the more generic phenomenon, which I shall refer to simply as economic growth. This reflects aggregate investment decisions by firms and individuals. It is typically measured in this literature by employment growth, increases in capital stock, or more indirectly, income growth. The second level of investment behavior, business-location decisions, is a particular subset of the first and has been the dominant object of interest in studies of policy influence. Location decisions involve the siting of the facilities of entirely new companies, of branch plants of existing companies, or of firms that relocate from one place to another. Development incentives were designed initially to influence location decisions,[1] but it became apparent almost immediately that they might be employed also to encourage the expansion of local companies, that is, to foster economic growth by eliciting additional investment by existing resident firms and capitalists. Bridges reports, for example, that in fact the bulk of state loans to industry in the earliest years of these programs went to firms already located within the state (Bridges, 1965a).

The distinction between the two aspects of growth—the general and the particular—is important for understanding the issue of policy impacts: the weight of evidence indicates that taxes and incentives are not very important in decisively influencing particular location choices, but they are often associated with higher rates of employment and income growth, suggesting that such policies are conducive to more expansive investment behavior by resident firms.

Another issue has to do with specifying the geographical scope of the competition for investment fueled by the offer of inducements or the maintenance of favorable tax rates. A long-established broad rule of thumb is that, as the geographical orbit within which competing jurisdictions lie diminishes in size, supply-side economic development subsidies become more influential with respect to business-location decisions.[2]

The choice of a site proceeds in several stages. In the first stage of the model search a broad regional comparison is made in which market factors, which may be understood in terms mainly of transportation costs, and the cost of other major inputs, such as labor and energy, dominate the decision process. As the Advisory Commission on Intergovernmental Relations points out, "Regional differences in construction, energy, and labor costs are generally too large to be outweighed by any differences in state and local taxes or fiscal incentives" (ACIR, 1981, p. 32). Cornia, Testa, and Stocker illustrate this point dramatically: in 1972, business paid about $20 in employee compensation for every dollar paid in state

---

1. James Cobb (1982) writes that "Mississippi's controversial BAWI plan contributed to an atmosphere of heightened interstate competition for new industry after World War II as the use of municipal industrial development bonds spread across the South and much of the rest of the nation. The search for the 'edge' needed to win industries away from competing states and communities also reconfirmed the use of tax exemptions and inspired the formation of local organizations committed to providing manufacturers with the capital needed to erect buildings and begin their operations" (p. 35). Later he observes that "the subsidy plans also created ill feelings not only in competing states but among established local manufacturers who wondered why newcomers were so much more appreciated and favored than they were" (p. 40).

2. McLaughlin and Robock (1949) were among the earliest analysts convinced that this was a valid rule of thumb. "[S]pecial inducements," they wrote, "play a successful role only if the primary attraction exists in an area" (p. 119).

and local business taxes. Thus, "a mere 2 percent difference in wages could offset as much as a 40 percent difference in taxes" (Cornia et al., 1978, p. 2).

The choice of a region serves to hold certain major factor costs more or less constant. For example, transportation charges from points of production to national markets will tend to cluster by region. Natural gas and electricity costs also exhibit regional patterns: the four most expensive states in one ranking were all from New England, while the energy-producing states of the Southwest and Rocky Mountain regions all had cheaper power and fuel (Alexander Grant and Co., 1982). And despite signs of regional convergence in labor costs, interstate similarities in wages will still tend to be greater within regions than among them. Average hourly manufacturing wages in every state in the South, with the exception of Louisiana, fell below 90 percent of the national average in the early 1980s. The same low-wage pattern prevailed in all the New England states, save Connecticut. In contrast, wages 110 percent of the national average have been the norm in most of the midwestern states around the Great Lakes (Browne, 1980, p. 41).

The second stage of the process of deciding business location occurs after firm officials have chosen a region. Then the question becomes one of comparing neighboring states and substate sites, the latter often within the same metropolitan area. At the subregional level differences in taxes and incentives that might be overwhelmed and rendered insignificant in regional comparisons of major factor costs seem to take on greater importance in investment decisions.[3] While most students of industrial location acknowledge this, there is some disagreement about the magnitude of influence. Schmenner, for example, tends to minimize government incentive policies, even in substate location choices, arguing that "taxes and financial inducements seem to be, at best, tie-breakers acting between otherwise equal towns or sites" (1982, p. 51).

But an analysis by Mark Schneider suggests that taxes, if not incentives, are more than simply tie-breakers in intrametropolitan location decisions. Schneider examines growth in the number of retail, wholesale,

3. Bartik and his associates (1986) sought to assess the economic rationality of the General Motors decision to locate its Saturn plant in Tennessee. The model initially examines the Saturn decision as if only access to markets mattered. The optimal site in the entire country by this criterion—that is, the one that achieves the lowest transportation costs consistent with serving the highest concentration of demand—was somewhere between Indianapolis and Terre Haute, Indiana. When the researchers added labor costs, particularly for suppliers (Saturn operations fall under union contract) and state and local taxes, the optimal site shifts to Nashville, Tennessee, not far from the actual choice.

and manufacturing establishments in 800 suburbs in 44 SMSAs (Schneider, 1985). These are by no means equivalent communities differentiated only by taxes, for they exhibit, among other things, wide variations in socioeconomic composition and in levels of expenditures for public services and infrastructure. Nevertheless, Schneider finds that the most important independent variable in the regression model is the property tax rate, which bears a negative relationship to business growth. Manufacturing firms in particular, he concludes, "shun high tax suburbs" (p. 599).

In short, any discussion of the influence of supply-side inducements on investment decisions must specify the scope of the geographical stage on which the decision is played out. Influence may be nil when a site search is conducted nationally but critical within a metropolitan area. In practical policy terms this lesson suggests the importance for jurisdictions of adjusting incentives and tax levels in relation to those of intraregional competitors rather than seeking to match inducements offered beyond the region. The latter strategy is likely to cost much and induce little.

A third issue has to do with sorting out the multitude of factors that influence investment behavior and establishing the ways in which factor costs are set as a way of determining which factors government can manipulate. Most of the work in this area has involved specifying the factors that affect business location decisions in particular.

Aside from purely idiosyncratic personal preferences of business owners or chief executives, there are four broad categories that seem to encompass most of the specific factors that influence business-location decisions. Each of these categories represents a set of factors whose "prices" vary from place to place. Although different firms may assign different priorities to specific location factors, it is safe to say that certain of these categories are generally more significant influences on location decisions than others. It is also the case that the prices of some of these factors are more susceptible than others to government manipulation. These four categories of factors are arrayed from left to right across the top of Chart 8-1, from those whose costs are most easily influenced by government (*processing costs*) to those whose costs are least easily influenced (*contextual elements*).

On the left-hand side of the table are listed three major price-setting determinants. Governments set or influence factor prices through *selective mitigation* and *general policies*. *Situational determinants* of factor prices, most of which have to do with supply and demand characteristics

Chart 8-1. Factors That Influence Business Location and Their Price-setting Determinants

	Categories of Factors			
Price-setting Determinants	Processing Costs • Taxes • Regulation	Primary Inputs • Land • Labor • Capital • Energy	Market Access • Transportation costs	Contextual Elements • Services • Amenities • Geography
Selective mitigation	Tax concessions Regulatory relief	Land write-downs Customized job training Capital subsidies	Customized transportation infrastructure	
General policies	General tax policies Regulations	Zoning laws Right-to-work laws Utility regulation	Transportation infrastructure maintenance and modernization	Taxing and spending policies
Situational determinants	Population size and affluence Industrial base	Real estate market Labor market Capital market Energy supply and demand	Transportation market Population density and growth Income growth Location	Climate Topography Political culture

of the market setting, are essentially beyond the influence of state and local governments. Specific examples of each category of factors are listed in the lower right-hand half of the four category boxes; specific examples of price-setting determinants are listed in the rows beneath the four category boxes. Let us examine the chart more closely.

Processing costs have mainly to do with taxes, fees, and regulatory requirements. These costs, which vary from place to place, are associated with business activities but are incidental to the actual production of goods and services. The initial prices of these factors are determined directly by state and local governments through their general tax and regulatory policies, although government must be sensitive to situational parameters in raising revenues. Thus, the establishment of a corporate income tax at a particular rate or the passage of a general industrial exemption from sales taxes on new equipment establishes a structure of tax "prices" to which all firms are subject. Certain of these prices, however, may be mitigated for some firms on a selective basis. For example, while most firms must pay property taxes, certain qualifying firms may be granted tax abatements. Regulatory relief or the waiver of various fees (e.g., for building permits or water and sewer hookups) available only to firms locating in certain enterprise zones are other examples of selective mitigation of processing factor costs.

Primary inputs include those factors essential to the actual production of goods and services. The classic factors are land, labor, and capital. We may add energy. The prices of each of these are initially established by the market situation. Market prices are a function to a large degree of a combination of local supply factors such as the availability of open land and energy resources, the size and skills of the labor pool, and the resources of the local financial community, as well as the presence of competitors for these factors. Various larger national and international supply and demand forces also influence local prices of these factors.

State and local governments may influence the prices that firms face on the local market for these factors through both selective mitigation and general policies. Land write-downs and IRB financing are typical examples of selective mitigation of land and capital costs, while rezoning prime land for industrial use is an example of general policy. Although no state or municipality offers long-term direct wage subsidies, one-time cash payments or tax credits for each new hire are offered under many state enterprise zone programs, and most states subsidize job training. More commonly, state governments employ general policies to reduce labor costs, for example, through vocational education systems to train more productive workers and right-to-work laws to dampen union strength.

Another category of primary inputs includes energy and water. It is clear that the prices of these vary by location. Governments may influence their prices by regulating utility rates and through investments in infrastructure, such as water supply and treatment systems.

Market access pertains to the costs a firm bears in gaining access to its customers and in assembling its raw materials or components for production. Market access is largely a function of transportation costs. Freight rates and passenger fares on common carriers that traveling sales personnel and executives must pay at any particular geographical location are established primarily by the transportation market, particularly since federal deregulation of the trucking and airline industries. State and local governments may influence certain transportation costs through general policies that provide a dense network of modern transportation facilities, such as good roads, ports, public terminals and warehouses, and airports.

Governments also try to mitigate the transportation costs of firms on a selective basis through the customized design of public facilities. Thus, for example, a state may agree to construct an interchange near an industrial site to provide quick access to an interstate highway as part of a package of inducements offered to a particular firm. Or industrial park officials may promise to tailor their internal road system and rail sidings to the specifications of a prospective industrial tenant.

Finally, there are contextual considerations that play an important role in influencing the location of investment. These have to do mainly with the availability of various public and private services and amenities, as well as climate and topography. Government can provide high-quality parks, schools, recreational facilities, and even health care through its general taxing and spending decisions. It can do little about the basic nature of topography and climate, both of which may have some bearing on industrial location choices, other than mitigate the harsh effects of the latter on athletic events (through the construction of a domed stadium, for example) or exploit scenic aspects of the former (say, through construction of riverside parks).

Let us now turn to a consideration of the crucial question of whether government is able to influence costs of factors to an extent that makes an important difference in choosing an industrial site or in making another sort of investment decision.

The Determinants of Investment Behavior: Market and Labor Factors

The great, often primary, importance of market access, by which McLaughlin and Robock first explained much of the movement of firms to the postwar South (1949, p. 122), has been reaffirmed in countless subsequent studies of plant-location determinants. Kieschnick's review of 24 surveys and interview studies of firms in all parts of the country, all conducted prior to 1964, found that access to the market consistently ranked as the most important consideration in choosing a site (Kieschnick, 1983, pp. 205–6). Moriarty reports on a similar survey of interview studies done prior to 1974 that found access to markets to be the most important location factor in 20 of the 23 investigations, which themselves were based on an aggregate of more than 17,000 responses (Moriarty, 1980, p. 96).

Kieschnick's own, more recent, survey (1979–80) of 1800 firms found a similar emphasis on market considerations, though the precise rank of such factors varied slightly according to the sort of investment in question. New firms seeking a location ranked access to customers, access to growing markets, and access to raw materials as the first, second, and fourth most important location factors. (The third most important factor here was the personal preferences of the owners or chief executive officers, which usually hinged on contextual considerations.) Access to the market was the second most important criterion for established firms contemplating expansion at a larger site, while maintaining the current labor force ranked first. The siting of branch plants seemed determined first by labor supply and the absence of unions; market factors were cited as the fourth and fifth most important considerations (Kieschnick, 1983, pp. 249–54).

Finally, Roger Schmenner, whose separate location studies cover firms in the Cincinnati metropolitan area, the New England region, and a national sample drawn from the *Fortune* 500, finds that market concerns are of prime importance. Although he warns that "a definitive assessment of the impact of any one factor on industry location is an extraordinarily difficult methodological task," he is nevertheless willing on the basis of his interviews and survey instruments to conclude that proximity to markets and labor climate are the critical factors in the choice of region (1982, pp. 143, 154).

A favorable labor climate appears to be less a function of low wages than of the absence of union activity. As Bluestone and Harrison observe,

"The business community fairly widely admits now that it consciously chooses locations in order to avoid unionization whenever possible" (1982, p. 165). Bartik's logit analysis (1985) of *Fortune* 500 decisions for siting of branch plants provides strong support for this claim. If the level of unionization among workers in a state were *not* taken into account in deciding where to locate plants, "the regional shares of new branch plants would change dramatically. . . ." The South's share of plant openings in the 1972–78 period would drop from 46 percent to 35 percent, and the share in the Northeastern census region would rise from 38 percent to 48 percent. Percentage unionized emerges as the single most important factor in Bartik's examination.

Schmenner offers various pieces of survey evidence to support the notion that firms prefer locales where unions are weak or absent. For example, he found that of 40 new plants where managers evinced a "desire to escape an unproductive labor situation at an existing plant," 27 (68 percent) opened in right-to-work states. And among all new plants located in right-to-work states, Schmenner found that 88 percent of their managers indicated that remaining nonunionized was of critical importance to them (Schmenner, 1982, p. 157).

That the search for sites where strong unions are not likely to flourish is more than an effort simply to reduce payroll costs is suggested by the finding in one of Schmenner's several studies that "favorable labor climate" ranked as the first or second most frequently mentioned among 18 factors (p. 51). Lynn Browne's analysis (1980) of manufacturing investment by state found that, although low wages were the single most important explanatory variable in the 1960s, labor supply, the existence of a right-to-work law, and the absence of strike activity were considerably more important in the 1970s. Where unions do exist, pliancy is considered a mitigating factor, as the following site evaluation of a Vermont county suggests:

Labor relations in Chittenden County are conditioned by the fact that a large part of the working force consists of rural people with a strong tradition of self-reliance. In the recent nationwide strike of one of the community's chief employers, the local union voted against the strike and over 90 percent of the workers crossed the picket lines. Many firms in the area are not unionized and those that are find union leadership reasonable in negotiations. City and state law enforcement agencies have a record of firmness in maintaining law and order in the few disputes that have taken place. (Stedman, 1961, p. 75)

Interest in locating in right-to-work states, especially those in the South, continues despite evidence of regional wage convergence in recent decades. Based on comparative location studies done over time by his firm, Charles Harding of the Fantus Company argues that "today, many well-managed Northern plants could achieve only modest reductions in labor costs by relocating in the South" (Harding, 1984, p. 111).[4] Nevertheless, interregional growth differences that favor the Sun Belt persist.

Labor climate may also be a function for some firms of the availability of appropriately skilled labor or the existence of good subsidized job-training programs. Kieschnick found in a survey of firms that access to an ample supply of trained workers was ranked as a location determinant above the cost of that labor (Kieschnick, 1983, pp. 222–23). Indeed, Premus shows that for high-tech firms in particular the presence of a well-trained labor pool may be the most critical factor of all (Premus, 1982).

Job training programs, in contrast, are not particularly important. Schmenner found that they are scarcely even used by most firms that make new investments: only 6 percent of the *Fortune* 500 firms that had moved used such assistance, as did 30 percent of the newly opened plants (Schmenner, 1982, p. 55).

To summarize, the weight of evidence from more than three decades of research on the determinants of plant-location indicates that markets and the labor situation are the two most important considerations in explaining plant-location decisions. What is important for economic development purposes is that most of the elements in both these categories—population size and migration patterns, freight rates, purchasing power, labor productivity, wages—are relatively immune to manipulation by subnational governments seeking to create comparative location advantages.

General Tax Policy

Taxes typically constitute the largest processing cost that firms bear. They also constitute the single factor cost most directly determined by public policy. For these reasons, government efforts to encourage plant location and expansive investment through manipulation of the tax structure represent the most common device to influence investment behavior. The key question, of course, is whether tax differentials among jurisdictions, generated by differences in types of taxes and tax rates, are significant enough to investors to influence their location choices or the

---

4. Harding cites studies done in the 1960s for two appliance manufacturing firms that indicated a southern site would result in payroll savings of between 35 and 45 percent over northern locations. But studies done for similar firms in the 1980s showed only a 12–25 percent savings (p. 112).

Chart 8-2.   Selected Studies of the Influence of State and Local Taxes on
Investment Behavior

Statistical Studies	
Little or No Influence on Economic Growth	Some or Great Influence on Economic Growth
Thompson and Mattila (1959)	Hodge (1978)
Sack (1965)	Genetski and Chin (1978; revised 1983)
Struyk (1967)	Vedder (1982)
Romans and Subrahmanyam (1979)	Wasylenko (1985)
Browne (1980)	Papke (1985)
Plaut and Pluta (1983)[a]	Bartik (1985)
Steinnes (1984)	
McHone (1984)	

Survey Studies	
Little or No Influence on Plant-Location Decisions	Some or Great Influence on Plant-Location Decisions
Morgan (1964)[b]	Premus (1982)
Stafford (1974)	
Schmenner (1982)	

[a]Plaut and Pluta have found that high tax effort is negatively related to growth but tax rate is not.

[b]Morgan reviews 17 survey studies: 13 showed taxes were insignificant, 3 found modest effects, 1 found that tax considerations were important.

magnitude of their outlays. An extensive literature has addressed the problem. (See Chart 8-2 for selected studies and their basic findings.)

The orthodox position on this issue has been that taxes simply represent too small a portion of business costs either to influence plant-location decisions or to affect more general investment patterns, except perhaps in intrametropolitan competitions. The best method of calculating business tax burdens is itself a matter of some disagreement, but any way it is done produces relatively small proportions compared, say, with labor costs. Bluestone and Harrison, among others, figure tax burden as a percentage of the total sales receipts of a firm. Combined corporate income and business property taxes amounted on average to only 1.69 percent of total sales in 1975. Regional variations were minor: the range was from 2.46 in New England to 0.96 percent in the East South Central states (Alabama, Mississippi, Kentucky, and Tennessee) (Bluestone and Harrison, 1982, p. 186).

William Wheaton (1984) has argued, however, that the resources businesses have from which to pay taxes are much narrower than total gross sales. He proposes instead that the proper way to measure tax burden is to calculate total taxes as a proportion of net income or profits. Using 1977 data on seven different state and local taxes levied on businesses (not including severance taxes and fees and licenses), Wheaton finds that taxes constituted an average of 7.65 percent of net business income. The state-by-state range varied from Wyoming's 3.1 percent to Michigan's 12.6 percent. Regional averages exhibited less variation. East South Central states were lowest at 5.6 percent; the New England states were at the high end at 10.2 percent.

Although variations in tax burden from place to place cannot be dismissed as entirely insignificant, the impact of such differences on firm-location calculations must be diminished by the fact that state and local taxes are deductible for federal tax purposes. The burden of location in a high-tax state may in fact be mitigated by a lower federal tax liability than the firm would pay after the smaller deduction available in a low-tax state (ACIR, 1981, pp. 6, 19–22).

Efforts to investigate empirically the impact of taxes on investment behavior go back at least to the 1950s. The benchmark study of the period, an analysis conducted by Thompson and Mattila (1959), found, using both simple correlation and ordinary least squares techniques, that neither state and local taxes as a proportion of personal income nor taxes paid by manufacturers per employee were significantly related to general investment behavior measured by manufacturing employment growth between 1947 and 1954. Despite the use of 1953 tax burden data as an independent variable to explain employment growth over the preceding seven years, the study was widely cited as evidence that tax burdens did not slow down manufacturing growth. In any event by the mid-1970s there was enough corroborative evidence to lead Cornia and his colleagues to conclude that "most statistical comparisons of interregional growth fail to support the hypothesis that low tax rates result in rapid economic growth" (1978, p. 15; for similar views see Moriarty, 1980, Ch. 11; and Wheat, 1973, p. 21).

Surveys of plant officials designed to explore the determinants of the more specific process of plant siting followed a similar history and provided complementary support for the notion that taxes were of minor significance in investment processes. After reviewing many of these investigations Kieschnick (1983) was able to conclude:

Taking into account the wide diversity of techniques, types of respondent's companies, and geographical areas, the consistency of findings from surveys and interviews is striking. Even disregarding the existence of reasons to overestimate the importance of business taxes and incentives, businesses themselves agree that fiscal considerations and incentives are of relatively little importance in their location decision. (p. 209)

A convincing illustration of the generally minor role of taxes in location decisions is provided by Schmenner (1982, p. 48) in a study that relies not on surveys or aggregate growth data but on careful efforts to track the actual movement of firms from one tax jurisdiction to another. Here are the basic findings:

- Among his sample of *Fortune* 500 long-distance movers, 44 percent ended up in places with lower tax rates than their previous location; but an equal proportion—44 percent—relocated to places with a higher tax rate.

- Among a different sample of firms that had moved into the New England region, 47 percent located in places where the tax rate was the same as in the previous location, 20 percent moved to higher tax jurisdictions, and 33 percent went to lower tax places.

- Short-distance movers (less than 20 miles) might be expected to be more sensitive to tax differentials. Among the short-distance *Fortune* 500 firms, however, the proportion relocating to lower-tax jurisdictions (21 percent) was the same as that relocating to higher-tax jurisdictions. Among the plants moving within New England (a different sample from the *Fortune* 500 group), short-distance movers were far more likely to end up in places where the tax rate was the same as or higher than their previous location. Only 18 percent of all the movers in this category went to lower-tax communities.

Only one major survey has provided any contradictory evidence on the role of taxes in firm-location decisions. In a study conducted for the Joint Economic Committee of the U.S. Congress, Robert Premus (1982) surveyed a national sample of high-technology firms about their location preferences. The availability of skilled labor and labor costs ranked first and second as regional factors, but 67 percent of respondents mentioned tax climate, placing it third among the various considerations. Taxes ranked second to skilled-labor availability when it came to choosing a specific site; at this second stage of the location process taxes were considered important by 85.5 percent of Premus' 691 respondent firms. Premus explains the importance of taxes for high-technology firms as a function primarily of the impact of the personal tax structure on the willingness of highly paid professionals and entrepreneurs to locate in a particular area. Taxes bear, therefore, on skilled-labor availability.

Around 1978 there began a sudden accumulation of econometric evidence suggesting, in direct contradiction to accepted wisdom, that a state's tax policies toward business did in fact have a direct bearing on its economic fortunes. According to Kieschnick (1983), an unpublished study done by Genetski and Chin (1978) for the Harris Bank of Chicago became the most politically influential of these early revisionist studies when it was picked up and cited by the *Wall Street Journal*. The research apparently showed that high-tax states which reduced their taxes slightly would increase their growth rate (measured by personal income change) relative to low-tax states that increased their taxes slightly. The study was attacked for failing to include other relevant variables in the regression models and for ignoring the possibility that relative change in taxes could just as plausibly be regarded in the analysis as the dependent variable, a function of income change, rather than the other way around (Beier-Solberg, 1984; Kieschnick, 1983). But subsequent studies lent weight to these findings that tax policy makes a difference in growth.

Vedder (1982), for example, regressed personal income growth during the 1970s in all 50 states against state and local tax burden per capita in 1980 and found that states with low taxes grew more than a third faster than states with relatively high taxes. High-growth states had lower income and personal property taxes than did low-growth states; the former also tended to have flat rather than progressive income tax rate structures. In another study Bartik (1985), using a logit analysis, found that corporate income tax rate is negatively related to the probability that one of the *Fortune* 500 firms would locate a branch plant in a state, though the tax effect is modest. An unpublished study reported by Wasylenko (1985) treats per capita annual expenditures on plant and equipment in 48 states from 1966 to 1978 as the dependent variable measuring investment. Independent variables included wage rate, per capita welfare expenditures, relative ratio of state and local tax to personal income, and the state's relative ratio of debt to personal income. The tax variable is also included in the regression equations as a lagged value. Taxes were found to be important determinants of capital investments; moreover, investment levels were found to respond with a lag to tax increases.

Finally, Leslie Papke (1985) generates a simulation model designed to explore variation in the after-tax rate of return on marginal manufacturing investment made in different locations. The model incorporates all the relevant characteristics of the different state and local tax systems and takes account of the interaction of state and local taxation and federal income tax deductibility. The dependent variable is new capital expenditure divided by production workers in 20 industries for 1978.

Papke finds that the after-tax rate of return accounts for a significant part of the geographic variation in investment patterns. "Investment," she writes, "is sensitive to the level of capital taxation. . . . the empirical findings here support the proposition that state and local tax cost differentials have a significant effect on investment location decisions" (pp. 16–17). While a measure of labor productivity is also a significant independent variable, it is notable that average wage and energy costs play no well-defined role in determining capital expenditures.

To draw firm conclusions about the effects of tax structure on various sorts of investment behavior would be exceedingly risky, despite this recent work. Not only is there no generally accepted method for measuring tax burdens on firms (Bahl, 1980), but there is a mass of conflicting evidence. A number of studies, contemporaneous with the revisionist claims that taxes influence investment, continue to show that taxes have no effect on growth. Steinnes (1984), for example, shows that the sales, income, and property tax burden on the average hypothetical firm in each of several different sectors (manufacturing, trade, and services) is not significantly related to employment change. He concludes that there is "very little empirical evidence to support the position that changing such taxes is an effective means of encouraging economic growth" (p. 46). And McHone (1984), who investigates differential employment growth in the various parts of multistate metropolitan areas, finds that job increases are significantly related *positively* to state and local taxes as a proportion of income, the opposite of what might be expected. Instead of shunning high property tax communities which spill into high tax states, many firms seek those places, he argues, that provide value in the form of good services for their tax dollars.

The policy implications of this substantial research effort of the past three decades do not support an aggressive or obvious course of action. Even in those instances where taxes are found to have significant effects on growth or location decisions, they are never regarded as *primary* determinants. Thus, for a state or city to build an economic development strategy with tax policy as its centerpiece is scarcely warranted. On the other hand enough evidence now exists to indicate that tax policy is probably not irrelevant to growth prospects. Crafting a tax profile that resembles one's regional or metropolitan neighbors may be the most rational way to balance economic development pressures that militate for a tax climate favorable to business and the public service demands that can be met only by maintaining a steady and reasonable flow of revenues.

Tax Concessions and Financial Incentives as Location Factors

Various tax incentives (mainly tax abatements) and financial inducements are often included as independent variables in the analytical models used to explore the determinants of investment behavior. In our terms tax incentives represent attempts to reduce processing costs, while financial inducements, among which are included subsidized loans and land write-downs, address primary input costs borne by business. As with investigations of the impact of the general tax structure on investment, the analysis of the effects of specific incentives produces mixed results. On balance, however, the efficacy of such devices in inducing plant location appears to be quite limited, though there are several studies that suggest positive effects on the volume of investment.

One of the earliest studies employed both archival and survey research to explore the effects of the state-run property tax abatement program in Louisiana (Ross, 1953). Ross concluded that about 50 percent of the firms that had received a tax abatement between 1946 and 1950 regarded it as a major factor in deciding either to locate in Louisiana or to expand there, and 5 percent of the 259 firms that answered Ross's questionnaire claimed that the abatement was in fact the deciding factor. However, 64.9 percent of the firms said they would finally have invested in the state even in the absence of the abatement. Furthermore, the 44 firms (17 percent) that said they would not have located without the tax abatement accounted for only 7 percent of the total dollars invested by all recipients of the abatements, or a bit less than $25 million. Foregone revenues from all of the abatements for firms in Ross's sample amounted to more than $51 million. Ross concluded from his survey that the limited importance and general expense of the abatement program made it a poor bargain for the state on all counts.

Bridges' review (1965b) of available evidence concerning tax exemptions, revenue bond financing, and various low-interest loan programs reaches a conclusion not inconsistent with Ross's work. Though he finds that financial inducements of this sort might significantly affect both location decisions and the volume of investment "in some cases . . . of a number of firms," he stresses that such subsidies are secondary factors in the choice not only of region but also of sites within a region. "Most studies of business investment," he points out, "show that the volume of investment is rather insensitive to changes in the cost and availability of capital" (p. 192); and actual location choices tend to be governed by cost differentials of primary factors such as labor and transportation.

Among more recent studies, findings on the effects of incentives are inconsistent. Steinnes (1984) finds no effects on job growth in various economic sectors of the number or volume of IRBs issued per year in a state. His analysis is based on a pooled time-series data set that covers 15 states during the 1970s. On the other hand a weak, but measurable, influence of incentives is found by McHone (1984) in an effort to relate differences in tax structure (discussed earlier) and availability of incentives among communities in multistate SMSAs to employment-growth differentials. He finds statistically insignificant relationships between the *magnitude* of these differentials and the availability of low-cost loan programs, property tax abatements, bond financing, and other inducements. But when he relaxes the requirements of his initial hypothesis to explore not magnitude of employment growth differentials but rather simply whether employment growth will be greater or less than that of the SMSA as a whole, his model generates significant coefficients for industrial bond programs, property tax abatements, and accelerated depreciation of industrial equipment.

Kale's approach (1984) involves first weighting 20 industrial development incentives on the basis of the relative importance accorded each one in a survey of industrial facility planners done by the Industrial Development Research Council. By awarding 10 points for each first place vote, 9 for each second, and so on, property tax abatements emerged as the most important incentive and right-to-work laws were second. Others in the top 10 in order included tax exemption on manufacturers' inventories, corporate income tax exemption, industrial bond financing, property tax exemption on equipment and machinery, accelerated depreciation, sales tax exemption on new equipment, subsidized job training, and tax exemption on raw material used in manufacturing.

Kale then derived a score for each state by summing the weights of all the programs in existence in that state, and this score served as the independent variable in a series of correlation analyses in which the dependent variable was manufacturing employment growth. Kale finds weak relationships at the national level between state incentive scores and employment growth using both parametric and nonparametric statistics. This is true even when he builds in a time lag between adoption of programs and employment growth. When he examines these relationships within a single region (West North Central states), however, he finds, first, a strong negative relationship between adoption of incentives and employment growth in the 1960s and early 1970s (suggesting, perhaps, that economic decline prompted adoption of incentives, an interpretation he does not make), and then in the 1970s a strong positive relationship which suggests their efficacy in inducing job-generating investment. The analysis is weakened, however, by the failure to include any other variables that might explain growth and decline, as well as by the artificiality of the weighting procedure.

A similar study done at the same time by Susan Hansen (1984) shows how tentative any conclusions from such investigations must be. Hansen performs a factor analysis to identify groups of states that rely on different clusters of incentives in their pursuit of investment. Although she finds that each of four clusters of incentives is correlated positively with the rate of new business formation, the existence of tax incentives and other inducements is *negatively* related to employment growth across the 50 states from 1977 to 1982. This finding is exactly counter to what we might expect given Kale's research.

Even if the findings of McHone, Kale, and Hansen were not inconsistent with one another, it could scarcely be said that any one of these studies provides strong support for the maintenance of a battery of tax and financial incentives to promote investment. But to draw serious policy implications from these investigations would be at best premature. Each of them is flawed and for the same critical reason: their independent policy variables are all based simply on the *availability* of incentives in each state or community. But what is crucial in exploring the relationship between these incentives and investment patterns is their utilization rate, their size in terms of funding, and their value to a firm.

Mere availability of a program in the statute books tells us nothing about its actual use. Schmenner's surveys indicate that only a small fraction of newly opened and relocating plants take advantage of government incentives (see also Kieschnick, 1983; and recall the discussion of Connecticut enterprise zones in Chapter 7). For example, among the *Fortune* 500 firms that Schmenner sampled, only 21 percent of new plants used industrial revenue bonds and only 14 percent used tax concessions. He presents similar figures for his sample of firms in the Cincinnati metropolitan area as well as his sample from the New England region (1982, p. 55). Not only does Schmenner show that few firms take advantage of available incentives, but he also indicates that utilization rates vary from region to region, though how much these broad differences might be a function of availability in particular states is not clear. Unfortunately, no comparative studies exist that examine the relationship between use rates in states that make these incentives available and investment patterns.

Several studies show, however, that the use of industrial revenue bonds at least results in a volume of investment that probably would not have taken place otherwise and in faster rates of growth than among firms that do not use such subsidies. Hellman and her colleagues (1976) use an approach that takes as its theoretical starting point the value of industrial incentives to the average firm. They develop a model to test the impact on rate of investment in Kentucky that includes total manufacturing investment in the state, by year, including time prior to the full operation of the industrial revenue bond program. They find the rate of investment and value added to be consistently related positively to the dollar amount of loans made annually through bond issues. (Using similar models, they find no effects of the Connecticut loan guarantee program and only modest impacts of the Pennsylvania low-interest industrial loans.)

A more recent survey of industrial revenue bond users in Massachusetts conducted by a consulting firm under contract to the state Industrial Finance Agency found striking positive impacts (Gunther-Mohr and Swoboda, 1985). Some of the basic findings of the study include the following:

- Manufacturing employment in the 63 respondent firms that provided job data grew from the date of bond approval to the time of the survey at a compound rate of 24.3 percent. By comparison manufacturing employment in the state as a whole declined by 1 percent. Growth among IRB users was greater even when industry type was controlled.

- Seventy-seven percent of the firms claimed that expansion would have been delayed without revenue bond financing, and an additional 6.2 percent said they would have reduced their expansions. For 13 percent of these firms the delay would have been three years or more.

- Firms resident in Massachusetts used industrial revenue bonds exclusively for expansion of facilities or acquisition of another company. Such financing was not used in one single instance to move a company from another state.

The authors conclude that the principal effect of IRB financing at the individual company level is to accelerate economic expansion (p. 14).

There is little warrant in these various studies to argue that tax and financial incentives play a role of much, if any, significance in plant-location decisions, but there is some evidence to suggest that these devices, along with a favorable tax structure, probably increase the volume of investment by indigenous firms. Until comparative econometric analyses take into account the variations in use by firms in a state and the volume of IRB loans made, more confident judgments about the effectiveness of such inducements will have to wait.

Other Location Factors

Most analysts agree that at the first stage of the decision process, labor and market considerations are the dominant factors in deciding where to locate new plants (Schmenner, 1982, pp. 37–38; Webber, 1984, p. 67; Vaughan, 1977, p. 42; Moriarty, 1980, p. 181). (See Chart 8-3) But for any individual firm the mix and ranking of factors are likely to be distinctive. Some factors will be entirely idiosyncratic, having to do, for example, with the owner's or chief executive officer's attachment to a particular place, a function of family history, schooling, or cultural or recreational tastes.

In a related vein, "quality of life" factors are critical for certain companies, particularly those that employ a high proportion of engineers, managers, and other professionals (Malecki, 1984). Quality of life is a notion that encompasses everything from recreational opportunities to freedom from congestion and crime to the character of the local schools (Vaughan, 1977, pp. 77–78). While many of these particular elements may be quantified or priced—hospital beds per population, crime rate, and so on—their relative value to a firm is a matter of subjective judgment.

Leonard Wheat (1973) has stressed the enormous importance of climate as a location factor. Indeed, it is second only to market considerations in his explanations of regional differences in growth. Climate is important per se because, Wheat argues, executives and professionals are unwilling to live in regions with harsh winters. But cold weather is also associated with higher energy costs, greater worker absenteeism, infeasibility of outdoor operations, and winter transportation problems. Climate also interacts with market factors, according to Wheat: warm climate attracts migrants and thus makes for a growing market. Climate in and of itself, however, seldom appears on others' lists of critical local considerations, although it is clearly germane to discussions of comparative energy costs and so on.

Chart 8-3. Ranking Location Factors: Selected Survey Results

Regional Location Factors in Rank Order of Importance	Local Site Factors in Rank Order of Importance
Market access	Trucking
Labor cost and availability	Reasonable cost of property
Raw materials	Reasonable or low taxes
Building availability	Ample area for expansion
Site considerations	Favorable labor climate
Transportation facilities	Favorable attitude of community
Distribution	and residents to industry
Living conditions	Nearness to present sales area
Climate	Reasonable cost of construction
Industrial fuel cost	Favorable climate for personnel
Water cost and availability	Availability of labor skills
Industrial power cost	Nearness to sources of raw materials
Financial help	Need for plant to service new or
Taxes	expanding area sales
Laws and regulations	Favorable political climate toward business
Miscellaneous	Pleasant living conditions
	Commercial services
	Rail facilities
	Zoning restrictions
	Cost of living and economic conditions
	Labor rates
	Educational facilities
	Favorable climate for production processes
	Inexpensive fuel or power
	Public transportation
	Recreational and cultural facilities
	Water supply
	Waste disposal
	Nearness to airport
	Topography
	Water transport

Source: Vaughan, 1977, pp. 42–3.

Energy and utility costs are not a major factor in choosing a site for most firms. Moriarty (1980, p. 217) points out that electricity, for example, costs the average firm less than eight/tenths of 1 percent of the value of finished products, although the cost is somewhat higher for a very few select industries. Water availability is perhaps a more important concern for a small percentage of firms. Ninety-seven percent of all manufacturing plants are minor water users whose needs can be easily satisfied by public water systems (ibid., p. 207). For the remaining 3 percent—steel, paper pulp, food processing, chemicals, for example—water is a major site determinant. Notably, the availability of abundant water in the Los Angeles metropolitan area, a result of its early waterworks program, attracted major industrial water users to the area in the 1920s, accounting in large part for the city's emergence as a national manufacturing center (Ostrom, 1953).

Conclusions

By and large supply-side economic development policy operates at the margins of private investment decision-making. This is not to say that such policies are always ineffective: although it is difficult to reach a definitive conclusion based on the conflicting evidence in the foregoing studies, the various subsidies apparently do help under certain conditions to shape or stimulate investment. But the specific incentives governments can offer and the contexts governments can create through their general tax and regulatory policies are simply not prime determinants in private decisions to invest, at least where the question involves choice of business location. The critical factors in deciding where to make investments among competing regions are essentially beyond the reach of state and local governments. It is possible that right-to-work laws and efficient transportation systems may in some degree reduce labor and marketing costs, but these primary considerations are basically shaped by migration patterns, shifts in consumer tastes and purchasing power, and labor supply and demand.

There is, of course, growing—though by no means conclusive—evidence that favorable state tax policies either stimulate or are associated with expansive investment behavior. That is, when the choice is not where to invest but rather whether to invest more or less, low-tax jurisdictions seem, according to more recent research, to have an edge. But there are limits to efforts to create a favorable tax climate in the eyes of business. Many high-tax states support elaborate systems of public services and facilities. Not only are these difficult to cut back in significant ways, but their very quality and availability may in themselves be attractive to certain firms and investors. There are in other words powerful incentives to maintain good public services even at (relatively) high cost. Many low-tax states are not unaware of the attractions of good services, particularly education, and are willing to spend more to improve. In the matter of tax policy, then, extreme cutting to attract investment is unusual, as we saw in Chapter 6. A state must identify the fine line between a favorable tax structure and good services. Regional norms rather than national extremes tend to serve as guidelines.

Using general tax policy—types of taxes and tax rates—to encourage investment is relatively unwieldy.[5] Without an elaborate set of specific exemptions and tax credits, the burdens or advantages of a particular tax system are experienced by all firms indiscriminately, making it a blunt development tool. It is also difficult to produce timely predictable results. This is so in part because the manipulation of the tax structure relies heavily on investors' willingness or ability to believe that a favorable investment climate has been forged by tax reforms or the creation of incentive subsidies. But perceptions of a state's tax profile seem often to lag behind actual changes in tax laws. Wisconsin is a case in point: it ranked 47th in the nation in the share of total tax liability borne by business, according to a study done in 1983, yet its reputation in the business community was as a high-tax state. In a comparison of the attitudes of business people in five states (Massachusetts, Indiana, Minnesota, North Carolina, and Wisconsin) a greater proportion of survey respondents in Wisconsin than in any of the other states was convinced that business taxes would increasingly shape their location decisions to Wisconsin's disadvantage. Such concerns existed in spite of the fact that Wisconsin had sought steadily through tax reductions and the implementation of various exemptions to signal business that it was responsive to its complaints (Wisconsin Strategic Development Commission, 1985, p. 92).

Another problem with the use of general tax policy and tax and financial incentives as location inducements is that, when they do come into play, their main impact is on intrastate—usually in fact intrametropolitan—location choices (see Chart 8-3). In other words, such policies seem to do little to lure investment across the border from out-of-state but may be influential in distributing investment within the state, although statistical studies (as opposed to surveys) never suggest that taxes and financial inducements are primary factors even in this context. Since most firms that change location are short-distance, within-state movers (Schmenner, 1982, p. 101), the net effect of the battery of inducements from the point of view of the state economy is zero-sum.

Ultimately, substate competition among local jurisdictions might in fact create a drain on the state's economy, a minus-sum situation, a problem that has not been addressed in the literature. It is possible at least

---

5. As John Zysman has argued, "[T]axation is not as flexible as credit allocation. Taxes can be used to target categories of action but they are difficult to manipulate toward specific industrial ends. Unless the principles of rational administration are violated, taxes cannot be bargained. Moreover, taxes operate to increase profits from gross earnings; they tend to follow rather than to lead new activities" (1983, p. 77).

that in foregoing future tax revenues or maintaining low tax rates simply to attract industry, communities will so reduce their revenues that they will be increasingly dependent on state aid to offer basic services. Alternatively, widespread competition among communities based on low taxes may mean that few if any jurisdictions will be able to finance the necessary infrastructure or education systems to attract industry at all. When many sites in the state are ruled out on the grounds of inadequate public services and facilities, the state economy as a whole pays the costs of substate tax competition.

The supply-side strategy has one more problem: even when there is evidence to suggest that such incentives influence investment behavior, the effects must be short-lived. After all, incentives are easily matched by competitor states, as the spread of incentives during the 1970s and 1980s shows. Competition for what mobile capital does exist becomes even more difficult to pursue successfully when a state is faced with a market differentiation problem.

To summarize, the traditional supply-side strategy to induce investment and influence location choices is burdened with certain liabilities. The positive effects of such incentives have not been established incontrovertibly, and there are even potentially perverse effects. In addition, incentives and tax profiles are relatively easy to match, thereby canceling out any advantage in the long run.

It is my argument that the uncertainties and problems associated with supply-side efforts have contributed to the impetus to generate strategies for economic development that avoid the head-to-head competition with other states to influence the disposition of existing investment dollars. It is thus partly out of the problematic experience of the supply-side tradition that the entrepreneurial state has emerged.

Part III

DEMAND-SIDE POLICY

IN ECONOMIC DEVELOPMENT

CHAPTER 9

Demand-Side Concepts and Their Policy Implications

VARIOUS shortcomings of the supply-side approach to encouraging private investment for development ends have led states and cities to explore policies based on the alternative notion that accommodating, manipulating, anticipating, or stimulating demand forces in the market may offer more effective solutions to the development problem. Among the problems of supply-side strategies, which stimulated the search for different approaches, are the uncertain impacts of particular investment incentives; the ease with which competitor jurisdictions can match subsidies for mobile capital in a bidding war; the fact that economic decline continued in some states even during decades of vigorous efforts to lure and keep industry through supply-side devices; and the failure of the private sector to sustain high rates of research and development spending and, in some regions, business formation.

The alternative strategy, based on demand concepts, requires government to play an unaccustomed entrepreneurial role. This is a role normally reserved in the American context for private individuals and institutions. In the iconography of capitalism the archetypal figure is the individual risk-taker who ventures all, who bets that a market exists for a good idea. It is the tinkerer in the backyard garage, the dreamer of big dreams, not government, who finds or creates a market and who mobilizes the resources to translate the idea into a commercial product. How is it possible, the capitalist asks, for government bureaucrats, who venture nothing of their own, to assess the market and the risks as accurately as the individual who puts his or her money on the line?

Such a question assumes, of course, that the entrepreneurial impulse is driven only by the profit motive, and that, lacking the possibility of private gain, governments, embodied by their bureaucratic and elected

227

functionaries, cannot or will not understand all that is at stake in a venture into the market or do what is necessary to increase the chances of success. But in fact the public stakes in market ventures are increasingly clear to state and local governments, and they lie less in the prospect of profit than in jobs and taxable resources. To secure these ends, state and local governments have begun to make serious efforts to develop the financing, investment, and marketing skills necessary to function in the world of entrepreneurship.

The virtues of demand-based policies appear plentiful in theory. A focus on the demand rather than the supply side permits earlier and more decisive intervention in private investment decisions, it helps to avoid the head-to-head competition inherent in competitive location inducements, and it promises to promote real capital formation more consistently than supply-side inducements that run a higher risk of simply relocating existing resources.

Consider the different stages in the investment decision at which government may intervene with its economic development tools. In the chronology of any private decision to invest, the actual outlay of capital occurs in response to a perceived opportunity. Supply-side policies bring government into the investment process *after an opportunity has been identified by an investor or firm.* The point of the policy is to hasten or increase the size of the investment or to create a location incentive such that the investor is induced to pursue the opportunity in a particular geographical locale. The problem for government here is that the opportunity pursued by the private investor may not produce dividends that maximize or even promote the public's long-run economic interests. But in the context of the supply-side strategy, government is commited to the proposition that opportunities are best defined by the private sector.

Demand-side intervention often occurs at an earlier stage of the investment process, at a point at which government discovers or creates an opportunity or assesses and ranks existing opportunities as a way of focusing investors' resources. Demand-side policies are designed to permit or encourage private investors to capitalize upon certain opportunities judged to be likely to produce significant benefits in the public's economic interests. The contrast in approaches here may be as simple as the decision to offer IRB financing to a low-wage hosiery producer which has announced its intention to relocate (the producer has defined the investment opportunity; the state simply seeks to capitalize on it) versus the decision to initiate the formation of a public-private consortium to explore and develop agricultural applications of new biotechnological research. Here the state has defined a potentially productive opportunity and sought to bring it to fruition. Financing the hosiery firm may gain a community a number of jobs in the precarious low-wage sector. The research consortium, however, holds out the promise of fostering a new industry with a diverse workforce and creating entirely new demands for biotechnology applications as yet unknown. Naturally, the consortium may come to nothing, but at least the state has used its resources to encourage an undertaking that may serve long-term development interests. The hosiery firm, in contrast, has all the earmarkings of a short-term proposition vulnerable to low-wage competitors abroad. The entrepreneurial state, sensitive to demand-side considerations, would decide, all things being equal, not to offer assistance to such an enterprise.

The difference in the two approaches is further illustrated by the fact that in the context of traditional policy it is assumed that opportunities for investment exist for the taking and that some actors in the market will clearly perceive and seek to capitalize upon them. The demand-side approach accepts the notion that the decision to invest is in great part a matter of perspicacity and courage but that such a decision nevertheless sometimes needs to be encouraged and focused. The demand-side approach is a response to the belief that actors in the private sector do not always perceive opportunities or may be hesitant to pursue those for which there is no immediately apparent, easily accessible market. The idea behind the demand-side policies of the entrepreneurial state is to discover or point out such opportunities and to assist investors to capitalize on them, if those investments promise enduring or long-term development benefits. As we shall see, efforts to encourage small business participation in export trade, to subsidize technology transfer from university laboratories to the market, and to underwrite research and production in technologically advanced fields are all examples of government attempts to ferret out opportunities or reassure and support investors, both individual and institutional.

Demand-based policies also appear advantageous to the extent that they greatly reduce the intensity of the sort of interjurisdictional competition that leads to ever-increasing capital subsidies. The object of demand-based development efforts is not so much to attract mobile capital when it weighs alternative locations as it is to create or clarify market opportunities for indigenous firms and entrepreneurs. Competition is not absent from the development enterprise, but its character is altered. States may find themselves promoting similar goods or services in the same consumer marketplace: competition among vacation states for tourist trade is an example. But this is a competition for consumers, not producers. In the demand-based framework the entrepreneurial state is concerned less with putting together the best possible deal to induce a firm to invest than it is to work out a way for someone in the private sector to produce a better, more competitive commodity or service.

One of the ironies of competitive bidding for private capital is not only that it is potentially very costly or even that "bids" or subsidies or low tax rates are likely to be matched by other states or cities, but rather that the actual movement of firms from place to place or the establishment of branch plants seem in most cases to have little to do with the kinds of inducements offered by government. Supply-side public policies in other words fail at some level to connect with the realities of investment decision-making. Demand-side concepts suggest a different focus: foster those indigenous capacities to serve new or expanding demands (rather than pursuing mobile capital) by providing resources that permit direct penetration or capture of a particular market (rather than providing peripheral subsidies of factor costs) or that permit a risky but potentially productive undertaking that would not have gone forward without government support.

Finally, demand-based policies seem more likely, at least in theory, to contribute to real capital formation. It is true that certain supply-side subsidies leverage entirely new private investment, thereby adding not only to the local economy but also augmenting the national capital stock. But many such policies are also associated with (and may on rare occasions actually *cause*) a shift simply in location of capital rather than its augmentation. Demand-based efforts are all designed at least to promote real growth by supporting or generating new capacity to produce goods and services, helping to develop the new goods themselves, or helping to find new markets to stimulate business expansion.

Demand Concepts and the Rise of the Entrepreneurial State

The policies of the entrepreneurial state draw sustenance from principles of export base theory present in the fields of urban and world system economics. The central thesis of export base theory is the intuitively appealing conviction that a local (or regional or national) economy will grow in response to increases in exogenous demand for the output of any resident sector. In his classic exposition Douglass North wrote that the growth of a region "is closely tied to the success of its exports and may take place either as a result of the improved position of existing exports relative to competing areas or as a result of the development of

new exports" (1955, p. 251). Or as Wilbur Thompson put it more suc-
cinctly, "As the export industry goes, so goes the total local economy"
(1965, p. 29). Indeed, Jaffee has shown empirically that the degree of
dependence on the export of processed goods, at least at the nation-state
level, is associated with growth in per capita GNP (Jaffee, 1985).

It would be incorrect, however, to say that the policies of the modern
entrepreneurial state are theoretically derived in any self-conscious way
or that they are constrained by any coherent theoretical framework.
Rather, state and local policy architects build programs on the basis of
key themes in export base theory and discard its constraining or trouble-
some elements.[1] Theory, insofar as it is apprehended, is merely a suggestive guide to action.

The central lesson derived from export base theory by the policy actors of the entrepreneurial state is not so much the value of exporting
goods but rather that the key to growth and development lies first in
understanding the structure and dynamics of the market as a prelude to
its exploitation. Export base theory assumes that a major outcome of the
successful identification and capture of a new or expanding market is the
generation of jobs in the export sector. The production of new goods for
export is also presumed to set into motion a local employment multiplier
as subsidiary businesses form to provide services to the export workers.
Empirically, the relationship between the proportion of employment in
the export sector and secondary jobs is unstable (Thompson, 1965, p.
38; Conroy, 1975, p. 42). The former is an unreliable guide to the size
of the latter. Furthermore, there has been considerable dispute in economics over which sector is more "basic"—export or services—in the
sense of which sorts of enterprises attract and support others. In fact,
neither the exact magnitude nor direction of causality are of much importance to economic development officials. What is significant is that
the fortunes of the two sectors of the labor force are linked.

One of the major practical adaptations of export base theory by the
entrepreneurial state is to broaden its policy efforts beyond the narrow
problem of generating the export of goods. The focus rather is on expanding *markets,* whether they lie beyond or within political borders.
Growth is assumed to come about not only through the infusion of exogenous income to pay for export goods but also by offering goods (and
services as well) that stimulate spending of indigenous income. In addi-

---

1. For a succinct, not wholly unsympathetic, critique of export base theory, see Richardson, 1973, pp. 16–22.

tion, while export base theory appears to ignore or underplay government spending and the role of local credit markets in capital formation, the entrepreneurial state operates on the assumption that these too initiate spending multipliers and thus help to promote growth. The entrepreneurial state is concerned furthermore with encouraging technological innovation in a long-run framework as a way of stimulating or anticipating eventual new demands whose locational origins are not yet known precisely.

Innovation relates to another key theme derived from export base theory, namely the importance of invention as a key to development. Schumpeter discussed the relationship between the inventive process and economic growth in *Capitalism, Socialism and Democracy* (1962), but the realization that American state and local governments could play a stimulus role in this domain is far more recent. Invention is important for several reasons. For one thing, the appearance of new goods may stimulate the formation of new demand. Furthermore, the invention of new products has locational implications, as the following passage from the Michigan strategic plan makes clear:

... state government has a special stake in the level of innovation, because the products and processes produced through innovation tend to be commercialized near the place they are invented. Existing firms in the region where an innovation occurs generally learn about it before more distant competitors. That means, if they move quickly, they can be, and generally are, the first to exploit these innovations in the marketplace. The more industrial innovations created in Michigan, the more likely that Michigan firms ... will be the first to commercialize them and thus become more competitive. That means more jobs for Michigan. (Michigan Task Force, 1984, p. 77)

Michael Conroy points out an additional implication of the fact that the invention of new products creates a short-run monopoly in the market for the producer: economic development is fostered in part through the ability of producers under such conditions to pay higher wages. New products also stimulate the formation of new supplier firms: the creator of a new agricultural enzyme, for example, will need a reliable producer of test tubes and other laboratory equipment. Much of the preoccupation of the entrepreneurial state with encouraging high-technology firms derives from the assumption that innovation stimulates and serves as yet unformed or immature markets. Borne on the back of the inventive process, growth possibilities appear unlimited.

That subnational governments perceive these demand-oriented policies as a break with past practice is quite clear. A few examples illustrate the sense of transition. The city of Houston, reeling from the decline in oil prices in the mid-1980s, hired a development consultant who told the community's leaders that there would be no recovery through a reliance on industrial relocation from other places. City leaders agreed that they must instead incubate Houston's small business sector and build and innovate on the base of the city's energy and space industries (*New York Times*, Nov. 2, 1985). In California, business and political leaders were distressed at the decision in 1983 of the Microelectronics and Computer Technology Corporation, an 18-company consortium, to locate in Texas rather than in southern California. Blaming their own complacency in part for this loss and others like it, the legislature sought to invest in the state's high-tech future by increasing the university system's budget by 30 percent to bolster its technology offerings. Such conscious efforts to support growth industries had been rare in California: "Five or eight years ago," a business leader told a magazine reporter, "most people only cared about reducing regulations and taxes" (*Inc.*, Oct. 1984, p. 119). The state of Ohio in its strategic planning document, *Toward a Working Ohio*, expressed explicit doubts about the efficacy of the old supply-side subsidies for mobile firms while laying out a timetable for the implementation of a series of entrepreneurial programs focused on home industries with growth potential (Ohio Office of the Governor, 1983, p. 16).

Taking a broader view, a report completed for the Joint Economic Committee of the U.S. Congress observes, "The engrained practice of chasing 'smokestack industries' with generous financial incentives has been giving way to a strategy that places much greater emphasis on problems encountered in product development, technology transfer, capital formation, and industrial innovation" (Premus et al., 1985, p. 54). And analysts at the Advisory Commission on Intergovernmental Relations note that "recent years have witnessed an expansion into new directions. State and local governments still fund physical infrastructure, but now they also promote high-technology, apply new technologies to mature industries, [and] support small business . . ." (Roberts et al., 1985, p. 22).

Entrepreneurialism as a Bridge between Export Base and Supply-Side Approaches

In the supply-side tradition the key to growth is the mobilization of additional capital, labor, and other input resources (Borts and Stein, 1964). More inputs mean more production, jobs, and income. In contrast, orthodox export base theorists "have little to offer in the analysis of the importance of the cost or availability of productive inputs . . ." (Vaughan, 1977, p. 33). Labor, presumably drawn in ample supply by new employment opportunities, and capital, attracted by investment possibilities, are thought to be "in infinitely elastic supply" (ibid., p. 27). In short, the existence of attractive markets will, it is assumed, elicit the commitment of sufficient resources necessary to their exploitation (Conroy, 1975, p. 44). The entrepreneurial state certainly acts on this assumption in its broker role: a governor who travels abroad to promote his or her state's products and returns to report to local firms that a market exists for their goods does so in the expectation that *in some cases at least* the necessary private-sector inputs can be mobilized to exploit these new demands.

But the entrepreneurial state also recognizes that the resources required to pursue new market opportunities do not always exist or exist only in a latent and inadequate form. Venture capital may be in short supply in certain states; resources to carry out research and development to meet a demand in the market may be lacking; knowledge about how to penetrate an export market in Asia may be rudimentary. In such circumstances, the entrepreneurial state seeks to make up the resource shortfall rather than have private-sector interests forego an attractive market opportunity. The price and availability of productive inputs are, in short, of vivid concern to the entrepreneurial state.

Thus, the state provides venture capital directly to start promising small businesses; it finances basic research and export ventures. It becomes in a variety of ways a direct and active participant in the market. As the *New York Times* observed in documenting these developments, "Many state and local officials are becoming so deeply involved in business activity that it is difficult to tell where government ends and private business begins" (Dec. 9, 1985).

Some of the efforts to remedy the inability of the private sector to generate enough capital or provide the skills or knowledge necessary to exploit a market resemble traditional supply-side devices: capital subsidies, tax credits, land write-downs, and so on. What makes them different in the hands of the entrepreneurial state, however, is that they are targeted to selected firms or sectors positioned to respond to market opportunities identified or legitimated by the state.

The Entrepreneurial State and the Job-Generation Studies

We have already examined a number of important forces that led to the shift from a virtually exclusive reliance on supply-side policies to the more economically interventionist efforts of the entrepreneurial state. A combination of opportunity and necessity has been critical. For example, the emergence of foreign-export trade possibilities, combined with the inability of most American firms to capitalize upon those opportunities, is one factor that impelled state and local governments to examine the structure of the market. Furthermore, the extraordinary international appetite for advanced technology—fueled by private demands for consumer goods, by industrial demands for automated production systems, by government demands for complex weapons and communications equipment—made the high-tech sector an obvious focus of state and local action, particularly as heavy manufacturing languished. The decline of federal aid lent urgent necessity to all these efforts.

But in addition to these situational influences that encouraged an interest in the demand side of the growth equation, the role of ideas cannot be discounted. It would be an exaggeration to say that the policies of the entrepreneurial state are informed by theory in the manner in which, say, national macroeconomic policy is the product of Keynesian economics or the Laffer curve. Rather these ideas are best understood simply as the conclusions of academic research, transmitted to the policy community at conferences, in trade journals, at public hearings, and through the efforts of itinerant consultants.

One such set of conclusions comes from the literature critical of supply-side location incentives that we examined in Chapter 8. Four decades of largely negative findings on the impact of such subsidies on industrial-location decisions finally began to penetrate the state capitals (ironically, just as the revisionist literature began to appear). By the early 1980s, substantial numbers of state and local economic development officials had at last begun to express doubts about the efficacy or at the very least the cost effectiveness of location inducements (see, for example, Beier-Solberg, 1984). While this did not lead to the wholesale abandonment of supply-side devices, as Chapters 6 and 7 demonstrate, the findings in the academic literature certainly helped to encourage the search for alternative approaches to development.

Another influential set of conclusions arises from the job-generation studies of David Birch. Birch's research on the sources of new jobs in the American economy has been conducted at the Program on Neighborhood and Regional Change at the Massachusetts Institute of Technology. The basic conclusions of this research are cited regularly in economic development trade publications, in strategic economic development planning documents, and in speeches and addresses by public officials and development consultants. The first major product of this investigation, and the most influential, *The Job Generation Process* (1979), was never published in full in widely available form, which makes its virtually universal currency in the economic development community all the more remarkable.

Architects of the entrepreneurial state tend to draw implications for policy from Birch's work with which he himself would disagree. While many policy-makers regard the job-generation studies as a rationale and guide for particular modes of aggressive, targeted state intervention, Birch rejects such an approach in favor of more traditional efforts to improve the business climate through lower taxes and fewer regulations (Birch, 1981).

The original study was based on data collected by the Dun and Bradstreet Corporation that pertain to the histories of 5.6 million business establishments from 1969 through 1976. Birch and his colleagues were able for each of these businesses to trace changes in location, employment, and corporate affiliation, among other characteristics. Later the data file was extended to cover 1977, 1979, and 1981 (Birch and MacCracken, 1984).

Birch's work has been criticized for his use of *establishments* as the unit of analysis rather than *firms*. Establishments are single-site businesses, which may or may not be independent firms. The latter refers to the corporate organization, which may or may not be organized as a single-site enterprise. Approximately 91 percent of all businesses with employees have only one location: that is, the firm and the establishment are the same. But the other 9 percent, according to Armington and Odle (1982), are multilocation—that is, multiestablishment—firms, and they are responsible for 62 percent of the private-sector workforce. Since decisions about expanding or contracting employment particularly tend to be made at the firm rather than at the establishment level, a focus on establishments as the units of analysis produces somewhat different conclusions about the contribution of different-sized businesses to the process of job generation. When the analysis concerns differences in establishment size, the role of "small business" in job generation is somewhat exaggerated, since in fact many of the key decisions are made by larger parent firms (U.S. SBA, 1983, p. 85). Nonetheless, this problem of choice of unit of analysis seems scarcely to have deflected the impact on policy of Birch's work.

Two major conclusions of Birch's job-generation research are critical for current economic development policy-making. One is that very little

Table 9-1. Percentage Distribution of Employment Changes, by Cause, U.S. Totals, 1969–76

	Firm Births	Firm Deaths	Firm Expansions	Firm Contractions	In-Migration	Out-Migration
1969–72	5.6	5.2	4.7	2.9	0.1	0.03
1972–74	5.5	4.5	5.3	2.6	0.1	0.05
1974–76	6.7	5.7	4.4	3.4	0.1	0.1

Source: Birch, 1979, p. 22.

job growth or loss in any particular locale can be attributed to the in- or out-migration of businesses. What is important instead in determining employment change is the local ratio of business births (start-ups) to deaths (failures) and expansions to contractions. The second key conclusion is that small businesses contribute disproportionately to job creation.

Birch presents his data on the sources of employment change by grouping the 50 states into fast-growing, moderate, slow, and declining categories based on their rates of job gain or loss per year. Then he shows that between 1969 and 1976 the out-migration of business establishments contributed no more than one-tenth of 1 percent to the annual rate of employment change in any of these four categories. To put this in another light, for every one job lost through out-migration of businesses between 1974 and 1976 in all 50 states, 57 were lost through business deaths and 34 through contractions. Similarly, for every one job in that period gained through the in-migration of businesses, 67 new jobs were created by business births and 44 by expansions. James Miller's analysis (1982) of this same data base shows even more graphically how insignificant the migration of businesses is in the job-generation process. He found that only 6639 out of 326,123 manufacturing plants actually moved in these years. Only 751 of these were interregional moves.

Birch construes migration here to mean only the physical relocation of the business establishment. Bluestone and Harrison (1982) and Sheets and his colleagues (1985), among others, have shown that much job growth and loss is the product of the migration of *capital* rather than the comparatively rare migration of business establishments themselves. Although Birch acknowledges this distinction, he includes the founding of a branch plant in one state by a parent company located in another—a common way in which capital is shifted—as a business birth rather than an instance of migration. These distinctions notwithstanding, the lesson drawn from these findings from the Birch study by economic development officials is that *job generation begins at home*. Efforts are best concentrated in helping local businesses expand and encouraging potential entrepreneurs to establish businesses, rather than in disbursing public resources in the effort to attract the rare mover. Arizona's strategic planning document expresses this new understanding in typical fashion: "According to almost every study on the subject of job creation, the single most critical factor in every state's economic growth is the extent to which new firms form, survive, and expand across the whole economy of the state" (Arizona Governor's Office of Economic Planning, n.d., p. 14; see also, for example, Rhode Island Strategic Development Commission, n.d., p. 105; Nebraska Governor's Task Force on Small Business Equity Financing, 1986; Pennsylvania Office of the Governor, 1985, p. 6).

Birch's data also indicate that it is the small business sector in particular where high employment growth is generated, a conclusion that has led economic development officials to target their efforts to this category of businesses. Of all net new jobs created in the U.S. between 1969 and 1976 fully 66 percent were generated by business establishments with 20 or fewer employees, and slightly over 80 percent were generated by establishments with fewer than 100 workers (Birch, 1979, p. 30). Birch and MacCracken have calculated that between 1977 and 1981 establishments of 20 or fewer employees accounted for 19.9 percent of all existing jobs in the United States, but they generated 51.3 percent of all new jobs. Businesses with more than 100 employees, which accounted for 63.9 percent of all employment, generated only 30.4 percent of all new jobs (Birch and MacCracken, 1984, p. 26).

The Dun and Bradstreet data file, despite its size, covers only those businesses that seek credit, that is, about 80 percent of all establishments in the country. Several investigators have attempted to explore the role of small business using more comprehensive data sets drawn from state unemployment compensation records filed with state labor departments. A 1981 study of California firms (cited in U.S. SBA, 1983, p. 64) and a 1984 study of the Wisconsin Department of Development (Wisconsin Dept. of Development, 1984,) use such data and confirm the disproportionate impact of small business. For example, the Wisconsin study found that establishments with fewer than 100 employees accounted for only 47.5 percent of the state's jobs in 1977 but generated 69.4 percent of all new jobs in the following year. Between 1979 and 1981 very small businesses (those with 20 or fewer employees) generated *all* net new jobs in Wisconsin, while every other size category produced net losses. And as if to underscore the proposition that growth is home-based, the Wisconsin study found that Wisconsin-owned businesses had higher growth rates than those of small branch operations of firms headquartered outside the state. During recessions between 1969 and 1981 Wisconsin-owned businesses experienced a lower rate of job loss than branches owned by out-of-state corporations.

Researchers at the Brookings Institution have analyzed the same Dun and Bradstreet data file used by Birch but applied a more restrictive definition of "small business" (Armington and Odle, 1982). They nevertheless confirm Birch's basic point. Their analysis of the performance of establishments in *firms* with fewer than 100 employees shows that while these small business units accounted for 36 percent of all jobs in 1976, they generated 51 percent of net job growth between 1976 and 1980 (Armington, 1983).

To discover that the small business sector is the major source of employment growth and ought therefore to command a significant policy commitment is potentially daunting for the economic development practitioner. The small business sector is extremely large, diverse, and decentralized. Reaching any substantial number of small businesses is time-consuming, and the chances that any single contact or offer of assistance will be cost-effective are not great. Business failure rates are high, and the course of growth and decline of such enterprises tends often to be violent. Business people in this large sector have few specific interests in common. Development officials are confronted, therefore, with the problem of focusing their efforts to stimulate the small business sector.

Some guidance may be inferred from the job-generation studies. The logic of the policy process suggests that economic development programs will have the greatest impact on the ability of small businesses to generate jobs among those firms or establishments with growth potential but which cannot on their own overcome barriers to expansion or market entry. Job-generation studies are careful to caution that the role of larger firms in creating jobs cannot be ignored by policy-makers (Birch and MacCracken, 1984, p. 23; Wisconsin Dept. of Development, 1984, pp. 14–15), but such firms are less likely to be responsive to local influences, more likely to migrate, and more likely to possess adequate financial and managerial resources of their own to which the addition of public assistance would be superfluous (Armington and Odle, 1982, p. 17). Only a small proportion of small businesses possess genuine growth potential.[2]

---

2. The job-generation studies are in general agreement that only between 12 and 15 percent of small businesses are responsible for creating all the net job growth in that sector. What proportion of these expanding businesses require public aid as a condition of growth is not known (U.S. SBA, 1983, p. 67).

The ability to create jobs is in part a function of the structure of the particular sort of market the business serves. Small enterprises offering traditional goods or services—grocery stores, taverns, hardware stores, barbershops, automobile repair shops—serve a predictably stable clientele. The structure of their markets is static; growth prospects are virtually nonexistent.

But some businesses or would-be entrepreneurs serve or promise to serve expanding markets. It is these enterprises that economic development officials believe to be appropriate targets of policy. To identify those select few, or to gauge the claims made by small businesses themselves that they have growth potential, state and local governments must be conversant with the structure of consumer markets and their probable evolution. Only through such a demand analysis can public officials hope to target policy in the most effective way.[3]

Policy Directions

The practical impact of embracing demand-side concepts has been to stimulate policy activity by the entrepreneurial state in at least three broad areas. These are venture capital, high-technology development, and foreign export. Venture capital policies, which may affect both high-tech firms and export businesses, as well as other sorts of enterprises, involve the subsidy of private capital as well as the investment of public funds in various sorts of private ventures. Most of these efforts are aimed at the creation or expansion of small businesses with growth potential. High-technology development represents an informed guess about the structure of future markets, as well as an effort to respond to current demands. State and local governments have increased education funding in the sciences, helped the private sector to develop new products, and supported the process of technology transfer from laboratory to the marketplace. Export trade, the third major policy area, has involved both promoting local products in new foreign markets and subsidizing exporters at home. These policy areas are the subjects of the three chapters that follow.

---

3. Gregory Daneke's observations are germane here: "Newly emerging state level economic development plans have begun to place unprecedented emphasis on the support of small business. Such an emphasis constitutes a radical departure from previous policies which tended to focus on enticing large manufacturing firms to locate a new plant within a particular state." The interest in small business, in Daneke's view, is a function of the "frenzy" for high-tech development (1985, p. 722).

CHAPTER 10

State Governments as
Venture Capitalists

THE belief that the future well-being of state economies depends heavily on the nurturance of small businesses with high growth potential was firmly established among state policy-makers by the mid-1980s (Daneke, 1985). At that time there was not only growing evidence that small enterprises are the major generators of new jobs but also mounting confirmation of their disproportionate importance as originators of new products and processes (U.S. SBA, 1983, pp. 121–28). In addition, small businesses also seemed well-suited to structural changes occurring in the patterns of economic activity. The declining importance of economies of scale in the less capital-intensive industries dependent on advanced technology, the growing tendency to contract out the manufacture of component parts to independent suppliers,[1] and the need for more flexible production and management systems to respond to the competitive challenges of rapid product innovation[2] all suggested not only a role but also the necessity of a strong small business sector and a public policy matrix to support it. Besides, fostering the establishment of a multiplicity of small companies rather than competing for a single major employer seemed to many state and local officials to offer a more sensible path to stable development. Explaining his commitment to small business in hearings before the Joint Economic Committee of Congress, for example, Governor Richard Thornburgh of Pennsylvania told how his state had managed in the 1970s to attract a major Volkswagen plant in the expectation that it would produce between 5000 and 7000 new jobs.

---

1. On the rise of "vertically disaggregated" corporations—that is, firms that rely on other companies for manufacturing their products as well as supplying various corporate services—see *Business Week,* March 3, 1986, pp. 64–71.

2. See for example, Reich, 1983.

"Today that facility is struggling and the job projections have not been realized. . . . I think there is a hint of a lesson there about putting all your eggs in one basket" (*State Policy Reports,* May 1985, p. 28).[3]

If, as Governor Thornburgh said on a later occasion, "[It would be better] to have 50 small companies with 100 employees each" than one with 5000 (Kotkin and Critser, 1985, p. 97), then the question arises of how best to work toward the achievement of such an economic base. Birch's work (1979) has suggested not only that small firms are the chief generators of new jobs but also that the specific processes by which they augment a state's employment base involve new business formation and expansion rather than in-migration of established firms from elsewhere. Thus, it seems to follow that, rather than pursuing migratory firms with ever more generous location inducements, the task for public policy ought to be to address the problems associated with business births and the dangerous period of infancy when business mortality rates are exceptionally high.

Both the justification for public intervention and its basic form derive from an analysis of the plight of small business in the established capital markets. In outline form the argument is as follows: business formation, survival, and expansion in the early years all depend heavily on access to adequate capital, particularly "patient" money in the form of equity or, less optimally, long-term debt. But most institutional vehicles for providing such capital—commercial banks, the stock exchanges, the bond markets—are closed to most small businesses. The problem is partly a reflection of rational risk-averse behavior, but it is also due, according to some, to imperfections in the market. The result is a pattern of discrimination against small firms in the allocation of financing that cannot be explained by the risk-return ratio alone. A state role is justified, according to this argument, when its purpose is to remedy market failure. The nature of that role is suggested by the diagnosis of failure of the capital markets in particular, namely, action to ensure greater access for entrepreneurs and small companies to financing for start-ups and early-stage operations.

To play out that role state governments have focused particularly on ways to use public authority to increase the availability of venture capital, that is, primarily high-risk equity financing, for new and young firms that promise to tap or create rapidly expanding markets. To augment the

---

3. The wisdom of Gov. Thornburgh's observation was brought home in 1987 when Volkswagen announced that it would close its Pennsylvania plant.

supply of capital is in general to approach the problem of development from the supply side. But to do so in a selective way only for firms that promise to serve or create expanding markets is to pursue an entrepreneurial course in which demand-side considerations govern strategy. In certain states the logical extension of this chain of reasoning is for the state itself to become a venture capitalist.

Small Business and the Problem of Capital

All but a minority of small businesses are initially capitalized by the personal savings of the entrepreneur and those of friends and relatives (Kieschnick, 1979). Raising equity capital through a public offering to finance a business start-up is virtually impossible, nor is it common for a new small business to manage to interest commercial banks or other lenders in supplying long-term-debt financing (Guenther, 1984, p. 183.) Organized capital markets at this level are simply closed to young small firms. Even after small businesses have been in operation for a period, their access to credit is more likely to be of the short-term variety than anything else, producing high ratios of debt to equity.

Some believe that the unwillingness of investors to purchase the liabilities of small firms reflects entirely rational estimations of the risks involved and does not therefore necessarily require remedial government intervention (see, for example, Saunders, 1984; and Horvitz, 1984). But others contend that the lack of access by small business to external capital is not always justified in economic terms (Litvak and Daniels, 1983, p. 44).[4] To some degree, therefore, the small business sector according to this latter view is burdened by market failure—the failure to allocate capital to its most productive uses—that prevents small business from realizing its full economic development potential (U.S. SBA, 1984c).

Surveys of small firms indicate that the inability to penetrate the capital market is in fact a serious concern of only a minority of enterprises, suggesting that most either do manage to raise capital externally or have no need or desire to do so. One national survey that tracked small business concerns annually between 1973 and 1979 found that only 8 percent of firms in the average year said that financing was their most sig-

---

4. This is certainly the case for venture capital investments, which may or may not be in small firms. Litvak's examination of the performance of a sample of 38 business development investors—all various sorts of private venture capital funds—found that between 1960 and 1980 their mean annual return was 25.7 percent (Litvak, 1983, p. 171). A survey of similar findings is contained in Rhode Island Strategic Development Commission, n.d., p. 952.

nificant problem (Andrews and Eisemann, 1981, p. 3). Another survey, this one by the National Federation of Independent Business (NFIB) based on quarterly soundings of urban small businesses from 1979 to 1983 and cited in testimony before the House Committee on Small Business, shows that "obtaining needed loans" ranked as only the 17th most pressing problem out of a total of 25 mentioned (U.S. Congress, House, 1983, pp. 59–61). A broader survey of small firms in small towns and rural areas as well as cities in 1982, also conducted by the federation, produced a list of 72 concerns (ibid., pp. 64–65). Obtaining long-term loans ranked 38th, short-term loans 45th, and investor financing (equity) 53rd. However, *new* firms in this survey cited financing problems as a serious problem more frequently than established small firms.

Access to external capital may not be an urgent concern for most small businesses, but for those for which it is crucial—firms engaged in extensive product-development research, for example, or those faced with a rapidly expanding market—there is strong support for the view that the conventional capital market is poorly equipped to serve their needs. For one thing, certain transaction costs involved in issuing public stock or selling corporate bonds are more or less fixed and thus represent a heavier proportional burden for small firms contemplating a modest deal (Litvak and Daniels, 1983). Andrews and Eisemann show, for example, that the flotation costs borne by a firm for the issue of debentures worth less than half a million dollars may amount to as much as 14 percent of the gross proceeds, while an issue of $5 million will cost only about 3 percent (1981, p. 16; see also Wisconsin Department of Development, 1985a, p. 9).

Investors are reluctant to consider committing money to small business in part because they face high information costs as they seek to make an assessment of the risks involved in backing a firm without a record in the public market. Discrimination against women and minority entrepreneurs, who are overrepresented among operators of small businesses, also accounts to some degree for small-business difficulties in the financial markets. As Litvak and Daniels write, ultimately "money flows on the basis of personal confidence in the borrower" (1983, p. 14).

One result of the workings of the capital market is to produce a financing profile for small business that is weighted more heavily in favor of short-term debt than that of larger firms. Examining data that employ the varying size limits used by the Small Business Administration, Andrews and Eisemann (1981, p. 4) have found that 38 percent of the financing of incorporated small firms is short-term debt, compared with

28 percent for large firms. Over 42 percent of large-firm financing is equity, compared with 35 percent for small companies. At least for small manufacturing firms debt loads had been steadily rising when these data were collected in the mid-1970s.

From the state's point of view the difficulties small companies face in obtaining financing pose a problem to the degree that there is simply less capital being invested in potential, job-creating small businesses. In seeking to encourage the capitalization of productive small businesses, many states have concluded that the existing financing programs that they have traditionally administered are not suited to the task. Industrial revenue bonds, for example, will seldom attract buyers when the proceeds are destined to finance a new or young business without a credit history. Similarly, industrial loan programs, whose funds have often financed comparatively small operations, nevertheless have seldom been employed for high-risk new business formation or early-stage capital. Furthermore, most public financing programs available to small business have traditionally offered only debt financing. Some states have concluded that the most effective way to help new small firms is to provide equity backing to underwrite the process of business planning, product development, initial production, and marketing. During this early stage new businesses typically run at a loss. Debt financing, which usually involves the immediate scheduled payback of the loan plus debt service, poses an extremely heavy burden in the early years of operation. In the search by state governments for alternative ways to support new business formation and the expansion of infant companies one obvious model has clearly come from the private venture capital industry.

The Rationale for State Venture Capitalism

"Venture capital" is a term used to denote the high-risk financing of small businesses at the gestation, start-up, and early-expansion stages. Such financing involves direct, long-term equity investment in a company where returns are greatly delayed while the business forms and takes off (Premus et al., 1985, p. 73). Returns are unpredictable. Venture capitalists—highly informed institutional and individual investors willing to take such risks—typically seek to support entrepreneurs who demonstrate the potential for building rapid-growth businesses or new young companies with financing needs associated with the problem of commercializing an innovative product or process for the market. Private venture capitalism usually requires substantial personal involvement both in the identification of likely investment opportunities and in the nurturance of new companies through the early years. The risks of investing in businesses at these early stages are extremely high. Thus, the possibility of raising equity by issuing public stock for purchase by a multitude of investors is virtually foreclosed. Venture capital is therefore regarded as "prepublic" financing. (Approximately 60 percent of the companies financed in this way eventually go public or merge upwards [Premus et al., 1985, p. xii; Stoll, 1984, p. 230].) Venture capitalists seek a high rate of return for bearing high risks: a minimum return rate of 30 percent per year is a common expectation (Premus et al., 1985, p. xii).

At least three problems of the private venture capital industry have led policy-makers to believe that state action in this field can fill a genuine need. One is that the industry is underfunded; a second is that its monies are unevenly distributed by region; and a third is that the private market often spurns investments that promise the greatest economic development benefits.

During much of the 1970s the private venture capital market actually appeared to be in decline. In 1970, $97 million in new private capital was committed to venture capital firms, but by 1975 this figure had fallen steadily to only $10 million. Although the industry seemed to recover in the following year with the commitment of $50 million in new funds, the infusion fell again in 1977 to $39 million (U.S. Congress, 1986, p. 19). The apparent evaporation of venture capital in this period became a major cause of concern among people interested in stimulating the process of industrial innovation as a strategy to enhance American economic competitiveness abroad (Premus et al., 1985). One effect of fluctuations in the amount of venture funds available is that the financing for higher-risk business start-ups and early-stage operations decreases as money becomes scarce and increases as it becomes plentiful (Premus et al., 1985, p. 11). Since it is in the states' interest to encourage business births, it follows that it is in their interest to expand the venture capital pool.

When the so-called Steiger amendment to the 1978 Tax Act reduced the maximum capital gains tax from 49 to 28 percent, the venture capital industry experienced a boom. In 1978, $600 million in new money was committed by venture investors. A further reduction in the capital gains tax to 20 percent in the 1981 Economic Recovery Tax Act produced another boost: $1.3 billion flowed in during 1981, a figure that rose to $4.2 billion by 1984. In that year the venture capital industry controlled a pool that totaled over $16 billion, up from $4.5 billion in 1980 (ibid.). Nevertheless, despite this record of growth in the 1980s, the president of the National Venture Capital Association could still testify before the

U.S. Senate that the nation faced an equity shortfall of more than $6 billion (U.S. Congress, Senate, 1983, p. 87). Furthermore, just as decreases in the capital gains tax seemed to encourage investment in venture funds, so may the tax increase that occurred in the tax reform of 1986 contract the venture pool. In that year the capital gains tax rate was raised back up to 28 percent, the same rate as that imposed on other income. It is also increasingly apparent that private venture investing fluctuates sharply with other elements of the economy besides the tax system. After the plunge in stock prices in October 1987, for example, private venture capital flowing to biotechnology enterprises dropped sharply. Analysts predicted that $400 million in private venture capital would be invested in biotechnology concerns in 1988, compared with $1.4 billion in the peak year of 1985 (*New York Times*, Feb. 2, 1988). Both federal tax reform and fluctuations in the market thus militate for a state role not only in augmenting but also in stabilizing the flow of funds to venture investments.

The claim that the national venture pool is underfunded gains some credence through the finding that, as the amount of money expanded after 1978, the number of business propositions increased in response without any decline in the quality of the proposals (Premus et al., 1985, p. 12). This suggests that a good deal of entrepreneurial energy was lying dormant for lack of capital. If the claim that there was a shortage of venture capital was spurious, then no such effect should have been observed.

A second problem concerns the uneven geographical distribution of private venture capital. In 1982 a single *county*—Santa Clara in California—was the site of *one-sixth* of all venture placements in the entire nation (Vaughan and Pollard, 1986, p. 277). Three states—California, Massachusetts, and Texas—accounted for 66 percent of all venture dollars invested in 1984. Eleven states accounted for 88 percent. The 23 states of the South and Midwest accounted for only 14 percent of the dollars invested (*Venture Capital Journal*, 1985). (See Table 10-1.)

Nationally, per capita venture investments came to $12.71 in 1984, but they reached $72.44 in Massachusetts and $51.52 in California. Illinois, which is among the top 11 states in venture dollars invested, fell far below these figures at $5.21 per capita (Wisconsin Dept. of Development, 1985c, p. 4). Intraregional disparities are common: for example, between 1969 and 1983 over $220 million in venture capital was invested in Minnesota, but only $55 million was invested by venture firms in neighboring Wisconsin. More than $67 million was invested in

Table 10-1.   Geographical Distribution of Venture Capital, 1984

Disbursement by State (% of all dollars invested)		Disbursement by Region (% of all dollars invested)	
California	44	West	60
Massachusetts	14	Northeast	26
Texas	8	Midwest	8
New York	5	South	6
Colorado	3	Total	100
Minnesota	3		
Oregon	3		
Connecticut	2		
Illinois	2		
New Jersey	2		
Pennsylvania	2		
Total	88		

Source: *Venture Capital Journal*, May 1985, p. 12.

Georgia in that period, but North Carolina was able to attract only $14.6 million (Wisconsin Dept. of Development, 1985a, p. 35).

Venture capitalists are not restricted by law to particular geographical areas, but the desire for personal monitoring of a firm's early years often results in a self-imposed limit on investments within a day's drive or less of the venture capital firm's headquarters (interview, Jackson, 1986; Susman, 1986). One explanation, therefore, for the bicoastal distribution of venture funds is that venture capital firms stay, by force of habit, in those areas where the agglomeration of high-technology enterprises fosters a lively entrepreneurial environment. But the finding that the availability of venture capital in itself elicits attractive business proposals suggests that there probably exist virgin territories in the nation's midsection where entrepreneurial impulses merely await the appearance of potential investors in order to blossom. Because private venture firms have not yet come to the interior in significant numbers, some states have themselves assumed the role of venture capitalist.

Finally, state-sponsored venture financing may be justified because private venture investors are more concerned with returns than with economic development goals. A profit-oriented investment strategy generally leads private firms to reject small proposals in the $50,000–$500,000 range: deals of this size are regarded in the private venture industry as not worth the costs of administration and monitoring. In contrast, state venture funds are aimed explicitly at small businesses with modest needs on the theory that it is this sector that is most likely to generate both jobs and product innovations.

Data also suggest that private venture funds are increasingly being invested in the service sector—fast food franchises, discount stores, athletic clothing outlets—rather than advanced technology or manufacturing companies. In 1981 approximately 16 percent of private venture funds went to firms in the personal and retail service sector; by 1986 the figure had risen to more than 25 percent (*New York Times,* Feb. 6, 1987). In addition, a third of new private capital flowing to venture firms was being used for leveraged buyouts. Neither in the service sector nor in leveraged buyouts does investment offer a maximally productive strategy for generating economic development benefits.

The States as Venture Capitalists

States employ at least five general types of venture capital programs, in which state commitment runs from the relatively tangential role involved in subsidizing privately capitalized business development corporations through the use of state income tax credits to full-fledged public participation in equity financing. Through 1986 at least 25 states, spread more or less evenly among the various regions, were operating one or more such programs. With the exception of Connecticut's Product Development Corporation, created in 1972, and the Massachusetts Community Development Finance Corporation, which dates from 1975, none of these programs began before 1977. Most are of more recent origin. While a number of states show little interest in becoming involved in venture financing, preferring to pursue industrial development financing through more traditional loan programs, the number of venture capitalist states seems likely to grow. Proposals for two such programs were among the main features of the platform of the unsuccessful Democratic gubernatorial candidate in Oklahoma in 1986 (*State Budget and Tax News,* 1986), and economic development commissions in other states, including Arizona and New Jersey, have recommended their adoption. Chart 10-1 lists the participating states in each of the five types of programs through 1986.

DEVELOPMENT CREDIT CORPORATIONS

These institutions, discussed in Chapter 6, are privately funded, privately managed,[5] for-profit venture capital funds chartered by their respective states. What distinguishes the corporations listed in the first col-

---

5. Iowa's Venture Capital Fund, administered by the Iowa Development Commission, a state agency, is the exception.

Chart 10-1. State Venture Capital Programs, 1986

Development Credit Corporations	Venture Capital Loan Programs	Product Development Corporations	Pension Fund Venture Pools	State Venture Capital Corporations
Massachusetts Capital Resource Co. (1977)	California Innovation Development Program (1981)	Connecticut Product Development Corp. (1972)	Washington (1981)	Massachusetts Community Development Finance Corp. (1975)
Maine Capital Corp. (1977)	Connecticut Innovation Development Loan Fund (1981)	Indiana Corporation for Science and Technology (1982)	Ohio (1982)	Massachusetts Technology Development Corp. (1978)
Indiana Corp. for Innovation Development (1982)	Oregon Business Development Fund (1983)	Iowa Product Development Corp. (1983)	Michigan (1982)	New Mexico Research and Development Institute (1986)[a]
Wisconsin Community Capital (1982)		North Carolina Innovation Research Fund (1983)	Illinois (1982)	Louisiana Small Business Equity Corp. (1981)
Montana Capital Companies (1983)		Massachusetts Product Development Corp. (1984)	New York (1983)	New York Corp. for Innovation Development (1982)
Iowa Venture Capital Fund (1983)		Illinois Business Innovation Fund (1985)[b]	Oregon (1983)	Illinois Venture Fund (1983)
Louisiana Capital Companies (1983)		Michigan Product Development Corp. (1985)	Utah (1983)	Utah Technology Finance Corp. (1983)
North Dakota Venture Capital (1985)			Pennsylvania (1984)	
Mississippi Cap. 459 (1985)			Kansas (1985)[c]	

Arkansas Capital
Development Corps.
(1986)

Kansas Venture
Capital Companies
(1986)

West Virginia Capital
Companies (1986)

Pennsylvania Seed
Capital Venture
Fund (1983)

Build Illinois Equity
Investment Pro-
gram (1985)

Arkansas Science and
Technology (1985)

Florida High Tech-
nology Innovation
Research and De-
velopment Fund
(1985)

Oregon Resource and
Technology Devel-
opment Corp.
(1985)

Kansas Venture Capi-
tal (1986)

Sources: Wisconsin Dept. of Development, 1987; Bettger, 1986; U.S. SBA, 1985.
[a]Originally established in 1981 as the New Mexico Energy Research and Development Institute.
[b]Funds must be used in cooperation with Illinois universities or nonprofit organizations.
[c]The Kansas Public Employee Retirement System board has mandated greater participation in venture capital financing of established firms that seek refinancing, but no specific set-aside is involved.

umn in Chart 10-1 from the 20 or so other business development credit corporations that date back to Maine's original 1949 program is that investors in the more recent corporations enjoy a state tax credit for their investment. These credits range from 5 percent of the investment in Iowa to 50 percent in Maine's modern successor arrangement, the Capital Corporation.

These corporations are not strictly state venture capital organs, for no public money is invested. Thus, unlike all the other venture arrangements discussed in this chapter, development credit corporations impose no financial risks on the states that initiate and subsidize them. But aside from their risk-free aspect from the government's point of view, development credit corporations qualify as creations of the entrepreneurial state. Not only is the purpose to expand financing for venture-stage operations, but also investments are targeted, according to the provisions of the respective charters, to small, in-state, risky firms with high-profit potential. Although several programs permit investment in firms in mature industries critical to the state's economy, the emphasis is on investing in innovative, technology-based companies. The development credit corporation, therefore, is very much guided by demand-based considerations.

Perhaps the most important characteristic of these corporations, however, is their small size: excluding the approximately $100 million pool controlled by the Massachusetts Capital Resource Company, a consortium of insurance companies, the other five programs actually operating in 1986 planned to administer a combined total of no more than $30 million. By the standards of the private venture capital industry, such a sum is easily absorbed by no more than a handful of deals.

VENTURE CAPITAL LOAN PROGRAMS

These programs rank just above development credit corporations in the level of risk to which the state is exposed in its venture investments. The programs in existence in 1986, all state-administered, were capitalized or endowed by a combination of state legislative appropriations (ranging from $2 million in California to $667,000 in Oregon) and Title IX grants of roughly similar magnitudes from the federal Economic Development Administration. Each of these programs targets its venture loans to firms in need of capital for the manufacture of a new product or the development of a new service, or in the case of Oregon, for small business expansion in areas in which growth and diversification are anticipated, such as aquaculture development and tourist facilities. These programs all qualify as efforts of the entrepreneurial state to the degree to which they offer debt financing to high-risk companies targeted for their growth potential.

PRODUCT-DEVELOPMENT CORPORATIONS

An arrangement in which the state provides financing for the development of a new product by an existing firm in return for a royalty represents a significant step across the risk threshold. It is also one of the clear cases in economic development policy of the emergence of mixed economic forms in which the public and private sectors conjointly hold an ownership stake. Product-development corporation financing is uncollateralized; returns to the state are entirely dependent upon the sales of the product financed. The arrangement falls short, however, of the private-sector venture capital model in that the state has no equity interest in the company whose product it finances and thus no voice in the management of the company.

Connecticut was the first to establish this sort of high-risk financing. In response to a gubernatorial task force recommendation, which took as its model Britain's National Research Development Corporation, the state legislature established the Connecticut Product Development Corporation in 1972 to create and preserve jobs, stimulate the innovation process, and encourage the diversification of the state's defense industries. Implementation of the CPDC program was delayed by three years by a suit challenging the ability under the state constitution to use public funds for what the plaintiff contended were purely private benefits. The Connecticut Supreme Court eventually ruled that the purpose of the act was in fact to promote the welfare of the state through job creation and that this constituted a legitimate "public purpose" (*Wilson v. Connecticut Product Development Corporation,* 355 A2nd 167 Conn., 1975). The CPDC made its first product-development investment in 1975.

The corporation operates much like a private venture capital firm: It receives about 400 proposals per year, all from existing companies, of which no more than a few are eventually funded. Once a decision to finance a product has been made, CPDC project directors maintain close personal contact with the business. Through the middle of 1986 CPDC had participated in the financing of 72 new products, which required a commitment of $17.4 million. Funding for the corporation comes from state-issued bond proceeds as well as from royalty income.

The CPDC will reimburse up to 60 percent of product-development costs of a firm and expects in return a royalty of 5 percent of net product

Table 10-2. Connecticut Product Development
Corporation Royalty Income (in
thousands of dollars), 1978–86

1978	5
1979	28
1980	52
1981	219
1982	456
1983	173
1984	357
1985	525
1986	555
Total	2400

Sources: CPDC *Annual Reports* for the years
shown.

sales up to five times the original investment. At that point the royalty
percentage declines to a nominal level. Royalty income through fiscal
year 1986 had reached an aggregate total of $2.4 million (see Table 10-
2) on an actual disbursement of $12.9 million to date. Administrative
costs have been paid out of royalty income since 1980, and officials expect eventually to pay off entirely the bonded indebtedness plus interest.
The average investment in a product reached slightly over $400,000 in
1985–86. The corporation estimates that about 960 full-time jobs have
been directly created as a result of product-development financing, at a
cost in invested funds of approximately $12,900 per job.

Connecticut's program is not targeted particularly to technologically
sophisticated products. Instead, the corporation is willing to consider
any product for which there is a verifiable market: "We evaluate market
size estimates, penetration prediction, cost and validity of plans for
achieving the predicted penetration, current and expected competitive
activity and product life" (Jonap, 1984, p. 10). Products financed range
from computer software packages and automated irrigation-control systems to molded plastic bathroom accessories and car-top ski carriers.

Despite a cautious assessment of demand factors, the corporation is
regarded as an extremely high-risk operation. The firms it finances have,
after all, been unable to obtain conventional financial backing for their
proposed new products. Nevertheless, the record of the CPDC is not
wholly unlike what one might find in the portfolio of a private venture
capital firm. In 1986, 25 of the 72 products were successfully marketed,
with aggregate sales over $50 million; 6 more were marginal but surviv-
ing; 18 products were still in the development stage; and 23 had either
failed or completed their life cycle.

CPDC funding covers only product-development costs; the financing of actual production and marketing of the new product was left entirely to the firm prior to 1981. Since then, however, firms with CPDC backing can obtain low-interest loans from the Connecticut Innovation Development Loan Fund, a venture capital loan program of the type already discussed, to purchase equipment or machinery, for inventory build-up, and for marketing. The loan fund is administered by the CPDC.

Having created fewer than 100 new jobs per year, the CPDC must be regarded as an extremely modest program. Yet Connecticut's foray into venture capitalism, relatively unnoticed in the 1970s, brought representatives in the 1980s from nearly all the remaining 49 states to Hartford to learn about the program. One of the first to act on what it had learned was the state of Iowa, which established a product-development corporation in 1983. Royalty returns on the predominantly agriculture-based products the corporation backs were minimal through 1986 (interview, Burmeister, 1986), but the program had leveraged over $3.8 million in private funds with an initial investment of $610,000 in state money. Officials report that the program had already created 95 new jobs.

The Massachusetts Product Development Corporation, established in 1984 but not implemented until late in 1986, is distinctive for its intention to finance new products made by small to midsized firms in mature rather than emerging industries, such as the needle trades, fishing, and machinery (interview, Leiken, 1986).

PENSION FUND VENTURE POOLS

The most common state venture capital arrangement involves earmarking a designated percentage of public employee pension funds to be invested as venture capital in local companies. Pension fund managers had typically been precluded from such investments by the need for strict adherence to a conservative interpretation of the "prudent man" rule,[6] a standard that normally served to limit investments to low-risk securities of large companies or the government. Most states at one time not only imposed the prudent man standard by statute but also supplemented the rule with so-called legal lists, that is, specific prohibitions against investing in certain assets unless they met various stringent quality criteria.

6. According to Litvak the prudent man rule derives from a Massachusetts court case of 1830, *Harvard v. Amory*, in which the court ruled that no investment in and of itself was sound or unsound. Rather the judiciousness of any investment decision was a matter of whether in the context of the trust's objectives and the state of investment management practices, the decision to invest made sense. The trustee "shall conduct himself faithfully and exercise a sound discretion. . . . He is to observe how men of prudence, discretion and intelligence manage their own affairs . . ." (Litvak, 1983, p. 202).

Among these are, typically, a five-year consecutive dividend history, a national stock exchange listing, or some prior earnings record (Litvak, 1983, p. 204). Some states—Indiana, for example—even go so far as to forbid their pension funds from investing in equities. At least 13 states still maintained legal lists in 1985 (Vaughan and Pollard, 1986, p. 278). A modest liberalization occurred in the 1970s when four states—Massachusetts, California, North Dakota, and Kentucky—moved to permit their pension fund managers to take into consideration the impact of their investments on the economy of the state, so long as what they did was "consistent with sound business practices"; but no provisions were made in this period for targeting in-state firms of a particular size or type or for a designated venture set-aside.

It took a change in the interpretation of the prudent man rule by the U.S. Department of Labor, acting on the recommendation of the Small Business Administration, to open the way for the current spate of venture fund pools. The role of the Department of Labor is a function of its responsibility to administer ERISA (the Employee Retirement Income Security Act of 1974), which declares that pension funds must be managed "with the care, skill, prudence and diligence under the circumstances then prevailing that a prudent man acting in a like capacity and familiar with such matters would use in the conduct of an enterprise of a like character and with like aims." The new interpretation of this standard, promulgated in regulations issued in 1979, declared that the prudence of an investment decision should not be considered in isolation but rather in the context of the entire portfolio in which price fluctuations of individual securities may offset one another (Stoll, 1984, pp. 201–2). A focus on the structure of the portfolio as a whole reflects the notion in modern investment theory that diversification substantially reduces risk. This idea, combined with the demonstration for the first time by professional venture capitalists in the late 1970s that they could achieve significantly higher rates of return than those on managed stock and bond portfolios (National Governors' Association, 1983, p. 43), prompted a number of states to invest some of their vast holdings in small, high-growth companies.

Ohio and Michigan in 1982 were the first states to earmark by statute a proportion of their public employee retirement funds for investment in local venture undertakings.[7] Ohio, which previously had limited pension

---

7. The state of Washington Investment Board began investing as a limited partner in 1981 in venture undertakings, but it acted on its own and without specific legislative autho-

funds for investment in large, publicly traded companies, now permits fund managers to invest up to 5 percent of the investment system's assets in any firm so long as it is headquartered in Ohio or maintains most of its assets or workforce in the state. The fund may finance young firms or start-ups directly or through the use of a private venture capital firm as an intermediary. The Ohio venture pool totals $350 million, of which only a small fraction had been invested by the mid-1980s.

Legislation creating the Venture Capital Division in the Bureau of Investments of Michigan's Department of Treasury was signed into law in 1982. It provides for the investment of up to 5 percent—approximately $600 million—in qualified small businesses on an equity or debt basis. The program is explicit in its use of market-demand criteria in making an investment decision: "Both high technology and existing technology businesses will be considered but the company should have a unique product, service or market position to give it a proprietary competitive edge" (Michigan Dept. of Treasury, 1986). At least half the firm's assets or personnel must be located in Michigan, a targeting requirement that would have been regarded as a dangerously reckless constraint a few years before.

Michigan was the only state in the mid-1980s to make any effort to monitor the impact of its pension fund venture investments on the state's economy, though the data it gathered were only rudimentary. By June 1986 the fund had invested over $172 million directly in 31 high-growth firms and indirectly through 16 different private venture capital companies (ibid.). The state Department of Treasury estimates that venture pool investments have created 3200 new jobs in the state and leveraged over $200 million in private investment in Michigan businesses. According to one official of the pension fund, one of the major impacts has been to attract branch offices of several California private venture capital firms to the state, thus greatly enlarging the community of such investment institutions in Michigan (interview, Sept. 25, 1986).

The eventual impact of such programs in state capital markets could be extraordinary: Litvak estimates that by 1995 state and local employee pension funds will reach $1 trillion (1983, p. 162). If in fact venture investments in the pioneer pension set-aside programs produce the high returns that typify private venture investment, stimulating business formation and job creation in the process, then other states are likely to join

---

rization. The board concentrates on computer-related companies and limits its venture pool to no more than 3 percent of the fund's assets.

in such activities. A number already have study commissions and task forces devoted to the subject. The universal embrace of venture fund arrangements may at this point flood the capital market with money in search of viable deals. Competition among states and between state funds and private venture companies may become intense, increasing incentives to invest in ever-riskier propositions. For the moment, however, such venture pools are still relatively modest contributors to the capital pool: the total available in earmarked funds probably amounted to a maximum of $3.5 billion in the mid-1980s, of which a majority was not yet invested in venture undertakings. Yet even at this size, such mechanisms are significant enough to help redress both regional imbalance in the distribution of venture capital and the financing gaps that hinder business formation in some states (see, for example, *Wall Street Journal*, June 24, 1986).

VENTURE CAPITAL CORPORATIONS

The two oldest state-owned venture capital corporations are products of the first governorship of Michael Dukakis in Massachusetts during the 1970s.[8] The two programs serve different purposes. The first to be established, the Massachusetts Community Development Finance Corporation, provides both venture loans and equity backing for small business start-up or expansion in designated distressed areas in the state. No particular industrial sector is targeted for assistance: projects are chosen rather for their potential for offering steady work at prevailing wages for area residents. The corporation works in conjunction with local community development corporations, which typically also own a share of the firms financed.

The Massachusetts Technology Development Corporation, established three years later, is directed specifically at high-tech companies expected to generate significant employment growth. The MTDC requires in fact that the principal products or services of the firms it finances "be sufficiently innovative to provide a competitive advantage." (Indeed, with the exception of the Massachusetts Community Development Finance Corporation and the Louisiana Small Business Equity Corporation, all of the state venture capital corporations target technology-based firms that promise "exceptional growth and success," in the words

---

8. For an excellent history of the genesis of these programs, see Ferguson and Ladd, 1986.

of the Illinois Department of Commerce and Community Affairs (1986, p. 23). Most of the investments of the MTDC involve start-up financing, where, according to state officials, the most persistent capital gap exists (Massachusetts Technology Development Corporation, n.d.) The corporation provides a combination of debt and equity backing, of which the former is usually in the form of unsecured, long-term, subordinated notes. Investments average around $250,000. The MTDC was initially capitalized by a combination of U.S. Economic Development Administration grants and state funds, a pattern shared by the Utah Technology Finance Corporation and the New York Corporation for Innovation Development. The New Mexico program is financed by the state's severance tax and royalties from successfully commercialized products of the firms financed. Other states have capitalized their funds by a combination of state appropriations and private investments. The Illinois Venture Fund, for example, is a partnership between the state, which put up $2 million, and a private venture company, which put up $5 million initially. The private firm manages the fund and is responsible for all investment decisions. The Louisiana program (LASBEC) also involves using a public appropriation to leverage private institutional investments in the SBA's Small Business Investment Companies or community development corporations. LASBEC provides an illustration of the capacity for invention in this whole policy domain: rather than investing directly in its targeted firms (small-growth concerns, small firms in distressed areas, or companies owned by disadvantaged persons), LASBEC will *guarantee* equity investments made in investment intermediaries such as Small Business Investment Companies by qualified financial institutions. LASBEC is a small operation. Although the state initially committed $2 million to it, only a few hundred thousand dollars were actually invested in the first several years (U.S. SBA, 1984d, p. 26). The Pennsylvania Seed Capital Venture Fund is also a combination of public ($3 million) and private ($9 million) money.

Most of the venture capital programs have been established too recently to evaluate. Some do not even publish annual reports. Experienced venture capitalists would also argue that, since "it takes a long time to make a pearl," the effects of successful ventures will not become evident for perhaps 7–10 years. But several conclusions are possible. Like all but the pension set-asides, these are extremely modest programs. No more than $30 million in state and federal funds were available for investment in the mid-1980s, although most of these programs do leverage about $5 in private investments for every $1 of public money. Several programs are making money: the MTDC managed a 25 percent rate of return between 1979 and 1984 (Hodgman, 1985), and both the New Mexico and New York programs report income from their investments. Of the programs that report data, only the Massachusetts Community Development Finance Corporation has lost money.

Return rates do not appear to approach those enjoyed by private venture firms, but the state programs are involved in a segment of the commercial market that the private investment community shuns as unprofitable. The point to be made, then, is not that public venture corporations do not match the productivity of their private counterparts but rather that the state entities have entered a very high-risk field and emerged, literally, with profit.

Economic development impacts, the primary object of these programs, tend, like the profits, to be modest. The Massachusetts Community Development Finance Corporation claims to have been responsible for about 500 new and retained jobs per year. The New York Corporation for Innovation Development had created only 250 new jobs altogether through 1985. Officials of the corporation initially projected 2000 new jobs by 1989 but in a subsequent report pushed the date back to 1991. The MTDC had accounted for about 1400 jobs through 1985.

Smart Investing: Mechanisms for Investment Decision-making

Investing in the market, it is widely believed, is best done when it is the product of abilities made sharp by professional experience and the risk of personal financial loss. Private venture capitalists are often skeptical about the capacity of public entities to make sensible or productive investment decisions, for bureaucrats, they argue, never have to face the consequence of financial loss, cannot anticipate personal gain, and seldom have been schooled in the business world (Steinbach and Guskind, 1984).

To counter these doubts state programs employ several strategies to increase the chances of making smart investment decisions. Two early programs that no longer exist, the Alaska Renewable Resources Corporation and the Kentucky Highlands Investment Corporation,[9] were allowed to spend money to hire private firms on retainer to search for investment opportunities (Litvak and Daniels, 1983, p. 108). Several of

---

9. The Alaska Renewable Resources Corporation was capitalized mainly by mineral lease revenues and royalties; the Kentucky Highlands Investment Corporation was funded by a federal Community Services Administration grant. Both programs operated very briefly during the 1970s.

the contemporary programs turn over the task of deciding when and where to invest to private co-investors or private investment managers. The Illinois Venture Fund and the Kansas and Ohio pension fund pools are examples.

Other programs are governed by boards of directors selected for their business experience. The Connecticut Product Development Corporation, whose board is appointed by the governor, must have at least five members with product development and marketing experience. The board in 1984 contained a banker, a mechanical engineer, a physicist, a patent attorney, two economists, and a venture capitalist. Administrative officials all had engineering and financial experience (Jonap, 1984). The MTDC board, also appointed by the governor, is a mix of private business executives, venture capitalists, academic scientists and engineers, and state officials. Final investment decisions are made by this body. The Michigan Venture Fund, which strives to operate like a regular private venture company, had a former Wall Street investment analyst as its first director (Bartsch, 1985, p. 42).

Failure rates among firms or products financed by these programs— at least for the few states that supply such data—indicate that investment outcomes are in line with private venture investing. Occasionally, a firm that began with the support of state venture funding experiences a growth boom, but these cases supply only anecdotal evidence of the smartness of state investment practices.

Keying Venture Programs to the Business Life Cycle

Traditionally, states have offered businesses a menu array of financing programs geared to different elements and stages of the typical plant construction project. Consider the range of Alabama's programs, a set of initiatives that target assistance to existing, primarily manufacturing firms. The state administers Industrial Site Preparation grants to pay for site improvements; a program of interest-free loans for building construction through its Industrial Development Authority Building Loan program; an industrial development bond program that helps to finance land acquisition, building construction, or new equipment; and the Economic Development Loan Fund that may be used to finance the same purposes as IDBs.

Other states finance far more than the standard manufacturing plant construction cycle, the heart of traditional supply-side approaches to economic development. Programs designed to finance different sizes and

Chart 10-2.   Illinois Business Financing Programs, by Size, Type, Function, and Life Stage of Businesses

---

Existing small business programs
   Micro Loan Program
   Small Business Development Program
   Small Business Fixed Rate Financing Fund
   Small Business Energy Conservation Loan Program
   Pooled Bond Program

Existing large and medium-size business programs
   Large Business Development Program
   Illinois Development Authority Direct Loan Fund
   Conventional Industrial Revenue Bond Financing

Start-up and infant firm programs
   Illinois Venture Fund

High-technology firm financing
   Equity Investment Fund
   Business Innovation Fund

Export financing
   Export Development Authority loans

Source: Illinois Department of Commerce and Community Affairs, 1986.

types of business and different stages of the business life cycle represent the elaboration of business financing by the entrepreneurial state. Illinois, for example, as Chart 10-2 shows, maintains at least five separate programs targeted at existing small businesses, two at existing high-technology firms, and one at start-up or infant companies, along with three more conventional financing programs for large to medium-sized firms. This more complex array of programs, along with the export loan fund, reflects the concerns of the entrepreneurial state for fostering small business births and growth, export activity, and high-technology firms.

Offering a range of business financing programs for high-risk enterprises is a hallmark of the entrepreneurial state, but entrepreneurial financing strategies may be pursued from state to state with varying degrees of program integration and planning. Illinois occupies one end of the spectrum: its programs are varied but are in no obvious sense the ultimate product of a coherent plan or perspective. Massachusetts presents a similar venture-financing profile. Connecticut is an example of a state that occupies a middle position on the program-integration spectrum. Although it maintains a much smaller array of particular financing schemes than Illinois, it offers an integrated two-program package for firms engaged in new product development. One program, the Connecticut Product Development Corporation, provides backing for new prod-

Chart 10-3.   Linking the Business Life Cycle with Risk Financing Programs:
the Michigan Strategic Fund

Business Life Stage	State Financing Program[a]
I. Research and development Proof of concept Prototype development	State Research Fund
II. Emerging stage Business pre-start-up Marketing/distribution plan Management team assembly	MSF Seed Capital Michigan Venture Capital Fund
III. Middle-risk growth stage Product development Early growth Market development Inventory buildup Diversifying Automating	MSF Capital Access Program Michigan Product Development Corporation Michigan Business and Industrial Development Corporations MSF Minority Business Fund
IV. Bankable stage Expansion	tax-exempt bonds

Source: Michigan Strategic Fund, n.d.

[a]Michigan also administers, but does not fund, a variety of federal programs, including CDBG, SBA 504 and 7(a) programs, and Small Business Innovation Research grants.

uct development. A follow-up program, the Innovation Development Loan Fund, offers assistance to recipients of product-development financing to manufacture, promote, and market the new product.

The most comprehensive integrated approach to financing venture undertakings has been pioneered by Michigan. Financing programs are linked to a number of different high- and middle-risk stages of the business cycle (see Chart 10-3). Oversight and coordination functions are the responsibility of the Michigan Strategic Fund, created by the legislature late in 1984 and implemented in the fall of 1985. The fund itself does not run the various financing programs, but it is designed to coordinate the process. In theory, a new, small, innovative business that cannot qualify for conventional financing could move through the system from program to program as its needs change. Assistance is available at each stage of the business cycle. If properly nurtured, a firm could presumably emerge from this system of state support to function on its own in the private capital market. The idea of keying separate programs to the different stages of business development rather than simply offering an array of programs designed to serve different sizes and types of firms in their early years is unique among the states.

Conclusions

At least since the initiation of industrial development financing programs in the 1950s, the states have functioned as commercial bankers of the last resort. In a limited sense, then, the new venture capital arrangements represent simply an expansion of that role. But I would argue that venture financing by the state constitutes a sharp departure from the traditional programs. Indeed, they are critical programmatic embodiments of the style and objectives of the entrepreneurial state.

What makes these programs entrepreneurial is first of all that they involve the state in high-risk financing. Whereas the traditional industrial development loans went mostly to existing firms, which backed their borrowing with collateral, the new programs focus on start-up operations, small business at the early stages of development, and new product development. Venture loans are generally of the subordinated variety and often do not require collateral. Many venture arrangements involve equity investments, a degree of involvement unknown in the old industrial financing programs. By focusing on high-risk propositions—a strategy that the entrepreneurial state justifies by the potential job growth such enterprises promise—the state has entered a domain that not only conventional financial institutions but even many private venture capitalists shun. The state is literally at the high-risk financing frontier, a position heretofore reserved for the boldest and possibly most reckless of the private venture capitalists.

If the element of risk distinguishes the new financing from the old, so too does the sensitivity of state venture capitalism to the structure of the market. Where traditional financing programs tended overwhelmingly to back standard manufacturing firms, the venture programs target companies that offer a unique product, a distinct market advantage, and high growth. Industrial financing was employed to induce the location or retention of any manufacturing employer. The venture capital programs, however, pose a simple question before they back a firm: does the company make something that is going to sell?

Finally, these financing arrangements are reflections of the entrepreneurial impulse to the degree that they are means by which the state plays midwife in the capital formation and birth process. This aggressive, participant role in the economic process contrasts with traditional industrial financing efforts, which seek simply to influence firms weighing alternative location decisions.

For all their relative boldness, these state venture capital programs are very small. The sums of money they have invested are modest, and the number of jobs any one program claims to have generated per year can seldom compensate for the employment losses caused by the average plant closing.

But to say this is not to suggest that these programs are trivial. With the exception, perhaps, of the forays into venture financing in Connecticut and Massachusetts, it is much too soon to offer reliable conclusions about the significance for economic development of these interventions. But I would argue that the way in which we will eventually be able to observe their development implications is in terms of what might be called the additive effects of "microimpacts." That is to say, in the short term the consequences of any single program are not likely to show up as measurable changes in the aggregate performance of a state's economy. But any single program intervention may have significant *localized* impacts. The implications for a small community or an urban neighborhood of the emergence of a fast-growing employer will be felt quickly. As these instances of localized intervention accumulate, then it is reasonable to expect to see measurable effects on the aggregate state economy over the long term. A state is likely to accelerate the process by which microimpacts accumulate by developing several venture programs, each of which corresponds to a different phase of the business life cycle. Aside from any learning benefits that might accrue from specialization in a narrow class of business problems, program proliferation is likely to increase the total resources devoted to venture financing, since in budgeting politics new programs are seldom created at the expense of existing ones. From the perspective of microimpacts, therefore, economic development as a process is best evaluated as the product of an increasing number of small interventions over time.

CHAPTER 11

Anticipating and Creating Markets: The States and High-Technology Policy

FROM the vantage point of an era in which people have become accustomed to the rapid adaptation of sophisticated technologies for everyday use, it takes a moment to remember that the advent of the computer age in the two decades after World War II was greeted by many as a development of quite ominous proportions. The popular press regaled readers with articles that warned that "machines are taking over" (*Life*, Mar. 3, 1961; see also, for example, *U.S. News*, Jan. 11, 1960; *Time*, Jan. 11, 1960), and scholars worried about the economic and social consequences of the cybernetic revolution. At the conference "The Impact of the Computer on Society" in the mid-1960s, a point at which some of these concerns had begun to moderate, the economist Garth Mangum (1966, p. 86) reflected on the increasing crescendo of dire possibilities that so frightened people in the early years: "The computer appeared to threaten jobs, the very concept of a full employment economy, the nature of work and the survival of political democracy."

In the 1980s the economic perspectives on the computer, still the most widely accepted symbol and component of "high technology," as well as on other less well-known emerging technological disciplines and products, were substantially altered. For public officials in state and local government in particular, "high-technology enterprise," a term I shall identify momentarily, had by now assumed a central role in planning for economic growth and development. Thus, as the state of Michigan broke ground in 1985 for its $17 million Industrial Technology Institute for the development and implementation of computer-integrated manufacturing systems, corporate, political, and academic leaders spoke not of the possibilities of automation-induced unemployment but rather of the hope that they were establishing "the seedbed for a whole new industry in Michigan" (Baba and Hart, 1986, p. 2). The implications for economic development of undertakings of this sort seemed clear to the governor of Pennsylvania, Richard Thornburgh, when he wrote in 1982 that "advanced technology is expected to generate one million jobs nationwide within this decade. Its innovations will not only spawn new enterprises that offer new products and services, but also modernize and expand the scope of traditional industries . . ." (Pennsylvania Governor's Office of Policy and Planning, 1982, p. i). The governor of Texas, explaining his enthusiasm for high technology put it more simply: "Research is the oil and gas of our future" (Jaschik, 1986b, p. 16).

State involvement in the promotion of high-technology activities as part of an economic development strategy is a comparatively recent phenomenon (National Governors' Association, 1983, p. S-1). The diverse state efforts that characterize this involvement are of interest from an economic development perspective on several grounds. High technology, understood in part as goods, services, and processes that result from efforts at the frontiers of scientific research, serves a rapidly expanding international market of household consumers, armies, businesses, industries, and agricultural producers. More striking, perhaps, than the state's efforts to help private firms respond to expanding demands for leading-edge goods and processes already on the market, however, is the possibility that states can help to stimulate demand for goods and processes not yet at a commercial stage or *not yet even conceived*. It is clear, to give one example, that the field of biotechnology—the use of living organisms in medical, industrial, and agricultural processes—is in its comparative infancy and will in all likelihood lead eventually to revolutionary techniques and products. By encouraging biotechnology and other sorts of advanced research, the state is essentially in the business of trying to create future markets.

The state role in the complex process by which ideas are translated into basic and applied research, which in turn leads to marketable innovations, is a pure example of state entrepreneurialism in the sense first that policy is devoted to identifying or targeting fields of endeavors or industries likely to serve or create expanding markets. State development planners seek to key such targeting to the resources already present in the state, such as specialized academic research capabilities or an agglomeration of industries prepared to capitalize on particular innovations. Thus, for example, a state whose universities have strong biochemistry and agricultural science components and whose economy has a strong agricultural base is more likely to target biotechnology research than, say, that in fiber optics or industrial robotics. By targeting particular disciplines, industries, or research areas for special policy attention, the entrepreneurial state seeks to establish a priority ranking among activities likely to lead to business formation or new products. "Certain types of advanced technology," Pennsylvania development planners have written, "hold particular promise for creating job opportunities in Pennsylvania" (Pennsylvania Governor's Office of Policy and Planning, 1982). They go on to list nine fields to be explored, ranging from robotics to telecommunications, in which Pennsylvania universities and industries have special capabilities and interests.

Certain industries or potential industries in other words are perceived as ascendant—or in the parlance of industrial policy, as "winners"—because they are more likely to produce economic development benefits for the state. Not only is targeting entrepreneurial in the sense that it involves identifying exploitable opportunities, but in the case of high technology particularly, it is entrepreneurial in the Schumpeterian meaning by virtue of the effort to exploit "an innovation . . . or untried technological possibility" (Schumpeter, 1962, p. 132).

Once a state has targeted particular areas it deems likely to flourish in the distinctive setting of the state, it seeks further to create conditions that make it possible for private actors to pursue opportunities for commercial application of research. These entrepreneurial activities might require mobilizing and supplying resources as necessary, such as research funds or institutes or even venture capital.

State efforts to generate development benefits from high technology are entrepreneurial in at least two other ways: policy in this particular field is characterized by high risk and by a long period between investment and payoff. To support basic or even applied research that may or may not lead to product development that in turn may or may not capture a share of the consumer market is both an uncertain enterprise and one calling for great patience. Evaluating the payoff of policy initiatives according to the scientific timetable rather than constraining judgment by the shorter electoral cycle is unusual in American politics. But such patience must necessarily become the norm—much as it is for the entrepreneur starting a new business—if states are to be involved in the field of high-tech economic development policy.

Besides offering a distilled example of the state entrepreneur identifying and seeking to create market opportunities for its residents to exploit, state efforts to encourage high-tech development for economic well-being are of concern because the elaboration of policy in this area is proceeding under the twin conditions of inadequate information and discouraging feedback. On the one hand little is known about how to stimulate innovation; on the other hand labor economists project extremely modest employment growth in high-tech industries through the end of the century. To wager that some infant technological research field, such as computer-integrated manufacturing or advanced polymer research, will lead to viable industrial activity of sufficient size to create the economic base of the future is a high-risk gamble for the entrepreneurial state.

Defining High Tech

Economic development programs aimed at encouraging high tech devote little effort to defining the term. Thus, the Illinois Business Innovation Fund, for example, simply "supports entrepreneurial activity involving technology and stimulates the development, marketing, and commercialization of new, technology-based products or services that have a significant potential for increased economic activity and employment creation and retention" (Illinois Dept. of Commerce and Community Affairs, 1986, p. 21). The Massachusetts Technology Development Corporation finances firms whose business is "technology-based" and whose products or services are "sufficiently innovative to provide a competitive advantage" (Massachusetts Technology Development Corporation, n.d., p. 2). North Carolina's Innovation Research Fund supports businesses doing "research leading to the development of products, processes, or services" (North Carolina Technological Development Authority, 1985, p. 19).

High technology is thought to inhere in any number of specific, relatively new research fields such as electronics, fiber optics, lasers, biotechnology, advanced materials, and so on. State policy architects, however, seldom provide standards for determining or limiting the composition of the list of such fields. Mississippi, for example, simply lists 14 two-, three-, and four-digit SIC industries[1] eligible for tax credits and exemptions under its Advanced Technology Initiatives Act without providing any sense of why some industries are eligible and others are not. In most states, policy-makers assume that they know a high-tech industry or firm when they see it.

---

1. SIC stands for Standard Industrial Classification. As the number of digits increases, so does the specificity of the classification.

The result of this sort of nominalism is a good deal of definitional ambiguity about what is really meant by high tech and what state governments have in mind when they seek to encourage it. Some programs are aimed at fostering the development of entire new industries; others are designed to stimulate the formation and expansion of particular firms. Some states construe high-tech employment, the chief policy goal, in terms of technical and professional occupations, though most states are just as interested in gaining workers engaged in the manufacture of goods that are the products of high-tech research, such as microchips or circuit boards.

An inspection of the objectives that states wish to achieve, however, clearly suggests that only a limited range of industries and types of firms can satisfy these goals. It is this restricted group that properly qualifies as high tech for economic development purposes. At a general level state economic development planners want a substantial high-tech economic base because they believe that innovation generates growth and improves the competitive posture of the state in national and international markets. More particularly, they want high rates of local job growth and the possibility for significant secondary employment in the production of high-tech products (see Birch and MacCracken, 1984). They seek industrial firms that are geographically stable and that spawn spin-off firms. High-tech companies are also attractive for their high concentration of well-paid professional and technical workers and their ability to attract government grants for research and development (R&D).

Conceptually, firms that promise to achieve these goals are those engaged in active research programs and/or in the nonroutine production of new, prototype, and specialty products informed by emerging technologies (Malecki, 1984, p. 263). They are companies whose activities are "knowledge intensive" (Browne, 1983) or that "integrate and apply scientific and engineering knowledge to complex problems" (Johnson, 1984, p. 6).

Operationally, scholars and some policy planners typically designate as high tech those industries with high proportions of scientific, technical, and engineering workers. To adopt alternative criteria, such as including firms whose workforce is principally engaged in the *production* of high-tech goods, is to fall prey to what Malecki calls "the illusion of high tech growth" (1986, p. 67), the fruits of which are often a low-paid, low-skill labor force. Another standard criterion for designating industries or firms as high tech is their degree of financial commitment to research and development. Riche, Hecker, and Burgan (1983), for example, use different cut-off points with these two variables (proportion of high-tech workers and financial commitment to R&D alone or in combination) to produce three alternative groups of high-tech industries. One group includes industries in which the proportion of "technology-oriented" workers is 1.5 times the average of all manufacturing industries. This produces a list of 48 three-digit industries, among which are tire manufacturing, farm machinery, and heavy construction.

A second group is derived by including all those industries in which R&D expenditures in relation to net sales are twice the average for all manufacturing industries. This produces a very short list of six industries. A third group is based on both variables: it is composed of industries in which both R&D expenditures and the proportion of technology-oriented workers are at or above the all-industry averages.[2] Twenty-eight industries qualify by this dual standard. For reasons of simplicity, as well as the fact that two variables provide more information about an industry than a single measure, job performance data are presented for the 28 industries only. The industries are listed in Table 11-1.

The actual number of jobs in these 28 industries, counting all occupations, is relatively small. In 1982 just under 5.7 million workers were employed by firms in this group, or 6.2 percent of the national workforce (ibid., p. 53). Nevertheless, employment growth *rates* in the previous decade were 36 percent higher than in the economy as a whole (27.3 percent in the 28-industry group compared with 20.1 percent from 1972 to 1982), and Riche and his colleagues projected higher-than-average increases in high-tech employment through the mid-1990s.

Firms engaged in R&D activities tend to be more stable locationally than production plants. Many of the former tend to gravitate to university settings in order to tap the steady stream of new, highly trained workers, whereas many production facilities, less dependent on other proximate institutions, are willing or impelled to migrate in search of lower-cost labor (Farley and Glickman, 1986, p. 409). Small R&D firms in particular are also likely to be established by an individual entrepreneur in his or her location of choice.

The presence of one firm engaged extensively in R&D activities is likely to give rise to the establishment of others in the área. Research for the Joint Economic Committee of Congress found that the "vast majority of the entrepreneurs that founded the many high-tech firms in Silicon

---

2. For all manufacturing industries the average proportion of technology-oriented workers in 1982 was 6.3 percent. The average proportion of R&D expenditures as a proportion of net sales in 1980 was 3.1 percent.

Table 11-1.   High-Tech Industries and Job Performance (percentage of growth or loss), 1972–84[a]

Industries with Job Growth		Industries with Job Loss	
Computers and data processing services	345.5	Radio and TV receiving equipment	35.3
Office computing and accounting machines	94.8	Plastic materials and synthetics	23.1
Medical instruments	93.9	Ordnance and accessories	17.6
Electronic components	93.0	Electric transmission and distribution equipment	11.1
Optical instruments	82.4		
Guided missiles and spacecraft	65.1	Paints and allied products	10.1
R&D laboratories	63.8		
Measuring and controlling instruments	57.8	Special industry machinery	4.7
Communications equipment	34.1	Engines and turbines	1.0
Drugs	26.1	Petroleum refining	0.9
Engineering, laboratory, and research instruments	24.3		
Miscellaneous electrical machinery	21.6		
Aircraft and parts	21.5		
Soaps and cleaners	21.0		
Industrial organic chemicals	14.3		
Industrial inorganic chemicals	11.3		
Agricultural chemicals	8.3		
Photography equipment	7.6		
Miscellaneous chemical products	3.9		
Electrical industrial apparatus	1.8		

Source: Burgan, 1985.

[a]Industries in this chart are those with a proportion of technology-oriented workers at or above the average for all manufacturing industries and with R&D expenditures close to or above the average for all industries.

Valley and Route 128 were previously employed in successful, established high-technology and electronics firms in the same locality. In fact, the corporate history of these regions can be pictured as an extensive genealogical family tree . . ." (Premus et al., 1985, p. 69).

Firms with a high concentration of technical and professional workers tend to have significant effects on personal income in an area and consequently on the spending multiplier.[3] A simulation of the impact of the Microelectronics and Computer Technology Corporation in Austin, Texas, found that every $1 paid in salary by the corporation would generate a personal-spending multiplier of $3.28 (in 1979 dollars), ranking

---

3. In contrast to production workers, whose wages tend to hover around the legal minimum. See Reich, 1983, p. 208.

the corporation higher in this regard than any Texas economic sector (Farley and Glickman, 1986).

High-tech firms are also magnets for federal R&D grants and thus serve as important sources of exogenous income in a community. Federal funds for industrial R&D—that is, funds to support research conducted by private firms—amounted to about a third of the total spent on such activities by all parties in 1985, or somewhat over $21 billion in current dollars (U.S. Congress, 1986, p. 16). How much of this sum actually went to high-tech firms is uncertain, but at least 75 percent of the total was granted to companies in just three industries within the 28-industry high-tech group: aircraft, missiles, and electrical equipment (ibid., p. 11).

On a variety of counts, therefore, state government interest in high-tech companies, a virtually universal phenomenon among the 50 states (Brody, 1985), is both understandable and justifiable—at least at first glance. High-tech activities appear to be potent job generators of the most desirable sort.

Justifying State Intervention

The state justification for intervening in the process that leads from scientific research to the marketplace revolves around a combination of arguments that stress market failure, the problematic character of federal government involvement in R&D, and the pivotal situation of state governments in this particular domain. All of these arguments are predicated on the assumption that high tech will both revitalize to some degree and replace declining industries and thus lay the basis for the American economic future, ample justification in itself.

The market-failure argument focuses on the contention that a market economy will tend to underinvest in R&D because the firm that produces the knowledge often cannot capture all of the profits that arise from its creation. To the extent that this is the case, it falls, therefore, to government to bear much of the cost of the production of knowledge. Whether in fact there is reason in the American experience to support this view is a matter of some disagreement. According to Robert Lawrence (1984, pp. 29–31), spending on R&D in manufacturing grew as rapidly in the United States between 1972 and 1980 as it did in other industrial countries. This was true not only of business-funded R&D but also, except by comparison with Japan, of R&D paid for by the national government.

A study done for the Joint Economic Committee of the U.S. Congress presents a more up-to-date and somewhat more mixed picture (U.S. Congress, 1986). On the positive side the study shows that in 1983 total U.S.

R&D spending greatly exceeded that in Japan, Germany, France, and Great Britain, the comparison group. Japan, for example, spent only 39 percent of what was spent in the United States. This study shows, however, that the nations of the comparison group all had higher annual rates of growth in R&D spending prior to 1979, although after that date, the rate of increase in the United States was higher than that in all of the countries except Japan. Although R&D as a percentage of the GNP rose in the United States from 2.22 percent in 1978 to 2.7 percent in 1985, it had not regained the high point of 2.96 percent achieved in 1964.

What is more problematic than rates of R&D spending is the fact that so much of the money in the United States is spent for defense. If defense R&D spending is excluded, then the United States had a smaller ratio of R&D spending to the GNP than either Japan or West Germany did, at least through 1983. Furthermore, U.S. nondefense R&D spending was expected to decline slightly as a percentage of GNP after 1983.

The contention that R&D is underfunded gains some support from the figures on the number of patents granted to corporations over time. This declined steadily between 1969 and 1984 from over 33,000 to about 29,000. And although the United States has many more scientists and engineers than its industrialized trading rivals, the pool of such workers as a proportion of the workforce *decreased* by 2.6 percent between 1968 and 1983, while the same measure increased in every other country in the comparison group by a high of 86.2 percent in Japan and a low of 48.1 percent in France (ibid., p. 40).

With R&D spending from all sources around $100 billion per year in the United States in the mid-1980s (Corrigan, 1984, p. 1720) and the rate steadily increasing, American industry is hardly facing a serious crisis. But as the Joint Economic Committee report points out, U.S. high-tech surpluses (exports minus imports) have begun to decline markedly in recent years (U.S. Congress, 1986, pp. 55–56). Many would argue that this is a sign of diminishing competitiveness in world markets, a condition that reflects a declining ability to innovate swiftly enough. Though R&D spending may not be a direct measure of the rate of production of innovations, the two variables are certainly related at some level. As the Joint Economic Committee report concludes, therefore, matters may have improved in this sphere since the 1970s, but there is still much room for progress (ibid., p. vi). State governments believe they can encourage such progress by increasing public support for R&D leading to marketable innovations.

That states have come to assume this burden rather than the federal government is a function of the nature of Washington's particular interests in the R&D enterprise as well as of the states' crucial role in the maintenance of institutions of higher education. According to the Congressional Budget Office, federal spending on high-tech R&D in 1983–84 came to $8.4 billion in direct expenditures and $1.5 billion in R&D tax credits (CBO, 1985, pp. xii–xiii, 19). But as Vaughan and Pollard (1986) have pointed out, there is no self-conscious federal policy for the support of high-tech R&D as a domestic economic undertaking. Furthermore, the great majority of federal R&D funds (64 percent) is spent on defense research, compared with only 2.4 percent in Japan, 9.4 percent in Germany, 33 percent in France, and 50 percent in Great Britain (U.S. Congress, 1986, p. 30). Although much of this money is spent to support research in private corporate laboratories, many of the results of the research cannot be marketed widely either at home or abroad for security reasons. Furthermore, federal priorities may serve to divert both public resources and private energies from the development of new civilian consumer and industrial products. Thus, state governments justify their involvement as brokers and patrons of the technology-transfer process on the grounds that *their* priorities lie in the development of innovations to be sold in the open market, transactions that will ultimately enhance the local economy.

As research and product development have become increasingly complex, drawing on a wide range of highly technical disciplines, the role of the large research university in the process of technological innovation has grown substantially. These are pivotal institutions in state high-tech policy for economic development. Many of these schools are state institutions, and their quality and capacity are direct functions of the level and nature of state support. Thus, state involvement in high-tech R&D is in large measure a function of the federal division of responsibilities that leaves public higher education in the hands of the states.

The Limits of High Tech in Economic Development

For all of the promise of high tech there are persistent signals that a development strategy based heavily on encouraging activity in this varied sector must take account of several critical limitations. Yet to observe the rate of policy invention and the intensity of expectations among the states is to come away convinced that these problems are either too painful to acknowledge or too little known to dampen state enthusiasm. This is not to argue that efforts to promote high-tech growth are misplaced, but rather only that they must be regarded, for most states, less as the means to economic salvation than as a very modest part of a larger development strategy. There are at least four general limits to a strategy primarily dependent on high tech:

1. High-tech industries promise to produce relatively small numbers of jobs.
2. Many of these industries of the future are not immune, as many believe, to fluctuations in the business cycle.
3. High-tech activity is geographically concentrated in just a few parts of the country and is unlikely to spread beyond these areas to a significant degree.
4. The role of public policy may only be tangential to the growth of high-tech industries, although not enough is known yet about its impacts to make a definitive statement.

Consider job-growth projections for the 28-industry group listed in Table 11-1. Riche and his colleagues (1983) at the U.S. Bureau of Labor Statistics estimate that total employment in these industries will grow from 6.2 percent of all U.S. wage and salary workers in 1982 to between only 6.5 and 6.7 percent, depending on economic growth patterns, by 1995. Although the economy is expected to generate around 29 million new jobs in this period, only 2.2 million at most will be in the 28-industry group. These projections encompass all occupations in these high-tech industries. Growth among technology-oriented workers—those with scientific training and knowledge—will, according to bureau projections, amount to much less. Such jobs will grow from 3.2 percent of the total workforce in 1982 to 3.8 percent, or slightly under 5 million jobs by 1995. Neither the number of jobs nor the occupational composition of the high-tech sector will serve to offset employment losses in traditional manufacturing industries. Between 1979 and 1984, nearly 11.5 million manufacturing workers, mainly in blue-collar occupations, lost their jobs because of plant closings, layoffs, or automation (Balderston, 1986, p. 2).

Economic development planners appear to have paid less attention to these numbers than to the spectacular rates of employment growth in certain particular industries, as shown in the left-hand column of Table 11-1. The high growth rates in computing and electronics employment during periods of generally sluggish economic growth also convinced many that high-tech fields were immune to drastic swings in the business cycle (Malecki, 1984). But Burgan's data (1985) show that at least 8 industries among the 28-industry group actually lost jobs between 1972 and 1984, and another 11 failed to match the 27.8 percent rate of growth in nonagricultural employment in the economy as a whole in this period.

Although the overall employment in the 28 industries grew by around 43 percent between 1972 and 1984, the growth curve actually dipped during the recessions of 1974, 1980, and 1981–82. Indeed, in that last recession the rate of job loss in high tech exceeded losses in the nonfarm sector as a whole (ibid.; see also Markusen, 1986).

Some industries seem to fluctuate in response not to larger forces but to their own idiosyncratic cycle. The computer and electronic chip industry, for example, flourished during the recession of 1981–82 but went into a severe slide beginning in 1984, just as the rest of the economy was starting to recover. By 1986 some 17,500 jobs had been lost in California's Silicon Valley, and 35 percent of the factory and research space was vacant, the highest industrial vacancy rate in the country (*New York Times,* Oct. 5, 1986). The causes are complex. Much of the problem has had to do with the maturation of the industry, a process that offers a cautionary tale to states that assume that *their* infant high-tech industry can grow limitlessly. Once the basic technological breakthroughs had been made—for example, in the development of the personal computer—firms began to enter the market at a rapid pace. The number of American firms alone making microcomputers rose from 8 in 1981 to 47 in 1985; software companies increased in number from 34 to 280; producers of hard-disk drives, from 11 to 54; and the number of local area network companies that link computers at high speeds grew from 9 to 61 (*New York Times,* June 10, 1985). Most of the enormous investment in computer companies and related businesses in the early 1980s went to firms that did not advance technology but rather simply offered variations on existing products. The result has been a massive oversupply in relation to demand. The same problems of oversupply plagued the memory chip market, where analysts estimated that production in 1985 had exceeded demand by over 40 percent (ibid.). Chances are that a similar maturation process, characterized by technological routinization, rapid market entry of new firms, and market saturation, will occur in other high-tech fields on which states currently hope to ensure their economic future.

A number of states are likely to find that they are unable even to begin to build a high-tech base because they cannot attract or nurture the necessary agglomeration of firms that provides the seedbed for growth. The geographic concentration of high-tech activity is a key factor in stimulating further growth by drawing skilled labor to the area (Markusen, 1986), by generating firm spin-offs, and by attracting complementary firms and government contracts. Most high-tech employment, including production workers as well as scientists and engineers, is found in the Northeast, especially New England, and in Texas and California (Browne, 1983; Riche et al., 1983).[4] Premus' study (1982, p. 8) for the Joint Economic Committee found that 83 percent of the nation's high-tech jobs are located in 24 states. These same states accounted for 82 percent of the net increase in jobs in those industries from 1975 to 1979. Although individual states in regions other than New England and the West sometimes appear among the top 10 states in numbers of high-tech jobs—Illinois, Texas, and Florida are examples—other regions generally do poorly in comparison to the coasts. Armington (1986), who defines high tech simply in terms of industries with a higher-than-average proportion of scientific and technical workers, finds sharp regional variations in high-tech job-growth rates, ranging during the latter half of the 1970s from 2.1 percent in the Middle Atlantic region to 45.3 percent in the Rocky Mountain states. Using a more restricted set of industries, Browne (1983) reports that the Great Lakes states actually lost high-tech jobs in the latter half of the 1970s, measured not only in proportion of total employment but also in absolute numbers. Although these various studies employ slightly different standards to designate high-tech industries, the conclusions are the same: certain areas account for a substantially disproportionate amount of employment in this sector and will continue to do so. States without a strong high-tech base are not likely to be able to establish one in the near term.

State high-tech policy operates finally under the burden of uncertainty. As Vaughan and Pollard point out (1986, p. 269), little is known about how to stimulate an innovative process through the application of public policy that leads to the creation of commercial products. After an extensive review of an earlier generation of federal government programs that bore on the research and innovation process, Roger Noll concluded that "no universal policy covering firms in differing market and technological environments is likely to lead to an efficient rate and direction of technological innovation" (unpublished report quoted in Wiewel et al., 1984, p. 294). Furthermore, the current programs that seek to stimulate

---

4. Browne's alternative lists of high-tech industries differ slightly from the one shown in Table 11-1, although her criteria for inclusion are not made clear. Her lists account for between 3 and 6 percent of all nonfarm employment in 1982, while the categories proposed by Riche and his colleagues (1983) range from 2.8 to 13.4 percent in the same year. The 28-industry group shown in Table 11-1 accounts for 6.2 percent. As Browne points out, however, "high technology is more a concept than a set of industries defined by SIC codes. The high technology industries of the future will not necessarily be those we call high technology today" (1983, p. 20).

innovation, though increasing in number and varied in character, are nearly all too recent and often too indirectly linked to job creation and business formation to permit reliable evaluation of their economic development impacts.[5]

Case studies of the growth of high-tech industries in Massachusetts suggest that factors other than economic development policies are primarily responsible for the vitality of this sector. High-tech employment accounted for nearly 12 percent of the state's workforce in 1982, according to Riche and his colleagues (1983, p. 57), a figure that placed the state just below Delaware, Connecticut, and New Hampshire. Massachusetts led the nation in the rate of growth in employment in the 28-industry group from 1975 to 1982. Malecki (1986) and Ferguson and Ladd (1986) explain this explosive growth—it amounted to 30.9 percent compared with a national growth rate of 11.3 percent in the 28-industry group in these years—first as a product of defense spending in the state and second as a function of the concentration of high-quality academic institutions in the Boston area. Per capita military R&D spending in Massachusetts is the highest in the nation (Malecki, 1986, p. 54). Massachusetts industries receive about double their share of prime military contracts based on the state's share of the U.S. population (Ferguson and Ladd, 1986, p. 38). The availability of venture capital is a third factor that explains the growth of high tech in the Massachusetts economy (ibid., p. 40). State policies to foster high-tech development, Ferguson and Ladd conclude, played at best a marginal role in the "economic miracle" (p. 43).

As it is presented in the Ferguson-Ladd case study, the Massachusetts evidence bears only on the question of the impact of policy on aggregate employment in a whole industrial sector. It tells us little about the impact of program initiatives on the innovation process in particular firms or industries or disciplines, for which microlevel investigations would be required. Furthermore, the question of whether public policy might serve to stimulate the emergence of nondefense high-tech industries, where constant federal demand is not the sustaining market force, has not been addressed by the Massachusetts case studies. At best, then, all we can conclude is that state high-tech policy operates in an uncertain realm with inadequate information about its role, its impact, or its possibilities.

---

5. The U.S. Office of Technology Assessment (1983, p. 20) reports that 85 percent of the programs it identified in a survey of initiatives that bore in some way on high-tech development had not been evaluated.

State High-Tech Policy in the Mid-1980s

None of these limitations and uncertainties has prevented a veritable stampede to adopt programs among states anxious to share in what they hope will be a high-tech boom. Various indicators suggest the recency and number of these initiatives. A content analysis of gubernatorial state-of-the-state speeches from 1976 to 1985, for example, has found that the first proposals by governors—two of them—for cooperative university-industry high-tech programs appeared in 1982 (Herzik, 1985). The next year another 14 governors made similar proposals; 6 more did so in 1984; and in 1985, 4 more.

One of the first efforts to conduct a comprehensive census of state high-tech programs was carried out in 1982–83 by the Office of Technology Assessment of the U.S. Congress (U.S. OTA, 1984).[6] The census identified 153 programs "with at least some feature directed toward HTD [High Tech Development]." These programs fell into several broad categories: research, development, and technology transfer; "human capital" or education and training programs; entrepreneurship training and technical assistance; physical capital in the form of industrial parks and incubators; and information-dissemination programs. Thirty-eight of the programs were "dedicated" initiatives, that is, designed exclusively for the purpose of creating or attracting high-tech firms. The census reported simply that "most of these initiatives have been launched in the last three years . . ." (ibid., p. 11).

A more recent survey, in which the results are also broken down by type of program and by state, was carried out for all 50 states by *High Technology* magazine in 1984 (Brody, 1985). Its main results are reported in Table 11-2. The only states without any high-tech programs in 1984 were Alaska and South Dakota. On the other hand one state—Utah—had at least one of each of the six types of programs shown in Table 11-2, and six states (Connecticut, Iowa, Massachusetts, New York, Pennsylvania, and Wisconsin) had at least one of each of five types.

Data on the *growth* in the number of specific state initiatives are piecemeal, and the categories and data-collection methods make longitudinal comparisons from one survey to another a tentative enterprise. Among these efforts that appear to be internally consistent, de Laski (1985) reports that before 1980 only 4 states had high-tech development

---

6. A slightly earlier survey conducted by the National Governors' Association provided descriptions of selected state initiatives but made no attempt at a thorough census (see National Governors' Association, 1983).

Table 11-2. Number of States Offering Selected High-Tech Programs, 1984

	Number of States Offering One or More of Each Type of Program
High-tech development programs[a] (includes well-developed science parks, high-tech development corporations, and councils that direct R&D activities)	34
Task force or council (includes nonfunded groups appointed to study a state's high-tech potential or standing commissions that make policy recommendations to the governor)	13
University-based centers	44
State research grants	24
Technical assistance (includes incubators, innovation centers to evaluate business proposals, brokerage services matching inventors and venture capitalists)	40
R&D tax credits	9

Source: Brody, 1985.

[a]Some of these programs were discussed in Chapter IX, such as the Massachusetts Technology Development Corporation and the New York Corporation for Innovation Development.

programs, compared with 34 in 1984. The annual survey of business incentives and assistance conducted by the *Industrial Development and Site Selection Handbook* reports only 7 states with R&D tax credits in 1976 but 19 in 1985 (the *High Technology* survey had counted only 9 such tax credits a year earlier). Plosila and Allen (1985) report the likelihood of a 53 percent increase—from 75 to 115—in the number of business incubators between 1984 and 1985, though not all of these would be reserved for high-tech companies. The Congressional Office of Technology Assessment reports that, through 1987, 30 states had established industrial programs in biotechnology. The oldest of these, North Carolina's Biotechnology Center, dates from 1981 (*New York Times,* Feb. 20, 1988). New initiatives of other sorts are announced continually. If efforts to track the growth of such programs are spotty, all indicators nevertheless point to the same conclusion: there has been rapid and constant diversified growth of programs to encourage high-tech development.

Many of the individual programs counted in the different surveys are relatively modest. Others involve great expenditures but are linked only indirectly to high-tech business formation or the development of particular emerging industries. In the former category are the research grant programs that provide funds either to firms or to university researchers or to academic-business partnerships to work on specific projects with commercial promise. Michigan initially budgeted only $250,000 for its state research fund, while New York allocated $750,000 for that purpose. Utah budgeted $1.2 million to endow its fund and made four grants in 1985. As with other economic development programs, these research grants are designed to leverage private-sector investment. Thus, the Wisconsin Technology Development Fund spent $1.5 million in state funds in 1985 for research grants to academic-business partnerships and managed to leverage $8 million in funds from the firms involved. Some programs of this sort—the Ohio Seed Development Fund and the Rhode Island Partnership for Science and Technology—require royalty paybacks on successfully marketed products. These differ from the product-development corporations discussed in the previous chapter in that those programs do not require an academic-business partnership. The largest of the academic-business partnership programs, a $35 million fund, was passed by the Texas legislature in the 1985–86 biennium (Jaschik, 1986b).

"Human capital" programs tend to involve far more substantial financial commitments, but their impact on economic development is likely to be difficult to measure in any direct sense. These efforts usually involve programs to up-grade science and engineering education by endowing faculty positions or building laboratories. Nearly every state has done something in this realm in the 1980s, ranging from New Hampshire's establishment of a graduate program in engineering at its state university to Arizona's $50 million commitment to make Arizona State University an "engineering center of excellence" (Brody, 1985). A number of states, particularly in the South, have also increased funding for science and mathematics training in the secondary schools. Other states have put money into vocational training of technical workers. Although it is indisputable that the Silicon Valley and Route 128 high-tech agglomerations owe their existence in part to the presence of high-quality universities in the region, the degree to which state efforts to up-grade science and technical education will produce other seedbeds for new industries and scientist entrepreneurs is simply not clear. In any case, tracing cause and effect from endowed engineering chairs in the university to high-tech business start-ups and employment growth will rarely be simple.

Gubernatorial task forces and commissions, whose function is to recommend programs to the governors to promote technological research and development, are a more common device than their anemic showing in Table 11-2 suggests. Most of these bodies were established as temporary organs, and a number of them had already gone out of business by the time of the *High Technology* survey. No evaluation of the impact of these task forces on policy-making exists, but historical precedents are discouraging. In the 1960s, 47 states established science advisory boards along much the same lines as the various commissions on science and technology of the current era. A study of nine of these original bodies has concluded, however, that "no state has found a useful and recognized role of science advisors in the formation of public policy" (quoted in Schmandt and Wilson, 1986, p. 15). All of the 47 were apparently dissolved with the exception of the New York Science and Technology Foundation and the North Carolina Board of Science and Technology,[7] both established in 1963. The New York institution is particularly active in the 1980s, functioning no longer simply as an advisory board but rather as the administrative umbrella for a host of programs, including the Corporation for Innovation Development Program, Research and Development Grants, the Centers for Advanced Technology, and the Supercomputer Program at Cornell University, among others (New York State Science and Technology Foundation, 1986).

The most costly and visible of the state programs designed to bear directly on the promotion of high-tech industrial development and business formation, besides the various targeted venture capital programs discussed in the previous chapter, are the university-industry cooperative research centers and science or research parks.

University-industry research centers are devoted primarily to the process of technology transfer, that is, to the effort to capitalize on scientific research for the purpose of creating commercial products for the private market. Such centers are located at both private and public universities. Those centers created for the purposes of fostering economic development have typically been established at the instigation of the state, rather than the university or industry, with financial cosponsorship from private industry. Each center is devoted to research and development in a particular targeted discipline or technology, such as microelectronics, robotics, optical circuitry, or agricultural biotechnology, that taps local academic and industrial interests and capacities.

Interactions between universities and private industry are scarcely

---

7. North Carolina's high-tech programs are administered by the North Carolina Technological Development Authority, established by the legislature in 1983. It was an outgrowth of a gubernatorial commission appointed in 1982, which itself was an inheritance of an advisory board from the 1960s.

novel (Dimanescu and Botkin, 1986). A rich history of relationships and institutional forms provides a backdrop for the current spate of technology centers. Agricultural and engineering extension services in land grant universities, established by the Morrill Act of 1862, are the first in a long line of efforts to bring higher education resources to bear on industrial and agricultural practices. During the 1960s the U.S. Department of Commerce provided funds to every state to establish technical extension services for industry, most of which were based in universities. In a report done for the National Science Board, Peters and Fusfeld (1982) document the variety of subsequent arrangements. These include cooperative research relationships between academics and industrial sponsors on a contract basis; cooperative institutes and research centers devoted to single, key local industries (e.g., textiles or forestry); innovation centers, funded by the National Science Foundation, to train and facilitate the work of young inventors and entrepreneurs; and a variety of research-dissemination services and personnel exchange programs, among others (ibid., pp. 71, 82, 98–99). Most of these university-industry links were forged at the initiative of industry or individual researchers. What is novel about the current establishment of technology centers is that by and large they have been initiated by state governments in the name of economic development. Furthermore, they represent judgments about what disciplines will give rise to the industries of the future.

The Centers for Advanced Technology in New York State grew out of recommendations made by Governor Hugh Carey's High Technology Opportunities Task Force (Black and Worthington, 1986). Michigan's Biotechnology Institute and Industrial Technology Institute are also the products of a technology task force (Bartsch, 1986). The Massachusetts Centers of Excellence program was designed in the Office of the Secretary of Economic Affairs as the mechanism "to help sustain the state's economic preeminence into the 21st century" (Ferguson and Ladd, 1986, p. 137). Virginia's Center for Innovative Technology (*New York Times,* Sept. 15, 1985), Ohio's Thomas Edison Technology Centers, Pennsylvania's Ben Franklin Partnership centers, and North Carolina's Microelectronics Center (Dimanescu and Botkin, 1986, pp. 9–10, 57) are other examples of state-initiated cooperative research centers. In the mid-1980s one state—Indiana—appears to have taken the lead in institutionalizing "technology forecasting" as an on-going process. Five hundred volunteer scientists and engineers, organized into more than a dozen committees in various technological fields, meet periodically to discuss future trends and to make recommendations to state officials.

No reliable census of such centers exists, but there are various indicators by which to gauge the growth of university-industry relationships of this sort. The National Governors' Association has reported that U.S. industry was expected to spend $300 million in 1983 alone on R&D in academic institutions, a fourfold increase over the prior decade (National Governors' Association, 1983, p. 23). Not all industrial R&D money is spent in the new technology centers, of course. But these new, visible, and often costly institutions clearly absorb a substantial share of such funds. For example, New York's seven Centers for Advanced Technology, located at the state's leading public and private universities, require matching funds at least equal to monies provided by the state. In 1985–86 alone private funds in support of this program came to nearly $10 million, more than matching state appropriations (New York State Science and Technology Foundation, 1986). Pennsylvania's Ben Franklin "challenge grants" program is significantly larger: private industry contributions to joint research projects at the four different university sites in the state grew from $3 million in the program's first year (1982) to nearly $54 million in 1985–86 (Jaschik, 1986b).

Peters and Fusfeld (1982, p. 22) document the surge in university-industry relationships by tracking the histories of 463 arrangements of all different types. Of these, 51 percent had been in existence for less than three years, and another 17 percent were between three and five years old. Dimanescu and Botkin report a fivefold increase in the number of consortia between 1982 and 1985 (1986, p. xix), a trend apparently facilitated in part by the passage in 1984 of the National Cooperative Research Act, which exempts companies that compete in the marketplace from antitrust actions when they join such arrangements (*New York Times,* Oct. 11, 1987). Clearly, the increasingly central role of the research university in state economic development strategies is a comparatively recent phenomenon.

There are two major variants of the university-linked technology center. One is the free-standing research institute, established in proximity to a university but separate from it administratively. Such institutes hire their own staff. The Michigan Industrial Technology Institute, located on the Ann Arbor campus of the University of Michigan, and the North Carolina Microelectronics Center, near the universities of the Research Triangle, are examples. According to Baba and Hart (1986) the independence of Michigan's ITI provides legal and organizational flexibility to enter quickly into joint ventures with business and to concentrate on industrial applications. By standing outside the university the ITI provides a setting for its researchers free of the academic pressure to excel in basic research. Its proximity to the campus, however, allows the institute to draw on faculty and graduate students and to engage in face-to-face discourse.

The more common type of research center is that which is integrated in a university, although it may be sponsored by a consortium of academic institutions rather than a single university. The mission of these programs, which draws support from university research budgets, state appropriations, and the private sector, is generally to apply the academic research skills of university faculty and students to practical industrial problems and to serve as well as seedbeds for individual entrepreneurs among the researchers.

Pennsylvania's Ben Franklin Partnership centers are widely regarded as prototypical of the new technology research institutes (Jaschik, 1986b). The Pennsylvania state legislature established the four centers in 1982 in the hopes that they would help to shift the state's economy away from dependence on the declining steel industry. Each center is organized as a consortium of universities, colleges, and private-sector interests. For example, the Western Pennsylvania Advanced Technology Center, located at the University of Pittsburgh, is a consortium of 23 academic institutions and over 100 private firms, labor unions, and economic development groups. The primary areas of R&D effort are robotics, high-tech materials, metals, and biomedical research. In addition to sponsoring research, the centers provide financing and management assistance to new companies, run incubators, and provide training for workers in the new industries.

Unlike the older university-industry arrangements, the new centers are presumably to be evaluated on the basis of their economic development impacts, though virtually no hard information was yet available in the mid-1980s. Through surveys of firms that have worked with the four Ben Franklin Partnership centers, however, Pennsylvania development officials were able to report that 1082 new jobs were created by the fall of 1985, while another 1518 were retained (ibid.).

Science or research parks represent another prong in the attempt to bring industry and universities into closer contact as a way of hastening the technology-transfer process. Research parks, variants of industrial parks, are reservations for firms engaged in high-tech research efforts that can profit from close proximity to a university's research talent, laboratories, and highly trained labor. Some parks have been established at the initiative of state government (e.g., Virginia's park at Virginia Tech

University), others by public or private universities themselves in the hopes that they will be able to attract state support eventually (e.g., the University of Wisconsin's Charmany Farms Park). The prototypical park is the undertaking in the 1950s by Stanford University, a private institution that sought not to further economic development through technology transfer but rather to augment its income in the face of rising education costs that strained its endowment (Boley, 1962). The Stanford Industrial Park was made possible by cooperative zoning actions by the city of Palo Alto, but there was no state subsidy for the park.

The first state-sponsored research park is the North Carolina Research Triangle, whose three points are represented by Duke, the University of North Carolina, and North Carolina State University. The state donated large tracts of land for the park in 1959 for use as a high-tech research park and provided funds for access and maintenance roads. The park eventually attracted more than 35 research facilities employing over 18,000 workers (Luger, 1984). By 1971 there were about 81 such parks in the United States. Many of these, however, failed to attract a significant number of tenants. A study for the Southern Regional Education Board conducted by the Battelle Institute of 27 university-based research parks that had been established in the 1960s classified only 6 of them as clear successes (Battelle Institute, 1983). Sixteen of these parks were classified as outright failures, of which 10 had yet to attract a single tenant after more than a decade of effort.

The chances that research parks will successfully stimulate technology transfer are, perhaps surprisingly, only slightly better than their chances of attracting a significant number of employers, according to one early study. Peters and Fusfeld (1982, p. 107) examined 14 university-based research parks and concluded that only 4 of them actually facilitated the transfer of even a single bit of technology to the marketplace.

The high rate of failure has done little to deter other universities from seeking to establish research parks, however. By 1984 there were an estimated 150 such developments around the country (Schmidt, 1984; Casteen, 1986).

Conclusions

Nothing is more striking to the observer about the growing state campaigns to stimulate high-technology undertakings than the extent to which these efforts represent a policy of investment for the distant future. In common with the venture capital programs discussed in the previous chapter, high-tech initiatives produced very few immediately visible economic development benefits. Their payoff—if there is one—lies in the future and only after a series of subsequent events occur over which the original policy implementors have little control. State and local officials, whose time line is understandably shaped more by electoral considerations than by concerns over the judgments of posterity, are not accustomed to thinking in such terms. Their perspectives are overwhelmingly shaped by the pressures of delivering a range of quotidian services to their constituents. But high-tech public policy is different. It represents an effort to lay a foundation for an economic order now only in its formative stages and still dimly perceived.

The metaphor of a foundation is, however, inadequate, for it implies that the builders at least know *where* to build for the future. But the whole domain of advanced scientific research involves the exploration of many sites that will ultimately not pan out, that is, that will neither support new discoveries nor provide the basis for the growth of new industries employing people. Thus, this policy of state investment is unusual, not only because it is very future-oriented, but also because it is very risky. Many initiatives may never come close to producing the jobs which provide the ultimate justification for state intervention in the technological enterprise.

What makes it possible for politicians to countenance these economic risks, however, is that these policies may not be particularly risky *politically.* Although these initiatives raise enormous expectations at their inception (Jaschik, 1986a), failure is not highly visible, nor is it easy even to define. For a political career, it is probably more important to *establish,* say, a center for the study of laser technology than to be able to claim that such a center spawned a new company in the medical-equipment field. In any event, any accounting in economic development terms is unlikely to occur until long after current political incumbents are out of office. The long time line of high-tech policy, then, may actually reduce the political liabilities of such an uncertain enterprise.

The union of the academy, business, and the entrepreneurial state for the development of the economy of the future raises other issues besides the risks inherent in a policy of investment. For example, it is legitimate for union leaders, politicians, and the public to wonder whether planning for the high-tech future includes a concern for displaced manufacturing and low-skilled workers. Some states build a job-training program for such workers into their high-tech programs (Ohio's Thomas Edison program, for example), and several states—Pennsylvania, Ohio, Massachusetts—are interested in using the new technology as part of a "mature industries" policy. Here the object is to save jobs by helping traditional industries adopt advanced technologies in their operations. But these elements are not central to most state high-tech policies.

Finally, there is a question of whether the enlistment of the universities in the technology-transfer process for economic development will distort or change the notion of the proper functions of institutions of higher education. The issue is not a new one for universities, but the urgency of economic development concerns suggests that the context has shifted. Basic research in the hard sciences and engineering has gained stock, for such activities are seen as leading eventually to industrial applications. But if disciplines do not contribute to new product development, industrial modernization, or the creation of new industries, there is a reasonable concern for their future, particularly in state institutions funded by legislatures preoccupied with job creation in their state economies.

CHAPTER 12

The Search for New Markets: State and Local Export-Promotion Activities

AS the balance of international trade in manufactured goods grew to America's disadvantage during the 1970s, the fact that the United States was nevertheless simultaneously developing a robust export trade was nearly lost on most observers. Not only did the value of exported manufactured goods alone grow by 516 percent between 1970 and 1984, but also if the value of such merchandise exported is combined with the value of services and agricultural products sold abroad, then the rate of growth of exports very nearly matched that of total imports through 1982. And in that year, as in all but two of the years in the prior decade, the value of all exports actually exceeded that of all imports.[1]

Another development in this decade and a half, scarcely remarked until the late 1970s, concerned the growth of direct foreign investment in the United States, more of which has been in manufacturing than in any other area of commerce. Total foreign investment in all sectors rose from nearly $13.3 billion in 1970 to $159.6 billion in 1984. Investment just in manufacturing grew from $6.1 billion to $50.7 billion, an increase of 725 percent (U.S. Bureau of the Census, 1986, p. 798).

Officials in Washington, observing the deepening penetration of international forces in the American economy, seem to have focused princi-

---

1. Exports of all goods and services rose from $66 billion in 1970 to $362 billion in 1984; imports rose more dramatically from $60 billion to $452 billion in the same years. Between 1970 and 1982, however, the rate of increase for the two trade flows was relatively close—433 percent for exports, 482 percent for imports. The dollar value of all U.S. exports in 1982 was slightly *over* $350 billion, while the value of imports in that year was just *under* $350 billion (U.S. Department of Commerce, 1986, p. 794).

pally on the unrelenting growth of the merchandise trade deficit. But state and local officials, ever alert for opportunities to exploit for economic development, appear to have adopted a more balanced view: although they have persistently worried about the loss of jobs to import competition, they have also seen in the growth of exports evidence of an expanding universe of markets for American producers and, in the expansion of foreign investment, a way to save domestic manufacturing jobs and industries. The dual perspective of state politicians is aptly illustrated by a recent meeting of the Southern Governors' Association. In one session the governors' central concern was the devastation of the textile industry in their region under the onslaught of imports. In the next session, however, the theme of the meeting was "The South Going Global—The Internationalization of the South" (*New York Times*, Sept. 8 and 15, 1985).

Growing state and local interest in international trade has taken two broad forms. One, the older of the two, has been the effort to encourage "reverse investment," that is, the location of foreign business operations and investments on American soil through the promotion of the local business climate and the offer of various subsidies.[2] The other, more recent, activity has been the attempt to stimulate export trade for local businesses. The former activities represent the familiar supply-side location-subsidy economic development strategy operating in an international context. The efforts to expand export trade on the other hand embody the more recent state entrepreneurialism.

State and local involvement in promoting export trade is entrepreneurial first of all in the sense that it is concerned with discovering and fostering new foreign markets for local producers to exploit. It is noteworthy in this regard that after President Nixon established relations with China in 1972 about half the nation's governors immediately sought early invitations to China, which appeared to them, according to Kincaid (1984, p. 95), to be "a vast untapped market for goods and services produced within the various states." The pattern by which states established overseas trade offices also illustrates the interest in identifying new markets. The earlier offices, set up in the late 1960s, were located in the capitals of established European trading partners. Later, states opened offices in Canada, Brazil, Mexico, and Japan. More recently, Ala-

---

2. One reason for the decision of Japanese executives to locate a Nissan plant in Tennessee, for example, was the $12 million spent by the state for new roads to the facility, the $7 million state job-training grant, and the $10 million county tax break (*New York Times*, Feb. 27, 1985).

bama, Iowa, and Illinois have located permanent representatives in Hong Kong, and Illinois opened the first state office in China. In 1986 Ohio became the first state to establish a presence on the African continent with an office in Lagos, Nigeria (National Governors' Association, 1985, p. 20; *Wall Street Journal,* Oct. 7, 1986).

Another characteristic of state entrepreneurialism in the international arena is the effort to market new products as a way of stimulating new tastes and new demands. The National Governors' Association warns that "traditional commodities have been important to the export sector, but dependence on these resources for export earnings does not make for an effective growth strategy" (National Governors' Association, 1985, p. 7). In what economists increasingly describe as an international "glut economy," a condition characterized by worldwide industrial overcapacity for the manufacture of any number of standard goods, the necessity of marketing innovative products and services is particularly strong. "How should the states approach international trade?" Governor Michael Castle of Delaware has asked. "By looking for niches no one else can fill quite as well as they can" (Castle, 1985).

To the degree that states seek to expand employment and economic activity by encouraging local producers to export goods that afford them a unique or advantageous market position, they exemplify yet another aspect of the entrepreneurial strategy, namely the effort to deemphasize the competition among states for economic development opportunities. The sense that export trade need not involve another round in the "war between the states" is in part attributable to the sheer size and number of markets only recently opened to American business. The expanding scope of opportunities in new markets is amply illustrated by the ongoing shift in the destination of U.S. exports. Between 1973 and 1983 the percentage of the value of merchandise exports to nations in the Organization of Petroleum Exporting Countries (OPEC) and other developing countries rose from 29 percent to 36 percent. The share of exports sent to Western Europe in the same period declined from 30 percent to 28 percent (U.S. SBA, 1984b, p. 295). By 1984 the countries of the Pacific Basin—Japan, China, Singapore, Taiwan, South Korea, Hong Kong, the Philippines—represented almost as large a market for American goods as traditional Western European markets (U.S. Dept. of Commerce, International Trade Division, 1985, p. 22).[3]

---

3. The total value of U.S. merchandise exports to Western Europe in 1984 was $62 billion; the countries of the Pacific Basin bought $59 billion worth of goods from American producers in that year (U.S. Department of Commerce, 1986, p. 22).

Table 12-1. Average Annual Percentage Growth Rates in Gross Domestic Product, 1975–81, Selected Countries

United States	3.1
Western European countries	2.9
Canada	3.1
Hong Kong	12.0
Japan	5.0
South Korea	7.2
Philippines	6.0
Singapore	9.0

Source: United Nations, 1985, pp. 148–52.

The competitive nature of the states' quest to secure foreign markets is also lessened by the conviction that the international economy represents an expanding pie (see, for example, Kline, 1984). Economic growth among the new Asian trading partners in particular has in fact been striking, as the data in Table 12-1 showing average annual increases in the gross domestic product indicate. This growth, which translates into increased purchasing power, has not gone unnoticed among state governments. Thus, according to the California Department of Commerce:

Our vigorous economy is due in part to our ability to send California products to the rapidly expanding economies of the Pacific Basin. . . . The Asian nations alone offer a consumer market larger than the entire population of the U.S. and their economies are growing at rates of 5–10 percent a year. (California Dept. of Commerce, n.d.)

The Shift from Supply-Side to Demand Strategies in International Trade

The evolution of state and local government interest in foreign trade offers a textbook case of the more general shift that has taken place in economic development policy from an exclusive preoccupation with supply-side inducements to a perspective shaped increasingly by demand considerations. In the realm of foreign trade, state policy has evolved from efforts to lure foreign investment with offers of various sorts of assistance to an interest in helping local producers to capitalize on opportunities in export trade.

Kincaid (1984) dates the earliest state initiative in foreign trade to a trip made to Europe in 1959 by the governor of North Carolina, Luther Hodges, in search of reverse investment. Prospecting trips abroad, viewed as a logical extension of state efforts to induce interstate industrial relocation (National Governors' Association, 1985, p. 11), soon became a staple gubernatorial activity. Not surprisingly, southern governors, major architects of the supply-side economic development strategy, were the most active travelers to foreign lands. Dennis Grady's survey (1985) of former governors from all parts of the country found that 25 percent of the 35 southern governors had made six or more trips abroad in their first term to prospect for footloose firms, compared with only 4 percent of their colleagues from the Midwest, 12 percent of those from the West, and just under 15 percent of the eastern governors.

During the 1960s at least three states established permanent trade offices abroad to provide a base from which to encourage reverse investment. Then in 1971 the National Association of State Development Agencies, backed by the U.S. Department of Commerce, launched its Invest in U.S.A. program to provide support for multistate investment missions abroad. Federal support for the program waned in the late 1970s, however, when the rising volume of foreign investment in the United States came to be regarded as a mixed blessing (Kline, 1983, p. 43).

The effort to attract foreign investment remained the primary state objective in international trade through much of the 1970s, but the blossoming interest in nurturing small businesses at home, combined with evident growth of export possibilities, gradually propelled the states into an export role. Dating the first formal attempts by states to promote export trade is not simple. Kline notes, however, that Illinois established an International Marketing Department in its Department of Business and Economic Development in 1967 expressly to promote Illinois industries abroad (ibid., p. 54). Most states initiated export-promotion activities much later.

By the early 1980s, the evolution to a demand-side strategy had thoroughly taken hold. The Congressional Budget Office (1984, p. 25), reviewing various state development initiatives, reported that "whereas during the 1970s most state involvement [in foreign trade] was concentrated on attracting foreign investment, *over two-thirds of these expenditures are now on export promotion*" (my emphasis). With total state spending on foreign trade programs having grown from $3.2 million in 1976 in 25 states to $27.5 million in 42 states in 1984, this would indicate that more than $18 million was spent annually for export promotion in the mid-1980s (Grady, 1985; National Governors' Association,

1985, p. 12). The function of trade offices on foreign soil has also shifted to reflect the change in strategy: originally designed to advertise their states' business climates, they have now become active publicists for their states' industries and, to the extent that they drum up business for their states' firms, export middlemen.

State departments of international trade, if they had existed before, also underwent the same transformation. The Massachusetts Foreign Business Council is a case in point. Originally established under the Dukakis administration in 1978 to promote reverse investment, its name was changed in 1984 to the Office of International Trade and Investment and its mission was altered dramatically. Three-quarters of its work is now on export promotion; only one-quarter concerns reverse investment, its original focus (interview, Bagley, 1986).

State organs, newly established in the 1980s, apparently regard export as their primary function. For example, California's World Trade Commission, formed in 1983, brings together the top elected officials of the state and business leaders to articulate "California's enormous stake in international trade." The commission is devoted exclusively to "stimulat[ing] overseas demand for California goods and services and encourag[ing] the state's many fast-growing businesses to market their products abroad" (California World Trade Commission, 1985).

The thoroughness of the transition to demand-oriented policy is illustrated finally by the fact that most of the different types of foreign-trade development programs put in place by states in the late 1970s and early 1980s are designed to encourage export, not to attract foreign investment. Of the 11 different types of programs shown in Table 12-2, 10 promote export activity. Only foreign trade offices perform both export promotion and reverse-investment functions.

City governments also became involved in international trade in an active way during the 1980s, but there are no effective means by which to gauge the primary focus of municipal efforts or shifts therein. A report issued by the National League of Cities' International Economic Development Task Force in 1983 asserts that "for local governments, the key factor is a willingness to develop an international awareness among local businesses, and *to help them move into foreign markets*" (my emphasis) (National League of Cities, 1983, pp. 3–4). This may suggest that export promotion is regarded as the principal course of action to pursue, however, the task force appears in fact to push just as forcefully for efforts to attract foreign investment in the section of the report concerning policy recommendations.

Andrew Young, elected mayor of Atlanta in 1982, is widely thought

Table 12-2. State Foreign-Trade Development Programs, 1985

	Number of States Involved
Export service programs	
Seminars and conferences for potential exporters	49
One-to-one export counseling	43
Referrals to local export services	31
How-to-export handbooks	24
Language bank translation services	13
Operational export financing	10
Market-development activities	
Dissemination of sales leads to local firms	45
Sponsorship or support of foreign trade shows	40
Permanent foreign offices	31
Export newsletters	23
Preparation of market analyses	23

Source: National Governors' Association, 1985, p. 17.

to be the pioneer local official in the development of international trade for cities, although Ernest Morial of New Orleans had made a successful trip to Africa and Europe to seek reverse investments as early as 1980 (*New York Times,* June 24, 1984; *New Orleans Times-Picayune,* Nov. 19, 1980). Young came to city office after having served in the Carter administration as ambassador to the United Nations. He drew on contacts made during those years, particularly among the nations of Africa and Latin America, frequently traveling abroad seeking both reverse-investment and sales opportunities for Atlanta firms. Mayoral junkets had become commonplace by the mid-1980s, as mayors from San Francisco to Newark, from Albuquerque to Washington, scattered around the globe to sell goods or woo foreign companies (*New York Times,* June 24, 1984, and Jan. 20, 1985).

The U.S. Conference of Mayors, like the National League of Cities, has also promoted both strategies. Since 1980 the organization has conducted trade exhibitions abroad at which city trade officials may promote goods made in their communities. At the same time it runs a program called Invest in America's Cities, a combination of trade fairs to tout the respective business climates of member cities and prospecting trips by delegations of mayors in search of foreign investors.

Justifying State Intervention in Foreign Trade

Export trade offers an obvious and richly productive means to business expansion and, by extension, to job creation. These are its chief attractions to state and local government development officials. Yet many potential exporters, particularly smaller companies, are excluded from international trade by their inability to obtain financing and by the disproportionately high costs of gathering information about the export process and overseas market conditions and characteristics. To the degree that viable deals cannot be consummated for these reasons, it may be said that a market failure has occurred. Intervention by government is justified as an antidote to these market lapses and inefficiencies. But public involvement in encouraging foreign trade may be rationalized on other grounds as well: some argue that policy in this arena helps to stabilize the economy by diversifying market outlets and by helping to reduce the trade deficit. Since growth and recession cycles seldom occur simultaneously from country to country, establishing export trade with a multiplicity of trading partners may provide the nation's businesses with a countercyclical hedge against domestic downturns (Kline, 1983, p. 54; CBO, 1984, p. 25).

Approximately 5.5 million jobs in the United States were directly related to export in the mid-1980s, and perhaps twice as many were related indirectly through the employment multiplier. According to U.S. Commerce Department estimates, each $1 billion of exports directly generates 25,000 jobs. On a smaller scale, more comprehensible in the context of state and local policy, one new job is created for every $40,000 in export trade (Pilcher, 1985). Between 1975 and 1980 American exports more than doubled in value, generating over 1.5 million new jobs and accounting for more than 80 percent of employment increases in manufacturing industries. Export-generated jobs in this period accounted for about a third of the growth in private-sector employment (National Governor's Association, 1985, p. 8).

State and local officials are convinced that they can improve on these impressive employment effects by expanding export trade through public intervention. As the National League of Cities' Task Force on International Economic Development put it, "[E]xport trade, while no panacea, offer[s] vast potential and promise[s] to expand American markets and create new investment, resulting in more jobs, business profits, and tax receipts" (National League of Cities, 1983, p. 6). What underlies their conviction is the notion that there exists a substantial but unrealized export potential among small and medium-sized businesses (see, for example, National Governors' Association, 1985, p. 15). Various market barriers prevent most of these firms from participating in foreign trade, but the magnitude of these obstacles is such that they may be diminished by relatively modest government actions.

The idea that the business world is filled with would-be exporters finds support in at least two Commerce Department studies. The first, conducted in 1978, involved an examination of the business behavior of 252,000 manufacturing companies. Only 12 percent actually engaged in any overseas trade, but the study indicated that at least another 11,000 firms, most with fewer than 250 employees, not only made exportable products but also "could probably be induced to try exporting if properly approached and assisted" (U.S. General Accounting Office, 1983, p. 5).

A second study, a 1980 survey of 387,000 firms of all types, determined that at least 19,000 firms not then involved in foreign trade were seriously interested in receiving information on foreign market conditions, specific customers, and trade leads. Before the Commerce Department could design an information bank to serve this interest, however, the program lost its funding (ibid., p. 6).

Participation in export trade is hampered, particularly for smaller firms, by inability to obtain affordable financing and by the sheer complexity of the export process. As in seeking to finance domestic transactions, small businesses find that they are frequently shut out of the credit market. Their relatively modest needs make them unattractive to larger banks, and smaller financial institutions seldom have the capacity to handle international business deals (U.S. SBA, 1984b, p. 307). Furthermore, the export process, often encumbered by political uncertainty, overseas and foreign internal transportation problems, and the complexities of international currency exchange and trade policy, is regarded as a high-risk undertaking. Some public financing assistance is available for export operations through the federal Export-Import Bank, but most of Eximbank's clients have historically been large firms. According to the Congressional Budget Office, only 3 percent of the dollar value of Eximbank's loans in 1982 directly involved small business (CBO, 1984, p. 27), although subsequent amendments to the bank's reauthorization now require a 10 percent set-aside for small business.

Even if a smaller firm is able to get the necessary financing to underwrite an export transaction and obtain the insurance to protect the deal, the complexity of the process is formidable enough to discourage most businesses at the outset. A firm must identify and analyze appropriate markets, adjust products to foreign specifications in many instances, set prices, work out a marketing plan, establish a network of distributors, arrange transportation, deal with customs, meet foreign regulations and licensing requirements, pay tariffs and other duties, and arrange for servicing the product once it is sold—all this in the context of a foreign language and culture. As the National Governors' Association observes: "It is almost impossible for most small companies to have knowledge of all these variables; hence the need for outside assistance. . . . Through educational seminars and other services, states can eliminate some of the mystery surrounding the export process . . ." (1985, p. 16).

The Federal Backdrop to State and Local Export Activity

Unlike efforts by subnational governments to intervene in the venture capital process and to encourage high-tech development, state and local export-promotion activities have enjoyed substantial federal support. Much of this initially was indirect in the sense that Eximbank loans, begun in 1938, and various trade-expansion activities by the Department of Commerce and the U.S. Trade Representative benefited firms rather than enhancing state and local capacities to foster export. Lately, however, the federal government has sought explicitly to help subnational governments in their export-expansion initiatives. According to testimony before Congress by an official of the International Trade Administration of the U.S. Department of Commerce: "We, at the Commerce Department, recognize the important role the states play in the international trade arena. We also recognize that by joining forces with the states the export position of the United States can be strengthened" (U.S. Congress, House, 1985, pp. 185–86).

Federal efforts to encourage state export activity can be traced to the Carter years. In 1978 Secretary of State Cyrus Vance exhorted the states to help expand foreign trade. Later that year the president himself, who as governor had spent considerable time promoting Georgia in the international marketplace, urged the National Governors' Association to establish a committee to focus on international trade issues (Kline, 1983, p. 48). Congress, too, has played a role, first during the Carter years and then during Reagan's presidency. With the passage of the Small Business Export Expansion Act in 1980, the Department of Commerce became authorized to award grants to public or private entities for the purpose of counseling small businesses interested in exports; and then in 1982 Congress passed the Export Trading Company Act to facilitate the formation and operation, both by private brokers and by states and cities, of export trading companies (ETCs). An export trading company is an intermediary organization designed to help small business export activity in particular by purchasing goods for overseas sale from a multitude of noncompeting private businesses and then assuming all the risks and complications of the export process, including market research, financing, transportation, and after-sales servicing. Several cities and port authorities have already taken advantage of the relaxed federal restrictions on the formation of ETCs (Steinbach and Pierce, 1984). In Philadelphia the catalyst for the establishment of a municipally sponsored ETC was the nonprofit Philadelphia Industrial Development Corporation, a partnership between the city and the chamber of commerce. PIDC worked to organize the ETC and obtain investors, but it does not have a controlling role in the for-profit ETC (National League of Cities, 1983, pp. 26–29). In contrast, the city of Newport News, Virginia, set up and runs an ETC, the profits of which are reinvested with the aim of expanding the company. The Newport News ETC takes possession of goods through contractual arrangements with local private firms, and it offers export services, ranging from the management of export logistics to the provision of financing and insurance and the generation of foreign-market intelligence. Firms using these services pay a modest fee (ibid., pp. 29–33).

Congressional initiatives represent only a minor part of the federal effort to enhance state and local export-promotion capacities, however. Washington's principal activities in this domain have been devised by the International Trade Administration of the Department of Commerce. The ITA, through its U.S. and Foreign Commercial Service (US&FCS), assists states and cities in organizing overseas trade and reverse-investment missions. The service is heavily subscribed: in 1984, 42 states received such help (National Governors' Association, 1985, p. 32). Since 1982 the US&FCS has worked with states seeking to establish export-finance programs and advises them in the development of other export-promotion policies and programs (U.S. Congress, House, 1985, pp. 189–90).

In 1985 ITA officials met several times with members of the National Association of State Development Agencies and the National Governors' Association, along with trade representatives of individual states, to identify problems in the formulation and implementation of state export programs (ibid.) As a result of these meetings the ITA developed an "action plan" for providing additional help to the states in this area. Much of the plan involves the provision to the states of market information and trade leads gathered by the US&FCS. The ITA also announced plans to track the results of its own activities in this sphere, an evaluative effort not hitherto undertaken (ibid., pp. 192–95).

One additional initiative involving the Export-Import Bank is noteworthy: in 1985 the bank embarked on a year-long experiment to allow four midwestern states to commit Eximbank loan guarantees to firms of their choosing (*New York Times,* Aug. 5, 1985). One of the consequences of putting the substantial resources of the Eximbank at the disposal of the states was to halt the development, at least in Wisconsin, of state-funded export-finance programs (interview, Lotharius, 1986). The purpose of the pilot program was to channel more Eximbank funds to small businesses.

What is significant about all of this federal activity is that in contrast to nearly all of the rest of the federal programs designed to aid subnational governments in their economic development efforts, policies to help states and cities to promote exports are apparently vital and growing in number. It is true that these federal policies are neither very far-reaching nor very visible, but by their very presence they seem to indicate first of all that federal officials, presumably under the weight of the growing trade deficit, perceive a clearer convergence of state and national interests in the field of foreign export than in any of the other areas in which states have sought to pursue development objectives. Furthermore, federal officials are peculiarly vulnerable politically when it comes to the matter of foreign-trade performance in a way that they are not in, say, the realm of small business formation or high-tech commercialization. Unlike the record in these latter two areas, data on export performance are published as indicators of *national* economic performance, providing an incentive for involvement not present in other areas in which states are active.

Federal support for state initiatives in export promotion also derives from a sense that the federal government has an unambiguous responsibility to maintain a major presence—and to reiterate its sovereignty, if necessary—where foreign affairs are concerned. This responsibility—a constitutional obligation—has been sharpened by growing state aggressiveness in the international marketplace. As more and more states have entered into trade agreements with foreign national and provincial governments,[4] federal officials have had to struggle with the question of whether such accords violate the constitutional prohibition in Article I, Section 10, against any state entering into a treaty, agreement, or compact with a foreign power.

At least through the mid-1980s many, if not most of these trade agreements have taken the form of—for example—the Massachusetts-Guangdong Province (China) Agreement of 1983 or the Texas-Mexico

---

4. There is no systematic reporting of state agreements with foreign governments.

bilateral trade accords signed in July 1985. The former agreement has involved Massachusetts officials in efforts to find markets for products made in Guangdong, mainly by locating appropriate local trade and craft shows where producers may exhibit. In return Massachusetts expects similar assistance from the Chinese on behalf of goods made in the state. The Texas-Mexico accord constituted little more than a memorandum of understanding between the Mexico minister of agriculture and the Texas agriculture secretary to create a commission to address trade problems and projects of mutual interest. No binding agreements to purchase agricultural products were signed, but the two parties did agree to provide trade leads of mutual interest. The Texas Department of Agriculture is able to document several million dollars worth of sales that resulted from information exchanged at Texas-Mexico Exchange Commission meetings, though no systematic records or follow-up data are collected (interview, Lewis, 1987).

These memoranda of understanding, as well as the stationing of state trade representatives in foreign capitals, have been regarded by the Department of State as constitutionally permissible actions, but the issue had not in fact been litigated in the courts in the mid-1980s.

State initiatives in foreign-trade promotion also run the risk of violating the supremacy clause of the Constitution (Article VI). The state of Mississippi, for example, sought to exempt income from exports from the state income tax, but this particular sort of tax concession violated provisions of the General Agreement on Trade and Tariffs to which the United States is a signatory. The Mississippi law could not be put into effect (*State Policy Reports,* May 1985, p. 32). On balance, however, state entrepreneurialism and national interests and impulses coincide in this domain, making export promotion one of the few economic development activities in which the two levels of government are moving in the same direction.

State Export-Promotion Programs

States facilitate export trade by local businesses through two general types of efforts: the provision of services to help firms negotiate the treacherous waters of overseas commerce and the pursuit of a variety of market-development functions.

Service activities are aimed at both novice exporters and experienced ones. As is typical of the entrepreneurial state, the chief focus of these services is small, local firms. Seminars, the most widespread service program, one-on-one counseling, and export handbooks all lead businesses through the export process, covering issues such as handling inquiries from abroad, pricing techniques, export documentation, insurance information, and even foreign translations of common packaging terms such as "Handle With Care" and "Keep Upright." Export handbooks typically include referrals to organizations that provide export services, ranging from agents who handle overseas shipping to export trading companies that handle every aspect of the export transaction. State officials believe that one-on-one counseling is the most effective means of helping inexperienced exporters (National Governors' Association, 1985, p. 18). Forty-three states offer such assistance (see Table 12-2). Seminars, however, function not only as occasions for providing specific assistance but also as recruiting forums, often attracting companies curious about foreign trade but without a firm commitment to export.

Besides providing information about the mechanics of exporting, the other major service offered by a few states is export financing. The earliest of such programs—those in Indiana, Minnesota, and Ohio—date only from 1983. State export financing, capitalized either by bonds or by appropriations, depending on the state, is aimed primarily at small businesses that cannot obtain conventional private loans or Eximbank backing. Financing may be provided for a variety of purposes and in a variety of different forms: preshipment working capital loan guarantees, loans to lending institutions to provide funds to loan to exporters, medium-term direct fixed-rate financing, and postshipment guarantees to banks.

California's Export Finance Program, which became effective in 1985, is a typical example. A legislative authorization of $10 million, of which $2 million was actually appropriated, provides backing for loan guarantees. The program is restricted to small to medium-sized businesses engaged in the export of California goods and services. The program will guarantee up to 85 percent of both pre- and postshipment financing with a limit of $350,000. Programs funded by bond issues tend to be much larger than those reliant on legislative appropriations. For example, the Illinois Export Development Authority, which administers that state's export loan program, is authorized to issue up to $100 million in bonds to raise funds. The authority is authorized to make direct loans to firms of no more than $500,000 to cover up to 90 percent of the pre or postshipment financing; the remainder must be supplied by a local financial institution. At least 25 percent of the final value of the goods or services exported must be produced in the state.

It would be difficult to make the case that state services to exporters are strikingly novel. States have, after all, been providing some form of counseling and financing assistance to businesses for many years. The new, entrepreneurial element in these export services is thus not so much their form as simply the fact that they are responsive to market demand perspectives. They are designed explicitly to enable small, local firms to exploit new overseas markets by offering technical help and capital difficult to come by through the private sector.

What does represent a significant substantive departure among the various export programs, however, is the states' efforts at market development. Here the state—and particularly the person of the governor—has emerged as a major sales agent overseas for local businesses and a scout in uncharted foreign markets seeking likely new customers. As a sales agent, the governor, or the state's office of international trade, serves both as publicist and broker for firms in the state. Particularly in the role of publicist the state government has put itself in the position of lending its stamp of legitimacy and credibility to particular goods produced by particular private firms. Although state officials seek to provide neutral information about the availability and character of local products rather than a sales pitch, the line between the two is often a fine one. Such activities raise a host of unexplored questions. To what extent will the state's reputation suffer if it promotes the sale of shoddy or defective goods? To what degree is the state liable to charges of favoritism if it promotes the sale of one firm's goods and not those of its competitor? (The same question arises with respect to the state's broker or matchmaking efforts to link buyers with local sellers: to what extent are some firms provided with sales leads that competitor firms are not?)[5] What are the limits to the claims that the state might make for the goods produced within its borders? To what extent does state promotion of particular firms or industries raise conflict-of-interest issues when the state is responsible for their regulation?

None of these potential problems has stemmed the rush to develop foreign markets for local goods. In 1985, 33 governors traveled abroad on trade missions, and half a dozen more were scheduled to go early in 1986 (*State Policy Reports*, Dec. 1985, p. 16). Many governors make at least one trip a year: Governor James Thompson of Illinois announced plans in 1985 to travel annually to Japan; Governor Anthony Earl of Wisconsin, in his single four-year term, traveled to the Far East, Israel,

---

5. When the state of Rhode Island plans to attend a trade show to promote local industries, it advertises its intention in its newsletter, *Export Quarterly*, which goes out to 3000 manufacturers in the state. Development officials, however, selectively invite some firms to attend by letter and telephone.

Mexico, and West Germany in successive years, marketing bull semen to help the Chinese develop a dairy herd as well as selling Wisconsin beer and plumbing fixtures. Governor Joseph Garrahy of Rhode Island traveled at least once a year, either to Japan or Italy.

State development officials consider the gubernatorial visits to be an especially effective way of developing trade contacts, although few, if any, states keep systematic records of deals actually made as a result of such trips. Evaluation of these and other market development efforts is based instead on anecdotal evidence generated for presentation before the legislature at budget time (interviews, Lotharius, 1986; Lewis, 1987; Lenehan, 1987; see also Kline, 1984, p. 86).

Gubernatorial trips abroad, foreign offices, and trade shows are the most glamorous aspects of state export-market development. In addition, states develop overseas markets by disseminating sales leads gathered from all sources (many leads are supplied by the U.S. Department of Commerce Trade Opportunities Program), and about half the states actually prepare market analyses of foreign countries.

Conclusions

Like other activities of the entrepreneurial state, the efforts to ferret out new markets abroad for locally produced goods are modest initiatives. Yet they derive a certain strength from their sheer novelty, from the cumulative potential inherent in encouraging members of the large community of small businesses to trade abroad, and from the promise offered by the huge, awakening consumer markets of newly industrializing nations. Furthermore, the multiplicity of state and local trade initiatives function as a form of modest subsidy for exporters, reducing the costs of information gathering, market development, and financing. Although this assistance scarcely serves to match the subsidies that foreign governments often provide to their key export industries, it nevertheless does represent a modicum of support that helps in a limited way to offset the disadvantage borne by unsubsidized American companies competing on world markets.

Unlike entrepreneurial programs to supply venture capital or underwrite corporate-academic research in high technology, however, the export-promotion programs must confront a degree of inertia in the small business community that poses a significant threat to the success of these efforts. Export trade is perceived as so dauntingly complex that even when the groundwork has been carefully laid by state trade officials, many businesses still shy away from entering the international marketplace. An official in the Rhode Island Division of International Trade offers typical testimony: The state promoted the products of a number of local jewelry firms at a major trade fair in West Germany and gathered numerous sales leads in the process. Six months after these leads had been reported to the various companies in the jewelry industry, however, only one firm had pursued any of them (interview, Lenehan, 1987).

Other policies of the entrepreneurial state converge with and play upon American perceptions of themselves as a nation of business people, tinkerers, and inventors. But the national self-image does not encompass the foreign trader. Americans do not celebrate the import-export broker. Nor is foreign trade a standard part of the business lexicon as it is in, say, the island economy of Britain. A survey of banks conducted by the National Foreign Trade Council found that only 60 percent of the institutions it contacted were actually doing any export financing and half of those did no more than a handful of transactions (*New York Times,* Jan. 20, 1987). It is thus not unreasonable to suggest that if state export-promotion activities are to become a major contributor to economic development, state and local officials will have to overcome these various inertial forces.

CHAPTER 13

Protective Economic Development: Plant-Closing Laws, Breach of Contract Suits, and Eminent Domain Seizures

ECONOMIC development policy in the United States has always taken as its fundamental principle the desirability of a partnership between government and business. This is so whether government has chosen to define its role as suitor and supplicant to business or as risk-taker and initiator. In either case the partnership may take formal dimensions in which government becomes financially involved with business, or it may simply refer to government's friendly, facilitative attitude toward business. These partnerships are, ideally, nonadversarial and cooperative—and, indeed, most seem in practice to work that way.

Not all partnerships, formal or informal, achieve their economic goals, of course: even with public financial assistance some businesses fail to grow, and some fail altogether. Some decide for one reason or another to move to other locales, even after they have been helped by various development subsidies. In all these cases, both where government has provided concrete assistance or where it has simply created a hospitable climate for business, it may be said that when a business folds or leaves the partnership has failed. This is particularly the case from the point of view of the government affected, for government tends to reify the partnership to a greater degree than business. Furthermore, government is likely to feel acutely the futility of having expended public resources or good will without producing the expected jobs.

A common perspective among businesses on such failures is that they represent an inevitable, if "heartbreaking,"[1] risk of the marketplace (McKenzie, 1984, pp. 84–87). For the government whose task it is to deal with the consequences of a plant closing or departure, no such benign interpretation is possible. But the anger and sense of betrayal induced by such economic dislocations is typically channeled into a range of responses that neither bear nor make demands on the firm that left or folded. Instead, the common response of state or local officials is to pledge to search for a new employer or to explore a way of recycling the abandoned facility.

In recent years, however, several state and local governments, many of them "disappointed partners," have begun to develop strategies that impose obligations on particular firms or that seek to interpose state power between a closing business and those who depend on it for their livelihood. There is a surprising novelty to the way states and cities are going about these efforts: in a policy domain noted for the often desperate attempts to establish amicable and cooperative business-government relations, these new initiatives are adversarial, constraining to business, and, in the view of many, a threat to a jurisdiction's business climate reputation. Nevertheless, these initiatives are driven by an emerging conviction that "fairness" standards ought to govern relations in the economic development public-private partnership, as well as by a gradually broadening notion of the scope of the government's appropriate responsibilities in maintaining employment. Thus, some of these new efforts represent an attempt to create and impose a new theory of private-sector responsibility to workers, community, and government. Others constitute a departure from the almost universal reliance in economic development policy on the private sector's ability and willingness to generate and maintain jobs by substituting the government as an owner and employer of the last resort. These novel actions are distinguished from the more common economic development programs in that they do not seek primarily to support or subsidize capital to enable it to create jobs. Rather the intent of these efforts is to shelter or assist particular workers jeopardized by corporate decisions or to preserve or recover public funds spent (fruitlessly) for development subsidies. We may refer to them generally, then, as "protective" economic development policies. Specifically, they include the imposition of plant-closing laws, efforts to exact specific performance from firms that have received public development assist-

---

1. These are the terms in which Otis Elevator described its decision in 1983 to pull out of Yonkers, New York (*New York Times,* May 15, 1983).

ance, and the novel use of eminent domain powers to protect jobs in the face of a firm's failure or departure.

Plant-Closing Laws

As an abstraction, the process of "creature destruction," the term by which Joseph Schumpeter (1962, pp. 81ff.) depicted the evolutionary cycle of economic obsolescence and regeneration in capitalist systems, has a thoroughly reassuring aspect. The decline of industries, production technologies, and products and their replacement by the new is the stuff of progress, "the fundamental impulse that sets and keeps the capitalist engine in motion" (ibid., p. 83). In the concrete, however, the events that precede regeneration in the process of creative destruction often have tragic dimensions for the workers and communities affected. For them the sudden closing or departure of a business is an occurrence whose shocking quality is seldom mitigated by the thought that their experience is prelude to the rise somewhere, sometime, of other, more efficient or market responsive, firms.

Beginning in the mid-1970s various political and labor leaders argued, therefore, that businesses that displaced workers through layoffs, shutdowns, or relocations bore some responsibility to help cushion the trauma of job loss. In most instances the proposed responsibility was exceedingly modest: firms that displaced workers would have to provide advance notice of any job-threatening change in business operations. As Owen Bieber, head of the United Auto Workers union, wrote in the *New York Times* (Nov. 10, 1985, p. 2-F): "People should be protected against the devastating consequences of corporate decisions. . . . the emotional impact of sudden plant closings and permanent layoffs would be lessened by a 90-day notice requirement." Beyond simple advance notification, some contended that firms also bore an obligation to help provide job retraining, severance pay, and the continuation of health insurance payments.

None of these is particularly unusual: nearly every industrialized nation in Western Europe has laws requiring advance notice of closings, and many have elaborate provisions for assistance for displaced workers (Hooks, 1984; Folbre et al., 1984). Even in the United States many firms provide notice of plant closings voluntarily. A recent survey by the Conference Board of company approaches to dealing with plant shutdowns found that 88 percent of the 224 firms that responded to the survey provided workers with advance notice; more than a quarter of these gave six months or more warning (Conference Board, 1986). In addition, advance notice of plant closings is increasingly the subject of collective bargaining. By 1980 between 15 and 25 percent of all major collective bargaining contracts contained such a provision, up substantially since the early 1970s (Wendling, 1984, p. 109; Harrison, 1984, p. 41).

The voluntary provision of severance pay and assistance in finding a new job is also relatively common. Clague and Couper (1934), whose pioneer study had documented the impact of severance pay and job-placement efforts of the Candee and Company rubber shoe factory in New Haven after its closure in 1929, indicate that some firms paid a "dismissal wage" as early as the beginning of the 1920s. By the early 1980s the Conference Board survey found that three-quarters of the firms in its survey at least continued payment of health-care benefits, the major concern of labor in plant-closing cases. A majority of the firms provided some form of assistance to employees in looking for other jobs, although only 11 percent actually offered retraining programs themselves. The point of these examples is to suggest that what is novel about plant-closing laws in the current period is not their substance particularly but rather that they call for state government involvement in the encouragement, design, and implementation of such arrangements.

Plant closings, from whatever cause, are relatively common events, although analysts disagree on the exact magnitude of the problem. Bluestone and Harrison (1982, p. 32) estimate on the basis of a sample of manufacturing plants drawn from Dun and Bradstreet files that the rate of closure in the 1970s was slightly over 4 percent annually. Others, using less comprehensive data sources, estimate the closure rate at around 1 percent of all manufacturing plants per year.[2] Harris (1984), however, uses data from the Brookings U.S. Establishment and Enterprise Microdata file and offers estimates of annual rates of closing that range as high as 13 percent, depending on the years under consideration, the size of the firm, and whether it is a branch establishment or independent.[3] Service establishments, according to Birch (1979, Appendix D), tend to exhibit a slightly higher rate of closure than do manufacturing firms. Nearly all studies show that regional differences in the incidence of plant closings tend to be relatively minor.

---

2. Wendling (1984, p. 9) cites a study by the Bureau of National Affairs based on information gathered through newspaper clippings, union reports, and "informed sources." Schmenner (1982) also arrives at a figure of less than 1 percent by analyzing a sample of *Fortune* 500 firms.

3. The highest rate of closure occurred among branch or subsidiary establishments with fewer than 100 employees in the years 1980–82 (almost 13 percent). The lowest annual rate of closure was among independent firms with more than 100 employees from 1978 to 1980 (1 percent).

The magnitude of job loss from plant closings is substantial. Harris (1984) eliminates from her analysis all business dissolutions caused by bankruptcy, financial failure, retirement or death of the owner, and insufficient profitability, all "normal" sources of turbulence in the economy. Focusing then only on closures of establishments that are affiliates of business enterprises with 100 or more employees, she estimates that between 3.5 and 4 million jobs were lost between 1978 and 1982, or one out of every four jobs in large, manufacturing branch plants. Bluestone and Harrison, using their more comprehensive data base, calculate that plant closings from all causes cost workers 22 million jobs over the seven-year period from 1969 to 1976, or 3.2 million per year.

Despite scholarly disagreement over what exactly to measure and what data to use, the actual magnitude of the problem may be politically less important than the fact that it occurs at all. The emotional and economic disruptions of even one or two plant closings can be wrenching enough to make regulation an appealing policy option.

The case for regulating plant closings and major layoffs rests on the general proposition that it represents a way of forcing firms to help defray some of the social costs involved in such economic dislocations. Far from representing an effort to prohibit plant closures, as some critics claim (McKenzie, 1984), such legislation seeks instead to regulate the *process* by which such events occur (Folbre et al., 1984). Advance notice mitigates the costs of employment loss by enabling workers to search for work or retrain while they are still employed, thus hastening reentry into the ranks of the employed (Balderston, 1986, p. 10). And the provision of severance pay and continuation of insurance benefits is designed to require private firms rather than public welfare agencies to pay for workers' maintenance costs at least for a brief period during the transition from one job to another.

The legislative movement to regulate plant closings at the national level began in the U.S. Congress in 1974 with the introduction of legislation by Senator Walter Mondale (D.-MN) and Congressman William Ford (D.-MI). Their bill died in committee, but subsequent versions were introduced in every Congress thereafter. Congress finally passed a plant closing provision in 1988 over President Reagan's objections. Although the 1988 version called only for advance notice of plant closings, the earlier required in addition some combination of measures calling for continuation of benefit payments, severance pay, payments in lieu of taxes to communities, and job-retraining or -search assistance. To make these regulations palatable to business the federal government would provide loans, loan guarantees, interest subsidies, and the assumption of outstanding debt for firms in danger of closing. Proponents argued not only that such regulations would cushion workers facing a shutdown and perhaps save the jobs in a few firms hovering on the financial edge, but also that a *national* law would eliminate the presumed unfair advantage to be gained by states that would refuse to regulate plant closings if the matter were left to them.

Activity at the state level, little of which initially bore fruit, occurred for the most part after the failure of federal legislation in the 1970s. Maine passed a plant-closing notification and severance-pay law in 1971, and Wisconsin began to require 60 days prior notice in 1976. But the state debate over this issue did not begin in earnest until the 1980s. Between 1982 and 1986 at least 40 states considered plant-closing laws (ibid., p. 11). Only three states actually passed laws in this period, although about half a dozen more worked out voluntary codes through negotiations among union leaders, state officials, and business organizations to govern plant-closing decisions.[4] At the same time several local governments also passed plant-closing laws, notably Vacaville, California, Philadelphia, and Pittsburgh. The latter, however, was overturned in the courts as a violation of Pennsylvania's home-rule provisions, and Philadelphia's law has been distinguished by its lack of enforcement.

The most important of the state legislative enactments in the early 1980s is the Massachusetts "social compact." Widely regarded among state officials outside Massachusetts as a model compromise approach to the regulation of plant closings (interview Balderston, 1987; *State Policy Reports,* Sept. 21, 1984, p. 24), the 1984 social compact requires that businesses which seek financing assistance from any of the myriad of Massachusetts programs agree first to pursue good-faith efforts to provide advance notice of closings and layoffs, continuation of health insurance benefits, and job retraining and reemployment assistance. No mandatory standards of notice or assistance are established by the law, but the state "expects firms to provide at least 90 days notice or equivalent benefits whenever possible before closing" (Massachusetts Industrial Services Program, 1985, p. 1). Even businesses that do not seek public fi-

---

4. The three states that passed laws in this period included Connecticut (1983), which compels firms closing down to pay health insurance coverage for 90 days after closure; Maryland (1985), which wrote into law voluntary guidelines for prenotification and continuation of benefits; and Massachusetts, which wrote a voluntary compact into law. Among the states that worked out voluntary guidelines outside of the legislative process were California, Indiana, Pennsylvania, Washington, and New York.

nancing are expected to observe these "principles of responsible corporate behavior."

For its part in the compact, the state not only offers businesses access to various financial subsidies, but it also provides direct assistance to troubled firms and their workers. Through the Massachusetts Industrial Service Program, the state will send a team to evaluate a firm's problems, prepare a remedial business plan, and oversee its application for financial help to the Economic Stabilization Trust Fund, the financing arm of the program. In the first 10 months of its existence, the program gave some form of assistance to 44 companies, all in "mature" industries.

State help for displaced workers is a companion to the social compact. These efforts are modeled loosely after the Canadian Industrial Adjustment Service, which Massachusetts officials visited prior to the passage of the law (interview, Balderston, 1987). Besides providing unemployment insurance supplements and payments for health insurance for laid-off workers when the closing firm is unable to provide severance benefits, the state has established a set of reemployment assistance programs. These typically operate at the plant site, in union halls, or in local storefronts, providing job-search assistance, information on training programs, personal counseling, and preretirement workshops.

These on-site dislocated-worker services strongly resemble the rapid-response economic adjustment teams that more than 20 states established by the mid-1980s. Created first in California by order of Governor Jerry Brown in 1980 (and enacted into law there in 1982), the economic adjustment team sends state officials at the request of communities, unions, and employers facing a major plant closing to help plan and coordinate a strategy to deal with the dislocation (ACIR, 1985c, p. 92; Fedrau, 1984). The California Economic Adjustment Team sets up workshops on job retraining, provides workers with personal and employment counseling, and may even help organize an employee buy-out of the threatened firm or offer management assistance in an effort to save the firm from closing. The options open to the California team are not fixed: assistance is geared to the particular local situation. Rapid-response teams in a number of states are supported in part by federal funds from Title III (aid for dislocated workers) of the Job Training Partnership Act of 1982.

Voluntary "compacts" among business, organized labor, and the state on the one hand and the rapid-response teams on the other have the virtue in the eyes of many observers of involving the private sector in the response to economic dislocation without resorting to the coercion underlying mandatory prenotification. Whether voluntary arrangements result, however, in more willing and generous compliance with regulatory guidelines than mandatory laws is not clear. But what is apparent is that the latter are not particularly effective. Folbre and her colleagues (1984) report that, between 1975 and 1981, 30 plants, each employing more than 100 workers, closed in Maine. Although the law requires such firms to give at least 60 days notice to the state Bureau of Labor prior to closing, 23 of the 30 failed to comply. The Maine law also requires the provision of severance pay based on employee seniority. Firms that go bankrupt or have severance pay provisions in their collective bargaining agreements are exempt. Of the 16 firms that were required to pay, only 9 complied with the law. No penalties are imposed for noncompliance.

Compliance with Wisconsin's plant-closing law has been no better. Passed in 1976, the law requires firms with more than 100 employees (such firms account for only 2 percent of Wisconsin businesses) to provide 60 days notice to the state Department of Industry, Labor, and Human Relations of any change in operations due to merger, liquidation, or relocation resulting in closure. A fine of $50 per day per employee may be levied for failure to make timely notification. The legislature set up a bipartisan study committee, including business and labor representatives, to draft the law; however, business interests have vigorously opposed enforcement of the law since its passage (Murphy, 1984). Fearing that enforcement would "send the wrong signals" to business, two governors—one a Democrat, the other a Republican—quietly ordered the department not to prosecute violators. As a result, in the period between 1976 and 1984 only 57 of 140 large manufacturing businesses that closed, merged, or relocated actually provided timely notification. No fines were levied in this period against any firms that failed to comply. The law was amended in 1984 to require notification not only of the department but also of workers, union officials, and affected local governments.

Enthusiasm among state officials for mandatory plant-closing laws appeared to have waned in the mid-1980s under the twin liabilities of reluctance to enforce the laws in the few places where they existed and continued opposition by free market interests who regard prenotification as an "affront" to individual freedom (see, for example, McKenzie, 1984, p. 183). Although some states were clearly interested in following the Massachusetts voluntary compact model, the National Governors' Association predicted that state energies would be channeled increasingly into dislocated worker programs rather than into the search for the optimal prenotification and severance-pay arrangement (interview, Balderston, 1987). Encouragement for this strategy came late in 1986 in the form of a demonstration project launched in nine states under the co-sponsorship of the National Governors' Association and the Department of Labor. Drawing on the experience of the Canadian Industrial Adjustment Service and the rapid-response teams in several American states, the project was designed to help the selected states to set up adjustment teams and labor-management committees at plant-closing sites to help workers find new jobs and deal with the stresses of dislocation (National Council for Urban Economic Development, 1986). A large federal program for this purpose was included in the President's budget proposal for the 1988 fiscal year.

Suing Plant Closers for Breach of Contract

In the still comparatively uncrowded field of protective economic development policy, variations on a regulatory model appear to have been the dominant state and municipal response to plant closings in the early 1980s. A few governments, however, have begun to explore an alternative response based not on the controversial, and possibly ineffective, effort to regulate capital mobility but rather on the attempt to exact specific performance by firms under the law of contracts. While the regulatory model requires bureaucratic enforcement of a statutory closing law or of a voluntary compact, the contract model is based on the resort to litigation in order to resolve what many states and cities see as the breach of contract implied by the closing of a plant that has received public development assistance. Few governments have actually initiated such lawsuits, and the legal theory behind this strategy is still in its formative stages. But there are at least three cases worth examining where state or local governments have actually chosen this means to protect jobs and the investment of public funds for economic development aid.

The first case concerns the closing of the Otis Elevator factory in Yonkers, New York. Here the issue at stake in a suit brought by the city in federal court was whether and to what degree the company bore any obligation to the city that had helped to finance its expansion. The remedy sought by the city was restitution of some portion of the economic development funds used to assist Otis in its modernization effort.

Otis Elevator had been a major industrial employer in Yonkers for more than a century when it announced in 1968 that its quarters were both too old and too small to permit the firm to achieve the efficiencies necessary to compete in the world elevator market.[5] Dense residential and commercial development abutting the plant, however, seemed to preclude expansion at its current site. Otis nevertheless was receptive to a city proposal to try to work out a mutually acceptable arrangement that would make it possible for the company to stay in Yonkers. The eventual result was a plan that involved the exercise by the Yonkers Urban Renewal Agency of condemnation and eminent domain powers to enable it to acquire and prepare the land adjacent to the Otis plant and turn it over to the company. Otis agreed in 1972 to this plan in a letter of intent, saying that it would expand and modernize its facilities on the land made available for the purpose of continuing its operations and maintaining local employment. Company documents indicate in fact that Otis officials believed that the proposed expansion would serve the firm's needs well into the next century.

The cost of acquiring and clearing the land came to nearly $16 million in federal, state, and local funds, about a sixth of which was put up by the city of Yonkers alone. Once the land was prepared, it was conveyed to Otis for $539,000 with the express understanding that the company would build new quarters and make certain additional site improvements. To create the nine-acre parcel of land approximately 60 businesses and several hundred families were relocated.

Just as the new plant was being completed in 1976, Otis Elevator was taken over by United Technologies after a hostile tender offer. Employment at the Yonkers plant, devoted entirely to the production of electromechanical elevators, was cut immediately, because United Technologies decided to invest in facilities in the South that manufactured the more advanced silicon chip elevators. In 1982 United Technologies announced that it would close the "technically obsolete" Yonkers plant within a year.

Angered by what he considered a betrayal of the city, the mayor, a Republican, appointed a task force to investigate the possibility of legal remedies (New York Times, May 15, 1983). After several months of deliberation the task force recommended a strategy that sought not to block the closure of the plant but rather to recover some portion of the public funds spent to assist the Otis expansion. Thus, the city brought suit in federal court alleging violation of an express agreement on the part of Otis to stay in Yonkers and seeking restitution of some of the

5. Information on the Otis case is based on an interview with the attorney litigating the case for the city, Vito Cassan, conducted on February 17, 1987, and on attorneys' briefs filed in the U.S. Court of Appeals for the Second Circuit, April 22, 1987.

city's money. The attorneys for the city faced a major problem, however: nowhere had any of the parties to the original agreement thought to specify how long Otis was to remain in Yonkers after it had received development assistance. The attorneys for Yonkers argued that besides the express contract in writing between Otis and the city there also existed an "implied in fact" contract, that is, an agreement inferred by the law from the acts or conduct of the parties or circumstances of the transaction. Based on these factors Yonkers believed that Otis was bound to stay in the city for a much longer period after its expansion than it actually did (the city's expectation was "at least sixty years"). To determine the pro rata share of the development assistance to be returned to the city, the courts in such a situation would supply a reasonable period of time for the life of the contract. Otis officials contended that the company had in fact stayed in its new facilities for six years and owed the city nothing.

No decision was announced for two full years after the case had been argued in federal district court. When at last the judge issued an opinion, he ruled against the city's claims on the ground that the contract between Otis and the city was void in light of the statute of frauds, the application of which in this case was based on an interpretation of that law which states that no suit or action will be maintained for a contract expected to last more than a year unless there is a written note or memorandum signed by the parties specifying the time period of the agreement. The city filed an appeal in 1987.

At least two features of the Otis case are important to note. One is that the city did not challenge the decision of the company to shut down its plant. The owner's right to relocate, divest, or reallocate capital was conceded. Yonkers thus sought to avoid the charge by opponents of plant-closing laws that it was trying to impose intolerable restrictions and costs on the market. Second, the case is notable as the first in which a municipal government has sought to recover funds on the grounds of "unjust enrichment," that is, the claim that Otis profited at the expense of the city without meeting its part of the bargain. The implications of this claim are, first, that public economic development assistance can be regarded as conditional on specific performance and, second, that the relationship between city and firm in this policy domain can be governed by some standard of "fairness." The notion that government can assume a role of equality in a partnership with a private-sector actor—that is, in this particular situation that government can make claims against or demands upon its partner wholly apart from the taxing and regulatory functions—is, of course, characteristic of the expectations of the entrepreneurial state. The idea of equality contrasts with the public role in the traditional supply-side model, where subsidies are finally unconditional and failure by a business to meet the public sector's expectations is met with nothing more than disappointment and anger.

A second legal action, brought by the state of Illinois against the United States Steel Corporation in 1984, makes a claim similar to that in the Otis case. The state argued that in 1982 it had entered into an oral agreement with the corporation to make certain expenditures on site and transportation improvements if U.S. Steel would build a rail mill at its South Works complex.[6] The state made the necessary expenditures, but soon thereafter U.S. Steel began to demolish certain of its production facilities at the South Works plant. The state sought a temporary restraining order and a preliminary injunction to prevent further demolition and specific performance of the oral contract.

Three weeks after the suit was filed, the state circuit court granted the injunction to stop further destruction of the steel plant. The court then refused to dismiss the state's complaint that there had been a breach of contract, but it did not rule on the merits of the state's argument. U.S. Steel then appealed both the preliminary injunction and the refusal of the court to dismiss the state's complaints. Four months later the appellate court upheld the preliminary injunction, not for reasons related to the state's claim, but rather in response to a motion by the United Steelworkers Union, whose suit against U.S. Steel on the same matter had been consolidated on appeal with that of the state.

Having demolished all but one blast furnace at the South Works facility prior to the issuance of the preliminary injunction, there was in fact very little to continue to fight over in practical terms. U.S. Steel decided not to appeal the court's affirmation of the lower court injunction but instead to work out an agreement with the state. Under the terms of the new bargain, U.S. Steel was permitted to raze the remaining blast furnaces and in return transform the site, using $3 million of its own funds, into an industrial park.

Because the state's claim that U.S. Steel was guilty of breach of contract was never examined on its merits, the case, in the context of the emergence of protective economic development initiatives, is a piece of

---

6. Information on the South Works case is based on an interview with Jim Carroll, Illinois Attorney General's Office, January 30, 1987, and on the state appellate court's opinion in *People of the State of Illinois, ex rel. Neil Hartigan v. United States Steel Corporation,* November 27, 1984.

unfinished business. Nevertheless, it is notable that the state asserted a quid pro quo arrangement and was willing to sue in court on the grounds that U.S. Steel had not met its part of the bargain. Furthermore, even though the parties were bound only by oral agreement, the district court did not dismiss the state's complaint. Finally, the case is of interest because it induced U.S. Steel to bargain with the state to make up in some way for its failure to perform as expected.

A third suit that alleged breach of contract in an economic development dispute was brought by the city of Chicago against the Playskool Company, a recipient of industrial revenue bond financing, whose parent company, Hasbro, unexpectedly announced plans to close the Illinois plant. In 1979 the city and the toymaker entered into an agreement whereby Chicago would issue $1 million worth of IRBs to help Playskool to modernize and expand its facilities.[7] The terms of the loan agreement state not only that "the financing of the project will induce [Playskool] to create additional jobs in the city of Chicago" but also that "the obligations of [Playskool] to perform and observe the obligations on its part . . . shall be absolute and unconditional." Specifically, among other obligations, "during the term of the Agreement [Playskool] . . . will not dissolve or otherwise dispose of . . . its assets." The term of the loan agreement was fixed at 20 years. In addition to securing IRBs for the company, the city also agreed to provide streets and sewers, street lighting, and various other municipal services.

Four years after the city issued the IRBs, Playskool paid off the bonds in their entirety and announced the closure. Chicago then sued, seeking an order to compel the company, according to the Verified Complaint, "to specifically perform and honor and comply with the terms of their development agreement with the city of Chicago, and continue to maintain and operate the agreed upon development project until the expiration of the term of the Agreement on February 1, 2000." Playskool argued that the city's contribution to the development project was extremely minor: the city bore no risk and no expenses and in any event the $1 million amounted to less than 4 percent of the cost of the capital expenditures made in the Playskool modernization. Furthermore, the

---

7. Information on the Playskool case is based on an interview with Herb Caplan, assistant corporation counsel, city of Chicago, January 20, 1987; and documents pertaining to the case including the Verified Complaint for Specific Performance, Injunction, and Declaratory Judgment (December 3, 1984); Defendant's Memorandum of Law in Support of Motion to Dismiss (no date); and the Stipulation between Parties (January 31, 1985). See also *New York Times,* January 13, 1985.

company contended in the Memorandum to Dismiss that, having paid off the bonds, the terms of the loan agreement no longer applied:

> Playskool's right . . . to abandon the project or facility without any accountability to the City emasculates the premise which permeates the City's entire complaint—that by becoming the conduit for a loan to Playskool, the City became vested with the right to participate as a business partner for the duration of the stated term of the Bond with powers to dictate where the business will operate and how money will be spent in the conduct of the business.

Playskool's language suggests an effort to rebuff the city's attempt to establish equal partnership status with the firm. Partnership is, indeed, in a general sense the objective that lies behind protective economic development initiatives, though it is unlikely that any city would state its claim in such bold terms. A claim to some sort of partnership rights— even those far short of the rights depicted in Playskool's motion to dismiss the suit—would not, of course, have been contemplated under the old rules of economic development policy.

Despite the vehemence of Playskool's counterargument, it nevertheless entered into negotiations with the city, the result of which was a stipulation made in and overseen by the court that the city would drop the suit in return for certain actions on the part of the company and its parent corporation. The firm agreed first to keep the Chicago plant in operation for nearly a year longer than it had intended. Furthermore, Playskool agreed to establish the Job Center (headed by local football hero, Gayle Sayers) to help employees find new jobs. The company agreed to pay any employer who hired one of Playskool's workers for a vacant or new position the sum of $500 for retraining and reorientation. The company also agreed to search for a charitable donee of the real estate on which the plant sat who would transform the facility into a business incubator or put it to some industrial use. Playskool employees would be the first source of workers in either case. Finally, Hasbro, the parent firm, agreed to establish a $50,000 fund to be used for grants and loans to Playskool employees experiencing financial hardship as a result of the closing.

Whether or not the city genuinely believed that it could prevent the closing of the Playskool for any significant period of time, it nevertheless was able to use the litigation process to elicit various concessions from the firm to ease the adjustment of the workers. It is clear that litigation to achieve these ends is more cumbersome than the application of a plant-closing statute that calls for severance pay and reemployment assistance. But cases where breach of contract might be claimed appear to be fairly rare: prior to the Playskool case, Chicago had never faced a situation where an IRB recipient announced its departure.

Litigation does have certain virtues. It creates powerful incentives for negotiations, and it permits the tailoring of a settlement to the particular situation. Furthermore, as plant-closing laws have been written to date, they make no distinction between firms that have received development assistance and those that have not. Cities or states that pursue lawsuits against plant closers that once received public aid have a strong moral claim, and perhaps a legal one, based on notions of fairness and contractual obligations. Proponents of plant-closing laws, of course, believe *all* companies that close plants have a clearcut responsibility to their workers, but it is probably more difficult to invest blanket plant-closing statutes with the same legal justifications and moral force of a suit against a company that took public money and left.

Resort to the courts to seek restitution, prevent plant closings, or gain assistance for displaced workers is still rare. Legal theories to support such suits appear to be still in a formative stage. And no court had yet ruled in the mid-1980s on the validity of a state or local government's claim that a plant closer had broken a contract by taking economic development assistance and then shutting down.

Plant Shutdowns and Eminent Domain Actions

The use of condemnation and eminent domain proceedings to acquire private property for economic development purposes is well-established. Eminent domain power was the key to the old urban renewal program, for it enabled local redevelopment authorities to assemble parcels of land that were both sufficiently large and attractively enough situated to be sold to private developers. In more recent times a number of cities have used eminent domain to provide expansion room or new industrial sites for local firms. Yonkers is a case in point. A well-publicized, controversial example of the 1980s—the "rape" of Poletown to some, the most important economic development program ever undertaken in Detroit to others—occurred when Detroit seized nearly 1700 pieces of residential and commercial property involving the relocation of more than 3500 people in order to prepare a new site for a Cadillac plant (Jones and Bachelor, 1986). The seizure was justified on the grounds that the alleviation and prevention of unemployment was a public purpose.

Eminent domain has typically involved the taking of dilapidated or blighted residential or commercial property and its redevelopment by public or private actors. The uses to which publicly acquired land is put are manifold: public and private housing, commercial developments, industrial parks, roads, stadiums, convention centers, public buildings, and so on. As the U.S. Supreme Court noted in 1954 in a case sustaining the condemnation of blighted areas for public housing projects, "the concept of public welfare is broad and inclusive enough" to allow the use of eminent domain to achieve any end within the authority of Congress.[8] The same principle has generally applied to actions by state or local governments in the pursuit of their broad police powers (Epstein, 1985, pp. 161–62). The exercise of this power frequently engenders controversy, but it is a widely accepted and common device.

At the beginning of the 1980s, however, several communities sought to expand the scope of the power of eminent domain beyond its conventional uses by seeking to use it to prevent the closing or departure of a local business. Their argument was that if a firm is in some way a significant contributor to the local economy, then its departure or failure threatens the public well-being. Yet since the state or city cannot bind the *owner* to a particular place, the solution is to seize the business. The owner, fully compensated, is free to leave. The city can then choose to run the business as a municipal enterprise or sell it to a new owner who promises to run it as part of the local economy. As in the case of the suits for breach of contract, the question of the legality of such takings has not been definitively settled. Several examples of efforts to use eminent domain powers in this novel way exist, but they do not go far in resolving the issues raised. Nevertheless, they allow us to view the first foundations on which such initiatives must be built in the future.

The first case concerns the effort by the city of Oakland, California, to seize its professional football team after its owner had declared his intention to move the franchise to Los Angeles. Arguing that the team made a critical contribution both to the local economy and to civic pride and identity, the city began eminent domain proceedings in February 1980 in Alameda County court. A tangled and lengthy process of litigation followed, resulting finally in a judgment against the city.

The city believed it first had to establish that it could seize intangible property—a sports franchise—and further that the taking was for a valid "public use."[9] The Oakland Raiders football team countered with

---

8. *Berman v. Parker,* 348 U.S. 26, 33 (1954)

9. Information on the Raiders case is based on two interviews with the former city attorney for Oakland, David Self, and on *City of Oakland v. Oakland Raiders,* 32 Cal. 3rd 60 (1982) as well as other cases cited in the text.

a narrow interpretation of the law of eminent domain arguing that it does not permit the taking of "intangible property not connected with realty." Furthermore, the team contended that the city could not condemn an *established* business (that is, a viable, ongoing concern) and in any event that its taking would not conform to any public use standard, particularly if the city acquired the team and then sold it to a new private owner.

In the trial court the Raiders moved for summary judgment, and the court, concluding that the city had no authority to acquire the team, dismissed the action. The city appealed to the California Supreme Court. In considering the appeal the supreme court first established that the eminent domain power does extend to intangible property, including patent rights, contracts, and franchises, a view supported by a substantial body of case law in both the federal and state courts. The city would therefore be acting within its authority in seizing intangible property, the court noted, but the question of whether its action satisfied the public use standard could not be resolved without a full hearing. The court pointed out that conceptions of public use shift over time and according to changing notions of the role of government, although in general it refers to "a use which concerns the whole community or promotes the general interest in its relation to any legitimate object of government" (*City of Oakland v. Oakland Raiders*, 32 Cal. 3rd 60 [1982]). The court contended that the acquisition of a professional sports franchise could *possibly* be an appropriate municipal function, but the city would have to establish this in a trial. Thus the supreme court remanded the case to the district court with instructions to afford both sides a chance to present their respective arguments during a trial on the merits.

The trial court eventually entered a judgment against the city on the grounds that the seizure did not constitute a public use, that the action violated antitrust law, and that it posed a burden on interstate commerce and thus violated the commerce clause of the U.S. Constitution. The state court of appeals upheld the trial court decision solely on the interstate commerce argument, a defense the Raiders had not broached in their original response to the city's action. Efforts to appeal to the state and federal supreme courts were unsuccessful.

Several things are noteworthy about this case. It is, to begin with, the first major effort to use eminent domain to condemn a business on the verge of departure from a community. But, second, the issue of the legality of such an application of eminent domain is *not* resolved. The trial court's argument that the seizure did not meet the public use standard was not the basis on which the appellate court upheld the lower court's decision. Thus, the trial court's view on the question of such a seizure in light of the public use standard is essentially dictum.

The grounds on which the city of Oakland lost, however, suggest a critical limitation on the use of eminent domain as a protective economic development tool. When the object to be condemned is a viable business simply seeking to relocate to a more profitable or hospitable locale, then eminent domain proceedings are likely to founder on the commerce clause. In this case it is clear that the business in question—a National Football League team—is involved in nationwide commerce. By barring indefinitely the relocation of such a business through its eminent domain authority, a city would be guilty, according to the court, of "the precise brand of parochial meddling with the national economy that the commerce clause was designed to prohibit" (*City of Oakland v. Oakland Raiders*, 174 Cal. Ap. 3rd 414 [1985]). Eminent domain authority, the appellate court concluded, must give way to the commerce clause when the burden on interstate commerce is direct and substantial.

The city's rejoinder to the interstate commerce argument is equally interesting from the perspective of the contention about the transformation of the state role in economic development policy. Oakland argued in the appellate court that it was "exempt from scrutiny under the commerce clause because it merely attempted to enter the market as a *participant,* not as a regulator" (my emphasis) (ibid., pp. 418–19). The claim of "participant" status to describe state purchase or sale of property in interstate commerce is not unknown in constitutional law. Unfortunately for the strength of Oakland's case, it does not seem to exempt the "participant" from review under the commerce clause (Rotunda et al., 1986, pp. 615–19). The validity of Oakland's claim notwithstanding, what is important is the city's view of its role in what is at base an economic development controversy. "Participant" indicates a more intimate and riskier level of market involvement than "regulator," a more conventional government role in the economy. Participant status is, of course, an attribute of the entrepreneurial state. Oakland's initiative, therefore, may be viewed as entirely consistent with the larger trends in the transformation of economic development strategy.

Subsequent efforts to use eminent domain as a protective economic development tool have for the most part focused on plants in danger of closing rather than on businesses seeking to relocate. Most of these efforts were resolved one way or another before litigation could occur, but memoranda of law prepared for these cases, as well as the public debates that surrounded them, do not raise the issue of whether eminent domain when used to prevent the loss of jobs threatens to burden interstate commerce. It would appear, therefore, that efforts to condemn businesses on the verge of shutdown represent actions less vulnerable to the issue on which the Oakland Raiders case was ultimately decided.

Not long after the Raiders case was under way in the courts, a series of abortive efforts to save jobs through plant condemnations took place in the Monongahela Valley near Pittsburgh (Portz, 1987). The instigator in each of these instances was the Tri-State Conference on Steel, a coalition of labor, community, and church groups formed in 1979 to address problems associated with plant closings in the steel industry in Ohio, Pennsylvania, and West Virginia.

In the first case, which occurred in 1982, Tri-State sought to persuade the borough council of Midland, Pennsylvania, to create or seek out an existing public authority to seize the Crucible Steel Mill, targeted for shutdown by its owner, Colt Industries. Concerned about the financial liability of any public entity that might undertake such a seizure, as well as the unlikely prospect of finding a private buyer to take the firm off the public authority's hands, the council declined to act.

Tri-State next tried to interest the Pittsburgh Urban Redevelopment Agency in condemning and acquiring a 650-employee Nabisco plant slated for closure. Despite support from several Pittsburgh city council members, the the agency was skeptical. Before the issue could be forced however, Nabisco announced that it would not close its Pittsburgh plant after all. A third case proceeded further: in 1983 the borough council in West Homestead, at the urging of Tri-State, actually voted to create a public authority to take over the Mesta Machine Company. The mayor vetoed the resolution, however, arguing that the municipality had neither the expertise nor the community support to contemplate a plant takeover.

None of these three efforts to use eminent domain failed on the merits of the strategy itself. No judicial judgment invalidated the use of eminent domain as a protective development tool. Rather, the problem in each case, a political one, lay mainly in the inability of the Tri-State Conference to find a public entity willing to test the eminent domain strategy. No such difficulty plagued the city of New Bedford, Massachusetts, however, as it confronted the possibility that it would lose the Morse Cutting Tools plant.

The New Bedford situation was resolved before such a use of eminent domain was tested in the courts, but it is important both for how em-

phatically the case for such protective seizures was made and for its demonstration of the potential of the threat of eminent domain as a bargaining chip in negotiations with corporations over the disposition of
unwanted plants.

Morse Cutting Tools had been the subject of a disinvestment strategy
by its owner, the Gulf and Western Corporation, almost since its acquisition by the parent company in 1968 (letter from Congressman Gerry
Studds to Mayor Brian Lawler, May 18, 1984). Employment had declined during the Gulf and Western period from 800 to 450 workers. In
1983 the conglomerate announced plans to sell Morse, but its antiquated
plant and equipment greatly reduced its market appeal. If no buyer could
be found, the larger corporation planned to close Morse altogether (*New
York Times,* June 5, 1984).

The city initially sought state help in exploring the feasibility of conversion of the company to employee ownership (letter from Mayor Brian
Lawler to Governor Michael Dukakis, Sept. 23, 1983), but officials decided instead to try to help Gulf and Western find a buyer for the plant
who was interested in rehabilitating it. Gulf and Western, however, rejected offers of help from both the city and the state (City of New Bedford, 1984). At this point the city pledged to continue the search for a
buyer on its own. If Gulf and Western refused to sell to someone the city
found, then the city announced that it would seize the plant by eminent
domain.

To support its possible resort to eminent domain the city contracted
with Georgetown University's Institute for Public Representation to prepare the case for such a strategy. The resulting memorandum, never put
to judicial test, offers a comprehensive analysis of the legality of eminent
domain proceedings in this novel situation (Buchsbaum, 1984). The case
is built first on a 1966 amendment to the Massachusetts Constitution
that established that "the industrial development of cities and towns is a
public function." Following that amendment, the state legislature enacted a number of economic development laws, one of which defined the
redevelopment of obsolete plants in order to reduce unemployment and
stimulate the economy as a public use or purpose and authorized the use
of eminent domain to acquire such property. "By appropriating the
plant," the memorandum goes on to argue, "the city intends to secure
the jobs of residents, . . . to maintain and improve the economic health of
the city, to preserve the city's tax base, and to prevent the dire social and
economic consequences of unemployment on a substantial number of the
city's residents" (ibid., p. 11).

In the meantime the city continued its search for a buyer, sending names of prospects, unbidden, to Gulf and Western. Facing the possibility of an eminent domain condemnation and the lengthy litigation that was sure to follow, Gulf and Western finally agreed to sell the plant to a buyer endorsed by the city, a Michigan company which agreed to upgrade the facilities. The issue of eminent domain now moot, the city proceeded to offer the new owner various forms of financial assistance, and the plant remained open.

New Bedford officials were convinced that the preservation of jobs constituted a legitimate and defensible public purpose by which to justify the seizure of Morse, even if the plant were taken from one private owner and sold to another. According to a briefing sheet prepared by the mayor's office, "the state and the courts have long recognized that for industrial development to be successful, the government must aid some businesses and not others" (City of New Bedford, 1984). Faced with a virtually identical situation a year later, however, Boston's corporation counsel advised the city *against* using its eminent domain powers in an attempt to seize the Colonial Provision Company. "It is conceivable," he wrote, "that, under proper circumstances, a valid 'public purpose' *could* even be shown for the taking of the 'label and business.' However, the taking proposed by EDIC [Boston's Economic Development and Industrial Corporation] . . . is for the purpose of selling or turning the property over to another private entity, one which will agree to maintain the label and business in Boston" (City of Boston, 1986). Despite initial strong mayoral and city council support for using Boston's eminent domain powers, the city decided finally not to make the attempt to seize the aging and unprofitable facility. The company, a meat-packing operation, was eventually sold by its owners to an out-of-state corporation interested in acquiring its trade name, New England customer base, and distribution network. The production facility, with its 600 jobs, was closed several months after the sale (interview, Sullivan, 1987; see also McLaughlin, 1986). Again, eminent domain as a protective development device was not tested in the courts on the grounds on which its proponents sought to justify its use.

A final case in the attempted use of eminent domain to save jobs provides a footnote of interest. The Tri-State Conference on Steel, rebuffed in its early efforts to find an authority willing to exercise eminent domain powers, managed finally to catalyze nine Monongahela Valley communities to create the Steel Valley Authority in 1986 for the purpose of acquiring or retaining industry. The authority, vested with eminent domain powers under Pennsylvania's Municipal Authorities Act of 1945, promptly sought in court to enjoin the American Standard Company from closing its Swissvale plant and moving its operations to existing branch plants in the South. The purpose of the injunction was to give the authority a chance to devise a condemnation plan and raise funds for an eminent domain action. The federal district court, while taking judicial notice that "the loss of jobs affects adversely not only citizens individually but other businesses and communities and local governments," nevertheless refused to grant the injunction. To enjoin the relocation *without a condemnation*, the court maintained, would be in effect to take private property for a public purpose without just compensation in violation of the Fifth Amendment (*Steel Valley Authority v. Union Switch and Signal Division*, June 17, 1986). The court nevertheless left open the possible use of eminent domain in such a case: "Should the situation change and should the Authority condemn the property, the complaint may be renewed."

Conclusions

The effort to regulate plant closings, the resort to contract law to exact specific performance from private-sector recipients of development assistance, and the use of eminent domain to seize businesses on the verge of shutting down all represent adversarial approaches to the economic development function. As such, these initiatives stand in contrast to the vast body of cooperative, facilitative programs and policies that constitute what state and local governments think of as the public-private partnership in quest of jobs and prosperity.

The cases in this adversarial realm represent no well-established trend; nor is it even clear that many of these initiatives are legitimate constitutionally or legally. Much has yet to be decided. But they are important, nevertheless, for all their inconclusiveness and tentativeness, as signs among the many other indicia of the broader and more active role of government in the economy now emerging at the subnational level.

Part of this new role is the assumption by government of a more equal relationship with the private sector in their partnership for development. The articulation of some sort of "fairness standard" that structures expectations and establishes norms of behavior for the public and private parties to mutual efforts in economic development is one manifestation of this new role. Concepts drawn from contract law—"unjust enrichment," "breach of contract," "implied in fact agreements"—are the legal expression of this governmental push for more equal status in the partnership.

A few state and local governments seem determined not to provide public subsidies without some means of holding business recipients accountable for their part in the relationship. However, not only is there an emerging sense that a private firm cannot accept assistance and then choose to leave the community that aided it, but there is also a growing effort to have business and governments share responsibility for cushioning the shocks of economic dislocation. This, too, is part of the thrust for equal status in the partnership, for government, through plant-closing legislation and even its eminent domain initiatives, has begun to explore ways of compelling business to share the liabilities of partnership as well as the benefits.

Instructing the business community about its expanded responsibilities to workers and communities and about its obligation as the beneficiary of public development assistance is part of a broader conception of the public economic development function than that which existed through the 1970s. The economic development function is no longer purely facilitative vis-à-vis capital; it now involves in addition a protective component vis-à-vis workers, though this latter aspect is still in its nascent form. Another indicator of the protective function is that the willingness to use eminent domain to save jobs suggests by implication that government is beginning to consider playing the role of employer as a last resort. Again, this role has scarcely been developed or carefully considered. Nor has any government actually had to face this situation in the context of eminent domain. But New Bedford, Oakland, and the Steel Valley Authority all considered and accepted the possibility that they would have to operate the businesses they hoped to seize until a private buyer could be found.

There is, of course, an alternative perspective on these various, largely unsuccessful and unresolved, "protective" development initiatives. Rather than viewing them as signs of an expanding and changing subgovernment role in economic development, it would be simple to make the argument that these cases present a record of abortive and frustrating defeats for governments in an adversarial posture. It would not be illogical to conclude that the prospect of lengthy litigation and a sullied reputation in the business community would discourage other states and municipalities from emulating the actions of Yonkers, Oakland, and the other communities. This view is supported, perhaps, by the diminishing interest in plant-closing statutes.

But the case that protective initiatives are better seen as experiments, early forays into a new territory that are likely to be followed by more careful explorations, is also a strong one. For one thing these thrusts toward equality in the public-private partnership are consistent with the burgeoning developments in the realm of entrepreneurial development policy. For another, it is clear that many of the issues raised by breach of contract suits and eminent domain and the like have not been resolved. Opportunities exist to adjust and refine the theories by which communities use the courts to protect workers and their own "investments" of economic development aid. Protective economic development from this point of view is an emergent phenomenon, not a dead end.[10]

10. It is interesting in this regard that a gubernatorial task force in Wisconsin, appointed by a conservative Republican governor, recommended in 1987 that the state seek restitution of development assistance when businesses fail to produce the expected benefits by including a "clawback" provision in all agreements to provide public aid. Such a device would eliminate the automatic resort to case-by-case litigation (Wisconsin Dept. of Administration, 1987).

CHAPTER 14

Conclusions

IN a treatise on political economy written early in the nineteenth century, Willard Phillips, a Massachusetts lawyer and tract writer, made a strikingly modern case for state entrepreneurialism. The introduction of new modes of production and new industries, he argued, is essential to the continued growth and well-being of the community. Yet the risks entailed in such undertakings are so high that individuals are more prone "to adhere to the accustomed employments of capital and industry." Individual and community interests run directly counter to one another. One remedy for this problem is for the state to bear some of what the modern economist calls the early-stage risks: "It would be folly," Phillips wrote, not to encourage, even through the use of "bounties" or direct grants, the "kinds of production . . . eventually useful to the community and profitable to the concerned, but which could not otherwise be undertaken without loss in the beginning, and therefore, would not be spontaneously undertaken at all" (Phillips, 1828, pp. 169, 92).

In the context in which Phillips wrote, such sentiments were not so unusual. For several decades after the Revolution the state of Massachusetts and its communities had provided, as their treasuries permitted, a variety of subsidies, including loans, tax relief, and outright "bounties" to support the growth and development of targeted firms and industries considered crucial to the young state's economic well-being. Similar efforts have been documented for this period in other states, including Georgia, Pennsylvania, and New Jersey (Scheiber, 1972). As the historian Robert Lively wrote, this was an era in which

the elected official replaced the individual enterpriser as the key figure in the release of capitalist energy; the public treasury, rather than private saving, became the major source of venture capital; and community purpose outweighed personal ambition in the selection of large goals for local economies. (Quoted ibid., p. 135)

331

Eventually in Massachusetts the desire to reduce taxes and limit the state's debt burden brought an end to these efforts to nurture fledgling industries. In other states public intervention withered with the rise of laissez-faire ideas around midcentury, and through the rest of the 1800s and the first 30 years of the present century state contributions to economic development were limited to little more than the effort to put in place a basic transportation network, a system of public higher education, and agricultural extension services. The microeconomic interventions of the postrevolutionary period were all but lost to memory. In the Great Depression, however, states began to embrace a broader range of economic development functions, most of them aimed at inducing particular industrial employers from outside the state to relocate. Thus was born the era of modern economic development policy.

Intervention in the years after the Great Depression was justified not as a way of fostering infant industries or stimulating the processes of industrial innovation but rather as a way of creating comparative location advantages by reducing factor costs on the supply side. For more than three decades states and their communities were preoccupied with the effort to invent evermore generous subsidies for land, capital, the tax burden, equipment, and labor training.

Matters began to change some time in the 1970s. States began to shoulder some of the risk of new product development and the founding of new firms, and they began to fashion a public role in the nurturance of entirely new industries. States and communities began to intervene in markets even where individual entrepreneurs feared to go. Without any self-conscious sense of the cycle of history, subnational governments had begun to come full circle to the early state entrepreneurialism of postrevolutionary Massachusetts.

The emergence, development, and transformation of subnational economic development policy since the 1930s have been the concerns of this study. Let me summarize the argument. Efforts to encourage business investment in the private sector as a means of generating employment, tax-base growth, and general prosperity in particular locales have been marked throughout the modern era by certain constant structural features:

- Initiatives are pursued through the vehicle of public-private partnerships.
- Policies are designed and implemented in a highly decentralized way.

- Planning efforts until recently were rare.
- Public intervention is designed largely to provide support, both direct and indirect, to capital rather than labor.
- Criteria for policy intervention and evaluation tend to be pragmatic rather than the products of dogma, ideology, or economic theory.

Within this fundamental framework the mix of forms of public subnational intervention has undergone a shift in recent years in response to a series of transformations in the American political and economic setting. The result has been the emergence of a model of public involvement in the economy quite different from any to which Americans have been accustomed in this century. The once exclusive reliance on supply-side factor subsidies designed to induce industrial relocation has given way to a more broad-based approach in which supply-side initiatives share the terrain with policies sensitive to structural dynamics of the market. These demand-side policies are not so concerned with shifting the location of established capital or even with retaining it (though the latter particularly is an important goal of all economic development bureaucracies) as they are with the effort to foster new business formation, business diversification, and new industries. Convinced that the key to local growth and well-being lies in exploiting and even creating new markets for local private businesses and entrepreneurs, state government has taken upon itself the task of identifying, ranking, and developing market opportunities. To bridge resource gaps that private actors cannot fill and to share some of the risks involved in new market ventures, state and local governments may subsidize or coinvest in these undertakings. To the degree that state and local governments have increasingly assumed the roles of market developer, broker, financial partner, and risk-bearer, we may speak of the rise of the entrepreneurial state.

The forces responsible for the embrace of state entrepreneurialism are manifold. The dispersion of population and industry across the nation set into high motion a competitive cycle which generated incentives for constant policy invention and elaboration among states and cities. The decline of manufacturing in relative terms—and its absolute diminution in some regions—stimulated subnational governments to think about fostering industries of the future, a high-risk research-intensive undertaking. Studies that raised doubts about the efficacy of location incentives and others that indicated that the local small business sector was the prime locus of job generation helped to shift the focus of policy away from established firms to local ventures that promised new capital formation. International competition in the market place, a phenomenon that began to take serious shape in the 1970s, put a premium on product innovation and technological pioneering, while the development of overseas domestic economies created new markets for American exporters. States and local governments responded to these forces by developing programs to finance new, small, young business ventures, to encourage basic and applied research in advanced technological fields with an eye toward product development for the commercial market and the fostering of new industries, and to facilitate export activity. Such policies define the entrepreneurial state in action.

This displacement of supply-side strategies for economic development by demand-oriented policies is important for several reasons. For one thing, without exaggerating either the current magnitude of demand-side programs or the thoroughness of their ascendance over supply-side policy, it is possible to argue that, in the ways these two approaches have evolved in this policy domain, the new approach offers greater potential for new capital formation than the older system of location subsidies. From a national point of view in particular, economic development pursued through demand-oriented policies is designed to function as a positive-sum enterprise by focusing on latent entrepreneurs, innovative products and processes, and the small business sector. This is not to say that infusions of resources on the supply side serve merely to shift the location of existing capital. Furthermore, eligible recipients of assistance, whether local or out of state, have tended in traditional programs to have well-established business and credit records. Established capital, although more stable in terms of its staying power than newer enterprises, is less likely to generate new employment and may even be less innovative in product development.

The emergence of a policy mix that prominently includes demand-oriented programs thus represents a genuine change—indeed, an advance in terms of sophistication and possibly in effectiveness—in notions about how government in the United States might stimulate growth and development in a mature industrial society. The entrepreneurial state may in fact be understood as an adaptation to an economic order in which manufacturing and the large industrial firm no longer seem to offer the principal keys to prosperity. The entrepreneurial state is a response to increasing technological complexity and to great international economic forces, whose mastery eludes the capacity and resources of most individual private entrepreneurs. The demand-based policies that we have examined are reflections, then, of diminished individual opportunity. Yet they are the policies of a society that nevertheless insists on preserving some possibility for private economic action. In this context the entrepreneurial state is a kind of compromise between the subsidized individualism of the traditional supply-side model and a state-run economy.

Demand-side policies also represent an advance in economic management techniques in the American political economy to the degree that they require the targeting of public resources to growth industries and potentially productive new technologies. Demand-side policy calls for a more highly rationalized system of public subsidy of private business in which planning, forecasting, technology assessment, and strategic analysis are the critical tools to guide selective interventions. The entrepreneurial state is a mechanism, though still institutionally rudimentary, for preparing for the economic future in a relatively self-conscious way.

The policies of state entrepreneurialism are significant for a third reason, and that is that they may be serving gradually to rescue states from the debilitating and unproductive interstate competition for private industry that so dominated the era of supply-side inducements.[1] Bidding wars are giving way to a politics of domestic husbandry. In the entrepreneurial state the market may often lie beyond state borders, but the seeds of growth and development are home-grown. States are less likely to commit to a course of policy that results in repeated contests with other states for industrial targets, though episodes such as the wooing of the General Motors Saturn plant remind us that these competitions may still on occasion be politically and economically tempting. But the burden of competition has clearly begun to shift from states in their quest for industry to the shoulders of private parties in public-private partnerships in the entrepreneurial state as they seek a niche in the larger marketplace.

All this means, of course, that the dynamic that leads to more and more costly inducements in bidding wars for industry is no longer so compelling. Public resources spent for economic development under the regime of state entrepreneurialism are less likely, theoretically, to exceed the margin of utility; that is, they are designed to cover only what is

---

1. Detroit's efforts to retain General Motors' Cadillac plant by creating a Poletown site offers an example of the Pyrrhic victories that often result from these competitions. To get General Motors to stay in Detroit the city offered such generous tax abatements and financing subsidies that even "under the optimistic assumptions of the city's economic-development officials, the project will do well to allow the city to recover its investment and to repay the loans that it arranged" (Jones and Bachelor, 1986, p. 135).

necessary to make possible the initiation or expansion of a business or research venture without the additional cost increment imposed by the challenge of bids from competitor states. In short, state entrepreneurialism promises a more rational and more efficient use of public resources in economic development simply because each state and locality seeks to stimulate growth through germinal elements present in their own local economies.

Despite these relatively positive assessments of the entrepreneurial state, several issues and problems remain. Some of these simply provide the basis for speculations about the future, while others suggest weaknesses in the entrepreneurial approach to economic development.

The Problem of Evaluation

Whether or not economic development policies actually "work," that is, whether they generate net new employment, is an abiding question in this policy domain. The question breaks down into a host of more specific queries. Do state expenditures to subsidize private capital elicit investment that would otherwise not have occurred? Do economic development policies create new employment, or do they mainly serve to shift jobs from one locale to another? Is economic development mainly an exercise in symbolic politics for the purpose of enhancing a state's business climate reputation?

Assuming that the answers to these questions provide reassurance as to the effectiveness of economic development policies in stimulating new growth, other questions follow. Do the public costs of generating a new job outweigh the benefits? Are the demand-based policies of the entrepreneurial state more effective than supply-side policies? Are some states more effective in stimulating employment growth than others?

This book is not, of course, an effort to address these questions directly through a new empirical analysis. Nevertheless, the foregoing overview provides both context and clues for suggesting some answers and making some forecasts.

To begin with, the questions about effectiveness were formulated during the era of supply-side location incentives and reflect concerns derived from experiences with those instruments. Two features of the supply-side approach suggest that its effects on new investment and job generation will be minimal. One of these features is that in most cases location incentives represent a very small portion of a firm's business costs, too little, indeed, to affect investment behavior. Occasionally, when all else is equal, the offer of an inducement is sufficient to make a firm choose among competing locations, but this outcome simply serves to shift the location of investment and jobs that would have been produced anyway *someplace* (Thompson, 1983).

Another feature of location inducements—tax abatements, IRBs, loan guarantees, and so on—is that they are almost invariably offered to established firms in the manufacturing sector or to established real estate developers. Since most enterprises of this sort are continually engaged in a series of investment behaviors—expansion, renovation, branching, new product development, diversification—it is hard to determine whether the offer of an inducement really stimulates any single behavior in this chain of on-going activity that would otherwise not have occurred.

From an economic point of view it is simple, therefore, to make the argument that location incentives are ineffective as devices for the generation of new investment and new jobs. Supply-side initiatives are best seen principally as the exercise of symbolic politics in the effort to fashion a hospitable business climate.

Now consider the same basic set of questions in the context of demand-oriented entrepreneurial policies. These are aimed mainly at encouraging business activity by those who could not pursue a project if they had to rely solely on the private investment community or their own resources. Private capital for the most part shuns such activities—small business, venture undertakings, new product development, basic R&D, foreign export—as too risky. Many analysts, particularly in the public sector, consider the risks involved in these investments to be overstated, especially because there are ways of cushioning investors from risk (e.g., portfolio diversification, R&D consortia, export-trading companies). Besides, the high growth potential should offset the real risks. Excessive private financial caution, however, creates a capital gap. Economic development officials in entrepreneurial states consider the reluctance of the private financial community to invest in these potentially productive activities to be a form of market irrationality, inefficiency, or failure. It is *only* when the entrepreneurial state offers to share the risks by committing some of its own resources that private investors may be willing to invest their own money in this high-risk sector. The targets of entrepreneurial state economic development policy are not, therefore, weighing bids among alternative competing locations for their investments; rather they are trying to determine whether they will be able to undertake any investment at all. We may conclude, then, that to the extent the entrepreneurial state focuses its resources on firms and entrepreneurs in the high-risk sector, the likelihood is that it will in fact elicit new investment that would not have occurred otherwise or in any other place. Furthermore, chances are that such an approach will be more effective than location incentives offered to established firms in the low-risk sector.

Although entrepreneurial policies seem generally to elicit new investment—thus adding to the national capital stock—it is less clear that they will always generate new jobs. Entrepreneurial policies have simply not been evaluated thoroughly enough to determine whether or not they produce jobs, but for some of the older economic development programs enough data exist to suggest that there seems to be something like a "two-thirds rule" in operation: that is, new jobs are created (or shifted from somewhere else) in about two-thirds of the projects supported; or alternatively, two-thirds of the jobs anticipated or projected actually materialize. This at least is the case for programs as diverse as the Economic Development Administration's public works grants, UDAG, and Wisconsin's Tax Increment Financing districts. It is not, of course, clear that this is an immutable law of nature. What it suggests simply is that not every economic development partnership will generate employment.

The direct costs of creating new jobs seem manifestly lower than the costs of unemployment, although as we saw in Chapter 3, new jobs create a host of indirect costs for a community. Bluestone and Harrison show data indicating that the cost of each industrial layoff to the state, local and federal treasuries in lost taxes plus the new social welfare expenses often ran as high as $18,000 annually in the early 1980s (1982, p. 75). Yet the direct public cost of generating a job in most economic development programs, supply- or demand-side, hovered in those years around $10,000 or less as a one-time expenditure. To the degree that new jobs are created, rather than shifted from one place to another, the public investment is easy to justify.

The conclusion that follows from this discussion is that demand-side economic development policies probably work in the sense that they stimulate new investment that leads in most cases to the creation of new jobs. Questions about the nature of the jobs created by entrepreneurial policies I leave until later, but one additional problem may be addressed here: how can such small programs, as most of the demand-oriented initiatives are, really promise to make a difference in the employment and well-being of a state?

The answer is that the chances of making a measurable difference in the economy of a given jurisdiction increases with the degree to which enough different programs are allowed to operate over a long enough period of time. Since most programs of the entrepreneurial state involve high-risk undertakings, it makes sense to keep any single program relatively small. Since small programs produce modest results—say, on the order of the Connecticut Product Development Corporation's 100 jobs per year—it is necessary to implement a number of different programs. The prudent course in a high-risk situation is not to stake everything by magnifying a single program with a good success rate but rather to diversify. Measurable impacts are unlikely to result from any one program but rather will come over time about from the additive effects of many different programs. The key to state economic development in the entrepreneurial mode, it seems logical to argue, is to initiate and sustain a multiplicity of programs on a broad front.

Economic Development and Popular Interests

In many respects supply-side economic development policy represents a tradition in opposition to popular interests. Although supply-side strategists seem to have had little role in the creation of low wage rates in certain states, they nevertheless showed no reluctance to capitalize on them in the competition for industry. Cheap labor was clearly regarded as a major asset for many states in their drive to publicize their business climate. And many states, particularly in the South, the bastion of the location inducement approach, at least attempted to maintain their wage-rate advantage through the passage of right-to-work laws. Many states have also acted to limit unemployment and worker-compensation levels (and welfare payments as well) on the assumption that the appearance of social generosity is an economic development liability.

The competition for industry took on an antilabor cast in the supply-side tradition, and other forms of economic development in this period followed a course antipathetic to the poor. During the years in which officials in state capitals were preoccupied with the problem of creating a comparative location advantage, city leaders pursued their own strategy of economic development in the form of downtown renewal. These efforts, like the right-to-work laws, also represented an assault on popular interests. The urban renewal program in particular destroyed vast numbers of low-income housing units, displaced a million poor and working-class people and uprooted many small businesses, and disrupted long-established lower-class community social systems (Fainstein et al., 1983; Friedland, 1983; Gans, 1962).

The class and labor implications of the newer state entrepreneurialism have not yet acquired a sharp focus, but several points can be made.

Like the traditional supply-side programs, demand-oriented initiatives are designed to generate jobs by supporting capital. Labor training, wage subsidies, and a national minimum-income policy are still not regarded as central components of an economic development strategy. Neither are large-scale public employment or worker-ownership programs. In other words a whole set of initiatives in which labor interests are paramount are still either tangential to the practice of economic development or fall off the spectrum of debatable alternatives altogether.

The interest of the entrepreneurial state in small business also poses a concern from the point of view of labor. Many of the jobs created in the small business sector are lower paid, command fewer fringe benefits, and afford less opportunity for advancement than jobs in larger firms. Furthermore, the effort to construct the economy of the future in part on the basis of small business is a high-risk strategy in which the high rate of firm failure will be a continuing source of employment instability. On the other hand the preoccupation with small business may free states committed to entrepreneurial strategies to some degree from the influence of large corporations. As big firms become relatively less important players in the economic development plans of states and cities, more explicit efforts to protect and promote labor interests may develop. The emergence of protective economic development initiatives is consistent with this scenario. But it is possible in addition that efforts to support new capital formation will eventually be integrated with worker protections and training and adjustment programs.

The involvement of the entrepreneurial state with small business with its attendant employment disadvantages may be offset too by the emphasis on just that part of the small business sector that offers genuine growth potential. Fostering small business development does not require a blanket commitment to the entire sector. The development initiatives of the entrepreneurial state are targeted frequently to concerns that require high-skill labor or entrepreneurial talents. Growing firms too offer better chances of long-term employment.

It is the case, however, that entrepreneurial policies are not geared to the employment and welfare needs of the very poor. The unskilled, the uneducated, the geographically and culturally isolated are not likely to benefit in substantial numbers from programs that enlarge the pool of venture capital or help to nurture a new high-tech industry. In the new economy some people in this large underclass may be absorbed by the direct production jobs that result or through secondary employment, but they do not constitute the featured constituency in this policy domain.

Economic development remains by and large a world apart from the welfare state.

Entrepreneurial economic development has shed the explicitly anti-labor cloak worn by its crasser predecessor tradition, and its current practitioners are seldom implicated anymore in the physical destruction of people's communities for the purpose of building office towers and expensive housing. But economic development is nevertheless a policy domain in which a middle-class vision defines both the nature of the problem and its solutions.

A New American Political Economy

What may in the end be the most important implication of the rise of the entrepreneurial state is that it offers a new model in the American context for structuring the government role in the economy. Robert Solo (1974) has suggested that the American political economy can be viewed as a series of successive but overlying modes of government intervention. These begin with a "housekeeping" function, in which the responsibility of government is simply to maintain the legal and physical infrastructure necessary to the orderly functioning of the market. Next there developed an "offset" function, mainly through the vehicle of Keynesian economics, in which government seeks to counterbalance the effects of private saving and spending choices that may on their own disequilibrate the market. A third function Solo calls planning and programming. This most recently developed form of economic intervention involves simply the organization of complex economic activity in the private sector for public purposes, such as the exploration of space. It does not entail the establishment of national goals or industrial priorities or the effort to allocate resources in any planned way. On the basis of these three models, the American state is regarded as a comparatively weak intervenor in the market.

The entrepreneurial state offers a fourth mode of government interaction with the economy. By its willingness to assume equity positions in private undertakings, to practice a principle of selectivity in assisting industries, to develop and even seek to create consumer markets for privately produced goods, and by its first tentative embrace of strategic planning, the entrepreneurial state has fashioned a far more intimate form of involvement in the private market than anything to which Americans have been accustomed. The product is, on a small scale, an American version of a "mixed economy"—modest levels of public participation in all phases of what were once almost exclusively private economic functions, from product development to marketing, for selected firms and industries, without the nationalization of key industries, as some European nations have done.

The advent of the entrepreneurial state has curiously gone almost unnoticed among the public. But this is perhaps not surprising: the initiatives that define this new intervention are small, technically complex, and difficult to evaluate. In addition the policy domain is inhabited by subnational actors, generally less visible to the casual public eye than those in Washington. Furthermore, the programs of the entrepreneurial state are not the products of mass political demands or the subjects of extended media debate or party platform planks. They appear instead to be technocratic experiments, emerging from the nexus of research institute, academic, and bureaucratic connections, to achieve highly general and almost universally popular employment goals articulated most often by political chief executives. All this said, these programs appear nevertheless to have achieved an institutionalized and growing presence in state and local government. For all their modest dimensions and uncertain impact, therefore, they represent the seeds of a genuine transformation in the American political economy.

BIBLIOGRAPHY

ATTRIBUTED INTERVIEWS

INDEX

Bibliography

Abbott, Carl. 1981. *The New Urban America: Growth and Politics in Sunbelt Cities.* Chapel Hill: University of North Carolina Press.

Abrams, Charles. 1966. "Some Blessings of Urban Renewal." In James Q. Wilson, ed., *Urban Renewal: The Record and the Controversy,* 558–82. Cambridge, MA: MIT Press.

Achtentuch, H., Frank Domurad, Ruth Messinger, and James Silver. 1984. *The Rich Get Richer: 421a Tax Breaks in New York City.* New York: New York Public Interest Research Group.

Advisory Commission on Intergovernmental Relations (ACIR). 1968. *Urban and Rural America: Policies for Future Growth.* Washington, DC: GPO.

Advisory Commission on Intergovernmental Relations (ACIR). 1979. *The States and Distressed Communities.* Washington, DC: GPO.

Advisory Commission on Intergovernmental Relations (ACIR). 1981. *Regional Growth: Interstate Tax Competition.* Washington, DC: GPO.

Advisory Commission on Intergovernmental Relations (ACIR). 1985a. *Significant Features of Fiscal Federalism, 1984.* Washington, DC: GPO.

Advisory Commission on Intergovernmental Relation (ACIR). 1985b. *The Question of State Government Capability.* Washington, DC: GPO.

Advisory Commission on Intergovernmental Relations (ACIR). 1985c. *The States and Distressed Communities: 1983 Update.* Washington, DC: GPO.

Advisory Commission on Intergovernmental Relations (ACIR). 1985d. *The States and Distressed Communities: State Programs to Aid Distressed Communities. A Catalog of State Programs, 1983.* Washington, DC: GPO.

Advisory Commission on Intergovernmental Relations (ACIR). 1986. *Significant Features on Fiscal Federalism, 1985–86.* Washington, DC: GPO.

Alabama Development Office. 1986. *Cut Out for Business.* Montgomery.

Alexander Grant and Co. 1979. *General Manufacturing Business Climates of the Forty-eight Contiguous States of America.*

Alexander Grant and Co. 1982. *General Manufacturing Business Climates of the Forty-eight Contiguous States of America.*

Alexander Grant and Co. 1984. *General Manufacturing Business Climates of the Forty-eight Contiguous States of America.*

Ambrosius, Margery. 1985. "Olson's Thesis and Economic Growth in the States: The Role of Interest Group Strength in State Economic Development Policy-Making, 1969–1980." A paper delivered at the meetings of the Midwest Political Science Association, Chicago, Apr.

Anderson, Martin. 1964. *The Federal Bulldozer.* Cambridge, MA: MIT Press.

Andrews, Victor, and Peter Eisemann. 1981. "Who Finances Small Business circa 1980?" A paper prepared for the Interagency Task Force on Small Business Finance, Washington, DC, Nov.

Anton, Thomas, and Darrell West. 1987. "Trust, Self-Interest and Representation in Economic Policy Making." *New England Journal of Public Policy* 3 (Winter/Spring): 73–88.

Arizona Governor's Office of Economic Planning. n.d. *Arizona Horizons: A Strategy for Future Economic Growth.* Phoenix.

Armington, Catherine. 1983. "Further Examination of Sources of Recent Employment Growth Analysis of USEEM Data for 1976 and 1980." Business Microdata Project, The Brookings Institution, Washington, DC. Mar. Mimeo.

Armington, Catherine. 1986. "The Changing Geography of High Technology Businesses." In John Rees, ed., *Technology, Regions, and Policy,* 75–93. Totowa, NJ: Rowman and Littlefield.

Armington, Catherine, and Marjorie Odle. 1982. "Small Business—How Many Jobs?" *Brookings Review.* 1 (Winter): 14–17.

Arthur Andersen and Co. 1983. *San Francisco's Strategic Plan: Making a Great City Greater.* Feb. San Francisco.

Avens, Oliver, Frank Domurad, Dan Kaplan, Ruth Messinger, Martin Rosenblatt, and James Silver. n.d. *The Rich Get Richer: J-51 Tax Breaks in New York City.* New York Public Interest Research Group.

Baba, Marietta, and Stuart Hart. 1986. "Portrait of a New State Initiative in Industrial Innovation: Michigan's Industrial Technology Institute." In D. Gray, T. Solomon, and W. Hetzner, eds., *Technological Innovation: Strategies for a New Partnership,* 89–110. Amsterdam: North Holland.

Bahl, Roy. 1980. *The Impact of Local Tax Policy on Urban Economic Development.* Washington, DC: U.S. Department of Commerce, Economic Development Administration, Economic Research Division.

Bahl, Roy, and Larry Schroeder. 1981. "Fiscal Adjustments in Declining Cities." In Robert Burchell and David Listoken, eds., *Cities under Stress,* 301–29. Rutgers, NJ: Center for Urban Policy Research.

Balderston, Kris. 1986. *Plant Closings, Layoffs, and Worker Readjustment: The States' Response to Economic Change.* Washington, DC: National Governors' Association.

Bakke, E. W. 1940. *Citizens without Work.* New Haven, CT: Institute of Human Relations, Yale University.

Bartik, Timothy. 1985. "Business Location Decisions in the United States: Estimates of the Effects of Unionization, Taxes, and Other Characteristics of States." *Journal of Business and Economic Statistics* 3 (Jan.): 14–22.

Bartik, Timothy, Charles Becker, Steve Lake, and John Bush. 1986. "Saturn Has Landed in Tennessee: Implications for State Economic Development Policy."

Working Paper 86-W25, Department of Economics and Business Administration, Vanderbilt University, Nashville, TN.

Bartsch, Charles. 1985. *Reaching for Recovery: New Economic Initiatives in Michigan.* Washington, DC: Northeast-Midwest Institute.

Bartsch, Charles. 1986. "Michigan: Reaching for Recovery." *Economic Development Commentary* 10 (Fall): 8–12.

Battelle Institute. 1983. *Sites for High Technology Activities.* Atlanta, GA: Southern Regional Education Board.

Battle, Virginia, and Jack Underhill. 1986. "Coming to Grips with the U.S. Enterprise Zone Experiment: A Summary of Ten Case Studies." *Enterprise Zone Notes* (U.S. Department of Housing and Urban Development), Fall, 11–14.

Beaumont, E., and H. Hovey. 1985. "State, Local, and Federal Economic Development Policies: New Federal Patterns, Chaos, or What?" *Public Administration Review* 45 (Mar./Apr.): 327–32.

Beier-Solberg, Ann. 1984. "State and Local Taxes and Economic Growth—Review of the Literature." Wisconsin Department of Revenue, Division of Research and Analysis. Madison. Sept. Mimeo.

Bettger, Gary. 1986. "State Venture Capital Initiatives." *State Legislative Report* 11 (Feb.). Denver: National Conference of State Legislatures.

Bergman, Edward. 1983. "Planning the Development of Local Economies." *Journal of the American Planning Association* 49 (Summer): 260–66.

Bernard, Richard, and Bradley Rice, eds. 1983. *Sunbelt Cities: Politics and Growth since World War II.* Austin: University of Texas Press.

Bendick, Marc. 1983. "Workers Dislocated by Economic Change." *The Urban Institute Policy and Research Report* 13 (Fall): 1–4.

Beyle, Thad. 1983. "Issues Facing the States and Governors, 1982." *State Government* 56 (2): 65–68.

Biermann, Wallace W. 1984. "The Validity of Business Climate Rankings: A Test." *Industrial Development* 153 (Mar./Apr.): 17–25.

Bingham, Richard, and John Blair. 1983. "Leveraging Private Investment with Federal Funds: Use and Abuse." *Policy Studies Journal* 11 (Mar.): 458–64.

Birch, David. 1979. *The Job Generation Process.* Cambridge, MA: MIT Program on Neighborhood and Regional Change.

Birch, David. 1981. "Who Creates Jobs?" *Public Interest,* Fall: 3–14.

Birch, David, and Susan MacCracken. 1984. *The Role Played by High Technology Firms in Job Creation.* Cambridge, MA: MIT Program on Neighborhood and Regional Change.

Black, Michael, and Richard Worthington. 1986. "The Center for Industrial Innovation at RPI: Critical Reflections on New York's Economic Recovery." In M. Schoolman and Alvin Magid, eds., *Reindustrializing New York State,* 257–80. Albany: State University Press of New York.

Blair, John, Rudy Fichtenbaum, and James Swaney. 1984. "The Market for Jobs:

Locational Decisions and the Competition for Economic Development." *Urban Affairs Quarterly* 20 (Sept.): 64–77.

Bluestone, Barry, and Bennett Harrison. 1982. *The Deindustrialization of America.* New York: Basic Books.

Blum, John Morton. 1976. *V Was for Victory: Politics and American Culture during World War II.* New York: Harcourt Brace Jovanovich.

Boley, Robert. 1962. *Industrial Districts: Principles in Practice.* Washington, DC: Urban Land Institute.

Borts, George, and Jerome Stein. 1964. *Economic Growth in a Free Market.* New York: Columbia University Press.

Bradbury, Katharine, Anthony Downs, and Kenneth Small. 1982. *Urban Decline and the Future of American Cities.* Washington, DC: Brookings.

Bridges, Benjamin. 1965a. "State and Local Inducements for Industry, Part I." *National Tax Journal* 18 (Mar.): 1–14.

Bridges, Benjamin. 1965b. "State and Local Inducements for Industry, Part II." *National Tax Journal* 18 (June): 175–92.

Brody, Herb. 1985. "States Vie for a Slice of the Pie." *High Technology,* Jan.: 16–28.

Browne, Lynn. 1980. "Regional Investment Patterns." *New England Economic Review,* July/Aug.: 5–23.

Browne, Lynn. 1983. "Can High Tech Save the Great Lakes States?" *New England Economic Review,* Nov./Dec.: 19–33.

Bryce, Murray. 1960. *Industrial Development.* New York: McGraw-Hill.

Buchsbaum, Andrew. 1984. "Power of New Bedford, Massachusetts, to Acquire the Morse Cutting Tools Plant through Eminent Domain." Memorandum. Institute for Public Representation, Georgetown University, May 9.

Burgan, John. 1985. "Cyclical Behavior of High Tech Industries." *Monthly Labor Review* 108 (May) 9–15.

Business Week. 1976. "A Counterattack in the War between the States." June 21: 71–74.

Business Week. 1978. "'One-Stop' Permits to Woo New Industry." Sept. 11: 55–56.

Business Week. 1985. "California, 1985: Taking Off the Gloves." Special Advertising Section. June 10: 21–38.

Business Week. 1986. "And Now, the Post-Industrial Corporation." Mar. 3: 64–71.

Buss, Terry, and F. Redburn. 1983. *Mass Unemployment: Plant Closings and Community Mental Health.* Beverly Hills, CA: Sage.

Butler, Stuart. 1981. "Enterprise Zones: Pioneering in the Inner City." In George Sternlieb and David Listokin, eds., *New Tools for Economic Development,* 25–41. New Brunswick, NJ: Rutgers University Center for Urban Policy Research.

Button, K. J. 1976. *Urban Economics.* London: Macmillan.

California Department of Commerce. n.d. *The Californias.* Sacramento.

California Department of Economic and Business Development. 1984. *Job Creation for California in the Decade of the Eighties.* Sacramento.

California World Trade Commission. 1985. *About the Commission* ... Sacramento.

Cameron, Gordon. 1970. *Regional Economic Development: The Federal Role.* Washington, DC: Resources for the Future.

Carey, Hugh. 1981. "State Policy and New Enterprise Development." In Robert Friedman and William Schweke, eds., *Expanding the Opportunities to Produce: Revitalizing the American Economy through New Enterprise Development,* 301–4. Washington, DC: Corporation for Enterprise Development.

Carlton, Dennis. 1979. "Why New Firms Locate Where They Do: An Econometric Model." Working Paper Number 57, Joint Center for Urban Studies of MIT and Harvard, Cambridge, MA.

Carlton, Dennis. 1983. "The Location and Employment Choices of New Firms: An Econometric Model with Discrete and Continuous Endogenous Variables." *The Review of Economics and Statistics,* Aug.: 440–49.

Casteen, John. 1986. "The Politics of Research Parks." A paper presented at a Conference of the National Council of Urban Economic Development, Atlanta, GA, Sept. 18.

Castle, Michael. 1985. "Delaware Recommends Public-Private Approach to Foreign Trade by States." *State Spotlight,* Oct.: 13–14.

Chi, Keon. 1983. *State Futures Commissions.* Lexington, KY: Council of State Governments.

City of Boston. 1986. *Opinion of the Corporation Counsel Re: Colonial Provisions Company—Eminent Domain.* Feb. 12.

City of Madison. 1981. *Policy Governing the Review of Industrial Revenue Bonds.* Madison, WI.

City of Madison. 1985. "Community Development Block Grant 1985 Program Framework." Madison, WI. Mimeo.

City of Madison, Department of Planning and Development. n.d. *Project Plan for Tax Incremental Dist. 13* (Rayovac Headquarters District). Madison, WI.

City of Milwaukee, Department of City Development. 1982. *Annual Report.* Milwaukee, WI.

City of New Bedford. 1984. Minutes of press conference of June 4. New Bedford, MA.

Clague, Ewan, and Walter Couper. 1934. *After the Shutdown,* Part I. New Haven, CT: Yale University Press.

Clark, Terry, and Lorna Ferguson. 1983. *City Money.* New York: Columbia University Press.

Cobb, James. 1982. *The Selling of the South.* Baton Rouge: Louisiana State University Press.

Committee for Iowa's Future Growth. 1984. *We Are Iowans First.* Des Moines.

Conference Board. 1986. *Company Programs to Ease the Impact of Shutdowns.* Report No. 878. New York.

Congressional Budget Office (CBO). 1985. *Federal Financial Support for High-Technology Industries.* Washington, DC: GPO.

Congressional Budget Office (CBO). 1984. *The Federal Role in State Development Programs.* Washington, DC: GPO.

Congressional Quarterly. 1983. "Reagan Sends to Congress Message on Enterprise Zones." Mar. 26: 634–35.

Connecticut Dept. of Economic Development. 1985. *Enterprise Zones: The Connecticut Experiment.* A preliminary report to the legislature. Oct. Hartford.

Connecticut Product Development Corporation. 1986. "Background Statement." Hartford. Mimeo.

Conroy, Michael. 1975. *The Challenge of Urban Economic Development.* Lexington, MA: Lexington Books.

Cornia, G., W. Testa, and F. Stocker. 1978. *State-Local Fiscal Incentives and Economic Development.* Urban and Regional Development Series Number 4. Columbus, OH: Academy for Contemporary Problems.

Corrigan, Richard. 1984. "Federal Government Getting into the High-Tech Research & Development Act." *National Journal,* Sept. 15: 1717–20.

Corrigan, Richard. 1985. "No Smoke, No Growth?" *National Journal,* July 27: 1732–36.

Corrigan, Richard. 1985b. "Business Focus." *National Journal,* Aug. 31: 1967.

Corrigan, Richard, and Rochelle Stanfield. 1984. "Casualties of Change." *National Journal* (Feb. 11): 252–64.

Daneke, Gregory. 1985. "Small Business Policy amid State Level Economic Development Planning." *Policy Studies Journal* 13 (June): 722–28.

Danielson, Michael, and James Doig. 1982. *New York: The Politics of Urban Regional Development.* Berkeley: University of California Press.

Danilov, Victor. 1971. "The Research Park Shakeout." *Industrial Research,* May: 44–48.

de Laski, Kathleen. 1985. "Trouble in Mecca: New Programs Threaten Established Strongholds." *High Technology,* Jan.: 24–25.

Dimanescu, Dan, and James Botkin. 1986. *The New Alliance: American R&D Consortia.* Cambridge, MA: Ballinger.

Dommel, Paul. 1984. "Local Discretion: The CDBG Approach." In R. Bingham and J. Blair, eds., *Urban Economic Development,* 101–13. Beverly Hills, CA: Sage.

Dommel, Paul, and Associates. 1982. *Decentralizing Urban Policy.* Washington, DC: Brookings.

Dommel, Paul, Michael Rich, Leonard Rubinowitz, and Associates. 1983. *Deregulating Community Development.* Washington, DC: Department of Housing and Urban Development.

Duerksen, Christopher J. 1983. *Environmental Regulation of Industrial Plant Siting.* Washington, DC: The Conservation Foundation.

Eisinger, Peter. 1985. "The Search for a National Urban Policy: 1968–1980." *Journal of Urban History* 12 (Nov.): 3–23.

Elazar, Daniel. 1962. *The American Partnership*. Chicago: University of Chicago Press.

Ellwood, John W., ed. 1982. *Reductions in U.S. Domestic Spending*. New Brunswick, NJ: Transaction Books.

Epstein, Richard. 1985. *Takings: Private Property and the Power of Eminent Domain*. Cambridge, MA: Harvard University Press.

Executive Office of the President, Domestic Council. 1972. *Report on National Growth*. Washington, DC: GPO.

Fainstein, Susan, Norman Fainstein, Richard Child Hill, Dennis Judd, Michael Peter Smith. 1983. *Restructuring the City*. New York: Longman.

Farley, Josh, and Norman Glickman. 1986. "R&D as an Economic Development Strategy." *Journal of the American Planning Association* 52 (Autumn): 407–18.

Feagin, Joe. 1984. "Sunbelt Metropolis and Development Capital: Houston in the Era of Late Capitalism." In Larry Sawers and William Tabb, eds., *Sunbelt/Snowbelt*, 99–127. New York: Oxford.

Fedrau, Ruth. 1984. "Responses to Plant Closures and Major Reductions in Force: Private Sector and Community-Based Models." *The Annals* 475 (Sept.): 80–95.

Ferguson, Ronald, and Helen Ladd. 1986. "Economic Performance and Economic Development Policy in Massachusetts." Discussion Paper D86-2, State, Local, and Intergovernmental Center, John F. Kennedy School of Government, Harvard University, Cambridge. MA.

Fields, Gary. 1976. "Labor Force Migration, Unemployment, and Job Turnover." *The Review of Economics and Statistics* 58 (Nov.): 407–15.

Finch, J. 1981. City of New York, interdepartmental memorandum to Carol Bellamy, City Council, Sept. 29.

Finsterbusch, Kurt. 1980. *Understanding Social Impacts*. Beverly Hills, CA: Sage.

Flores y Garcia, Ramon. 1969. *The Industrial Park as an Industrial Incentive*. Engineering thesis, Stanford University.

Foard, Ashley, and Hilbert Fefferman. 1966. "Federal Urban Renewal Legislation." In James Q. Wilson, ed., *Urban Renewal: The Record and the Controversy*, 71–125. Cambridge, MA: MIT Press.

Folbre, Nancy, Julia Leighton, and Melissa Roderick. 1984. "Plant Closings and Their Regulation in Maine, 1971–1982." *Industrial and Labor Relations Review* 37 (Jan.): 185–96.

Francis, A. Denise. 1975. "Land Banking: Development Control through Public Acquisition and Marketing." *Environmental Law* 6 (Fall): 191–216.

Friedland, Roger. 1983. *Power and Crisis in the City*. New York: Schocken.

Funkhouser, Richard, and Edward Wise. 1985. "Progress Report on Maryland's Enterprise Zones." A paper prepared for presentation at the Atlantic Economic Society Conference, Washington, DC, Aug. 29.

Gans, Herbert. 1962. *The Urban Villagers*. New York: Free Press.

Gatons, Paul, and Michael Brintnall. 1984. "Competitive Grants: The UDAG Approach." In Richard Bingham and John Blair, eds., *Urban Economic Development,* 115–40. Beverly Hills, CA: Sage.

Gelfand, Mark. 1975. *A Nation of Cities.* New York: Oxford.

Genetski, Robert, and Young Chin. 1978. "The Impact of State and Local Taxes on Economic Growth." Chicago: Harris Bank. Rev. ed. 1983.

Georgia Governor's Office of Planning and Budget. 1984. *Georgia's Top Priorities.* Atlanta.

Gerweck, John, and Donald Epp. 1974. "The Effect of Industrial Growth on the Local Real Estate Tax: An Expanded Model." *Land Economics* 50 (Nov.): 397–402.

Gilmore, Donald. 1960. *Developing the "Little Economies."* New York: Committee for Economic Development.

Ginsburg, Helen. 1983. *Full Employment and Public Policy: The United States and Sweden.* Lexington, MA: Lexington Books.

Gold, Steven. 1979. *Property Tax Relief.* Lexington, MA: Lexington Books.

Goldsmith, William, and Mary Derian. 1979. "Is There an Urban Policy?" *Journal of Regional Science* 19 (Feb.): 93–108.

Goodrich, Carter. 1961. *Canals and American Economic Development.* New York: Columbia University Press.

Gordus, Jeanne. 1984. "The Human Resource Implications of Plant Shutdowns." *Annals of the American Academy of Political and Social Science* 475 (Sept.): 66–79.

Grady, Dennis. 1985. "Marketing the State: The Governor's Role in State Trade Promotion." A paper presented at the annual Midwest Political Science Association meetings, Chicago, Apr. 18.

Greenwood, Michael. 1981. *Migration and Economic Growth in the United States.* New York: Academic Press.

Groberg, Robert. 1966. "Urban Renewal Realistically Reappraised." In James Q. Wilson, ed., *Urban Renewal: The Record and the Controversy,* 509–31. Cambridge, MA: MIT Press.

Guenther, Harry P. 1984. "Some Ramifications of Bank Regulation for Small Business Financing." In Paul Horvitz and R. Richardson Pettit, eds., *Small Business Finance,* 173–86. Greenwich, CT: JAI Press.

Gunther-Mohr, John, and Joe Swoboda. 1985. "IDBs and Job Growth: The Massachusetts Experience." *Industrial Development* 154 (Sept./Oct.): 11–14.

Hacker, Louis. 1970. *The Course of American Economic Growth and Development.* New York: John Wiley.

Hagstrom, Jerry, and Robert Guskind. 1984. "Playing the State Ranking Game—A New National Pastime Catches On." *National Journal,* June 30: 1268–74.

Hamilton, William, Larry Ledebur, and Deborah Matz. 1984. *Industrial Incentives: Public Promotion of Private Enterprise.* Washington, DC: Aslan.

Handlin, Oscar, and Mary Flug Handlin. 1969. *Commonwealth: A Study of the Role of Government in the American Economy: Massachusetts, 1774–1861.* Cambridge, MA: The Belknap Press of Harvard University Press. Revised edition.

Hansen, Gary. 1984. "Ford and the UAW Have a Better Idea: A Joint Labor-Management Approach to Plant Closings and Worker Retraining." *The Annals* 475 (Sept.): 158–74.

Hansen, Susan. 1984. "The Effects of State Industrial Policies on Economic Growth." A paper delivered at the annual meeting of the American Political Science Association, Washington, DC, Sept. 2.

Hardie, Claire, 1985. "Cost Impacts of Development on Local Municipalities." A paper prepared for Political Science 974, University of Wisconsin—Madison.

Harding, Charles. 1983. "Business Climate Studies: How Useful Are They?" *Industrial Development* 152 (Jan./Feb.): 22–23.

Harding, Charles. 1984. "New Plant Location Strategies." *Dun's Business Month* 121 (Nov.): 111–26.

Harris, Candee. 1984. "The Magnitude of Job Loss from Plant Closings and the Generation of Replacement Jobs: Some Recent Evidence." *The Annals* 475 (Sept.): 15–27.

Harrison, Bennett. 1984. "Plant Closures: Efforts to Cushion the Blow." *Monthly Labor Review* 107 (June): 41–43.

Hawaii Governor's Committee on Hawaii's Economic Future. 1985. *Hawaii's Economic Future.* Honolulu.

Heath, Milton. 1954. *Constructive Liberalism: The Role of the State in the Economic Development of Georgia to 1860.* Cambridge, MA: Harvard University Press.

Hegg, David. 1973. "Tax-Increment Financing of Urban Renewal—Redevelopment Incentive without Federal Assistance." *Real Estate Law Journal* 2 (Fall): 575–84.

Hellman, Daryl, Gregory Wassall, and Laurence Falk. 1976. *State Financial Incentives to Industry.* Lexington, MA: Lexington Books.

Herzik, Eric. 1983. "Governors and Issues: A Typology of Concerns." *State Government* 56 (2): 58–64.

Herzik, Eric. 1985. "The Governors' State-of-the-State Addresses: A Focus on Higher Education. *State Government* 58 (Summer): 65–66.

Hirschman, Albert. 1958. *The Strategy of Economic Development.* New Haven, CT: Yale University Press.

Hodge, J. 1978. "A Study of Industries' Regional Investment Decisions." Unpublished paper. New York: Federal Reserve Bank.

Hodgman, John. 1985. Remarks Made at a seminar on State Initiated Technology Development Programs, Brown University, Mar. 1. Mimeo. transcript.

Holland, Stuart, ed. 1972. *The State as Entrepreneur.* London: Weidenfeld and Nicolson.

Hooks, Gregory. 1984. "The Policy Response to Factory Closings: A Comparison of the United States, Sweden, and France." *The Annals* 475 (Sept.): 110–24.

Horvitz, Paul. 1984. "Problems in the Financing of Small Businesses: Introduction and Summary." In P. Horvitz and R. Richardson Pettit, eds., *Small Business Finances*, 3–18. Greenwich, CT: JAI Press.

Howard, S. Kenneth. 1984. "De Facto New Federalism." *Intergovernmental Perspective* 10 (Winter): 4, 39.

Huddleston, Jack. 1984. "Tax Increment Financing as a State Development Policy." *Growth and Change*, Apr.: 11–17.

Hulkonen, John. 1974. "Tax Increment Financing: A Total Community Approach to Economic Development." *AIDC Journal* 9 (Apr.): 49–67.

Illinois Department of Commerce and Community Affairs. 1985a. *Jobs for the Future*. Springfield.

Illinois Department of Commerce and Community Affairs. 1985. *Illinois Enterprise Zones: Second Annual Report*. Nov. Springfield.

Illinois Department of Commerce and Community Affairs. 1986. *Business Financing Programs*. Springfield.

Indiana Department of Commerce. n.d. *In Step with the Future . . .* Indianapolis.

Industrial Development. 1965. "States Launch Science Programs." V. 134 (Aug.): 28.

Industrial Development. 1985. "Scoreboard." V. 154 (Nov./Dec.): 28–29.

Industrial Development and Site Selection Handbook. 1985. "Foreign Offices of Area Development Organizations in the United States and Canada." V. 154 (Aug.): 11–12.

Industrial Development Research Council. 1977. *The Industrial Facility Planner's View of Special Incentives*. Atlanta: Conway Publications.

International Association of Assessing Officers. 1978. *Urban Property Tax Incentives: State Laws*. Research and Information Series, Chicago.

Jacob, Herbert, and Kenneth Vines, eds. 1965. *Politics in the American States*. Boston: Little, Brown.

Jacobs, Susan, and Elizabeth Roistacher. 1980. "The Urban Impacts of HUD's Urban Development Action Grant Program, or, Where's the Action in Action Grants?" In Norman Glickman, ed., *The Urban Impacts of Federal Policies*, 335–62. Baltimore: Johns Hopkins University Press.

Jaffee, David. 1985. "Export Dependence and Economic Growth: A Reformulation and Respecification." *Social Forces* 64 (Sept.): 102–18.

James, Franklin. 1984. "Urban Economic Development: a Zero-Sum Game?" In Richard Bingham and John Blair, eds., *Urban Economic Development*, 157–74. Beverly Hills, CA: Sage.

Jaschik, Scott. 1986a. "University-Industry-Government Projects: Promising Too Much Too Soon?" *Chronicle of Higher Education*, Jan. 29: 12–13.

Jaschik, Scott. 1986b. "Universities' High-Technology Pacts with Industry Are

Marred by Politics, Poor Planning, and Hype." *Chronicle of Higher Education,* Mar. 12: 15–17.

Johnson, Chalmers. 1982. *MITI and the Japanese Miracle: The Growth of Industrial Policy, 1925–1975.* Stanford, CA: Stanford University Press.

Johnson, Lynn. 1984. *The High-Technology Connection: Academic/Industrial Cooperation for Economic Growth.* ASHE-ERIC Higher Education Research Report No. 6. Washington, DC: Association for the Study of Higher Education.

Jonap, Burton. 1984. Remarks on the Connecticut Product Development Corporation made at the Governor's Conference on Economic Development and Employment, Lincoln, NE, Feb. 4. Mimeo.

Jones, Bryan, and Lynn Bachelor. 1986. *The Sustaining Hand.* Lawrence: University of Kansas Press.

Jones, Susan, Allen Marshall, and Glen Weisbrod. 1985. *Business Impacts of State Enterprise Zones.* A report prepared for the U.S. Small Business Administration by Cambridge Systematics, Cambridge, MA, Sept.

Kahn, Joseph. 1986. "Growing Places." *Inc.* Oct.: 57–66.

Kale, Steven. 1984. "U.S. Industrial Development Incentives and Manufacturing Growth during the 1970s." *Growth and Change* 15 (Jan.): 26–34.

Kamm, Sylvia. 1970. *Land Banking: Public Policy Alternatives and Dilemmas.* Washington, DC: Urban Institute.

Kantrow, A., ed. 1983. "The Political Realities of Industrial Policy." *Harvard Business Review* 61 (Sept./Oct.): 73–86.

Kaplan, Barry. 1983. "Houston: The Golden Buckle of the Sunbelt." In R. Barnard and B. Rice, eds., *Sunbelt Cities,* 196–212. Austin: University of Texas Press.

Kasarda, John. 1985. "Urban Change and Minority Opportunities." In Paul Peterson, ed., *The New Urban Reality,* 33–68. Washington, DC: Brookings.

Kieschnick, Michael. 1979. *Venture Capital and Urban Development.* Washington, DC: Council of State Planning Agencies.

Kieschnick, Michael. 1983. "Taxes and Growth: Business Incentives and Economic Development." In Michael Barker, ed., *State Taxation Policy,* 155–280. Durham, NC: Duke University Press.

Kincaid, John. 1984. "The American Governor in International Affairs." *Publius* 14 (Fall): 95–114.

Kindleberger, Charles, and Bruce Herrick. 1977. *Economic Development.* New York: McGraw-Hill.

Kline, John. 1983. *State Government Influence in U.S. International Economic Policy.* Lexington, MA: Lexington Books.

Kline, John. 1984. "The International Economic Interests of U.S. States." *Publius* 14 (Fall): 81–94.

Komarovsky, Mirra. 1940. *The Unemployed Man and His Family.* New York: Dryden.

Kotkin, Joel, and Greg Critser. 1985. "Capitol Ideas." *Inc.* 7 (Oct.): 96–104.

Kraft, Michael, Bruce Clary, and Richard Tobin. 1988. "The Impact of New Federalism on State Environmental Policy: The Great Lakes States." In Peter Eisinger and William Gormley, ed., *The Midwest Response to the New Federalism*, 204–33. Madison: University of Wisconsin Press.

Krasner, Stephen. 1978. *Defending the National Interest*. Princeton, NJ: Princeton University Press.

Kurihara, Kenneth. 1959. *The Keynesian Theory of Economic Development*. New York: Columbia University Press.

Kuznets, Simon. 1955. "Economic Growth and Income Inequality." *American Economic Review* 45 (Mar.): 1–28.

Ladd, Helen. 1981. "Municipal Expenditures and the Rate of Population Change." In R. Burchell and D. Listokin, eds., *Cities under Stress*, 351–68. Rutgers, NJ: Center for Urban Policy Research.

Lawler, Mayor Brian. 1983. Letter to Governor Michael Dukakis. New Bedford, MA. Sept. 23.

Lawrence, Robert Z. 1984. *Can America Compete?* Washington, DC: Brookings.

Lepawsky, Albert. 1949. *State Planning and Economic Development in the South*. Washington, DC: National Planning Association.

Levitan, Sar. 1964. *Federal Aid to Depressed Areas*. Baltimore: Johns Hopkins University Press.

Levy, John. 1981. *Economic Development Programs for Cities, Counties, and Towns*. New York: Praeger.

Lindblom, Charles. 1977. *Politics and Markets*. New York: Basic.

Liston, Linda. 1967. "States Spar in Sizzling Contest for Industry." *Industrial Development and Manufacturers Record* 136 (Nov./Dec.): 22–28.

Litvak, Lawrence. 1983. "Pension Funds and Economic Renewal." In M. Barker, ed., *Financing State and Local Economic Development*, 159–301. Durham, NC: Duke University Press Policy Studies.

Litvak, Lawrence, and Belden Daniels, 1983. "Innovations in Development Finance." In M. Barker, ed., *Financing State and Local Economic Development*, 3–158. Durham, NC: Duke University Press Policy Studies.

Luger, Michael. 1984. "Does North Carolina's High-Tech Development Program Work?" *Journal of the American Planning Association* 50 (Summer): 280–89.

Lupsha, Peter, and William Siembieda. 1977. "The Poverty of Public Services in the Land of Plenty." In D. Perry and A. Watkins, eds., *The Rise of the Sunbelt Cities*, 169–90. Beverly Hills, CA: Sage.

Lyne, Jack. 1985. "Survey Suggests Law on Reuse of Industrial Sites Toughening in Many States." *Site Selection Handbook* 154 (Sept./Oct.): 884–88.

McHone, W. Warren. 1984. "State Industrial Development Incentives and Employment Growth in Multistate SMSAs." *Growth and Change* 15 (Oct.): 8–15.

McKenzie, Richard. 1984. *Fugitive Industry: The Economics and Politics of Deindustrialization*. San Francisco: Pacific Institute.

McLaughlin, Glenn, and Stefan Robock. 1949. *Why Industry Moves South*. Washington, DC: National Planning Association.

McLaughlin, Mark. 1986. "Colonial Fate Unclear as Boston Rejects Use of Eminent Domain." *New England Business*, Apr. 7: 40–41.

Magaziner, Ira. 1986. "Rhode Island: The Defeat of the Greenhouse Compact." *New England Journal of Public Policy* 2 (Winter/Spring) 48–63.

Malecki, Edward. 1984. "High Technology and Local Economic Development." *Journal of the American Planning Association* 50 (Summer): 262–69.

Malecki, Edward. 1986. "Research and Development and the Geography of High-Technology Complexes." In John Rees, ed., *Technology, Regions, and Policy*, 51–74. Totowa, NJ: Rowman and Littlefield.

Mandelker, Daniel. 1980. *Reviving Cities with Tax Abatement*. New Brunswick, NJ: Rutgers Center for Urban Policy Research.

Mangum, Garth. 1966. "The Computer and the American Economy," in Thomas Naylor, ed., *The Impact of the Computer on Society*, 86–100. Chapel Hill, NC: Southern Regional Education Board.

Margolis, Nell. 1985. "Report on the States." *Inc.* 7 (Oct.): 90–93.

Markusen, Ann. 1986. "High-Tech Plants and Jobs: What Really Lures Them?" *Economic Development Commentary* 10 (Fall): 3–7.

Marlin, Matthew. 1985. "Industrial Revenue Bonds: Evolution of a Subsidy." *Growth and Change* 16 (Jan.): 30–35.

Massachusetts Technology Development Corporation. n.d. Report. Boston.

Massachusetts Industrial Services Program. 1985. *The Industrial Services Program and the Massachusetts Social Compact*. Boston.

Michigan Department of Commerce, Office of Economic Development. 1982. *The Plant Rehabilitation and Industrial Development Districts Law: An Evaluation of Its Use and Economic Impact on Three Communities in Michigan*. Lansing.

Michigan Department of Commerce, Office of Economic Expansion. 1976. *A Guide to Michigan's Plant Rehabilitation and Industrial Development Districts Law of 1974*. Lansing.

Michigan Department of Treasury, Venture Capital Division. 1986. Summary sheet on Venture Capital Division operations. June. Lansing.

Michigan Strategic Fund. n.d. Untitled brochure. Lansing.

Michigan Task Force for a Long-Term Economic Strategy for Michigan. 1984. *The Path to Prosperity*. Lansing.

Mier, Robert, and Scott Gelzer. 1982. "State Enterprise Zones: The New Frontier?" *Urban Affairs Quarterly* 18 (Sept.): 39–52.

Miller, James P. 1982. "Manufacturing Relocations in the United States, 1969–75." In Richard McKenzie, ed., *Plant Closings: Public or Private Choices*, 29–48. Washington, DC: Cato Institute.

Milwaukee Department of City Development. 1979. *Developments.* A newsletter. July.

Minnesota Department of Energy and Economic Development. 1985. *Minnesota: A Strategy for Economic Development.* St. Paul.

Minnesota Department of Energy and Economic Development. 1985b. *Minnesota Enterprise Zone Status Report 1984.* St. Paul. Sept.

Minnesota Department of Revenue. 1985. *Property Taxes Levied in Minnesota, 1984 Assessments.* Property Tax Bulletin No. 14. St. Paul.

Mississippi Ad Hoc Committee. n.d. *Mississippi: 2036.* Jackson.

Mississippi Department of Economic Development. 1985–86. *Selling Mississippi: An Economic Development Marketing Plan.* Jackson.

Moes, John. 1962. *Local Subsidies for Industry.* Chapel Hill: University of North Carolina Press.

Mollenkopf, John C. 1983. *The Contested City.* Princeton, NJ: Princeton University Press.

Montana Office of the Governor. 1985. *Build Montana.* A report to the 49th Legislature. Helena.

Morgan. W. 1964. "The Effects of State and Local Taxes and Financial Inducements on Industrial Location." Ph.D. dissertation, University of Colorado, Boulder.

Moriarty, Barry. 1980. *Industrial Location and Community Development.* Chapel Hill: University of North Carolina Press.

Muller, Thomas. 1975a. *Fiscal Impacts of Land Development.* Washington, DC: Urban Institute.

Muller, Thomas. 1975b. *Growing and Declining Urban Areas: A Fiscal Comparison.* Washington, DC: Urban Institute.

Muller, Thomas. 1981. "Changing Expenditures and Service Demand Patterns of Stressed Cities." In R. Burchell and D. Listokin, eds., *Cities under Stress,* 277–300. Rutgers, NJ: Center for Urban Policy Research.

Murphy, Bruce. 1984. "The Little Law That Governors Don't Like." *Isthmus,* Apr. 20: 1, 10–11.

Muth, Richard. 1971. "Migration: Chicken or Egg?" *The Southern Economic Journal* 37 (Jan.): 295–306.

Nathan, Richard, Paul Dommel, Sara Liebschutz, and Milton Morris. 1977. *Block Grants for Community Development.* Washington, DC: U.S. Department of Housing and Community Development.

Nathan, Richard, and Jerry Webman, eds. 1980. *The Urban Development Action Grant Program.* Papers and conference proceedings on its first two years of operation. Princeton, NJ: Princeton University Urban and Regional Research Center.

National Council for Urban Economic Development. 1986. "Nine-State Demo Project Follows Northern Example." *Economic Development* 11 (Nov. 30): 1, 6.

National Governors' Association. 1983. *Technology and Growth: State Initia-*

tives in Technological Innovation. Final report of the Task Force on Technological Innovation of the National Governors' Association. Washington, DC: NGA. Sept. 30.

National Governors' Association. 1985. *States in the International Economy.* Prepared for the 77th Annual Meeting of the National Governors' Association. Washington, DC: NGA.

National League of Cities. 1983. *International Trade: A New City Economic Development Strategy.* A report of the National League of Cities International Economic Development Task Force, Washington, D.C. Nov. 26.

Nation's Business. 1972. "Milwaukee: Branching Out with the Land Bank." V. 60 (Oct.): 67–68.

Nebraska Governor's Task Force on Small Business Equity Financing. 1986. Report. Lincoln.

Nelson, Joel, and Jon Lorence. 1985. "Employment in Service Activities and Inequality in Metropolitan Areas." *Urban Affairs Quarterly* 21 (Sept.): 106–25.

Nevada Commission on Economic Development. 1985. *Nevada State Plan for Economic Diversification and Development.* Carson City.

New Jersey Economic Development Authority. 1985. *Guidelines for Financial Assistance.* Trenton.

New York Legislative Commission on Public-Private Cooperation. 1985. *Rebuilding Our Cities: The Case for Enterprise Zones.* Sept. Albany.

New York Office of Economic Development. 1985. *Rebuilding New York: The Next Phase for Recovery to Resurgence.* Albany.

New York State Science and Technology Foundation. 1986. *Annual Report, 1985–86.* Albany.

North, Douglass. 1955. "Location Theory and Regional Economic Growth." *The Journal of Political Economy* 63 (June): 243–58.

North Carolina Department of Commerce. n.d.-a. *North Carolina Industrial Revenue Bonds.* Raleigh. Pamphlet.

North Carolina Department of Commerce. n.d.-b. *The North Carolina Story.* Raleigh.

North Carolina Technological Development Authority. 1985. *Biennial Report, Fiscal Years 1984 and 1985.* Raleigh.

North Dakota Economic Development Commission. 1985. *An Economic Development Plan for North Dakota,* Vol. 1 and 2. Bismarck.

Norton, R. D. 1979. *City Life Cycles.* New York: Academic Press.

Norwood, Christopher. 1974. *About Paterson.* New York: Harper and Row.

Noyelle, Thierry, and Thomas Stanback. 1984. *The Economic Transformation of American Cities.* Totowa, NJ: Rowman and Allanheld.

O'Connor, Michael. 1985. "New Survey Reveals Emerging Trends for Prepared Sites of the Future." *Site Selection Handbook* 154 (Dec.): 1148–58.

Ohio Office of the Governor. 1983. *Toward a Working Ohio: Jobs and Ohio's Economy.* Columbus.

Oklahoma Department of Economic Development, Office of the Governor. 1985. *Annual Report and Marketing Plan*. Oklahoma City.

Olsen, J., and J. Eadie. 1982. *The Game Plan*. Washington, DC: Council of State Planning Agencies.

Ostrom, Vincent. 1953. *Water and Politics*. Los Angeles: Haynes Foundation.

Pack, Janet. 1973. "Determinants of Migration to Central Cities." *Journal of Regional Science* 13 (Aug.): 249–60.

Padda, Kuldarshan. 1981. "Report Card on the States." *Inc.* 3 (Oct.): 90–98.

Papke, Leslie. 1985. "The Measurement and Effect of Interstate Business Tax Differentials on the Location of Capital Investment." Center for Tax Policy Studies, Working Paper No. 5, West Lafayette, IN, Purdue University.

Parris, Addison. 1968. *The Small Business Administration*. New York: Praeger.

Patrick, L., director of Industrial Finance, Arkansas Industrial Development Commission. 1985. Letter to the author, Apr. 8.

Peltz, Michael, and Marc Weiss. 1984. "State and Local Government Roles in Industrial Innovation." *Journal of the American Planning Association* 50 (Summer): 270–79.

Pennsylvania Governor's Office of Policy and Planning. 1982. *Advanced Technology Policies for the Commonwealth of Pennsylvania*. Aug. 5. Harrisburg.

Pennsylvania Industrial Development Authority. 1986. *Summary of Loan Projects*. Harrisburg.

Pennsylvania Office of the Governor. 1985. *Choices for Pennsylvanians*. Office of Policy Development. Harrisburg.

Pennsylvania Office of the Governor. n.d. Cover letter accompanying Ben Franklin Partnership material. Harrisburg.

Perry, David, and Alfred Watkins, eds. 1977. *The Rise of the Sunbelt Cities*. Beverly Hills, CA: Sage.

Peters, Lois, and Herbert Fusfeld. 1982. "Current U.S. University/Industry Research Connections." In National Science Board, National Science Foundation, *University/Industry Research Relationships*, 1–162. Washington, DC: GPO.

Phillips, Willard. 1828. *A Manual of Political Economy*. Boston: Hillard, Gray.

Pilcher, Dan. 1985. "State Roles in Foreign Trade." *State Legislatures* 11 (Apr.): 18–23.

Plaut, Thomas, and Joseph Pluta. 1983. "Business Climate, Taxes and Expenditures, and State Industrial Growth in the United States." *Southern Economic Journal* 50 (Sept.): 99–119.

Plosila, Walter, and David Allen. 1985. "Small Business Incubators and Public Policy: Implications for State and Local Development Strategies." *Policy Studies Journal* 13 (June): 729–34.

Pollack, Charles. 1982. "Property Taxation on IRB-Financed Facilities." *Industrial Development* 151 (Jan./Feb.): 20–21.

Pomeroy, Miles, Community Development Agency, St. Louis, MO. 1984. Letter to the author, Oct. 24.

Portz, John. 1987. "Politics, Plant Closings, and Public Policy: The Steel Valley Authority in Pittsburgh." A paper presented at the annual meeting of the Midwest Political Science Association, Chicago, IL, Apr. 9.

Potter, David. 1954. *People of Plenty*. Chicago: University of Chicago Press.

Premus, Robert. 1982. *Location of High Technology Firms and Regional Economic Development*. A staff study prepared for the Subcommittee on Monetary and Fiscal Policy, Joint Economic Committee, U.S. Congress. Washington, DC: GPO.

Premus, Robert, Charles Bradford, George Krumbhaar, and Wendy Schact. 1985. *The U.S. Climate for Entrepreneurship and Innovation*. A report prepared for the Joint Economic Committee, U.S. Congress. Washington, DC: GPO.

President's Commission for a National Agenda for the Eighties. 1980. *Urban America in the Eighties: Perspectives and Prospects*. Washington, DC.

President's Commission on Industrial Competitiveness. 1985. *Global Competition: The New Reality*. Vol. 2. Washington, DC: GPO.

Ralph Andersen and Associates. 1983. *Debt Financing by California Cities and Counties: Past and Projected Trends, Issues and Needs for Technical Assistance*. Prepared by the California Debt Advisory Commission. Sacramento.

Ralph Andersen and Associates. 1984. *The Use of Redevelopment and Tax Increment Financing by Cities and Counties*. A report prepared for the California Debt Advisory Commission. Sacramento.

Rausch, Jonathon. 1985. "Small Business Agency Alive and Well Despite White House Attempt to Kill It." *National Journal*, Aug. 19: 1845–48.

Reich, Robert. 1983. *The Next American Frontier*. New York: Times Books.

Reinshuttle, Robert, n.d. *Economic Development: A Survey of State Activities*. Lexington, KY: Council of State Governments.

Rhode Island Strategic Development Commission. n.d. *The Greenhouse Compact*. Providence.

Richardson, Harry. 1973. *Regional Growth Theory*. London: Macmillan.

Richardson, Harry, and Joseph Turek. 1984. "The Scope and Limits of Federal Intervention." In H. Richardson and J. Turek, eds., *Economic Prospects for the Northeast*, 211–42. Philadelphia: Temple University Press.

Riche, Richard, Daniel Hecker, and John Burgan. 1983. "High Technology Today and Tomorrow: A Small Slice of the Pie." *Monthly Labor Review* 106 (Nov.): 50–58.

Roberts, Jane. 1984. "States and Localities in 1983: Recession, Reform, Renewal." *Intergovernmental Perspective* 10 (Winter): 10–23.

Roberts, Jane, Jerry Fensterman, and Donald Lief. 1985. "States, Localities Continue to Adopt Strategic Policies." *Intergovernmental Perspective* 11 (Winter): 19–29.

Rodwin, Lloyd. 1970. *Nations and Cities*. Boston: Houghton, Mifflin.

Romans, Thomas, and Ganti Subrahmanyam. 1979. "State and Local Taxes,

Transfers and Regional Economic Growth." *Southern Economic Journal* 46 (Oct.): 435–44.

Rosenthal, Neal. 1985. "The Shrinking Middle Class: Myth or Reality?" *Monthly Labor Review* 108 (Mar.): 3–10.

Ross, Douglas. 1987. Speech given at Wayne State University, Detroit. Apr. 16.

Ross, William. 1953. "Tax Exemption in Louisiana as a Device for Encouraging Industrial Development." *The Southwestern Social Science Quarterly* 34 (June): 14–22.

Roth, Dennis. 1985. "Enterprise Zone and Alternative Area Redevelopment Legislation." Congressional Research Service Brief, Dec. 24. Washington, DC.

Rotunda, Ronald, John Nowak, and J. Nelson Young. 1986. *Treatise on Constitutional Law.* Vol. 1. St. Paul, MN: West.

Sack, S. 1965. "State and Local Finances and Economic Development." In Charles Conlon, ed., *State and Local Taxes on Business,* 209–24. Princeton, NJ: The Tax Institute of America.

St. Louis Community Development Agency. 1980. *Chapter 353: Development Incentive Program: Developer's Information.* St. Louis.

Sale, Kirkpatrick. 1975. *Power Shift: The Rise of the Southern Rim and Its Challenge to the Eastern Establishment.* New York: Random House.

Samuelson, Robert. 1983. "The Old Labor Force and the New Job Market." *National Journal* 15 (Feb. 26): 426–31.

Saunders, Anthony. 1984. "The Demand for Small Business Loans." In Paul Horvitz and R. Richardson Pettit, eds., *Small Business Finance,* 51–74. Greenwich, CT: JAI Press.

Savas, E. S. 1982. *Privatizing the Public Sector.* Chatham, NJ: Chatham House.

Scheiber, Harry. 1969. *Ohio Canal Era.* Athens, OH: Ohio University Press.

Scheiber, Harry. 1972. "Government and the Economy: Studies of the 'Commonwealth' Policy in Nineteenth Century America." *Journal of Interdisciplinary History* 3 (Summer): 135–51.

Scheiber, Harry. 1975. "Federalism and the American Economic Order, 1789–1910." *Law and Society Review* 10 (Fall): 57–118.

Schmandt, Jurgen, and Robert Wilson. 1986. "State Science and Technology Policies: An Assessment." A paper prepared for the association of Public Policy Analysis and Management meetings, November 1, Austin, TX.

Schmenner, Roger. 1982. *Making Business Location Decisions.* Englewood Cliffs, NJ: Prentice-Hall.

Schmidt, Peggy. 1984. "The Greening of Research Parks." *New York Times National Employment Report,* Oct. 14: 37.

Schneider, Mark. 1985. "Suburban Fiscal Disparities and the Location Decisions of Firms." *American Journal of Political Science* 29 (Aug.): 587–605.

Schumpeter, Joseph. 1962. *Capitalism, Socialism and Democracy.* New York: Harper and Row. Originally published in 1942.

Shannon, John. 1985. "Fiscal Federalism after the California Taxpayers' Revolt: A Sorting Out of Sorts." In Charles Warren, ed., *Urban Policy in a Changing Federal System,* 71–90. Washington, DC: National Academy Press.

Shapero, Albert. 1981. "The Role of Entrepreneurship in Economic Development at the Less-Than-National Level." In Robert Friedman and William Schweke, eds., *Expanding the Opportunity to Produce, 25–35.* Washington, DC: Corporation for Enterprise Development.

Sheets, Robert, Russell Smith, and Kenneth Voytek. 1985. "Corporate Disinvestment and Metropolitan Manufacturing Job Loss." *Social Science Quarterly* 66 (March): 218–26.

Sherrod, Clinton. 1978. "Tax Increment Financing: Its Use as a Tool to Encourage Industrial Development." *AIDC Journal* 13 (Apr.): 53–78.

Silver, Hilary. n.d. "Deindustrialization and Metropolitan Income Distribution." Unpublished paper, Department of Sociology, Brown University, Providence, RI.

Simon, Herbert. 1981. *The Sciences of the Artificial.* Cambridge, MA: MIT Press.

Slayton, William. 1966. "The Operation and Achievements of the Urban Renewal Program." In James Q. Wilson, ed., *Urban Renewal: The Record and the Controversy,* 189–229. Cambridge, MA: MIT Press.

Solo, Robert. 1974. *The Political Authority and the Market System.* Cincinnati, OH: Southwestern.

Sorkin, Donna, Nancy Ferris, and James Hudak. n.d. *Strategies for Cities and Counties: A Strategic Planning Guide.* Washington, DC: Public Technology, Inc.

Stafford, H. 1974. "The Anatomy of the Location Decision: Content Analysis of Case Studies." In F. E. Ian Hamilton, ed., *Spatial Perspectives in Industrial Organization and Decision Making,* 169–88. New York: John Wiley.

Stanback, Thomas, and Thierry Noyelle. 1982. *Cities in Transition.* Totowa, NJ: Rowman and Allanheld.

Stanfield, Rochelle. 1978. "A Capital Idea?" *National Journal,* Apr. 22: 643.

Stanfield, Rochelle. 1979. "EDA—The 'Perfect Vehicle' for Carter's Urban Strategy." *National Journal,* June 23: 1032–35.

State Budget and Tax News. 1986. V. 5, No. 16 (Aug. 29).

Stedman, Frank. 1961. "New England's Gateway to the St. Lawrence." *Industrial Development and Manufacturers Record* 130 (Feb.): 73–76.

Steinbach, Carol, and Robert Guskind. 1984. "High-Risk Ventures Strike Gold with State Government Financing." *National Journal* 16 (Sept. 22): 1767–71.

Steinbach, Carol, and Neal Pierce. 1984. "Cities Are Setting Their Sights on International Trade and Investment." *National Journal,* Apr. 28: 818–22.

Steinnes, Donald. 1977. "Causality and Intraurban Location." *Journal of Urban Economics* 4 (Jan.): 69–79.

Steinnes, Donald. 1984. "Business Climate, Tax Incentives, and Regional Economic Development." *Growth and Change* 15 (Apr.): 38–47.

Sternlieb, George. 1981. "Kemp-Garcia Act: An Initial Evaluation." In G. Sternlieb and David Listokin, eds., *New Tools for Economic Development,* 42–83. Piscataway, NJ: Rutgers University Center for Urban Policy Research.

Stoll, Hans. 1984. "Small Firms' Access to Public Equity Financing." In Paul Horvitz and R. Richardson Pettit, eds., *Small Business Finance,* 187–238. Greenwich, CT: JAI Press.

Struyk, R. 1967. "An Analysis of Tax Structure, Public Service Levels, and Regional Economic Growth." *Journal of Regional Science* 7 (Winter): 175–84.

Studds, Congressman Gerry. 1984. Letter to Mayor Brian Lawler. New Bedford, MA. May 18.

Sundquist, James, 1975. *Dispersing Population.* Washington, DC: Brookings.

Susman, N. Bradley. 1986. "Venture Capital: Are Locally Managed Funds Important?" *Economic Development Commentary* 10 (Fall): 13–16.

Swanstrom, Todd. 1982. "Tax Abatement in Cleveland." *Social Policy* 12: 24–30.

Thomas, William. 1975. *Historical and Functional Aspects of State Industrial Development Organizations.* Division of Research, Bureau of Business and Economic Research, University of South Carolina.

Thompson, Lyke. 1983. "New Jobs versus Net Jobs: Measuring the Results of an Economic Development Program." *Policy Studies Journal* 12 (Dec.): 365–75.

Thompson, Wilbur. 1965. *A Preface to Urban Economics.* Baltimore: Johns Hopkins University Press.

Thompson, Wilbur, and J. Mattila. 1959. *An Econometric Model of Postwar State Industrial Development.* Detroit: Wayne State University Press.

Todaro, Michael. 1977. *Economic Development in the Third World.* New York: Longman.

United Nations, Department of International Economic and Social Affairs. 1985. *Statistical Yearbook.* New York: United Nations.

U.S. Bureau of the Census, Department of Commerce. 1953. *Statistical Abstract of the United States.* Washington, DC: GPO.

U.S. Bureau of the Census, Department of Commerce. 1970. *Statistical Abstract of the United States.* Washington, DC: GPO.

U.S. Bureau of the Census, Department of Commerce. 1972. *County and City Data Book.* Washington, DC: GPO.

U.S. Bureau of the Census, Department of Commerce. 1975. *Statistical Abstract of the United States.* Washington, DC: GPO.

U.S. Bureau of the Census. Department of Commerce. 1977. *County and City Data Book.* Washington, DC: GPO.

U.S. Bureau of the Census. Department of Commerce. 1983. *County and City Data Book.* Washington, DC: GPO.

U.S. Bureau of the Census. Department of Commerce. 1985a. *Current Population Reports. State Population Estimates, 1980–84.* Washington, DC: GPO.

U.S. Bureau of the Census. Department of Commerce. 1985b. *Statistical Abstract of the United States.* Washington, DC: GPO.

U.S. Bureau of the Census. Department of Commerce. 1986. *Statistical Abstract of the United States.* Washington, DC: GPO.

U.S. Congress. House. 1983. *Employment and Investment Incentives for Small*

Businesses in Distressed Areas. Hearings before the Subcommittee on Tax, Access to Equity Capital and Business Opportunities of the Committee on Small Business. 98th Congress, Apr. 27. Washington, DC: GPO.

U.S. Congress. House. 1985. *Federal and State Roles in Economic Development. Hearings before a Subcommittee of the Committee on Government Operations.* 99th Congress, 1st Session, Dec. 2, 4, and 5. Washington, DC: GPO.

U.S. Congress, Joint Committee on Taxation. 1983. *Trends in the Use of Tax-Exempt Bonds to Finance Private Activities Including a Description of H.R. 1176 and H.R. 1635.* Washington, DC: GPO.

U.S. Congress, Joint Committee on Taxation. 1985. *Tax Reform Proposals: Tax Treatment of State and Local Government Bonds.* Washington, DC: GPO.

U.S. Congress, Joint Economic Committee. 1986. *Technology and Trade: Indicators of U.S. Industrial Innovation.* A study prepared for the Joint Economic Committee. Washington, DC: GPO.

U.S. Congress. Senate. 1983. *Hearings before the Senate Committee on Small Business, Subcommittee on Urban and Rural Economic Development.* 98th Congress, 1st Session, July 13. Washington, DC: GPO.

U.S. Congress. Senate. 1985. *Small Issue Industrial Development Bonds as a Source of Capital for Small Business Expansion. Hearings before the Subcommittee on Small Business: Family Farm.* 99th Congress, May 22 and June 11. Washington, DC: GPO.

U.S. Department of Commerce, International Trade Division. 1985. *United States Trade: Performance in 1984 and Outlook.* Washington, DC: GPO.

U.S. Economic Development Administration (EDA), Department of Commerce. 1966. *Annual Report,* Washington, DC: GPO.

U.S. Economic Development Administration (EDA), Department of Commerce. 1970. *The Economic Development Administration's Public Works Program: An Evaluation.* Vol. 1. Washington, DC: GPO.

U.S. Economic Development Administration (EDA), Department of Commerce. 1975. *Annual Report.* Washington, DC: GPO.

U.S. Economic Development Administration (EDA), Department of Commerce. 1977. *Annual Report.* Washington, DC: GPO.

U.S. Economic Development Administration (EDA), Department of Commerce. 1979. *Annual Report.* Washington, DC: GPO.

U.S. Economic Development Administration (EDA), Department of Commerce. 1983. *Annual Report.* Washington, DC: GPO.

U.S. Economic Development Administration (EDA), Department of Commerce. 1984. *Annual Report.* Washington, DC: GPO.

U.S. Economic Development Administration (EDA), Department of Commerce. 1985. *Annual Report.* Washington, DC: GPO.

U.S. Department of Housing and Urban Development (HUD). 1974. *Urban Renewal Directory.* Washington, DC: GPO.

U.S. Department of Housing and Urban Development (HUD). 1975. *Statistical Yearbook.* Washington, DC: GPO.

U.S. Department of Housing and Urban Development (HUD). 1979a. *Fourth*

Annual Community Development Block Grant Report. Washington, DC: GPO.

U.S. Department of Housing and Urban Development (HUD). 1979b. *Urban Development Action Grant Program: First Annual Report.* Washington, DC: GPO.

U.S. Department of Housing and Urban Development (HUD). 1980a. *Fifth Annual Community Development Block Grant Report.* Washington, DC: GPO.

U.S. Department of Housing and Urban Development (HUD). 1980b. *President's National Urban Policy Report.* Washington, DC: GPO.

U.S. Department of Housing and Urban Development (HUD). 1981. *Sixth Annual Community Development Block Grant Report.* Washington, DC: GPO.

U.S. Department of Housing and Urban Development (HUD). 1982a. *An Impact Evaluation of the Urban Development Action Grant Program.* Washington, DC: Office of Policy Development and Research.

U.S. Department of Housing and Urban Development (HUD). 1982b. *Consolidated Annual Report to Congress on Community Development Programs.* Washington, DC: GPO.

U.S. Department of Housing and Urban Development (HUD). 1982c. *President's National Urban Policy Report.* Washington, DC: GPO.

U.S. Department of Housing and Urban Development (HUD). 1983. *Consolidated Annual Report to Congress on Community Development Programs.* Washington, DC: GPO.

U.S. Department of Housing and Urban Development (HUD). 1984a. *Consolidated Annual Report to Congress on Community Development Programs.* Washington, DC: GPO.

U.S. Department of Housing and Urban Development (HUD). 1984b. *President's National Urban Policy Report.* Washington, DC: GPO.

U.S. Department of Housing and Urban Development (HUD). 1986. *Consolidated Annual Report to Congress on Community Development Programs.* Washington, DC: GPO.

U.S. General Accounting Office. 1983. *Efforts to Promote Exports by Small, Non-Exporting Manufacturers.* Washington, DC: GPO.

U.S. Office of Technology Assessment (OTA). 1984. *Technology, Innovation, and Regional Economic Development.* Background Paper 2, Feb. Washington, DC: GPO.

U.S. Small Business Administration (SBA). 1979a. "An In-Depth Study of Eight Small Business Development Centers." Washington, DC. Mimeo.

U.S. Small Business Administration (SBA). 1979b. *The States and Small Business.* A report on the 1st national conference on state small business programs. Washington, DC: GPO.

U.S. Small Business Administration (SBA). 1980a. *Directory of State Small Business Programs.* Washington, DC: GPO.

U.S. Small Business Administration (SBA). 1980b. "White House Conference on Small Business." Washington, DC. Mimeo.

U.S. Small Business Administration (SBA). 1983. *The State of Small Business: A Report of the President*. Washington, DC: GPO.

U.S. Small Business Administration (SBA). 1984a. *Annual Report*. Washington, DC: GPO.

U.S. Small Business Administration (SBA). 1984b. *The State of Small Business: A Report to the President Transmitted to the Congress*. Mar. Washington, DC.

U.S. Small Business Administration (SBA). 1984c. *State Activities in Venture Capital, Early-Stage Financing, and Secondary Markets*. May. Washington, DC: GPO.

U.S. Small Business Administration (SBA). 1984d. *State Export Promotion Activities*. Office of Advocacy. Oct. Washington, DC: GPO.

U.S. Small Business Administration (SBA). 1984e. *State Policies and Programs to Enhance the Small Business Climate*. Washington, DC: GPO.

U.S. Small Business Administration (SBA). 1985. *State Activities in Capital Formation: Venture Capital, Working Capital, and Public Pension Fund Investments*. Washington, DC: GPO.

Utah Department of Community and Economic Development. 1985. *Developing Utah's Economy: Guidelines, Policies and Plans*. Salt Lake City.

Varaiya, Pravin, and Michael Wiseman. 1983. "Reindustrialization and the Outlook for Declining Areas." In J. V. Henderson, ed., *Research in Urban Economics*, Vol. 3, 167–90. Greenwich, CT: JAI Press.

Vaughan, Roger J. 1977. *The Urban Impacts of Federal Policies*. Vol. 2. *Economic Development*. Santa Monica, CA: Rand.

Vaughan, Roger, and Robert Pollard. 1986. "State and Federal Policies for High-Technology Development." In John Rees, ed., *Technology, Regions, and Policy*, 268–81. Totowa, NJ: Rowman and Littlefield.

Vedder, Richard K. 1982. "Rich States, Poor States: How High Taxes Inhibit Growth." *Journal of Contemporary Studies*, Fall: 19–32.

Venture Capital Journal. 1985. Special Report. May: 9–15.

Vernez, George. 1980. "Overview of the Spatial Dimensions of the Federal Budget." In Norman Glickman, ed., *The Urban Impacts of Federal Policies*, 67–102. Baltimore: Johns Hopkins University Press.

Vorsanger, Debra. 1983–84. "New York's J-51 Program: Controversy and Revision." *Fordham Urban Law Journal* 12: 103–49.

Walton, John. 1982. "Cities and Jobs and Politics." *Urban Affairs Quarterly* 18 (Sept.): 5–18.

Wasylenko, Michael. 1985. "The Effect of Business Climate on Employment Growth: A Review of the Evidence." A paper presented at the Conference on Financing Economic Development, Chicago, IL, Feb. 1–2. Sponsored by the Cooperative Extension Service, University of Illinois at Champaign-Urbana.

Watkins, Alfred. 1980. *The Practice of Urban Economics*. Beverly Hills, CA: Sage.

Webber, Melvin. 1984. *Industrial Location*. Beverly Hills, CA: Sage.

Webman, Jerry. 1980. "UDAG: A Targeted Urban Economic Development Program: Initial Directions and Prospects." In R. Nathan and J. Webman, eds., *The Urban Development Action Grant Program,* 87–110. Princeton, NJ: Princeton University Urban and Regional Research Center.

Weicher, John C. 1972. *Urban Renewal.* Washington, DC: American Enterprise Institute.

Weinstein, Bernard, and Robert Firestine. 1978. *Regional Growth and Decline in the United States.* New York: Praeger.

Wendling, Wayne. 1984. *The Plant Closure Policy Dilemma.* Kalamazoo, MI: W. E. Upjohn Institute.

West Virginia Economic Development Authority. 1984–85. A report on WVEDA programs. Wheeling.

Wheat, Leonard. 1983. *Regional Growth and Industrial Location.* Lexington, MA: Lexington Books.

Wheaton, William C. 1983. "Interstate Differences in the Level of Business Taxation." *National Tax Journal,* Mar.: 83–94.

Wiewel, Wim, Jane deBettencourt, and Robert Mier. 1984. "Planners, Technology, and Economic Growth." *Journal of the American Planning Association* 50 (Summer): 290–96.

Wildavsky, Aaron. 1986. "Industrial Policies in American Political Cultures." In Claude Barfield and William Schambra, eds., *The Politics of Industrial Policy,* 15–32. Washington, DC: American Enterprise Institute.

Wildavsky, Aaron, and Jeffrey Pressman. 1983. *Implementation.* Berkeley, CA: University of California Press.

Wilson v. Connecticut Product Development Corporation. 355 A2nd 167 Conn. 111, 1975.

Windsor, Duane. 1979. *Fiscal Zoning in Suburban Communities.* Lexington, MA: Lexington Books.

Wisconsin Department of Administration. 1987. *Wisconsin's Strategic Development Commission: An Update.* Madison.

Wisconsin Department of Development. 1984. *The Job Generation Process in Wisconsin: 1969–1981.* Dec. Madison.

Wisconsin Department of Development. 1985a. *Capital Formation and Distribution in the Wisconsin Economy.* A report prepared for the Strategic Development Commission. Feb. Madison.

Wisconsin Department of Development. 1985b. *Biennial Report on Tax Incremental Financing (TIF).* Mar. Madison.

Wisconsin Department of Development. 1985c. *Entrepreneurial Culture in Wisconsin.* Technical Report TR85-1. Nov. Madison.

Wisconsin Department of Development. 1987. *Models of Entrepreneurial Development Programs.* Madison.

Wisconsin Office of the Governor. 1985. "The Wisconsin Way" (a proposal to the Saturn Corporation). Madison. Mar. 12. Mimeo.

Wisconsin Strategic Development Commission. 1985. *The Final Report.* Aug. Madison.

Wolkoff, Michael. 1983. "The Nature of Property Tax Abatement Awards." *Journal of the American Planning Association* 49 (Winter): 77–84.

Yankelovich, Skelly, and White. 1984. *Wisconsin Business Climate Study.* Apr. Madison.

Zysman, John. 1983. *Governments, Markets, and Growth.* Ithaca, NY: Cornell University Press.

Attributed Interviews

Bagley, Andrew. Deputy Director, Massachusetts Office of International Trade and Investment. Boston. Dec. 11, 1986.

Balderston, Kris. Formerly of the National Governors' Association staff. Washington, DC. Feb. 11, 1987.

Brooks, Jean. Deputy director of Economic Development, city of San Francisco. Sept. 9, 1985.

Burmeister, Glenn. Iowa Product Development Corporation. Des Moines. Oct. 10, 1986.

Caplan, Herb. Assistant corporation counsel, city of Chicago. Jan. 20, 1987.

Carroll, Jim. Illinois Attorney General's Office. Chicago. Jan. 30, 1987.

Cassan, Vito. Attorney retained by city of Yonkers. New York. Feb. 17, 1987.

Hudak, James. Arthur Andersen and Company. San Francisco. Jan. 15, 1985.

Jackson, William. Brown University Research Foundation. Providence. Sept. 15, 1986.

Leiken, Sam. Massachusetts Product Development Corporation. Boston. Sept. 16, 1986.

Lenehan, Ed. Rhode Island Department of Economic Development, Division of International Trade. Providence. Jan. 9, 1987.

Lewis, Paul. Deputy director, International Marketing, Texas Department of Agriculture. Austin. Jan. 7, 1987.

Lotharius, Steve. Wisconsin Department of Development. Madison. Dec. 10, 1986.

Ortlieb, Renee. Michigan Department of Commerce. Lansing. Jan. 1985.

Self, David. Attorney retained by city of Oakland, California. Feb. 1986 and Feb. 2, 1987.

Steinbach, Carol. *National Journal* writer. Washington, DC. Jan. 30, 1987.

Sullivan, Neil. Office of the Mayor, city of Boston. Jan. 23, 1987.

Weinberg, Bob. Former director of Massport, Boston. Feb. 2, 1987.

Index

Advisory Commission on Intergovernmental Relations, 140, 142

Alabama, 16, 28n, 37, 171; industrial development assistance programs, 261; and establishment of foreign trade office, 292

Alaska, 28n, 141, 144, 156, 158

Alaska Renewable Resources Corporation, 260

American Federation of Labor, 159

Andrews, Victor, 244

Area Redevelopment Act of 1961, 100–101n, 123

Arizona, 137, 249, 282; commitment to indigenous business growth, 238

Arkansas, 28n, 155, 165; IRB guarantee program, 164

Armington, Catherine: job generation studies, 236, 239, 278

Atlanta, Georgia, 25, 113

Baba, Marietta, 285

Baltimore, Maryland, 194

Bartik, Timothy, 203n, 209, 214

Battle Creek, Michigan, 151n

Beaumont, E., 31

Bergman, Edward, 16

Bieber, Owen, 309

Biermann, Wallace, 135

Birch, David: and job generation studies, 235–39, 242, 310; criticisms, 236, 237

Bluestone, Barry, 51, 52, 208, 211, 237, 310, 311, 338

Bradbury, Katherine, 46

Bridges, Benjamin, 155, 156n, 163, 202, 216

Brown, Jerry, governor of California, 313

Browne, Lynn, 209, 278n

Burgan, John, 276

Business climate: defined, 130; comparative state surveys, 130, 134 (table); effects of surveys on economic growth, 135–38; mentioned in strategic plans, 135–36

Business development corporations, 156–57

Buss, Terry, 51

Cadillac, Michigan, 151n

California, 99, 150, 154, 170, 171, 247, 256, 278; growth of, 56; growth of economic development incentives in, 63–64; Proposition 13, 68; Innovation Development program Title IX grant, 105; role in initiating business climate surveys, 131; tax increment financing in, 185–88; and embrace of demand-based strategies, 233; job generation study, 238; fortunes of electronics industry in, 277; and export promotion, 293; export promotion efforts, 295, 303; dislocated worker program, 313

Cambridge Systematics, 194

Canadian Industrial Adjustment Service, 313, 315

Candee and Company, 310

Capital investment: impact on job growth, 42–43

Capital subsidies: as central feature of economic development, 29–30; in EDA Title II program, 103–4; in CDBG program, 110; in UDAG program, 117–19; focus of federal economic development programs, 124; debt financing as a location incentive, 153; direct loans to business, 154–56; business development corporations, 156–57; loan guarantees, 157; industrial revenue bonds (IRBs), 157–65; as tool of the entrepreneurial state, 234